PROMETHEUS IN MUSIC

For my Family and Friends

Prometheus in Music
Representations of the Myth in the Romantic Era

PAUL A. BERTAGNOLLI
University of Houston, USA

LONDON AND NEW YORK

First published 2007 by Ashgate Publishing

2 Park Square, Milton Park, Abingdon, Oxon OX14 4RN
711 Third Avenue, New York, NY 10017, USA

Routledge is an imprint of the Taylor & Francis Group, an informa business

Copyright © 2007 Paul A. Bertagnolli

Paul A. Bertagnolli has asserted his moral right under the Copyright, Designs and Patents Act, 1988, to be identified as the author of this work.

All rights reserved. No part of this book may be reprinted or reproduced or utilised in any form or by any electronic, mechanical, or other means, now known or hereafter invented, including photocopying and recording, or in any information storage or retrieval system, without permission in writing from the publishers.

Notice:
Product or corporate names may be trademarks or registered trademarks, and are used only for identification and explanation without intent to infringe.

British Library Cataloguing in Publication Data
Bertagnolli, Paul
  Prometheus in music : representations of the myth in the romantic era
  1. Music – 19th century – History and criticism
  2. Prometheus (Greek deity) – Songs and music 3. Mythology, Greek, in music
  I. Title
  780.9'034

Library of Congress Cataloging-in-Publication Data
Bertagnolli, Paul, 1956-
  Prometheus in music : representations of the myth in the romantic era / Paul Bertagnolli.
    p. cm.
  Includes bibliographical references (p.) and index.
  1. Music–19th century–History and criticism.
  2. Prometheus (Greek deity)–Songs and music–History and criticism. I. Title.

  ML196.B38 2007
  781.5'6—dc22

ISBN 978-0-7546-5468-1 (hbk)   2006032548
ISBN 978-1-138-26497-7 (pbk)

Contents

List of Figures

List of Tables

List of Music Examples

Acknowledgments

In writing a book whose subject encompasses multiple composers and genres while spanning international borders, I have naturally incurred debts to scholars, archivists, librarians, colleagues, and publishers scattered across two continents. For their invaluable help and patience I thank the staff members at the Music Division of the Library of Congress, the Staatsbibliothek zu Berlin Preußischer Kulturbesitz, the Goethe- und Schiller-Archiv, Weimar, the Anna Amalia Bibliothek, Weimar, the Stadtbibliothek, Leipzig, the Österreichische Nationalbibliothek, Vienna, the Franz Liszt Memorial Museum and Research Centre, Budapest, the Hungarian State Opera House, Budapest, the Salle de musique at the Bibliothèque nationale, Paris, the British Library, London, the Library of the Royal College of Music, London, the Bodleian Library at Oxford University, and Morris Martin and his colleagues at the Music Library at the University of North Texas, Denton. The Small Grants Program at the University of Houston funded travel to these institutions.

On a more personal note, I would like to express special thanks to Laura Ponsonby, Kate Russell, and Ian Russell of the Shulbrede Priory, Lynchmere, Sussex, for their generosity and hospitality during the summer of 2003, when they offered me unrestricted access to their collection of the correspondence, diaries, and musical manuscripts of Sir C. Hubert H. Parry. Their lively interest in perpetuating and promoting their ancestral legacy is certainly a boon to an ongoing florescence in nineteenth-century British music studies, one they magnanimously extended to an American interloper.

Among many colleagues who have expressed interest in the book's topic and have offered welcome advice in general and in their specific areas of expertise, I especially thank Michael Beckerman, Scott Burnham, David Butler Cannata, Barbara Rose Lange, Ralph Locke, Mary Sue Morrow, Rena C. Mueller, and Mary Ann Smart.

Deserving special gratitude at Ashgate Publishing are Heidi May, who not only stewarded the project through the submission and editing processes, but also offered substantive comments regarding content and style, particularly regarding the history of published atheism (Chapter 6), and Adam Richardson, who tackled the book's complex layout with aplomb. In a similar vein, Lorne Dechtenberg prepared the musical examples with scrupulous attention to detail and adept knowledge of the processes involved.

For permission to publish extracts from texts and music scores, I thank Bärenreiter-Verlag and the Musikwissenschaftlicher Verlag, Vienna, as noted in the list of music examples. I have made every effort to trace the original copyright holders of material printed in this book for their permission to do so. The publishers will rectify any inadvertent lapses in future editions.

Chapter 1

Promethean Legacies: The Myth in Literature and Music Prior to the Romantic Era

The Olympian gods of Greek mythology rose to power in a cataclysmic battle against the Titans, divine progeny of the primordial Sky God and Earth Mother. One of their clan, Prometheus, remained defiant in defeat, boldly stealing heavenly fire as a gift for mortals, a boon denied them by Zeus, the triumphant Olympian ruler. As punishment, Zeus had Prometheus chained to a cliff, where in perpetual solitude he suffered the daily torment of an eagle feasting on his liver. Lamenting his fate but never recanting, he was ultimately freed by Hercules and celebrated as mankind's champion.

Thus outlined, the myth seems tailor-made for the romantic era. Indeed, it elicited original literary works or critical commentaries from the period's seminal authors, including Goethe, Schlegel, Byron, the Shelleys, the Brownings, and Longfellow, plus musical scores from composers as celebrated as Beethoven, Schubert, and Liszt or as unjustly neglected as Reichardt, Halévy, Holmès, and Parry. Two modern tropes commonly account for the legend's appeal.[1] First, Prometheus was both rebel and liberator, an attractive double identity during the age of Napoleon, whose original ambition to free European nations from aristocratic oppression resembled the Titan's quest to rescue humanity from Olympian tyranny, as Vincenzo Monti definitively recognized in his epic poem, *Il Prometeo* (1797).[2] An identical fusion of revolutionary and emancipator achieved its most famous musical embodiment eight years later in Beethoven's "Eroica" Symphony, a score initially dedicated to the Corsican general

---

[1]   Helen Archibald Clarke and Charlotte Porter, "The Prometheus Stories as Treated by Aeschylus, Shelley, Goethe, Milton, Byron, Lowen, and Longfellow," *Poet Lore*, 9 (1897): 589–606; Herbert Antcliffe, "Prometheus in Literature," *Nineteenth Century and After*, 96 (1924): 815–23; Karl Heinemann, "Prometheus," in Otto Immisch (ed.), *Die tragischen Gestalten der Griechen in der Weltliteratur* (2 vols, Leipzig, 1920), vol. 1, pp. 12–39; John Cann Bailey, "Prometheus in Poetry," in *The Continuity of Letters* (Oxford, 1923), pp. 103–38; Karl Kerényi, *Prometheus: Archetypal Image of Human Existence*, trans. Ralph Manheim (New York, 1963), pp. 15–18; Gerald Gillespie, "Prometheus in the Romantic Age," in Gerhart Hoffmeister (ed.), *European Romanticism: Literary Cross-Currents, Modes, and Models* (Detroit, 1990), pp. 197–210.

[2]   Vincenzo Monti, *Il Prometeo: Edizione critica, storia, interpretazione*, ed. Luca Frassineti (Pisa, 2001), pp. 63–8, 346–9; Pantaléon Deck, *Vincenzo Monti, un grand chantre de Napoléon 1er* (Strasbourg, 1948), pp. 116–17; Harold Bloom, "Napoleon and Prometheus: The Romantic Myth of Organic Energy," in *The Ringers in the Tower: Studies in Romantic Tradition* (Chicago, 1971), pp. 81–4.

and confirming its Promethean heritage with a finale based on a theme from the composer's ballet, *The Creatures of Prometheus*. With equal power but less renown, the same duality of insurrectionist and savior resonated in Franz Liszt's symphonic and choral settings of the myth, composed in the wake of failed campaigns for Hungarian independence during the late 1840s, and in a cantata by Augusta Holmès, written when her native Paris was under siege during the Franco-Prussian War.

A second frequently encountered interpretation of the myth reflects the romantic imagination's darker side. The Titan's exile, imprisonment, and torture are often read as metaphors of the epoch's notion of the genius or artist as an outcast who endured an uncomprehending public's criticism, a view that appealed to Goethe during his youthful *Sturm und Drang* period, and especially to Byron and the Shelleys because of their unorthodox, heavily censured lifestyles.[3] Composers likewise identified with Promethean martyrdom: Beethoven's deafness isolated him from society, driving him to write bold new music; Schubert considered himself an outsider in Viennese social circles long before syphilis confined him to a sickbed, where he finished his *Winterreise*, a song cycle of anguished loneliness; and Liszt was harassed by the press, first for romantic scandals, then for daring to infuse the tradition of German instrumental music with specific literary meaning in his innovative symphonic poems, until he retreated to a Catholic monastery's seclusion. Likewise attesting to the period's emphasis of the myth's punitive elements are graphic depictions of the Titan's imprisonment or torture in paintings by Peter Cornelius, Henri Lehmann, Théodore Caruelle d'Aligny, William Edward Frost, and Thomas Cole, and an eagle's presence in Max Klinger's statue of Beethoven, a reminder not only of the composer's engagement with the myth, but also of his titanic struggle against a fate that would have prevented a lesser musician from completing his life's work.

In truth, however, the myth supported far more than two familiar viewpoints, instead allowing authors, composers, artists, and commentators to express remarkably diverse attitudes toward culture, politics, philosophy, and aesthetics, all of which changed during the nineteenth century in response to broader social trends. These varied perspectives are mirrored and even amplified in musical works that are examined in ensuing chapters. Beethoven's ballet, for example, largely observes conventions of two eighteenth-century dance genres, the divertissement and the *ballet d'action*, with music cast in a pastoral idiom and a scenario allegorizing Empress Marie Therese's patronage of the arts in Vienna. Lieder by Reichardt, Schubert, and Wolf, on the other hand, violate generic norms, employ audacious harmonic practices, and advocate transgression against multiple authorities, thereby matching radical literary features and central thoughts of their shared text, Goethe's *Sturm und Drang* ode. Liszt's incidental music for Herder's *Der entfesselte Prometheus* recalls a Golden Age, embracing the idealistic legacy of eighteenth-century Weimar Classicism even while illustrating the quintessentially romantic traits of rebellion, redemption, and artistic marginalization. In sharp contrast, French

---

[3]   Edith Abel Braemer, *Goethes* Prometheus *und die Grundposition des Sturm und Drang* (Weimar, 1959), pp. 147–53, 206–28; Heinrich Düntzer, *Goethes Prometheus und Pandora* (Leipzig, 1874), pp. 10–21; Leslie A. Marchand, *Byron: A Biography* (New York, 1957), pp. 643–7.

composers addressed contemporary topics, including reactions to romantic excess in the theater and an awakening of scholarly and popular interest in Greek antiquity (Halévy), their nation's emerging industrial prowess (Saint-Saëns), the tragedy of the Franco-Prussian War (Holmès), and a synthesis of Christian theology and Parnassian aesthetics that served to advance Languedoc's regional identity (Fauré). Radicalism resurfaced as atheism and Wagnerism in Parry's settings of scenes from Shelley's *Prometheus Unbound*, but at virtually the same time, the conservatism of absolute music influenced overtures by Woldemar Bargiel and Carl Goldmark, whose compositions pleased the century's leading formalists, Eduard Hanslick, Josef Joachim, and Johannes Brahms. Indeed, the breadth and depth of the myth's romantic interpretations doubtless contributed to a florescence of Promethean music during the twentieth century, when at least 74 composers turned to the legend.

Western European literature and its attendant critical discourse, however, had rarely neglected the myth prior to the 1770s, when intense reactions against the French Enlightenment heralded the romantic movement's advent in Britain and Germany. From as early as the eighth century BCE, when Hesiod recorded the first known account of the Titan, through the mid-eighteenth century, when the *Philosophes* sought to reconcile mythic thought with reason, the fable supported indefatigable explication.[4] Indeed, literary and critical traditions of previous eras furnish precedents, though sometimes in nascent form, for many ideas that shaped distinctly romantic attitudes toward Prometheus. Political and religious revolution, progress through culture and technology, the human spirit's animation through the arts, and the creator as outcast— all are themes that originated in earlier times and continued to engross the romantics. My exploration of nineteenth-century representations of the myth accordingly draws upon the distinguished literary bequest of classical antiquity, the Middle Ages, the early modern era, and the Enlightenment, plus an incipient musical tradition that emerged in the seventeenth century. Three broad trends nonetheless coalesce within the vast historical continuum of the Titan's portrayals and related commentaries: a humanist outlook, three specific exegetic practices (biblical, material, political), and a tendency toward satire or burlesque.

Hesiod, a Greek epic poet active during the eighth century BCE, recorded the earliest surviving references to Prometheus. His *Theogony*, a book of creation stories, established the myth's essential features.[5] Prometheus, an ancient Titan, is a thief and prankster who tricked Zeus into accepting a sacrifice from man that seemed worthy because it was presented as meat covered with glistening fat. The fat instead concealed bones, a deception that provoked Zeus into punishing the Titan's followers with the first mortal woman and her attendant evils. Prometheus responded by giving humanity fire, whose secret he stole from the heavens. Zeus then had him shackled to a pillar where he would endure the daily torture of an eagle consuming his liver. Hesiod's *Works and Days*, an account of Greek pastoral life, reinforces

---

4   The definitive historical study of the Prometheus myth in literature remains Raymond Trousson, *Le Thème de Prométhée dans la littérature européenne* (2 vols, Geneva, 1964). Volume 1 covers antiquity through the Enlightenment.

5   Hesiod, *Theogony, Works and Days, Shield*, trans. Apostolos N. Athanassakis (Baltimore, 1983), pp. 26–8.

the concept of divine retribution and names Pandora as the first mortal woman.[6] Prometheus accordingly became the source of mankind's problems, a view prevalent during the Middle Ages and Enlightenment, but antithetical to romantic perceptions of the Titan. Both narratives also mention supporting characters who populate the myth's later renditions, including nineteenth-century musical settings. Most notable are references to the Titans who survived their battle with Zeus: Oceanus, who personified the river encircling the Earth; the Oceanids, his nymph-like daughters; Themis, the incarnation of justice; and Iapetus, father of Prometheus and his brother Atlas, whose shoulders bore the world. Pandora seldom participates in romantic versions of the legend, but is omnipresent in earlier literary and musical works. Her scarce appearances in the nineteenth century thus help define one of the era's broad perspectives on the myth.

Some two hundred years later, the Athenian tragedist Aeschylus (ca. 525–426 BCE) wrote the next and easily the most important version of the legend, *Prometheus Bound*. Indebted to Hesiod and perhaps to earlier Indo-European mythologies, it comprised the second play in a trilogy whose first and third dramas no longer survive.[7] Produced in or about 465 BCE, *Prometheus Bound* develops a rich, continuous narrative that nonetheless divides into seven scenes based on entrances and exits of characters (Table 1.1).

In an expository dialogue (scene 1), the allegorical character Might urges Hephaestus, the Olympian smithy, to chain Prometheus to rocks in the Scythian desert as punishment for having stolen fire to give to mortals. Hephaestus, a deformed outcast among more perfect deities, identifies with Prometheus and is reluctant to comply. But after alluding to the Titan's rescue by a nameless and as yet unborn hero (Hercules), Hephaestus obeys Might's command. Abandoned, Prometheus delivers a soliloquy (scene 2), invoking the four elements to witness the injustice of divine retribution. He bemoans his imprisonment, yet vows to endure his trials because he foresees the future (his name translates as forethought). Offstage rustling interrupts his ruminations, heralding the arrival of the Oceanids, who fulfill the traditional role of the Greek chorus (scene 3). After hearing the clang of iron as Hephaestus shackled the Titan to the rocks, the alarmed nymphs had raced to him on winged chariots. Seeing him in bondage, they react in fear and condemn Zeus' oppression, which Prometheus claims will only hasten the tyrant's downfall. The Oceanids then ask him to explain his predicament, a request he obliges by describing the war against the Olympians, mankind's ensuing subjugation to the will of Zeus, and his own efforts to aid humanity. He begins to disclose the future to the Oceanids, but their father's arrival postpones his revelations (scene 4). Oceanus counsels discretion, since Zeus could overhear the Titan's obstinate remonstrations and devise an even harsher punishment. Renewing his protests with greater intensity, Prometheus dismisses Oceanus, who exits hastily. In an elaborate exchange with the Oceanids (scene 5), Prometheus claims he was no instigator of ill-fated events, as in Hesiod, but rather mankind's benefactor: mortals were blind, mute, and ignorant until he granted them sight, hearing, reason, and forethought. He also taught them practical

---

6   Ibid., pp. 68–9.

7   Paul Roche, introduction to *Prometheus Bound: A New Translation, Introduction, Commentary* by Aeschylus (Waucondo, Ill., 1990), p. xii.

Table 1.1   A Synopsis of *Prometheus Bound*, by Aeschylus

Scene	Characters	Action
1	Might Hephaestus Prometheus	Might compels Hephaestus to imprison Prometheus for stealing fire.
2	Prometheus	Prometheus condemns Zeus as unjust, laments his incarceration, and foresees the future.
3	Oceanids Prometheus	Oceanids express fear and pity. Prometheus predicts Zeus' downfall and narrates past actions.
4	Oceanus Prometheus	Oceanus fears divine retribution. Prometheus renews protests.
5	Prometheus Oceanids	Prometheus, claiming he is mankind's benefactor and educator, remains defiant despite the Oceanids' warnings.
6	Io Prometheus	Io illustrates divine retribution. Prometheus prophesies his rescue by Hercules.
7	Hermes Prometheus Oceanids	Hermes, seeking the rescuer's name, threatens Prometheus with threefold torture. Prometheus, joined by the Oceanids, remains defiant.

skills, including how to build homes, work with wood, measure the seasons, chart the heavens, calculate with numbers, write with letters, domesticate animals, and interpret dreams. Like their father, the Oceanids advise against further opposition toward Zeus, but Prometheus reasserts his stance: he will remain defiant, enduring 10,000 agonies before casting off his chains, as decreed by Fate, a power stronger than Zeus. Shuddering at the prospect of relentless torture, the Oceanids repeat their warnings until Io, the embodiment of divine retribution's potency, enters (scene 6). Once a beautiful maiden, Io was coerced by her father to satisfy Zeus' sexual desires, transformed into a cow by the Olympian's jealous wife Hera, condemned to wander in exile, and suffers intermittent madness because of her transgression. Prometheus sees no relief from her plight, but prophesies that in 13 generations one of her descendants will overthrow Zeus, a third reference to Hercules. Beset with madness, Io flees, leaving the chorus to infer a moral from her story, namely that marriage should be based on class. Prometheus, however, draws another conclusion: unlike Io, he is immortal and does not fear speaking out, even after witnessing a punishment more terrible than his own. Faced with immutable defiance, Zeus sends Hermes, messenger of the gods, to learn the name of the hero who will end Olympian rule (scene 7). Prometheus dismisses Hermes as a slave of Zeus, whom he still resists, whereupon the messenger utters the Titan's dire threefold destiny: thunder and lightning will shatter the cliff where he is bound, surrounding him in pillars of rock; Zeus' eagle will torment him; and he will regain freedom only after some god assumes his burdens and descends into Hades (tasks ultimately fulfilled by Hercules). Ignoring further threats from Hermes, the chorus remains loyal to Prometheus, who calls for the thunderbolt to strike where it may and invokes the Air, his mother, to witness his suffering. Immediately thunder and lightning plunge the stage into darkness.

Prometheus Bound supplied the model for the vast majority of later versions of the myth, including several nineteenth-century musical settings. Nearly all its characters inhabit the literature and criticism of ensuing eras, although the legend's romantic treatments rarely feature Io, perhaps because her digressive tale simply reinforces the theme of divine retribution. The play's dialogues, soliloquies, and choruses likewise suggest straightforward counterparts in ensembles, arias, and choral numbers of vocal works. But instrumental compositions also depict facets of the myth, particularly the Titan's defiance and redemption, by resorting to musical imitation. Goldmark's overture, for example, graphically portrays the Aeschylean drama's opening soliloquy and final cataclysm. More often, however, the Titan's unrepentant rebellion and beneficent role in humanity's development are paramount in the myth's romantic literary and musical traditions.

Later Greek and Roman authors rarely granted the legend centrality in their writings, instead mentioning its details in general mythologies or exegetic works. The genealogy and marital status of Prometheus, for example, aroused recurrent interest: the Oceanid Asia was his mother according to Lycophron and Apollodorus, but his wife according to Herodotus; Hyginus named the Titan Themis as his mother.[8] Few, however, preserved Hesiod's attribution of maternity to another Oceanid, Clymene.[9] Equally popular were variants of the myth's essential episodes: Prometheus obtained fire by hiding it in a fennel stalk, accepting an eagle's help, or may not have performed the heroic deed himself; Hermes supposedly executed his punishment, not Hephaestus; the site of his imprisonment was more often the Caucasus than Scythia; and although Prometheus usually incurred Zeus' wrath in part because he formed the entire human race, Lucian, Menander, and Hyginus claimed divine scorn resulted from creating women alone or Pandora in particular.[10] Debates

---

[8]   Lycophron, *Alexandra*, in *Callimachus: Hymns and Epigrams; Lycophron*, trans. A.W. Mair (Cambridge, Mass., 1960), pp. 426–7; Apollodorus, *Gods and Heroes of the Greeks: The Library of Apollodorus*, trans. Michael Simpson (Amherst, 1976), p. 14; Herodotus, *The History*, trans. David Green (Chicago, 1987), p. 297; Hyginus, *Fabularum liber* (New York, 1976), p. 9.

[9]   Hesiod, *Theogony*, pp. 25–6.

[10]   Regarding each episode, see the listed sources: fire's theft, Apollodorus, p. 32; Plutarch, *Moralia*, trans. Frank Cole Babbitt (15 vols, Cambridge, Mass., 1957), vol. 2, p. 85; punishment by Hermes, Hyginus, p. 42; imprisonment on Caucasus, Apollodorus, p. 99; Marcus Tullius Cicero, *Tuscan Disputations*, trans. A.E. Douglas (Warminster, 1990), pp. 82–3; Virgil, *Bucolics*, in *The Works of Virgil*, trans. A. Hamilton Bryce (London, 1914), p. 29; Hyginus, p. 42; punished

over such minutiae continued during later stages of the myth's development, but rarely escalated into serious disputes. The exception was Goethe's ode, which raised creative, political, and religious autonomy to the status of cardinal issues and hence precipitated vociferous debate.

Among several late classical works that developed the myth more fully, the most sensational is imbedded in a satire written by Lucian of Samosata during the second century CE.[11] Discussing Prometheus in a misogynist lampoon of life in a brothel, Lucian deemed the creation of women the Titan's worst offense, allowed defiance to degenerate into mockery when Prometheus resists Hermes, and diminished the sacrilege of stealing from a deity by claiming it was not serious enough to warrant such severe retribution. Indicative of the satire's late date and transitional nature is that Prometheus is crucified, not chained to a rock. The myth's Christian overtones naturally gained importance during the Middle Ages and resurfaced occasionally in later cultural periods, most notably during the nineteenth century in Shelley's *Prometheus Unbound*, Parry's related *Scenes*, and several Parnassian literary works, including the libretto of Fauré's opera.

Prometheus rarely appears in Latin or vernacular literature of the early Middle Ages. Antagonism toward pagan culture may explain this dearth, but even in centers such as Seville, where Archbishop Isidore (570–636) preserved knowledge of Greek language and civilization, the myth incited controversy. Isidore, Lactantius, Fulgentius, and Clement of Alexandria denounced the Titan's rebellion against Zeus and refusal to submit to divine rule as blasphemous assaults on papal authority.[12] The legend also evinced satanic elements, most obviously the Titan's fiery associations, hatred for Zeus, and endowment of mankind with a forbidden gift, the latter comparable to Lucifer's temptation of Eve.[13] Enmity toward religious authority, an important theme throughout the fable's history, aroused virulent dispute when Goethe's critics detected pantheism in his ode and when Shelley voiced his atheism by exploiting satanic associations.

Several early Christian exegetes nonetheless successfully reconciled facets of the myth with their theological orientation. Frequently noted parallels between the Titan's afflictions and Job's trials implied Prometheus should accept a just god's punishment, as in Tatian's early Christianized version of the legend (third century CE).[14] Pandora assumed a new role in the writings of Philo of Alexandria (first century CE), Tertullian

---

for creating women, Menander, cited in Lucian of Samosata, *Les Amours*, in *Dialogues des courtisanes*, trans. Belin de Ballu, ed. Jacques Nicolas (Paris, 1929), p. 218; Hyginus, p. 42.

[11]   Lucian of Samosata, *Selected Satires of Lucian*, trans. Lionel Casson (New York, 1962), pp. 125–35.

[12]   For references to Fulgentius (*Mythologiae*), Lactantius (*De opificio dei*), Clement of Alexandria (*Stromatum*), and Isidore (*Opera*), see John Gower, *The English Works*, ed. G.C. Macaulay (2 vols, London, 1900), vol. 1, pp. 366, 443.

[13]   Karl Federn, "Satan und Prometheus," in *Neun Essays* (Berlin, 1900), pp. 196–7; André Bonnard, "La Revolte de Prométhée et le devenir de la justice," *Suisse contemporaine*, 6 (1946): 436.

[14]   William A. Irwin, "Job and Prometheus," *Journal of Religion*, 30 (1950): 90–108; Johannes Lindblom, *Job and Prometheus: A Comparative Study* (Lund, 1939), pp. 28–87.

(born ca. 150 CE), and Plotinus (203–62 CE).[15] No longer the mere instrument of Zeus' revenge, she became a pagan Eve, who by unleashing evil upon the world embodied the doctrine of original sin. At least one leading Christian writer, however, maintained a positive view of the legend. Tertullian observed similarities between the myth and the life of Christ: Prometheus founded a new order and educated mortals; he felt compassion and sacrificed himself for mankind; he was chained to a cliff just as Christ was crucified on Calvary; and he was ultimately redeemed. Tertullian's insights were scarcely widespread, but they exerted tremendous influence on comparative mythology as the discipline emerged during the seventeenth century, and on the ideology of several romantic authors, including Samuel Taylor Coleridge, Elizabeth Barrett Browning, Edgar Quinet, and the Parnassians.

While not entirely absent from medieval literature, the myth suffered lingering neglect because the plays of Aeschylus remained untranslated longer than those of other Greek authors, even after humanist impulses prompted the emergence of early modern European cultures. Hesiod's complete writings, for example, were published in Latin by Niccolò Valle in 1471 and ran to 25 editions in 50 years.[16] Latin and vernacular translations of Aeschylus, however, were attempted at least two generations later (ca. 1518–52) and achieved adequate editorial standards only in 1557, when Petrus Victorius and Henri Estienne produced all his surviving plays.[17]

The Aeschylean revival's most distinguished forerunner was Giovanni Boccaccio (1313–75), a Florentine merchant's son whose literary juvenilia secured his entry into aristocratic circles. From 1350 onward his intense classical studies with Petrarch resulted in poems based on an episode in the Trojan War (*Filostrato*) and the story of Theseus (*Teseida*), plus a mythological compendium (*De geneologia Deorum*). Boccaccio devoted a whole chapter of his compilation to Prometheus, developing a humanist perspective on a conflation of sources.[18] Thus the Titan formed men

---

[15]   Philo of Alexandria, *De aeternitate mundi*, in *Philo*, trans. F.H. Colson and G.H. Whitaker (12 vols, Cambridge, Mass., 1929), vol. 9, p. 227; Tertullian, *De corona*, ed. Jacques Fontaine (Paris, 1966), pp. 94–5; Plotinus, *The Enneads*, trans. Stephen MacKenna (New York, 1962), pp. 272–3, 388–9, 538–40.

[16]   Dora and Erwin Panofsky, *Pandora's Box: The Changing Aspects of a Mythological Symbol* (New York, 1962), p. 14.

[17]   Marie Delcourt, *Etude sur les traductions des tragiques grecs et latins en France depuis la renaissance* (Brussels, 1925), p. 19; Bruno Costantini, "La fortuna di Eschilo in Italia," *Dioniso*, 12 (1949): 154–5; Ruth Bunker, *A Bibliographical Study of the Greek Works in Translations Published in France during the Renaissance: The Decade 1540–1550* (New York, 1939), pp. 197–200; José Maria de Cossio, *Las fábulas mitológicas en España* (Madrid, 1952), pp. 38–71; for a date of 1663 for the first Latin translation of Aeschylus undertaken in England, see Henry Burrowes Lathrop, *Translations from the Classics into English from Caxton to Chapman, 1477–1620* (Madison, 1935), p. 142; for references to 26 English translations of *Prometheus Bound* undertaken between 1822 and 1900, see Finley Melville Kendall Foster, *English Translations from the Greek: A Bibliographical Survey* (New York, 1918), pp. 2–7; Lawrence S. Thomson, "German Translations of the Classics between 1450 and 1550," *Journal of English and Germanic Philology*, 42 (1943): 348.

[18]   Giovanni Boccaccio, *Genealogiae deorum gentilium libri*, ed. Vincenzo Romano (2 vols, Bari, 1951), vol. 1, pp. 196–202.

and women from clay as in Ovid, taught them astronomy, morality, and civics as in Aeschylus, endowed them with a lion's violence as in Horace, and accepted an invitation from Minerva, the goddess of wisdom, to present his creations before the Olympians as in Sirvius and Fulgentius.[19] The legend consequently remained a creation myth, but one in which Prometheus bestowed intelligence on mankind, a role he had rarely fulfilled during the Middle Ages but assumed routinely in Renaissance texts and the Enlightenment's literature and music. Indeed, Boccaccio's widely disseminated conception of Prometheus as a benevolent animator and teacher of formerly lifeless beings made of clay resonates in many eighteenth-century representations of the myth, most notably Goethe's ode and Salvatore Viganò's scenario for Beethoven's ballet, whose action revolves around the presentation of the Titan's "creatures" before the Olympian court.[20]

Boccaccio's ideas more directly influenced the sixteenth century's three great Italian mythographers: Lilio Giraldi credited Prometheus with creating men and inventing the arts; Natalis Comes likewise attributed many inventions to the Titan and emphasized Minerva's mentorship; and Vincenzo Cartari recounted mankind's presentation before the Olympians.[21] Other Renaissance anthologists largely preserved the myth's darker medieval traditions, though the humanist version flourished among Florentine academicians, particularly Filippo Villani, Marsilio Ficino, and Pietro Pompanazzi, who rediscovered in Prometheus embodiments of the artist as creator, organized society's latent power, the search for truth, the human condition of perpetual struggle, and the dynamism of human consciousness.[22]

Northern writers also helped reconstitute the Titan's Greek humanist identity. The great Dutch scholar Desiderius Erasmus judged Prometheus a hero of self-determined destiny, an incarnation of human potential, and an illustration of persistent struggle's value,[23] thereby approaching a heroic conception of the Titan that would thrive during the nineteenth century. Another romantic notion of the myth was anticipated by Charles de Bouelles, a northern French humanist who astutely observed Prometheus was indeed a symbol of wisdom acquired through adversity, but he was by nature solitary and meditative, an image that appealed to Goethe and those he influenced, including Beethoven, Schubert, and Liszt.[24] Most modern in his outlook, however, was the English statesman and prolific author Francis Bacon,

---

[19]   Trousson, vol. 1, p. 88.

[20]   Ernest Hatch Wilkins, "The Genealogy of the Editions of the *Geneologia Deorum*," *Modern Philology*, 17/8 (1919): 65–78.

[21]   Lilio Gregorio Giraldi, *De deis gentium, Basel 1548* (New York, 1976), pp. 37, 572, 691; Natalis Comes, *Mythologie, Paris 1627*, trans. Jean Boudouin (2 vols, New York, 1976), vol. 1, pp. 298–302; Vincenzo Cartari, *Le imagini ... degli dei, Venice 1571* (New York, 1976), p. 387.

[22]   August Buck, "Ueber einige Deutungen des Prometheusmythos," in Heinrich Lausberg and Harald Weinrich (eds), *Romanica, Festschrift für Gerhard Rohlfs* (Halle, 1958), pp. 90–92; Trousson, vol. 1, pp. 101–6, 109.

[23]   Desiderius Erasmus, *Opera omnia*, ed. Joannis Clericus (10 vols, Hildesheim, 1961), vol. 1, p. 327A, vol. 2, p. 39B, vol. 4, p. 357B, vol. 5, pp. 29, 787E.

[24]   Charles de Bouelles, *Liber de sapiente*, ed. Raymond Klibansky, in Ernst Cassirer, *Individuum und Kosmos in der Philosophie der Renaissance* (Leipzig, 1927), p. 320.

who saw the Titan's flame not as a mere symbol, but as an essential element of a scientific society.[25] Prometheus stole fire from the heavens, but purposely left the task of discovering how to make it to mankind. Sequential technological developments were thus integral to humanity's progress. Bacon's viewpoint would predictably resurface as Europe industrialized, but its most concrete nineteenth-century musical realization is found in a cantata that Saint-Saëns composed to celebrate French industrial accomplishments at the Paris Exhibition of 1867.

Further Renaissance anthologies compiled by Hermannus Torrentinus in Antwerp, Charles Estienne in Geneva, Celio Calcagnini in Basel, and Geoffrey Whitney in London added little to humanist attitudes toward Prometheus.[26] These and other authors nonetheless established a foundation for comparative mythology's florescence during the seventeenth century. Likewise anticipating future developments were various sixteenth-century poems that mentioned but rarely focused on the Titan. Instead Pandora captivated the myth's readers, whether her evils again signified vices as in medieval allegories, or whether she evolved into an unattainable womanly ideal, thus reducing the Promethean flame to a symbol of romantic love. In such poems by Mellin de Saint-Gelais and Joachim Du Bellay, myth degenerated into burlesque, an event encountered regularly during the next two centuries but rarely in the romantic era, at least in musical genres.[27] Indeed, the myth's only nineteenth-century satirical treatments were John Barnett's *Olympic Revels, or Prometheus and Pandora* (1831), which inaugurated the heyday of British burlesque, and Joseph Lanner's *Prometheus Funken, Grätzer Soirée Waltzer* (1837), a set of unpretentious dances for piano.

Widespread interest in mythology during the seventeenth century produced myriad sources concerning Prometheus. Editions, translations, and manuals occupied encyclopedists for generations, while comparative mythographers likened the Greek fable to myths originating in Asia, northern Africa, and elsewhere in Europe.[28] Authors often explained the legend as an allegory of actual events in historical antiquity, renewing exegetic impulses that had motivated writers of the Middle Ages, though they normally sought to discover secular rather than

---

[25]   Francis Bacon, *The Wisedome of the Ancients, London 1619* (New York, 1968), pp. 127, 129, 142.

[26]   De Witt T. Starnes and Ernst Talbert, *Classical Myth and Legend in Renaissance Dictionaries* (Chapel Hill, 1955), pp. 119–23, 154–8; Henry Green, *Shakespeare and the Emblem Writers* (New York, [1870]), pp. 265–9.

[27]   Mellin de Saint-Gelais, *En la mort d'Anne Huillier*, in *Œuvres complètes*, ed. Prosper Blanchemain (3 vols, Nendeln, 1970), vol. 2, pp. 157–8; Joachim Du Bellay, *L'Olive*, in *Œuvres poétiques*, ed. Daniel Aris and Françoise Joukovsky (Paris, 1933), p. 70.

[28]   Seventeenth-century compendia include Jean Desmarets de Saint-Sorlin, *La Verité des fables* (Paris, 1648); Armand Maichin and Henry Boysset, *La Théologie payenne* (Saint-Iean d'Angély, 1657); Etienne Morin, *Stephani Morini dissertationes octo, in quibus multa sacrae et profanae Antiquitatis monumenta explicantur* (Geneva, 1683); David Nerreter, *Ursprung der Abgötterey* (Nuremburg, 1701); Alexander Ross, *Mystagogus poeticus, or the Muses interpreter, London 1648* (New York, 1976). Regarding the emergent study of Asian, African, and pan-European myths, see Otto Gruppe, *Geschichte der klassischen Mythologie während des Mittelalters und während der Neuzeit* (Leipzig, 1921), pp. 45–7.

biblical counterparts for mythic events and characters. The German philosopher and mathematician Gottfried Wilhelm Leibniz, for example, linked the struggle between the Titans and Olympians with the Scythian invasions of Greece during the seventh century BCE.[29] Louis Thomassin, a Parisian priest, and Alexander Ross, a Forfarshire schoolmaster, perpetuated a medieval belief that Prometheus was originally Egyptian, although they determined he was not a scholar, but a governor or king of the ancient civilization.[30] Antoine Furetière and Louis Moréri, authors of two of the seventeenth century's ubiquitous dictionaries, agreed Prometheus was a famous astronomer.[31] Such interpretations transformed the myth into a chronicle of mundane events, diminishing the humanism it had regained throughout the early modern era. They nonetheless set precedents for equating the Titan with heroes from secular history and a proliferation of Napoleonic comparisons during the late eighteenth century.

Biblical exegesis, invigorated by scientific philology, reached varied but equally material conclusions. Iapetus, father of Prometheus and his brother Epimetheus, was revealed to be Japhet, father of Magog and Gog, the heroes of Genesis who battled Satan after he escaped 1,000 years of captivity.[32] The name Prometheus, meaning forethought, encouraged comparisons with Noah, who divined the future and fathered a new order.[33] Prometheus was also a pagan Moses: both spoke to God, endured hardship, and ended their people's captivity.[34] Another popular correlation with an event in Genesis, the murder of Abel (Prometheus) by his brother Cain (Zeus), resurfaced as romanticism gained momentum, most conspicuously in Byron's poetic drama, *Cain, A Mystery* (1821). Such disparate biblical identifications, like their historical equivalents, were advanced sporadically prior to the seventeenth century and throughout the eighteenth and nineteenth. But biblical comparisons generally concerned the romantics less than earlier writers,

---

[29]   Gottfried Wilhelm Leibniz, *Opera omnia*, vol. 1, *Theologica* (Hildesheim, 1989), p. 236.

[30]   Louis Thomassin, *La Méthode d'étudier et d'enseigner chrétiennement et solidement les lettres humaines par rapport aux lettres divines et aux Ecritures* (2 vols, Paris, 1681), vol. 1, p. 288, vol. 2, pp. 669–72; Ross, p. 368.

[31]   Antoine Furetière, *Dictionnaire universel* (4 vols, Hildesheim, 1972), s.v. Prométhée; Louis Moréri, *The Great Historical, Geographical and Poetical Dictionary* (London, 1999), s.v. Prometheus [*Le Grand dictionnaire historique* (Amsterdam, 1692), translated by "several learned gentlemen"].

[32]   Samuel Bochart, *Opera omnia, hoc est Phaleg, Canaan, et Hierozoicon* (Leiden, 1692), p. 12.

[33]   Gerardus Joannes Vossius, *De theologia gentili, Amsterdam 1641* (New York, 1976), p. 74; Theophilus Gale, *The Court of Gentiles, or, A Discourse Touching on the Original of Human Literature* (Oxford, 1672), p. 72; Abraham Cowley, *Prometheus ill-painted*, in *Poems*, ed. A.R. Waller (Cambridge, 1905), p. 25. Other advocates of Noah include Guillaume de Lavaur, Samuel Bochart, and Edward Stillingfeet. See Trousson, vol. 1, pp. 149–50, 183.

[34]   Vossius, p. 74; Philipp von Zesen, *Coelum astronomico-poeticum, sive, Mythologicum stellarum fixorum* (Amsterdam, 1662), pp. 176–8; Pierre-Daniel Huet, *Demonstratio evangelica ad serennissimum delphinum* (Amsterdam, 1680), pp. 162–6.

except toward the nineteenth century's end, when their revival marked a retreat from the era's prevailing attitudes.

Few seventeenth-century authors emphasized humanist representations of the Titan as rebel, creator, or benefactor. The celebrated exception was Milton, whose portrayal of Satan in *Paradise Lost* (1667) reveals striking Promethean affinities.[35] Most obviously, both protagonists defy supreme deities, endure punishment for transgression, refuse to recant, and play roles in shaping mankind. Milton's satanic characterization and elegant blank verse influenced British romantics, particularly Byron and Shelley, who drew inspiration from the epic for their versions of the myth. Likewise addressing a traditional humanist issue was the philosopher Thomas Hobbes, who believed Prometheus embodied a specific type of human intelligence that precipitated the founding of democracy.[36] Controversial in its day, his republican identification became routine during the Napoleonic age.

Otherwise many seventeenth-century literary treatments of the myth followed Renaissance poetry's blithe trends. In an anonymous Spanish poem entitled *Eccos de la Musa Trasmonatana, o Prometheo, Fábula Alegórica*, for example, the Titan is punished not for defying Zeus, but rather for expressing affection for Pandora and thereby incurring the jealous wrath of Venus.[37] Likewise reflecting the century's frivolous approach is a Latin play by the Belgian humanist André Catulle, who flattered local magistrates to win support for the Collège de De Vaulx by setting one act in his native Louvain, where Prometheus extols current governmental policies.[38] William Killigrew devised a comic setting of the myth in *Pandora*, a play in which the title character's vices are deemed virtues by two libertines who attempt to usurp the throne of Syracuse.[39] These satirical tendencies strengthened during the Enlightenment, but as already noted, rarely attracted the romantics.

Dating from the seventeenth century are the myth's first modern musical treatments, as opposed to the recitation, choruses, and instrumental accompaniment that doubtless embellished the Aeschylean trilogy's festival productions during Greek antiquity but no longer survive.[40] Prometheus made his modern musical debut as a supporting character in two theatrical works. In *The Lord's Masque* by Thomas Campion, he is merely one of many mythological guests at the wedding of Elizabeth, daughter of James I of England, and Frederick V, Elector Palatine of the Rhine and King of Bohemia, in 1613.[41] His attributes are noteworthy, however, because he is

---

[35]   Raphael Jehuda Zwi Werblowsky, *Lucifer and Prometheus: A Study of Milton's Satan* (London, 1952), pp. 47–66.

[36]   Thomas Hobbes, *On the Citizen*, trans. and ed. Richard Tuck and Michael Silverthorne (New York, 1998), pp. 117–18.

[37]   Regarding this long poem, now preserved at the Biblioteca nacional de Madrid (Ms. 2 573), see Trousson, vol. 1, pp. 155–6.

[38]   Regarding Catulle's *Prometheus sive de origine scientiarum* (1613), see Félix Nève, *Prométhée, drame latin d'André Catulle* (Gand, 1862), pp. 7–14.

[39]   William Killigrew, *Pandora: A Comedy*, in *Four Plays* (London, 1664).

[40]   Thomas J. Mathiesen, *Apollo's Lyre: Greek Music and Music Theory in Antiquity and the Middle Ages* (Lincoln, 1999), pp. 122–5.

[41]   Thomas Campion, *The Works of Thomas Campion*, ed. A.H. Bullen (London, 1889), pp. 191–209.

touted as humanity's father and he animates eight inert female statues that come to life and dance with male courtiers, action duplicated in Viganò's scenario for Beethoven's ballet. In observing the masque's conventions, arrangements of music by a half dozen composers entail dances, choruses, and songs, none performed by Prometheus.[42] In Carlo Caprioli's opera-ballet *Le nozze di Peleo e di Teti* (1654), Prometheus was a singing role undertaken by Thomas Stafford, an English composer and performer active in Rome. But because the score disappeared after eight performances, little else is known about the lavishly produced opera.[43]

Prometheus achieved the rank of title character in three seventeenth-century operatic works. Italian organist and singer Antonio Maria Viviani composed perhaps only part of a Spanish-language comedy, *Aun vencido vence Amor, ò El Prometeo* (1669) for a performance honoring Queen Mariana of Spain at the Habsburg court in Vienna, where he was employed until his death in 1683.[44] Juan Hidalgo provided music for the great Spanish dramatist Pedro Calderón de la Barca's *La estatua de Prometeo* (1670 or 1674), an elaborately staged, partly sung, partly spoken semi-opera, a genre cultivated at the Madrid court.[45] Emphasizing the chaos mankind experiences after Prometheus steals a ray of sun and Minerva's restoration of order through an appeal to Zeus, *La estatua* honors noble patrons by comparing their beneficent acts to those of Prometheus. The state's glorification is also paramount in *Prometeo liberato* (1683), neither an oratorio nor an opera, but a hybrid vocal work with a libretto by Antonio Bergamori and music by Gianbattista Bassani, which inaugurated a festival in Bologna.[46] Here the Titan's liberation correlated not with aristocratic accomplishments, but rather with political freedoms the city secured 400 years earlier in a popular uprising. Thus Prometheus temporarily regained his status as a revolutionary, one of his dominant romantic attributes.

Specific seventeenth-century perspectives remained viable during the age of the *Philosophes*. Ongoing searches for the myth's concrete historical parallels, for example, yielded an indirect association with Sesostris, the leader of a Greek expedition pre-dating the Argosy's voyages, who left Prometheus "with a body of men at Mount Caucasus, to guard that pass," a theory postulated by Sir Isaac Newton.[47] Several French and Italian classicists, Giambattista Vico the best known among them, independently determined Prometheus was a king, but disagreed over whether he ruled Peloponnesus, Thessaly, or an undetermined empire.[48] Biblical exegesis waned

---

[42]   Andrew J. Sabol (ed.), *A Score for* The Lord's Masque *by Thomas Campion* (Hanover, 1993), pp. 49–315.

[43]   André Tessier, "Giacomo Torelli a Parigi e la messa in scena della *Nozze di Peleo* di Carlo Caprioli," *Rassegna musicale*, 1 (1928): 584–8.

[44]   Herbert Seifert, *Die Oper am Wiener Kaiserhof im 17. Jahrhundert* (Tutzing, 1985), pp. 69–70.

[45]   Louise K. Stein, *Songs of Mortals, Dialogues of the Gods: Music and Theatre in Seventeenth-Century Spain* (Oxford, 1993), pp. 177–84.

[46]   Richard Haselbach, *Giovanni Battista Bassani* (Kassel, 1955), p. 67.

[47]   Isaac Newton, *The Chronology of Antient Kingdoms Amended* (Dublin, 1728), p. 67.

[48]   Giambattista Vico, *The New Science of Giambattista Vico*, trans. Goddard Bergin and Max Harold Fisch (Ithaca, 1984), p. 503; Etienne Fourmont, *Réflexions sur l'origine,*

in an era marked by anticlericalism and the slavish adulation of reason, but no less an authority than Voltaire likened Prometheus and Pandora to Adam and Eve, thus completing a typically one-sided explication that concentrated on the women and their evils.[49] Numerous didactic pieces likewise demonized Pandora. But exegetic traditions declined as the eighteenth century progressed, largely because comparative studies demonstrated that resemblances among mythologies often merely disclosed common historical sources or sometimes originated by pure chance.

The myth nonetheless supported material associations of a more contemporary nature during the eighteenth century. Ippolito Zanelli, for example, judged the Florentine d'Este family and the Titan equally magnificent benefactors of mankind.[50] Resorting to similar flattery, Voltaire declared in verse that his patron Frederick the Great had reignited the Promethean flame, a compliment he paid in prose to dance master Jean-Georges Noverre.[51] In diametric contrast, Jonathan Swift criticized a prominent politician in his epigrammatic poem, *Prometheus, On Wood the Patentee's Irish Half-Pence* (1724).[52] Swift revived Hesiod's portrayal of the Titan as a robber, comparing his fiery theft to the financial policies of William Wood, a nefarious tradesman who profited from the dominant Whig Party's repression of Ireland through devaluation of the country's currency. Nearly a century later, Byron would make a similar political reference in *The Irish Avatar* (1821), a poem that restored the Titan's heroism by comparing him to Irish statesman Henry Grattan, whose brilliant oratory secured the repeal of Poynings' Law, which had subjected all Irish legislation to British parliamentary approval.[53] Each poem articulates its era's distinct attitude: during the early eighteenth century the myth was often a vehicle for satire, whereas the romantics typically emphasized an oppressed people's liberation by a redeemed hero.

Indeed, the myth's progressive message was surprisingly unappealing in an age as preoccupied with moral and social advancement as the Enlightenment. Indifference toward the Titan's role in humanity's development is partially explained by a debate over material progress, which many *Philosophes* considered necessary for achieving goals in ethical and political evolution. Jean-Jacques Rousseau dissented, however, deeming materialism a source of European cultural corruption. In his *Discours sur les sciences et les arts* (1750) Rousseau cited the Prometheus myth's transmission from Egypt to Greece as evidence of society's historical contamination through the

l'histoire et la succession des anciens peuples (2 vols, Paris, 1747), vol. 1, p. xxvii; Augustin Calmet, *Abrégé chronologique de l'histoire sacrée et profane* (Nancy, 1729), p. 4.

49   François-Marie Arouet de Voltaire, *Dieu et les hommes*, in *Œuvres complètes*, ed. Louis Moland et al. (52 vols, Paris, 1879), vol. 28, p. 189.

50   Ippolito Zanelli, *Prometeo: Serenata in onore di due felicissimi giorni natalizi delle altezze serenissime delle Principesse d'Este Benedetta e Amalia* (Modena, 1728).

51   See letters of 5 June 1740 and 11 October 1763 in Voltaire, *Les Œuvres complètes de Voltaire*, ed. Theodore Besterman et al. (Geneva, 1968–), vol. 91, pp. 193–4, vol. 111, p. 27.

52   Jonathan Swift, *The Poems*, ed. William Ernst Browning (2 vols, London, 1910), vol. 2, pp. 201–3.

53   Lord George Gordon Byron, *The Poetical Works of Byron*, ed. Robert F. Gleckner (Boston, 1975), pp. 201–4.

exchange of art and technology,[54] thus offering a rationalist alternative to Christian allegories of the legend as the source of original sin. Rousseau was not alone in casting an unflattering light on the Titan. In Jean-Jacques Lefranc de Pompignan's five-act tragedy after Aeschylus, Prometheus abuses his artistic talent, accepts punishment, and even apologizes for his transgressions.[55] The Titan likewise recants to gain freedom in *Der befreyte Prometheus*, a poem by the Swiss cleric Georg Christoph Tobler, a translator of Athenian playwrights.[56]

New eighteenth-century translations of Aeschylus rarely represented improvements over their precursors, especially in France, where the poet's coarseness was held in disdain until the 1830s.[57] The situation nonetheless scarcely precluded theatrical productions featuring the Titan in supporting roles. Compatible with the art of the divertissement, such plays typically involved Prometheus animating Pandora, a ploy capitalizing on an analogous episode in the Pygmalion myth, one of the period's most popular stories.[58] Adaptations of the legend by authors such as Anne-Marie Meusnier de Querlon (1748) and Pigeon de Saint-Paterne (1785) were brief, idyllic, and suited to spectacle, with characters expressing naïve astonishment as they first encounter nature.[59] Evincing more ambition, Alain-René Lesage's satire, *Boëte de Pandore* (1721), raised issues of class struggle by mixing commedia dell'arte characters with Olympian deities.[60] Similarly but less seriously, an anonymous English lampoon entitled *Pandora's Box* (1718) was merely a tirade against snuff and tobacco's evils.[61] Theatrical parodies, however, dropped sharply in number when Aeschylean translations achieved unprecedented accuracy and aroused interest in modern-language productions.

Several eighteenth-century authors nonetheless foreshadowed ideas the romantics would embrace and intensify. In one of the era's most influential commentaries on the myth, Lord Anthony Ashley Cooper Shaftesbury declared the fable was invented

---

[54] Jean-Jacques Rousseau, *Discourse on the Sciences and Arts*, in *The Collected Writings of Rousseau*, ed. Roger D. Masters and Christopher Kelly, trans. Judith R. Bush et al. (12 vols, Hanover, 1990–), vol. 2, pp. 12–13.

[55] Jean-Jacques Lefranc de Pompignan, *Prométhée*, in *Œuvres* (4 vols, Geneva, 1971), vol. 3, pp. 209–62.

[56] Georg Christoph Tobler, "*Der befreyte Prometheus*," *Der teutsche Merkur*, 82 (April 1782): 41–3.

[57] Howard Lee Nostrand, *Le Théâtre antique et à l'antique en France de 1840 à 1900* (Paris, 1934), p. 52.

[58] Regarding the Pandora myth's settings as divertissements, see Trousson, vol. 1, pp. 194–7; regarding the Pygmalion myth's relative neglect during the early eighteenth century and its popularity after Rousseau completed his play (1762), see Essaka Joshua, *Pygmalion and Galatea: The History of a Narrative in English Literature* (Aldershot, 2001), pp. 33–5.

[59] Anne-Gabriel Meusnier de Querlon, *Les Hommes de Prométhée* (London, 1748; reprint, Paris, 1894), pp. 117–31; Pigeon de Saint-Paterne, *Pandore: Scène lyrique* (Paris, 1785; reprint, Paris, 1888).

[60] Jean-Augustin-Julien Desboulmiers, *Histoire du théâtre de l'Opéra comique* (2 vols, Paris, 1769; reprint, New York, 1970), vol. 1, p. 79.

[61] Trousson, vol. 1, p. 212.

to explain divine Creation's inherent evil, a conviction Goethe and Shelley echoed.[62] Christoph Martin Wieland, a luminary of the German Enlightenment, countered Rousseau's interpretation of the legend as a parable of cultural corruption, claiming the Titan symbolized a perpetual struggle that was both an innate part of the human condition and the very means whereby mankind transcended new obstacles.[63] Wieland's idealism, destined to shape the historiography of Beethoven's achievement, epitomized the romantic approach to the myth, though Prometheus was likewise a progressive revolutionary in Voltaire's play *Pandore* (1740).[64] But easily the most radical formulation of the myth appeared in Thomas Blackwell's *Letters concerning Mythology* (1748), wherein the Titan receives assistance from "his spouse Celero the daughter of Atlas, the mighty prop of heaven," to create mortals, wean them from savagery, and usher in the dawn of civilization.[65] With Blackwell, Prometheus again became a creator, comparable to a god. Thus Shaftesbury, Wieland, Blackwell, and several other Enlightenment writers restored the Titan's humanist attributes, anticipating the effusion of heroic portrayals in romantic literature and music.

Virtually all eighteenth-century musical settings of the Prometheus myth, however, reflect the era's proclivity for superficiality and satire by exploiting the legend's scenic potential and relying heavily on dance or pantomime. In *Peleus and Thetis* (London, 1740), a masque with a libretto by George Granville and music by William Boyce, Peleus, a mortal tenor, consults Prometheus, an immortal countertenor, who, true to his name, foresees the future. But the Titan, a minor character, performs no heroic deed except persuading Jupiter to renounce his love for Thetis so Peleus may court her.[66] Joseph-Nicolas-Pancrace Royer's music for Voltaire's *Prometheus*, now lost, was composed without the author's consent and rehearsed as a divertissement at the home of the Marchioness of Villeroy in 1752 and 1754.[67] An identically named reform ballet with choreography by Calzevaro and music by Joseph Starzer played at the ducal court in Oranienbaum in August 1761.[68] Another Austro-Italian collaboration was *Prometeo assoluto* (1762), a serenata performed at the Viennese

---

[62]   Oskar Walzel, *Das Prometheussymbol von Shaftesbury zu Goethe* (Munich, 1932), pp. 32–4.

[63]   Christoph Martin Wieland, *Beiträge zur geheimen Geschichte des menschlichen Verstandes und Herzens*, in *Sämmtliche Werke*, ed. J.G. Gruber (53 vols, Leipzig, 1824–8), vol. 31, pp. 43–79. The sixth "contribution" is subtitled "Ueber die von J.J. Rousseau vorgeschlagenen Versuche den wahre Stand der Natur des Menschen zu entdecken nebst einem Traumgespräch mit Prometheus."

[64]   Hans Urs Balthasar, *Prometheus: Studien zur Geschichte des deutschen Idealismus* (Heidelberg, 1947), p. 45; Ronald S. Ridgway, *La Propagande philosophique dans les tragédies de Voltaire*, Studies on Voltaire and the Eighteenth Century, ed. Theodore Besterman, vol. 15 (Geneva, 1961), p. 15.

[65]   Thomas Blackwell, *Letters Concerning Mythology* (London, 1748; reprint, New York, 1976), pp. 49–50.

[66]   Ian Bartlett, "*Peleus and Thetis*," in Stanley Sadie (ed.), *The New Grove Dictionary of Opera* (4 vols, New York, 1992), vol. 3, p. 933.

[67]   Ronald S. Ridgway, "Voltaire's Operas," in *Studies on Voltaire and the Eighteenth Century*, vol. 189, ed. Haydn Trevor Mason (Oxford, 1980), pp. 119–51.

[68]   Lisbeth Braun, "Die Ballettkompositionen von Joseph Starzer," *Studien zur Musikwissenschaft*, 13 (1926–7): 38–56.

court with choreography by Migliavacca and music by Georg Christoph Wagenseil.[69] (In 1801 Beethoven and Viganò would form another Austro-Italian alliance for their ballet.) John Abraham Fisher's overture to *Prometheus* introduced a pantomime at Covent Garden on 26 December 1775.[70] And scarcely a week before the Bastille was stormed in July 1789 Franz Beck supplied background music for Aumale de Corsenville's melodrama *Pandore*, in which the title character's animation again constitutes the Titan's primary action.[71]

With the advent of the "long century" that comprises the romantic era, facile musical settings and depictions of Prometheus as a cultural corruptor or a naïve mankind's animator soon became scarce.[72] Indeed, by 1800 the phrases "new" or "second Prometheus" were already watchwords for fresh creative impulses that signaled distinct changes in broad intellectual sensibilities, which coincidentally revitalized the legend's humanism, rehabilitated Aeschylus, and fostered appreciation of his "savagery."[73] The indisputable fount of modern representations of the myth was Goethe's ode (1775), though Shaftesbury had prefigured its radical conception of the Titan's creative autonomy. In his *Soliloquy, or Advice to an Author* (1711) Shaftesbury likened a "master" poet—one capable of forming "a whole, coherent and proportion'd in it-self"—to "a just Prometheus, under Jove."[74] Shaftesbury thus linked the Titan with the creative artist, establishing a union that would inform an authentically romantic perspective on the fable. But in characterizing Prometheus as "a second maker" who occupied a subordinate position "under Jove," Shaftesbury left the task of granting Prometheus genuine autonomy to Goethe, who achieved this aim in two stages.[75]

Goethe's interest in the myth first manifested itself in a fragmentary play written in 1773. Drawing on Hesiod, Aeschylus, and other classical and modern writers, it portrays a rebel who defies the Olympians, sculpts men from clay, educates mankind, and founds a new society. Prometheus, however, animates Pandora with Minerva's help, and consequently relies on an external power. Goethe then abandoned the drama and turned to his epoch-defining ode, completing it no later than 1775, when

---

[69]   Walther Fetter, "Der deutsche Character der italienischen Opern Georg Christoph Wagenseils," in Heinrich Hüschen (ed.), *Festschrift Karl Gustav Fellerer zum sechzigsten Geburtstag* (Regensburg, 1962), pp. 558–72.

[70]   Paul F. Rice, "Fisher, John Abraham," in Stanley Sadie and John Tyrell (eds), *The New Grove Dictionary of Music and Musicians*, 2nd edn (29 vols, New York, 2001), vol. 8, p. 906.

[71]   Trousson, vol. 1, pp. 188–9.

[72]   Literary historians generally designate the 1770s and 1780s, when the American and French Revolutions were accompanied by reactions against the French Enlightenment among English and German writers, as the onset of the romantic era. In music Oskar Bie's designation of 1814, the year Schubert composed *Gretchen am Spinnrade*, has been ratified by Carl Dahlhaus and Jacques Barzun and extended by others back to the 1770s. See Steven Paul Scher, "The German Lied: A Genre and Its European Reception," in *European Romanticism: Literary Cross-Currents, Modes, and Models*, p. 127.

[73]   Gillespie, p. 203.

[74]   Shaftesbury, "Soliloquy, or Advice to an Author," in *Characteristicks of Men, Manners, Opinions, Times* (3 vols, [London], 1711), vol. 1, p. 207.

[75]   Regarding Goethe's ode, see Chapter 3, pp. 93–9.

it circulated among close colleagues. Unlike the incomplete play, the ode features a Titan who vows perpetual defiance against Zeus, condemns the Olympian's oppression of humanity, and predicts his annihilation. Pointedly noting he has always worked in solitude, without Zeus' aid, Prometheus resolves to form men in his own image, to produce a race whose members, like him, will revile the Olympian. Implicit in the Titan's proclamation is that humanity will inherit his autonomous creativity. Published without Goethe's consent, the ode provoked incendiary reactions among his contemporaries, who regarded its advocacy of transgression against authority and poetic unorthodoxies as embodiments of the *Sturm und Drang* revolt. It retained its potency, influencing generations of German and English romantics.

Outside Goethe's intimate circle, one of the earliest and foremost promulgators of the ode's conception of Prometheus was August Wilhelm Schlegel, who invigorated German romanticism with seminal Shakespearean translations and co-founded *Das Athenäum*, a journalistic forum for early romantic manifestos. In a poem entitled *Prometheus* (1798) the Titan opposes a return to humanity's childish Golden Age; instead mankind must learn to trade, create, and endure privation, aided by the gift of fire.[76] Themis revives Rousseau's argument, fearing humanity will acquire the vices of pride, crime, war, and treason by embracing technology. Prometheus, however, refutes her eighteenth-century contention, claiming mankind's evolution depends on acquiring the sacrilegious attribute of free will: "to guide himself is the lot of the free, knowledge nourishes him, where he blunders, climbs with increasing strength out of the flood of deception, and is hardened in wisdom through resolve." Thus humanity's independence is paramount in Schlegel's poem, just as the Titan's autonomy was in Goethe's ode.

Schlegel also discussed Prometheus in his most celebrated critical work, the *Vorlesungen über dramatische Kunst und Literatur*, a series of lectures delivered in Vienna in 1808, published to great Continental acclaim in 1809, and translated into English in 1815.[77] The sixth lecture's survey of classical plays begins by describing the *Prometheus Bound* of Aeschylus as "the representative of constancy under suffering," a theme underscored throughout the drama's ensuing synopsis: Prometheus "suffers and is resolute from beginning to end"; he remains silent when imprisoned "under the harsh inspection of Strength and Force"; his complaints are "solitary"; he contemptuously dismisses advice from Oceanus; Io is "a victim of the same tyranny as Prometheus himself suffers under"; and the final cataclysm, hurling the Titan into "the abyss of the netherworld," comprises a "triumph of subjection" that "was never perhaps more gloriously celebrated."[78] Thus the iconic image of the persecuted genius suffering in solitude looms large in Schlegel's lecture, recalling bold declarations in Goethe's ode. Such tribulations, Schlegel contends, serve not to establish a cult of followers in the manner of a "self-devoting deity," but rather to demonstrate the Titan's defiance of

---

[76]   August Wilhelm Schlegel, *Prometheus*, in *Sämmtliche Werke*, ed. Eduard Böcking (12 vols, Hildesheim, 1971), vol. 1, pp. 49–60.

[77]   Edgar Lohner, foreword to *Vorlesungen über dramatische Kunst und Literatur* by August Wilhelm Schlegel (Stuttgart, 1966), pp. 5–8; John Black, preface to *Lectures on Dramatic Art and Literature* by August Wilhelm Schlegel (London, 1909), pp. 1–3.

[78]   Schlegel, *Lectures on Dramatic Art and Literature*, pp. 93–4.

divine authority is "nothing but the attempt to give perfection to the human race." Prometheus consequently reassumes his role as champion of a progressive mankind.

Johann Gottlieb Fichte likewise echoed Goethe in *Die Anweisung zum seeligen Leben*, a set of religious commentaries presented in 1806 at the Friedrich-Alexander University in Erlangen. Previously dismissed from the University of Jena on charges of atheism, the philosopher again flouted authority by lecturing on Sundays, in violation of school policy. His view of Prometheus reflects his radicalism:

> You require nothing except yourself; not even a god; you yourself are your own god, your savior and your redeemer. ... A venerable representation of this manner of thinking is ... Prometheus, who, aware of his just and beneficial deed, of the thunderer above the clouds, and of all the torments the latter will heap upon his head, laughs, and with undaunted courage watches the world's rubble collapse around him.[79]

Fichte then quotes the conclusion of Goethe's ode, wherein Prometheus vows to form men in his image. Like Goethe, Fichte boldly advocated mankind's metaphysical independence, reiterating tenets of a purely idealistic philosophy he had broadly expressed prior to his appointment in Jena in his *Wissenschaftlehre* (1794): the thinking self constitutes the only form of reality; quotidian existence is nothing more than a medium for self-emancipation.[80] While Fichte's sovereign, pre-Freudian ego would intrigue many later romantics, his atheistic interpretation of the myth appealed most directly to Shelley and other early nineteenth-century authors who rejected an unjust deity.

Ernst von Feuchtersleben, a philosopher, poet, and pioneer of clinical psychology's development in Vienna, also addressed the topic of Prometheus. Identifying with the Titan in his diary, Feuchtersleben claimed he had "learned to be free in the school of bondage" and "had mastered the spark and nourished it" just as "boldly as Prometheus."[81] In a poem (1829) confirming the physician's affinities with Goethe, Prometheus threatens Zeus with a destiny that will make him tremble: strengthened by hope, mankind will defy Zeus and suffer like their benefactor.[82] Feuchtersleben and earlier Austro-German writers consistently emphasized the Titan's individualism and bond with humanity, which ultimately fostered some type of freedom, often metaphysical in nature. British authors had meanwhile developed similar perceptions, establishing a foundation for evolving attitudes toward the legend's innate humanism.

A genuinely romantic approach to Prometheus began modestly in England with a passing reference in William Wordsworth's *The Excursion* (1814), a nine-book poem

---

[79]   Johann Gottlieb Fichte, *Die Anweisung zum seeligen Leben*, in *Gesamtausgabe der Bayerischen Akademie der Wissenschaften*, ed. Reinhard Lauth and Hans Gliwitzky (Stuttgart-Bad Cannstatt, 1995), p. 138.

[80]   Fichte, *Foundations of Transcendental Philosophy (Wissenschaftslehre) nova methodo (1796/99)*, trans. and ed. Daniel Breazeale (Ithaca, 1992), pp. 108–20.

[81]   The excerpt appears in a collection of "Umrisse zu seiner Biographie und Charakteristik" in Ernst von Feuchtersleben, *Sämmtliche Werke*, ed. Friedrich Hebbel (7 vols, Vienna, 1853), vol. 7, p. 236.

[82]   Feuchtersleben, *Prometheus*, in *Sämmtliche Werke und Briefe*, ed. Herbert Seidler and Hedwig Heger, vol. 1, *Dichtungen*, ed. Hermann Blume (Vienna, 1987), p. 204.

narrating a cynical poet's encounters with characters from different walks of life. In the sixth book a pastor relates stories of people interred in his churchyard, praising a steadfast yet unrequited love, perseverance, spiritual peace obtained in solitude, and religious faith. The skeptical poet surprisingly sympathizes with a tale of two political exiles who became comrades in their isolation and now lie buried beneath a monument they built to their friendship: if "their blended influence be not lost upon our hearts," then "the more are we required to feel for those among our fellow men, who, offering no obeisance to the world, are ... cut off from peace like exiles on some barren rock."[83] Immediately the poet clarifies his allusion to "that ancient story of Prometheus chained to the bare rock, on frozen Caucasus," where a vulture made an "inexhaustible repast drawn from his vitals." For the poet, Greek myths were "fictions in form, but in their substance truths, tremendous truths," with the Titan's ordeal illustrating "the dread strife of poor humanity's afflicted will struggling in vain with ruthless destiny." Wordsworth accordingly conceived Prometheus as an exiled rebel who offered no "obeisance" to authority and symbolized mankind resisting an oppressive fate, traits already ascribed to him by Goethe and other German authors.

Prometheus occupies a more substantial position in the literary output of Lord George Gordon Byron, a name synonymous with Hellenism's revival in Britain. Not only do his works frequently engage with classical traditions, but he also devoted much of his life and fortune to emancipating Greece from Turkish rule and died at Missolonghi while supporting Greek insurgents.[84] As early as 1804, during youthful studies at Harrow School, he paraphrased a chorus from the Aeschylean play, the first of numerous Promethean encounters.[85] But Byron most directly expressed personal ideas on the myth in a poem written in 1816, just after debts and accusations of incest involving his half-sister compelled him to leave England, never to return, and join the Shelleys in Switzerland.[86] Its first stanza attributes the pity Prometheus felt for mortals to his silent suffering, agonized torture, and loneliness. In the second stanza, however, the Titan's defiance is paramount: the "deaf tyranny of fate" and the "ruling principle of hate" initially comprise his rhymed objects of contempt, but soon the thundering menace of Zeus draws his scorn. The godlike crime of Prometheus, the final stanza relates, was to "strengthen Man with his own mind." Mortals thus became "in part divine," able to foresee their fate and yet persevere despite adversity, their spirit "triumphant where it dares defy." Thus Byron's threefold romantic stance toward the myth stresses the Titan's tortured isolation, unswerving defiance, and beneficence as mankind's champion.

Byron's Swiss sojourn spawned another Promethean product. Mary Wollstonecraft Shelley recounted that she, her husband, and Byron agreed to write

---

[83]   William Wordsworth, *The Excursion* (New York, [n.d.]), p. 214.

[84]   William St. Clair, "Byron and Greece," in Tom Winnifrith and Penelope Murray (eds), *Greece Old and New* (New York, 1983), pp. 153–68.

[85]   Byron, *From the* Prometheus Vinctus *of Aeschylus*, in *The Poetical Works of Byron*, p. 89.

[86]   Byron, *Prometheus*, in *The Poetical Works of Byron*, p. 191.

supernatural tales after reading German ghost stories in 1816,[87] a pact she alone fulfilled with *Frankenstein, or the Modern Prometheus* (1818), an epistolary novel that inverts the myth's key attributes. As the subtitle indicates, the protagonist, Victor Frankenstein, overtly resembles the Titan: during medical studies he learns the secret of reanimating lifeless matter, just as Prometheus steals fire to imbue mortals with the spark of humanity. Frankenstein's altruistic experiments yield an extraordinarily large and strong creature, but its gruesome appearance elicits universal hatred. Denied intimacy in imposed isolation, the creature commits several murders before fleeing to the Arctic. Now considered the science fiction novel's prototype, the Gothic tale supports various modern and postmodern explications.[88] But for many nineteenth-century readers, it reenacted the myth of the Noble Savage, illustrating unspoiled nature's corruption through dangerous technology.[89] Other cultural hazards exacerbated the tragedy. Near his hovel the creature discovers three books, doubtless left by Frankenstein: Plutarch's *Parallel Lives* teaches him to admire "peaceable lawgivers" and abhor vice; Goethe's *Werther*, climaxing in a young artist's suicide, confounds him with existential anguish; and *Paradise Lost* prompts him to identify not with Adam in the benevolent yet lonely protectorate of Eden, but rather with a Satan consumed by "the bitter gall of envy."[90] Victor Frankenstein is consequently a flawed Prometheus, a brilliant scientist but failed educator. That his error was more social than technological in nature was a view espoused by the novel's first critic, Percy Bysshe Shelley, who blamed an intolerant society for the outcast's misfortunes in an essay written in 1817 in anticipation of hostile reviews.[91]

Mary and Percy Shelley shared another point of literary contact regarding the myth. His *Prometheus Unbound*, a four-act lyric drama begun after they settled in Italy in 1818 and published in 1820, amplifies similarities between the Titan and Milton's protagonist in *Paradise Lost*. As Shelley's preface explains, "the only imaginary being resembling in any degree Prometheus, is Satan," an assertion based on Lucifer's defiance of God, expulsion from heaven, imprisonment in hell, and refusal to recant—events with unmistakable parallels in the Greek legend.[92] Milton's hero, however, is tainted by "ambition, envy, revenge, and a desire for personal aggrandizement," whereas Shelley's Titan is "impelled by the purest and the truest of motives to the best and noblest ends." An idealized satanic Prometheus thus joins Faust in the pantheon of romantic antiheroes. More broadly, *Prometheus Unbound*

---

[87]   *The Journals of Mary Shelley*, ed. Paula R. Feldman and Diana Scott-Kilvert (Baltimore, 1987), p. 126.

[88]   Essays encompassing psychoanalytic, feminist, gender, Marxist, and cultural criticism appear in Mary Shelley, *Frankenstein: Complete, Authoritative Text with Biographical, Historical, and Cultural Contexts, Critical History, and Essays from Contemporary Critical Perspectives*, ed. Johanna M. Smith (Boston, 2000), pp. 237–449.

[89]   Terry Jay Ellingson, *The Myth of the Noble Savage* (Berkeley, 2001), pp. 237–42.

[90]   Shelley, *Frankenstein*, pp. 115–17.

[91]   Percy Bysshe Shelley, "On Frankenstein," in *Complete Works*, ed. Roger Ingpen and Walter E. Peck (10 vols, New York, 1965), vol. 6. pp. 263–5. The essay remained unpublished until 1832.

[92]   Shelley, preface to *Prometheus Unbound*, in Prometheus Unbound: *A Variorum Edition*, ed. Lawrence John Zillman (Seattle, 1959), pp. 120–21.

blends Shelley's social ideology, Neoplatonism, and idiosyncratic opinions on conflicts between materialism and idealism, physics and metaphysics, and science and religion, all expressed in assorted verse forms confirming his mastery of classical idioms. But central to its densely allegorical action is that the redeeming power of self-regenerating love can extricate humanity from political, scientific, and sexual turmoil.[93] The play accordingly spans extremes in the Promethean spectrum, employing a satanic Titan to promote Shelley's notions of spirituality.

Following the flurry of poetry and fiction indebted to the myth, two British romanticists evaluated Aeschylus in critical essays. Samuel Taylor Coleridge's "On the *Prometheus* of Aeschylus" (1825) addresses issues ranging from new archeological evidence for dating antiquity's monuments to advances in biblical philology, but nonetheless includes concrete observations on the myth's basic substance and the Titan's character. As an allegory of "the tree of knowledge of good and evil," the legend discloses human reason was "superadded or infused," not produced by "mere evolution."[94] Fire, the symbol of reason, was stolen, making it different in kind from other faculties, and originated in the heavens, distinguishing it as superior to earthly human traits. The pilfered spark was also the gift of a benefactor whose dynasty preceded that of Jove, thus corroborating the existence of spiritual thought prior to the perception of objects by the senses.[95] In less devoutly Christian terms, Coleridge's Titan was the clan's leader, counselor, lawgiver, and bestower of productive energy and the ability to learn. Yet he was also a solitary figure removed from earthly existence, more of an ideal abstraction than even Shelley's satanic Prometheus, at least until he was tethered to his rock, a counter-symbol of barrenness and non-productivity.

Elizabeth Barrett Browning, a formidably erudite classicist as a youth, was particularly drawn to Aeschylus. In a preface to her anonymously published translation of *Prometheus Bound* (1833) she revisited Shelley's fusion of Prometheus and Satan, contending they stood on ground "as unequal as do the sublime of sin and the sublime of virtue":

> Satan suffered from his ambition; Prometheus from his humanity: Satan for himself; Prometheus for mankind: Satan dared peril which he had not weighted; Prometheus devoted himself to sorrows which he had foreknown. "Better to rule in hell," said Satan; "Better to serve this rock," said Prometheus. But in his hell, Satan yearned to associate with man; while Prometheus preferred a solitary agony.[96]

---

[93] Douglas Bush, *Mythology and the Romantic Tradition in English Poetry* (New York, 1937), p. 146.

[94] Samuel Taylor Coleridge, "On the *Prometheus* of Aeschylus," in *The Literary Remains of Samuel Taylor Coleridge*, ed. Henry Nelson Coleridge (4 vols, London, 1835; reprint, New York, 1967), vol. 2, p. 336.

[95] Ibid., vol. 2, pp. 352–5.

[96] Elizabeth Barrett Browning, preface to *Prometheus Bound* by Aeschylus, in *The Complete Works of Elizabeth Barrett Browning*, ed. Charlotte Porter and Helen A. Clarke (6 vols, New York, 1900), vol. 6, pp. 85–6.

Shelley underscored the protagonists' similarities, Browning their differences. She praised the Titan's sacrifice, self-awareness, and beneficence, though his solitary character still reflected a romantic perspective. But in her preface to *The Seraphim and other Poems* (1838), she explicitly compared his sacrifice with its biblical counterpart: "had Aeschylus lived after the incarnation and crucifixion of our Lord Jesus Christ ... he would have turned ... to the victim, whose sustaining thought beneath an unexampled agony was not the Titanic 'I can revenge,' but the celestial 'I can forgive.'"[97] Browning's Christian parallels not only shed positive light on an exegetic practice that had engendered negative associations during the Middle Ages; they also anticipated trends that intensified as the romantic era progressed.

Identical sentiments appeared simultaneously in *Prométhée* (1838), an epic poem by French historian Edgar Quinet. Although its versification betrays the author's scholarly vocation, its preface articulates his religious sentiments clearly: the myth represents one stage in the evolution of humanity's religious consciousness. Beyond prefiguring Christ, Prometheus "embodies the interior drama of God and man, faith and doubt, creator and created; and it is thereby that this tradition applies to all eras and this divine drama will never end."[98] Quinet's universalized Titan epitomizes French romantic penchants for depicting Christ as both a victim of a cruel God and a collaborator in mankind's struggle against metaphysical despotism.[99] French proclivities for a Christ-like Prometheus, rejuvenated by the Parnassians during the 1860s, still resonated in Symbolist writings as the nineteenth century waned.

Otherwise the Titan's literary representations changed noticeably in Europe and America as the romantic era progressed, reflecting the rise of positivism, the increasing value society accorded science, and realism's dominance in the arts.[100] Thus in Henry Wadsworth Longfellow's poem, *Prometheus, the Poet's Forethought* (1858), the Titan still gains wisdom through suffering, but he is a "bard," a "poet, prophet, and seer," not a rebel, his flame a torch of progress, not a spark igniting humanity's metaphysical independence, and the myth itself an "old classic superstition."[101] Robert Browning likewise preserved vestiges of Promethean romanticism in *Parleyings with Gerard de Lairesse* (1887), initially describing a rebel defiantly standing erect amid "thunders on thunders, doubling and redoubling," impervious to lightning's "sharp white fire," the voracious eagle actually cowering at his side.[102] Later, however, Prometheus shows "not one spark of pity" for Io, uncharacteristically denying sympathy to mankind. Removed from modern life,

---

[97] Browning, preface to *The Seraphim*, in *The Complete Works*, vol. 1, pp. 164–5.

[98] Edgar Quinet, preface to *Prométhée*, in *Œuvres complètes* (10 vols, Paris, 1858), vol. 8, p. 19.

[99] Gillespie, pp. 207–8.

[100] Bernard Weinberg, *French Realism: The Critical Reaction, 1830–1870* (New York, 1937), pp. 1–4, 130–41; René Wellek, "The Concept of Realism in Literary Scholarship," in *Concepts of Criticism* (New Haven, 1963), pp. 222–55; Donald Pizer, introduction to Donald Pizer (ed.), *Realism and Naturalism in Nineteenth-Century American Literature* (Carbondale, 1966), pp. 6–14.

[101] Henry Wadsworth Longfellow, *The Poetical Works of Longfellow*, ed. H.E. Scudder (Boston, 1975), pp. 185–6.

[102] Robert Browning, "With Gerard de Lairesse," in *Parleyings with Certain People of Importance in Their Day* (Boston, 1887), pp. 122–3.

Browning's Titan is already a nostalgic figure: Mount Caucasus is "lost now in the night; away and far enough lies that Arcadia." His flame, once an embodiment of myth's power, is extinguished: "the dead Greek lore lies buried in the urn where who seeks fire finds ashes." Prometheus, neither a rebel nor a humanitarian, merely symbolizes perseverance.

Mixed motives of a different nature had already appeared throughout *Prometheus the Firegiver* (1883), a book-length poem by Robert Bridges.[103] Bridges still portrayed Zeus as a tyrant who withholds fire from the residents of Argos, but he reverted to Hesiod's image of Prometheus as a thief and prankster. Concealing celestial embers in a reed, the disguised Titan enters Argos and offers them to King Inachus, Io's father and a worshiper of Zeus. Formerly aware of fire's secret, Inachus concedes it would serve his subjects well, but poses two deeper questions: will fire compel nature to divulge "the cause of life," and had it once belonged to the earth, just as the heavens now possess its "airy essence?" Prometheus submits evolutionary answers: fire was once "a raging power that held both heaven and earth," but while it still governs heaven, it was succeeded on earth by air, which in turn brought forth water and plants as flames dwindled into coals. The romantic era's celestial spark thus acquired terrestrial properties that mankind could reclaim. Moreover, Prometheus suggests mortals could use fire to develop "the cunning of invention and all arts in which thy hand instructed may command, interpret, comfort, or ennoble nature." Greece was already "far fairer now, clothed with the works of men," he observes, implying fire would make it fairer still. Inachus, after learning Zeus will exact revenge on Io, reluctantly agrees to sacrifice her for his people's welfare. Prometheus then ignites the flame, but hidden by smoke, he defaces the altar, deleting the Olympian's name, inscribing his own, and vanishing unseen. Fire is accordingly a mere tool acquired in a bargain as part of a new era's technological arsenal, and Prometheus becomes a principled vandal.

Increasingly materialistic perspectives adopted by additional late nineteenth-century authors such as Karl Marx, Alexandre Saint-Yves, and Richard Watson Dixon may represent the "defeat" of Prometheus, as Raymond Trousson suggests in his peerless study of the myth.[104] Mythic language, however, is a "conceptual tool" capable of expressing diverse, abstract ideas and combining them "in the form of propositions of universal significance," an assertion Claude Lévi-Strauss supports with empirical investigations of myth's structure in traditional cultures.[105] Certainly evolution, technological progress, human persistence, and the classical legacy's dissolution rank among romanticism's great themes, and adapting the Prometheus myth to elaborate these subjects need scarcely be judged a "defeat." Nor are Lévi-Strauss's manipulations of mythic language's phonemes essential for realizing a particular myth endures by flexibly addressing the foremost concerns of its collective

---

[103]   Robert Bridges, *Prometheus the Firegiver: A Mask in the Greek Manner*, in *Poetical Works of Robert Bridges* (London, 1936), pp. 1–48. For relevant quotations and plot developments, see lines 9–11, 119, 519–35, 579–92, 610–15, 693–8, 736–42, 1131–41, 1270–1360.

[104]   Trousson, vol. 2, pp. 389–91.

[105]   Claude Lévi-Strauss, *The Raw and the Cooked*, trans. John and Doreen Weightman (Chicago, 1969), pp. 1–3.

authors and the seemingly inconsequential realities of daily life. Indeed, the same observation was advanced by Victor Hugo, arch-romantic of the July Monarchy, exile of the Second Empire, and (eventually) repatriated politician of the Third Republic, in his study of William Shakespeare (1864). Prometheus and Hamlet are similar, Hugo claims, because both face existential obstacles, though the Titan's are external and accordingly elicit action, while the Dane's are interior and thus prompt hesitation.[106] Hugo then declares, "nothing can be more fiercely wild than Prometheus stretched on the Caucasus," a punishment imposed for one reason: "What is his crime? The Right. To characterize right as crime, and movement as rebellion, is the immemorial skill of tyrants; he has taken a little knowledge. Jupiter ... punishes this temerity of having desired to live."[107] Finally, Hugo considers Prometheus, like Shakespeare's Queen Mab, a "wonderful fable, which with a profound meaning unites the sidereal with the microscopic, the infinitely great and the infinitely small."[108] Hugo's remarks apply equally well to the romantic era's musical representations of Prometheus, which reveal conflicts between interior and exterior impulses, embody fierce rebellion and dreadful punishment, portray unjust tyranny and redeeming heroism, and in so doing, unite the universal with the topical, the "sidereal with the microscopic," and "the infinitely great" with "the infinitely small."

---

[106]   Victor Hugo, *William Shakespeare*, trans. Melville B. Anderson (Chicago, 1887), p. 228.

[107]   Ibid., p. 230.

[108]   Ibid., p. 281.

Chapter 2

Gesture and Convention in Beethoven's *Ballet d'action*

Die Geschöpfe des Prometheus [*The Creatures of Prometheus*] holds threefold significance for Beethoven's life, compositional development, and the historiography of his achievement. The ballet's Viennese premiere on 28 March 1801 marked a turning point in his career, as his foremost biographers agree, beginning with his amanuensis Anton Schindler and extending from Alexander Wheelock Thayer to Maynard Solomon.[1] Already a celebrated pianist when he arrived from his native Bonn in 1792, Beethoven soon found patrons among Vienna's leading aristocrats. But the ballet was his first major commission from Emperor Francis II and Empress Marie Therese, who urgently requested the score on 7 March 1801, two weeks before the anticipated premiere.[2] Beethoven consequently suspended other activities until the rescheduled debut on 28 March. The imperial behest's fulfillment thus signified his acceptance in Viennese nobility's highest echelon, a standing he never relinquished.

Commentators likewise invariably deem the ballet a harbinger of Beethoven's burgeoning compositional ambitions. It was his first genuine theatrical endeavor, except for piano variations on operatic themes, two substitution arias, and a *Ritterballet* produced in 1791 in Bonn as a sequence of disjunct, generic dances, not a continuously danced drama. Despite Beethoven's inexperience, his Promethean ballet achieved modest success, playing at Vienna's Kärntnertortheater 23 times in two years and attracting Emanuel Schikaneder's attention. Mozart's famous librettist for *Die Zauberflöte* invited Beethoven to compose an opera for the recently opened Theater-an-der-Wien,[3] an abortive collaboration that nonetheless awakened Beethoven's interest in his only opera, *Fidelio*, which would require a decade to complete. And as my discussion of the ballet reveals, several of its numbers prefigure pivotal instrumental works, namely the "Eroica" and "Pastoral" Symphonies, the Fourth Piano Concerto, and the Variations and Fugue in E-flat major, Op. 35.

The ballet also marks an important historiographical juncture. Schindler was the first to suggest it inaugurated Beethoven's all-important middle period,[4] an idea subsequently developed in two ways. First, his work on the score coincided with or perhaps even stimulated

---

[1]   Anton Schindler, *Beethoven as I Knew Him*, ed. Donald MacArdle, trans. Constance S. Jolly (Chapel Hill, 1966), p. 91; Alexander Wheelock Thayer, *Thayer's Life of Beethoven*, ed. Elliot Forbes (Princeton, 1964), p. 271; Maynard Solomon, *Beethoven*, 2nd rev. edn (New York, 1998), pp. 145–50.

[2]   Ludwig van Beethoven, *Briefwechsel Gesamtausgabe*, ed. Sieghard Brandenburg (7 vols, Munich, 1996), vol. 1, p. 68.

[3]   Solomon, p. 247.

[4]   Schindler, p. 92.

his growing symphonic aspirations, doubtless encouraged by the reception of several of its numbers whose repeated performances on the Augarten concert series were greeted "with uncommon applause, an honor ... heretofore never ... accorded to ballet music."[5] Previously he had focused on solo, chamber, and concerted keyboard compositions and had even postponed fulfilling a commission to write his first string quartets in a seemingly conscious effort to avoid genres in which Mozart and Haydn had excelled. But after 1800, as he grappled with increasingly profound deafness, he embraced large-scale orchestral, choral, and theatrical works, indulging his predilection for heroic subjects, especially "beneficent saviors of mankind."[6] In the decade following the ballet's debut he extolled Christ's valor in the oratorio *Christus am Ölberge*, paid tribute to Napoleon in the "Eroica" Symphony, idealized conjugal love's triumph over despotism in *Fidelio*, and recounted a Flemish aristocrat's defiance of Spanish oppression in incidental music to Goethe's *Egmont*. The ballet accordingly initiated a pronounced shift toward symphonic genres and a lasting involvement with heroism, hallmarks of the middle period.

Thus previous study has emphasized the ballet's foreshadowing of Beethoven's future development, virtually excluding its appraisal as dance music. Indeed, critics have rarely noted as basic a feature as the score's cultivation of familiar dance types such as the minuet and polonaise, much less whether the ballet observes prevailing dance conventions. Even Constantin Floros, author of the only monograph on the subject and the first to analyze relevant sketches systematically, examined the period's broadest dance categories (heroic, comic, grotesque) primarily to illuminate analogous passages in the "Eroica."[7] Earlier Hugo Riemann had largely discounted the score's reliance on dance traditions, instead positing variation technique as its fundamental compositional impulse and thereby affirming its status as non-representational, absolute music.[8]

Such approaches, though predictably insightful when adopted by the likes of Floros and Riemann, ignore a context vital to the ballet's understanding, since Vienna was a leading dance center, second only to Paris, throughout the eighteenth century.[9] More importantly, the Habsburg court surpassed Paris in developing the *ballet d'action*, which articulated a continuous narrative through extensive pantomime, unlike customary interpolations of decorative dance numbers in spoken or sung dramas.[10] Four choreographers active in Vienna between 1737 and 1803 were instrumental in the new genre's founding and florescence: Franz Hilverding, Gaspare Angiolini, Jean-Georges Noverre, and Beethoven's collaborator, Salvatore Viganò. My intent, therefore, is to draw on conventions governing contemporary scenarios, choreography, and music to show that Beethoven's ballet participates in two traditions: the eighteenth-century divertissement, as its allegorical scenario,

---

[5]   *Letters to Beethoven and Other Correspondence*, trans. and ed. Theodore Albrecht (3 vols, Lincoln, 1996), vol. 1, p. 90.

[6]   Marion M. Scott, *Beethoven*, rev. Jack Westrup (London, 1977), p. 51.

[7]   Constantin Floros, *Beethovens Eroica und Prometheus-Musik* (Wilhelmshaven, 1978).

[8]   Hugo Riemann, "Beethovens Prometheus Musik: Ein Variationenwerk," *Die Musik*, 9/13–14 (1909–10): 19–34, 107–25.

[9]   David Lynham, *The Chevalier Noverre: Father of the Modern Ballet* (London, 1972), p. 72.

[10]   Robert Haas, "Der Wiener Bühnentanz von 1740 bis 1767," *Jahrbuch der Musikbibliothek Peters*, 44 (1937): 77–93.

pastoral music, and final dance sequence illustrate; and the new *ballet d'action*, as evinced by extant sources for the narrative, dance typologies, pantomimic episodes, and Beethoven's sketches and full score. These neglected lines of inquiry offer new perspectives, not only on an early critical assessment of the music as "too learned" for a ballet, but also on Beethoven's representation of the Prometheus myth.[11]

Integral to drama since Greek antiquity, theatrical dance maintained alliances with plays and operas well into the eighteenth century. During the reign of Louis XIV elaborate dance sequences, or divertissements, appeared throughout court operas, enhancing generic dramatic events such as massed entrances and celebrations or depicting stereotyped characters, including shepherds, warriors, and mythological beings. Soloists were usually nameless or occasionally minor characters. Dancers' actions typically received verbal explanations in prefatory recitatives or from offstage choruses whose members remained stationary as their words were enacted.[12] After Jean-Baptiste Lully's death in 1687, an already circumscribed use of pantomime declined, and his successors emphasized the divertissement's celebratory function.[13] Somewhat different circumstances prevailed in Italy, where ballets normally occurred between an opera's acts rather than interrupting or concluding them. Their plots consequently shared little or no connection with operatic storylines, instead providing celebratory, supernatural, allegorical, exotic, or pastoral vignettes. And these frequently static *intermedi* often featured more pantomime and athleticism than divertissements.

Seventeenth-century choreographers catalogued multitudes of intricate steps that temporarily remained small and close to the ground because dancers wore bulky costumes and heeled shoes, not slippers. Men portrayed heroes wearing perukes and cumbersome *tonnelets*, the stylized attire of Roman soldiers, while women donned headdresses and full-length skirts.[14] Male dancers nonetheless overcame restrictive costumes to perform *la danse haute*, which involved familiar leaps such as cabrioles, tours en l'air, and entrechats. Earthbound women rarely executed the pirouette's turns and waited until the early nineteenth century to dance on *pointe*. Symmetry governed the choreography of the corps de ballet, whose minutely detailed steps embellished balanced global designs. Equally stylized ballet music entailed common Baroque dances, including minuets, passapieds, and courantes in prescribed binary, rondeau, and variation forms. Composers nonetheless tailored music to suit particular characters or situations.

Subjected to zealous Enlightenment reforms, theatrical dance experienced comprehensive change beginning in the 1730s and culminating 30 years later in the *ballet d'action*. These independently produced ballets narrated complete stories without explanatory recitation, instead reflecting characters' moods and motives with pantomime, gestures, and expressive steps. Naturalistic choreography replaced symmetrical patterns, requiring new dance types and freer musical forms. Minor characters and the corps

---

[11]   See the unsigned review published as *"Die Geschöpfe des Prometheus,"* in *Die Zeitung für die elegante Welt*, 1 (April 1801): 485–7, reprinted in Wayne M. Senner (ed.), *The Critical Reception of Beethoven's Compositions by His German Contemporaries* (Lincoln, 1999), p. 216.

[12]   Jean-George Noverre protested such practices in *Letters on Dancing and Ballets*, trans. Cyril W. Beaumont (New York, 1966), pp. 49–51.

[13]   Rebecca Harris-Warrick, "Ballet," in *The New Grove Dictionary*, vol. 2, p. 571.

[14]   Regarding his objections, see Noverre, pp. 73–6.

contributed to the plot, interacting with the principals. Simpler costumes, styled to enhance the dramatic setting and characterization, supplanted *tonnelets* and long skirts, liberating dancers' bodies. Coordinating these parameters within a coherent plot is an achievement often attributed exclusively to Noverre, whose influential treatise, *Lettres sur la danse et sur les ballets* (1760), codified the *ballet d'action*'s principles. Nonetheless deserving credit are the English dance master John Weaver, Jean-Philippe Rameau's collaborator Louis de Cahusac, and Noverre's predecessors in Vienna, Hilverding and Angiolini.

Born in Vienna but trained in Paris, Hilverding (1710–68) served the Habsburg court as dancer, choreographer, and dance master beginning in 1737. By 1740 he purportedly conceived autonomous ballets based on serious plays of remarkable expressive potential by Racine, Voltaire, and Crébillon.[15] But until 1752, when he verifiably produced independent ballets, he embellished pre-existent operas with dance episodes that rarely relate to ongoing plots, sometimes entail interpolated songs, and often emulate divertissements with stately entrance processions and loosely connected dance sequences. More notably, however, Hilverding exploited pantomimic interludes and replaced generic troupes of shepherds, peasants, and soldiers with characters who advance the plot or establish local color, especially Tyrolean woodcutters, love-struck millers, gardeners, and exotic national groups.[16] Cultivating these character types sharply reduced reliance on trite allegorical themes such as the Seasons and the Hours. Moreover, Hilverding arranged dancers asymmetrically and employed dynamic gestures, unlike French dance's balanced patterns and predetermined upper-body movements.[17] Further details regarding his choreography are scarce: he published no scenarios, believing dance could convey a narrative without them.[18] Hilverding accordingly deserves his reputation as a pioneer of the *ballet d'action* and founder of a distinctly Viennese school of ballet.

Inaugurating his career as a dancer and choreographer in Italy, Angiolini (1731–1803) accepted a position in Vienna, perhaps in 1752, and quickly became Hilverding's protégé.[19] After Hilverding left for Saint Petersburg in 1758, Angiolini acted as dance master in Vienna for eight years before traveling restlessly between Russia and Italy. Like his mentor, Angiolini digressed from the main plot in operatic interpolations of a light pastoral, mythological, or allegorical nature.[20] Somewhat anomalous, then, were his momentous collaborations with opera seria's reformers, Christoph Willibald Gluck and Ranieri di Calzabigi.

Angiolini expounded his aesthetics in prefaces to two Gluck ballets, *Don Juan* (1761) and *Sémiramis* (1765), respectively adapted from Molière and Voltaire.[21] The first granted pantomime an exalted status:

---

[15]   Marian Hannah Winter, *The Pre-Romantic Ballet* (New York, 1974), p. 92; Haas, "Der Wiener Bühnentanz," pp. 78–9.

[16]   Haas, "Der Wiener Bühnentanz," p. 81.

[17]   Winter, pp. 94–5.

[18]   Gaspare Angiolini, *Dissertation sur les ballets pantomimes des anciens*, ed. Walter Toscanini (Milan, 1956), pp. C5, D1–D3.

[19]   Debra Craine and Judith Mackrell, *The Oxford Dictionary of Dance* (Oxford, 2000), p. 17.

[20]   Harris-Warrick, p. 575.

[21]   Previously disputed, the first preface's ascription to Calzabigi seems secure in Manfred Krüger, *J.G. Noverre und das "Ballet d'action"* (Emsdetten, 1963), p. 107.

The sublimity of ancient dance was pantomime, which was the art of imitating the habits, passions, and actions of gods, heroes, and men by movements and attitudes of the body, by gestures and signs made in rhythms and appropriate for expressing what one intends to represent.[22]

These movements, Angiolini continued, "must form a coherent discourse," a "type of declamation made for the eyes, which is rendered intelligible to spectators through the means of music."[23] He also insisted that ballets observe neo-Aristotelian unities of action, time, and place, but conceded action might be compressed for dancers, who, unlike actors, could not perform for long periods.[24]

In the second preamble Angiolini developed identical points, asserting "if there is something sublime in dance, it is incontestably a tragic event represented without words and rendered intelligible by gestures."[25] A dancer's goal was to assimilate a vocabulary of motions capable of expressing "all the passions and all the states of the soul," not to cultivate athletic or intricate steps, which accounted for dance's degeneration in modern times.[26] Music, "the poetry of the pantomime ballet," allowed dancers to speak,[27] justifying Gluck's replacement of conventional binary and rondo forms with freer structures involving through-composed passages, instrumental recitatives, frequent tempo changes, and open harmonic cadences at the ends of numbers—all to mirror nuanced actions.[28] Although both ballets initially elicited confused reactions, their aesthetic ultimately prevailed throughout Europe. Angiolini nonetheless lost favor after returning to Vienna in the 1770s, when audiences had grown accustomed to the more refined style of his successor, Noverre.[29]

Born and classically trained in Paris, Noverre (1727–1810) first performed at fairs and in comic theaters, pantomime-laden venues that shaped his theories.[30] Beginning in 1747 he produced his first ballets in Marseilles and Lyons before returning to Paris in 1754, when the renowned English actor David Garrick dubbed him "the Shakespeare of the dance."[31] At Garrick's invitation Noverre visited London in 1755, producing several ballets and consulting the actor's magnificent library of modern and classical writers, who inspired Noverre's seminal works. Garrick's Shakespearean acting, especially his "rare gift for pantomimic expression," supplied a model for Noverre's revolutionary treatise, begun after his return to Lyons and completed in 1759.[32] It established principles that

---

[22]   See the preface's facsimile in Christoph Willibald Gluck, *Libretti: Die originalen Textbücher der bis 1990 in der Gluck-Gesamtausgabe erschienenen Bühnenwerke, Textbücher verschollener Werke*, ed. Klaus Hortschansky (Kassel, 1995), p. 172.

[23]   Ibid.

[24]   Ibid., pp. 172–4.

[25]   Angiolini, pp. A3, B4–B5.

[26]   Ibid., pp. A5, C4.

[27]   Ibid., p. D3.

[28]   Winter, p. 91.

[29]   Lynham, pp. 75, 185.

[30]   Ibid., p. 15.

[31]   Lynham, pp. 16–18; Lillian Moore, *Artists of the Dance* (New York, 1975), p. 42.

[32]   Noverre, pp. 82–5.

experienced no equally comprehensive revisions until 1820, when Carlo Blasis codified classical ballet's techniques.[33]

Above all Noverre opposed divertissements, "which express nothing, present no story, sketch no connected or logical plot, and possess nothing dramatic," but instead merely display the art's mechanics.[34] His alternative, the independent *ballet d'action*, "should be divided into scenes and acts, and each act should possess ... a beginning, central portion, and conclusion," like a spoken drama.[35] As serious subjects Noverre advocated myth, history, and an inferior source, the choreographer's imagination.[36] Noverre's fellow men, however, were preferable to ballet's traditionally idyllic, chimerical, and fantastic characters, a naturalistic precept that required subsidiary players to assume important roles connecting them to heroes and choreographers to conceive "a different action, expression, and character" for each dancer.[37] These ambitions mandated the "sacrifice" of complex, virtuosic steps that Noverre repeatedly blamed for ballet's decline.[38] Instead dancers would "speak" through differentiated steps, replace a long-standing "abuse of symmetry" with nature's "ravishing disorder," and discard perukes, *tonnelets*, skirts, and masks to don costumes and makeup that would promote free movement, enhance characterization, and contribute to a natural setting.[39] Music, likewise integral to the *ballet d'action*, would "fix and determine all the dancer's movements" in "time and tone."[40] To depict varied and suddenly changing passions, "music must entirely abandon the feeble movements and modulations which are generally employed for dance music. ... The harmonic succession of sounds ... must imitate those of nature and suggest the dialogue."[41] Thus Noverre championed an "alliance" of balletic arts that has drawn comparisons with Wagner's *Gesamtkunstwerk*.[42]

Noverre realized his ideals first at Stuttgart's grand ducal court (1765–6), where he directed 20 renowned soloists, a 100-member corps, and talented designers in every branch of stagecraft, and then in Vienna, where he produced over 60 ballets in eight years.[43] His combination of traditional choreography, pantomime, strongly characterized music, spectacle, and individualistic performers justified the *Wiener Theater-Almanach*'s boast: no city equaled Vienna as a dance center, no company matched Noverre's in expressive range or the capacity to "awaken every passion in the spectators."[44] Ultimately, however, Noverre's achievement and influence lie more in his progressive theories than in his ballets, whose detailed scenarios disclose conservatisms: operatic interpolations outnumber independent works; largely mythological subjects often involve

---

[33]   Carlo Blasis, *Traité élémentaire théorique et pratique de l'art de la danse* (Milan, 1820).
[34]   Noverre, pp. 50–57.
[35]   Ibid., pp. 19–22.
[36]   Ibid., pp. 4–5, 77.
[37]   Ibid., pp. 23, 76–7.
[38]   Ibid., pp. 1, 29, 50, 99, 102, 106.
[39]   Ibid., pp. 3, 12.
[40]   Ibid., pp. 36, 60.
[41]   Ibid., p. 72.
[42]   Regarding the "alliance," see Noverre, pp. 5, 11. For Wagnerian comparisons, see Krüger, p. 51; Lynham, p. 70.
[43]   Moore, pp. 43–7.
[44]   Ibid., pp. 47–8.

divertissements; conventional steps and positions abound; and finales routinely comprise massed contredanses, vestiges of French court ballet.[45]

He nevertheless transformed Vienna into Europe's foremost ballet center, and his methods spread throughout Europe by 1800.[46] But after 1776, when imperial nationalistic reforms privileged German-language plays and *Singspiele* over costly ballet and Italian opera,[47] Viennese dance entered a period of decline, and Noverre achieved his lifelong ambition as the Paris Opéra's dance master. Ballet began regaining prestige only in 1790, when Leopold II ascended the throne, reinstated a permanent dance troupe, and selected its Italian personnel himself.[48] Leopold's reign ended with his unexpected death in 1792, but his successors, Francis II and Marie Therese, promoted his agenda by hiring two artists who induced a veritable dance mania in Vienna: Viganò and his lovely Spanish wife, Maria Medina.

Descended from a prolific ballet family and exposed to Noverre's precepts as a youth, Viganò (1769–1821) debuted in female roles in Rome, where the Pope prohibited women theatrical performers, and as a teenager choreographed ballets in Venice.[49] In 1789 he performed at the coronation of Charles IV of Spain, meeting Medina and Jean Dauberval, Noverre's foremost protégé. After touring with Dauberval's company for two years and producing Venetian ballets for two more, the couple arrived in Vienna as internationally acclaimed dancers and choreographers. During their three-year engagement (1793–5) Medina's flimsy costumes, styled by Viganò to cling to her shapely body and expose her calves in the manner of Grecian veils, attracted considerable public attention.[50] But her dancing scarcely suffered in comparison. As the poet Heinrich von Collin noted, she displayed "an art until then without precedent," a type of dance that was "natural, lively, and unconstrained."[51] Johann Gottfried Schadow's contemporary engravings capture her novel execution and Viganò's ingenious choreography (Figure 2.1). Natural attitudes and movements include a flexible torso, a mobile head, unrestrained arm positions, and legs turned both outward and inward, all within a balanced formal construct.[52] Such comportment drew throngs to eight ballets that Viganò produced before he and Medina toured central Europe (1795–8) and then separated.[53]

---

[45]   Noverre, pp. 4–5, 152, 159, 162; Krüger, p. 8.

[46]   Krüger, p. 123.

[47]   W.E. Yates, *Theatre in Vienna: A Critical History, 1776–1995* (Cambridge, 1996), p. 2.

[48]   John Arthur Rice, "Emperor and Impresario: Leopold II and the Transformation of Viennese Musical Theater" (Ph.D. diss., University of California, Berkeley, 1987), pp. 65, 207–8.

[49]   Viganò's biographers invariably rely on Carlo Ritorni, *Commentarii della vita e delle opere coredrammatiche di Salvatore Viganò* (Milan, 1838). Two studies revived interest in Viganò during the 1920s: Andrei Levinson, *Meister des Balletts*, trans. Reinhold von Walter (Potsdam, 1923), pp. 69–94; Henry Prunières, "Salvatore Viganò," *Revue musicale*, Numéro spécial (1 December 1921): 71–94.

[50]   Prunières, p. 76.

[51]   André Levinson, "Le Ballet de *Prométhée*: Beethoven et Viganò," *La Revue musicale*, 8/6 (1927): 90–91.

[52]   Krüger, p. 135.

[53]   Robert Haas, "Zur Wiener Ballettpantomime um den Prometheus," *Neues Beethoven-Jahrbuch*, 2 (1925): 85–8.

Figure 2.1   Johann Gottfried Schadow, Maria Medina

Returning to Vienna in 1799 as the Hofburgtheater's choreographer, Viganò achieved standards that again rivaled the Paris Opéra in sheer brilliance.[54] But seven new ballets, some to his music, aroused contention. Orthodox factions condemned departures from Noverre's principles, citing virtuosic indulgences and lapses in the pseudo-Aristotelian unities, though Noverre was flexible in these matters.[55] If Viganò exceeded Noverre's practices, it was by infusing pantomime sequences with formal dance steps, thus replacing a static alternation between dance and mime with an expressive "mime-dance" now recognized as one of his greatest accomplishments.[56] Modern critics agree Viganò was a faithful disciple of Noverre and Dauberval, not only because he believed ballet was "a type of poem, expressed through the means of pantomime,"[57] but also because he insured each character's individuality by rehearsing soloists and groups within ensembles separately.[58] He likewise arranged the corps asymmetrically and synchronized their actions with music.[59] And his free movements and unrestrictive costumes represent an extension of Noverre's naturalism. Controversy persists, however, regarding whether Viganò synthesized Noverre's precepts in his new vision of ballet before or after 1803, when he left Vienna for Italy.[60] Reactions to his Milanese debut in 1804 nonetheless indicate his skills were already fully developed. In a balletic rendering of Shakespeare's *Coriolanus*, Viganò reportedly mimed a "soliloquy" so effectively that everyone understood it, even without reading the libretto.[61] Thus Viganò's "mime-dance" probably emerged in Vienna and enhanced the choreography of Beethoven's ballet.

Viganò's libretto for the ballet has not survived, though it undoubtedly existed in Italian and German, since Beethoven's sketches contain detailed, multilingual stage directions.[62] Five sources nonetheless help reconstruct the plot: a program note included in the playbill for the premiere on 28 March 1801; an unsigned review that appeared the following month in the Viennese belletristic journal, *Die Zeitung für die elegante Welt*; Carlo Ritorni's detailed scenario, published in his biography of Viganò in 1838; annotations in Beethoven's sketchbook; and the music itself, which often unambiguously imitates stage actions.[63] These sources reveal *Die Geschöpfe des*

---

[54]   Winter, p. 189.

[55]   Friderica Derra de Moroda and Monika Woitas, "Viganò, Salvatore," in *The New Grove Dictionary*, vol. 26, p. 600.

[56]   Levinson, *Meister des Balletts*, p. 87.

[57]   Salvatore Viganò, "Argomento" to *Prometeo: Ballo mitologico inventato e posto sulle scene del R. Teatro alla Scala* (Milan, 1813), p. 3.

[58]   Moore, pp. 65–8.

[59]   Winter, pp. 190, 262.

[60]   For contrasting opinions see Prunières, p. 173; Winter, p. 71.

[61]   Prunières (p. 77) gives the fullest account.

[62]   Beethoven drafted the ballet in the sketchbook known as Landsberg 7 (D-Bsb), which has been transcribed as Karl Lothar Mikulicz (ed.), *Ein Notierungsbuch von Beethoven aus dem Besitze der Preußischer Staatsbibliothek zu Berlin* (Hildesheim, 1972). Stage directions appear on pp. 73–5, 85, 89–91, 98, 109–11, 114–15, 119, 154, 160.

[63]   For the German playbill see Floros, p. 37; an occasionally inaccurate English translation appears in Thomas K. Scherman and Louis Biancolli (eds), *The Beethoven Companion* (Garden City, NY, 1972), p. 128. The review is translated in Senner, pp. 215–16. Ritorni's scenario

Prometheus observes the *ballet d'action*'s principles regarding a serious subject (the human spirit's animation through the arts), a well-structured plot divided into equally well-designed scenes, the depiction of a tragic event, individualization of interrelated characters, and the insertion of formal dances and sequences at appropriate narrative junctures. Reconstructing the storyline also discloses its adherence to eighteenth-century conceptions of the Prometheus myth, as multiple levels of allegory and the Titan's specific attributes illustrate. The ballet's claims on both distinguished legacies, however, would remain invalid unless the music "renders the gestures of the dancers intelligible" and "fixes their movements in time and tone." Beethoven's score fulfills such expectations, as analysis of its separate numbers demonstrates.

Comprising a slow introduction and an allegro cast as a sonata form without development, the overture emulates the structure of theatrical preludes by Gluck, Mozart, and Salieri. Recent critics, however, often ignore its conventionality and instead discern an encapsulation of the impending drama, undoubtedly prompted by perceptions of coherent narrative trajectories in Beethoven's later, "heroic" overtures, especially *Egmont* and *Leonore No. 3*. Thus the overture alternatively embodies "Prometheus the educator," an identity revealed in the allegro's "vigorous agitation" and "bright C-major key"; "the serious grand appearance of Prometheus (adagio) and his leading mankind toward joy (allegro molto con brio)"; or even "man's development out of chaos and liberation from dark forces of the subconscious."[64] Reconciling essentially Mozartean music with Beethoven's later works nonetheless seems anachronistic because the ballet's overture eschews its successors' transparent sequences of conflict, crisis, and triumph, and their thematic borrowings from attendant dramas. Instead the overture's largely abstract themes remain "resistant to all exegesis in the function of a program,"[65] with two exceptions, one rarely if ever observed, the other frequently recognized.

The opening chord tonicizes the subdominant, F major, not the tonic, C (Example 2.1), duplicating the unorthodox harmonies that inaugurate Beethoven's First Symphony, premiered in Vienna on 2 April 1800, a year before the ballet's debut. According to Schindler, Beethoven often recalled that any entrenched Viennese music teachers who did not already consider themselves his enemies—particularly Joseph Preindl, Dyonis Weber, and Maximilian Stocker—were sufficiently antagonized by this single chord to join the rest.[66] The recurrent tonal effrontery thus represents Beethoven's willful violation of old-guard musical sensibilities, a transgression with an obvious but overlooked parallel in the Prometheus myth: the Titan defied Zeus by stealing heavenly fire. Beethoven's petite tonal insurrection resonates in the legend's later romantic treatments: Reichardt, Schubert, and Wolf matched *Sturm und Drang* traits of Goethe's ode with extraordinary chromaticism; Liszt began his symphonic poem with quartal harmonies; French composers evoked Greek antiquity's

---

appears in his *Commentarii*, pp. 47–9. Because these sources occupy very few pages, further references to them and the sketchbook will occur in the text. Longer secondary reconstructions, particularly those of Riemann and Floros, will be cited in notes.

[64]   Riemann, p. 24; Paul Bekker, *Beethoven* (London, 1927), p. 326; Paul Nettl, *The Dance in Classical Music* (New York, 1963), p. 153.

[65]   Levinson, "Le Ballet de Prométhée," p. 93.

[66]   Schindler, p. 92.

Example 2.1   Beethoven *Die Geschöpfe des Prometheus*, Overture, mm. 1–4

atmosphere with quarter tones and modes; Parry infuriated staid Victorian critics with Wagnerian chromaticism and leitmotifs; Bargiel quoted Beethoven's initial chords in his overture; and Skryabin expanded Liszt's quartal harmonies to form his idiosyncratic symphony's "mystic chord." For the romantics, Prometheus became synonymous with unusual sonorities, beginning with Beethoven.

Example 2.2a   Beethoven *Die Geschöpfe des Prometheus*, Overture, mm. 17–25

A universally recognized programmatic association links the sonata form's principal theme with the ballet's concluding fugato (Example 2.2a–b). While not identical, both themes share similarities of tempo, meter, rhythm, motive, melodic contour, and key, all defining a lively character suitable for the "festive dances" that end the ballet in Ritorni's scenario. Thus the overture's principal theme foreshadows a celebration of the creatures' animation through the power of the arts. Although obvious, these thematic resemblances and dramatic connotations attracted little notice from early critics, who instead judged the overture too long for a divertissement, particularly compared to the ballet's shorter pieces.[67] Doubtless the overture's length and brilliance likewise informed the opinion of Beethoven's music as "too learned" for a ballet, criticism also leveled at several dance numbers.

In contrast to the largely abstract overture, the ensuing *introduzione* indulges in graphic musical pictorialization. Bearing the inscription "La Tempestà" in the piano reduction Artaria published in 1801, the *introduzione* depicts a storm, as surviving scenarios confirm, by exploiting conventional figuration used in eighteenth-century stage works and characteristic symphonies, and which Beethoven would fully cultivate in the "Pastoral" Symphony's fourth movement. Low string tremolos, marked piano in the remote key of A-flat, portend distant thunder. Unison strings make repeated crescendos while arpeggiating diminished triads, a standard means of portraying a storm's approach. Timpani rolls intimate closer thunder, now answered by quick, ascending woodwind arpeggios that unmistakably represent lightning

---

[67]   *Die Zeitung für die elegante Welt*, pp. 215–16.

Example 2.2b   Beethoven *Die Geschöpfe des Prometheus*, No. 16, mm. 192–9

flashes. And additional unisons lead to the storm's outbreak in fortissimo tremolos, sustained blaring of woodwinds and brasses, and wide-ranging broken chords in the violins. But as explicit as the tempest's depiction is, the introduction's conclusion more clearly illustrates Beethoven's close engagement with combining music and stage action (Example 2.3).

Above a pedal tone on G, a diminuendo and staggered chromatic descents in strings and woodwinds lead to paired fermatas, events usually interpreted as the storm's subsidence. The playbill, the review in *Die Zeitung für die elegante Welt*, and Ritorni's scenario, however, indicate the fermatas correspond to Prometheus placing fire on the hearts of the creatures, described in all three sources as lifeless statues, and the earlier staggered descents accompany the Titan's entrance as he flees the "thundering wrath of heaven," perhaps already weary from labor. Following the fermatas a unison string descent effectively portrays his collapse, whereupon a softer, slower descent played in thirds by violins and bassoons reflects his "breathless" exhaustion on a rock, with hairpin dynamics evoking a sigh. Thus Beethoven mirrored body movements with stock figuration drawn from an arsenal of eighteenth-century musical clichés that would remain central to the nineteenth-century operatic vocabulary, as Mary Ann Smart has adroitly demonstrated, notwithstanding objections critics ranging from Rousseau to modern operatic apologists have perennially raised against stereotyped coordination of music and body motion.[68] Beethoven's commentators even more staunchly discount his supposedly uncharacteristic forays into programmaticism, yet some of his most admired music is rooted in imitation of movement, as the next number illustrates.

Example 2.3   Beethoven *Die Geschöpfe des Prometheus*, Introduction, mm. 46–66

---

[68]   Mary Ann Smart, *Mimomania: Music and Gesture in Nineteenth-Century Opera* (Berkeley, 2004), pp. 70–78.

Example 2.3 continued.

Example 2.3 continued.

Example 2.3 concluded.

The first numbered piece verifies the composer's systematic coordination of music and action, affects perceptions of other works, and consequently warrants thorough consideration. Beethoven's sketchbook contains a running commentary above 107 measures of music whose basic structure is retained in the published score, though details vary greatly. As in a rondo, or more aptly a Baroque ritornello form, a passage for the creatures alternates with episodes involving Prometheus (ABACA'C'BA"B). The former (A), obviously designed for pantomime, shifts from the tonic, C major, for its last two statements. Of the latter, one is likewise recurrent (B), but suits formalized dance and remains in the tonic; another (C) again changes key, contributing to an imperfect symmetry.

As the sketchbook discloses, the number begins as the newly awakened creatures slowly cross the stage, their halting steps depicted in largely scalewise lines punctuated by eighth rests (Example 2.4a). Upbeats soon destabilize their gait, which deteriorates in increasingly sporadic rhythms. Nevertheless, a clear pattern emerges: two eight-measure periods, each comprising a pair of two-measure units and a four-measure phrase, respectively cadence in the dominant and tonic. The published version, now harmonized for strings, preserves the sketchbook's phrasing and cadences, but its rhythm is more precarious because rests and upbeats vary in length (Example 2.4b). This ill-balanced ostinato closely resembles its famous counterpart in the ballet's finale, where the fully human creatures perform a contredanse (Example 2.4c). Here, however, the bass line's "steps" alternate between notes and rests of equal length until they acquire the rhythmic momentum and melodic profile that propel them toward the retained half cadence. Thus the ostinato functions programmatically, first portraying awkward, insensible creatures, then full-fledged human beings capable of stylized dancing.

The deceptively straightforward depiction of bodies taking their first, tentative steps developed an even richer genealogy after serving as the renowned contredanse's prototype. Three additional works exploit the finale's theme: the seventh of Twelve Contredanses, WoO 14 (1802); the Variations and Fugue on an Original Theme, Op. 35 (1802), which Beethoven claimed were written in an entirely new manner owing to their use of Baroque contrapuntal procedures and ambiguities regarding whether the theme's bass line or its treble melody is the principal subject; and the "Eroica" Symphony's finale (1804). The last-named movement spawned its own exegetic tradition, whereby "festive dances" commemorate the achievements of a hero, normally an apotheosized Napoleon, or more idiosyncratically an idealized Homeric champion, as Arnold Schering once imaginatively suggested.[69] In both cases, the quotation of the ballet's finale at the symphony's conclusion connotes fulfillment or renewal of the acts of mankind's "beneficent" champion, either the pre-dictatorial Napoleon, or the archetypal protagonist of Greek epic.

---

[69]   Arnold Schering, "Die *Eroica*, eine Homer-Symphonie Beethovens?" *Neues Beethoven Jahrbuch*, 5 (1933): 159–77.

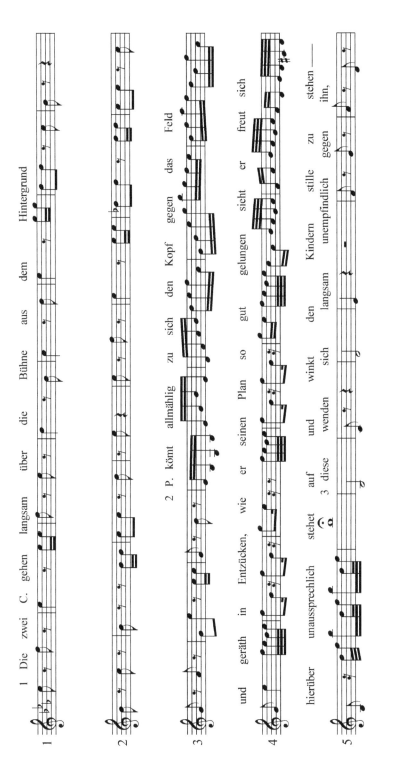

Example 2.4a   Beethoven Sketch for *Die Geschöpfe des Prometheus*, No. 1, mm. 1–37

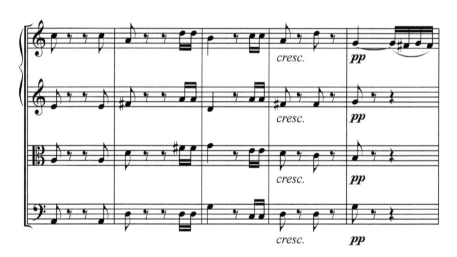

Example 2.4b   Beethoven *Die Geschöpfe des Prometheus*, No. 1, mm. 1–10

Example 2.4c   Beethoven *Die Geschöpfe des Prometheus*, No. 16, mm. 1–8

Heroic progressivism, as the anthropomorphic trope maintains, is reflected in the "Eroica" finale's basic sequence of events. Following a unison fortissimo introduction indebted to accompanied recitative, pizzicato strings softly play the ostinato. It then supports four increasingly sophisticated variations before its emergent countermelody (Example 2.4c, Violino I) dominates six more variations and a coda. Routinely overlooked in this familiar allegorization is that the fundamental impulse behind the "Eroica" finale's initial conception was mimetic: the ostinato originally imitated the unsteady footfall of the ballet's proto-human creatures, though it assumes its regular, stylized form in the symphony's finale. Thus one of Beethoven's most admired sets of "abstract" variations is rooted in movements of the body.

The ballet's first number actually initiates a comparably progressive process that connects the creatures' halting steps with an ensuing contredanse. When the ostinato ends on a dominant pedal tone, ascending scales embellish a seventh chord, acquire doublings in thirds, and gradually crescendo, all in synchronization with pantomime. Beethoven's sketchbook reveals this transitional passage accompanies Prometheus, posed with his head on the ground, as he regains his senses, presumably by rising and demonstrating renewed awareness. Thus nondescript figuration again depicts simple physical motions immanently well. But when the tempo changes to allegro con brio, Prometheus experiences rapture over his creatures' awakening and rejoices inexpressibly, emotions that precipitate the ballet's first formal dance (B), a specifically English type of contredanse in duple meter, lacking an upbeat, and displaying a formulaic rhythm of two eighth notes followed by a strong cadence on every second measure's downbeat.[70] Linked by the transition, the ostinato and contredanse also feature identical phrase lengths and cadential patterns—formal correspondences that strengthen the progressive dramaturgical connection.

A contredanse, however, is an unusual solo vehicle: in social settings women and men face each other in lines, executing synchronous steps. Moreover, the contredanse's straightforward duple meter and simple choreography (walking steps, skips, and perhaps small hops) suited the abilities of untrained amateurs who popularized the dance during the eighteenth century's last two decades much better than the smaller, quicker steps, turns, and hemiola patterns of the aristocratic minuet, which lost favor as the century waned. Viganò's choice of a contredanse, capably realized by Beethoven, accordingly implies the creatures should join their animator in facile, egalitarian dancing, in accordance with the sketchbook, where Prometheus coaxes them to stop moving aimlessly and approach him. But in ensuing episodes they respond to multiple entreaties, set to the contredanse's recurrences, with stiff, prolonged toddling, marked by the ostinato's return in various keys (I, vi, i)—repetition that fatigued the critic for *Die Zeitung für die elegante Welt*.

The contrasting episodes (C) among these varied restatements abjure dance style. Decidedly vocal in nature, they present a cantabile melody above repeated chords and another ostinato-like bass line. Between two melodic statements in the dominant and submediant, the ostinato reappears, a sequence the sketchbook thoroughly explains. Prometheus repeatedly addresses the creatures, expresses divine, paternal love for them, and again urges them to

---

[70]   Sarah Bennett Reichart, "The Influence of Eighteenth-Century Social Dance on the Viennese Classical Style" (Ph.D. diss., City University of New York, 1984), pp. 246–7.

draw near (V), but they merely contemplate a tree (ostinato). He then loses heart, becomes anxious, and leads them by the hand downstage, where he clarifies their relationship and embraces them (vi). Thus an expressive vocal style matches the rhetorical mode of the Titan's gestural discourse and his overtly emotional attachment to his "children."

Models outside the realm of dance likewise shape the second number. A slow introduction (adagio) derives from opera seria, while the main body of the movement (allegro con brio) adopts a specific symphonic idiom. Unlike the previous number's divisions, however, these two sections bear no dramaturgical explanations in Beethoven's sketchbook, despite the presence of several drafts of their melodic lines. Ritorni's scenario nonetheless elucidates a series of contrasting episodes that rapidly unfold in just 50 measures. Pantomime again predominates, virtually excluding recognizable traces of formalized dance.

The adagio begins in F major with two measures of double-dotted rhythms and fragmentary rushing scales recalling the French overture's *intrada* figure, a comparison strengthened by Baroque scoring for unison strings and bassoons. Synonymous with pomp and ceremony, such figuration typically attends imposing, authoritarian characters in opera seria,[71] as in *Idomeneo* when the high priest enters in Act III, and in both finales of *Don Giovanni*, first when the aristocratic masqueraders conspire to enter the Don's home, and then as the Commendatore's statue knocks at his door. Thus the Titan's demeanor changes from paternal benevolence to domineering power. Too short to accompany movement, the *intrada* passage probably reinforced a static pose, a mainstay of acting well into the nineteenth century.[72] More animated figuration, however, immediately interrupts the stately rhythms, suggesting that body motion resumes. Fortissimo repeated notes and tremolos, linked with psychological agitation since Monteverdi's time, accord with Ritorni's reference to an angry Prometheus, while nine ensuing repetitions of three-note scale fragments, punctuated by sforzandos, plainly represent "menaces" he directs toward the creatures, perhaps with matching arm gestures and stereotypical clenched fists. The adagio accordingly depicts a static affect's intensification into volatile emotions, a process realized harmonically by movement away from the tonic to the relative minor's dominant.

In contrast, the allegro con brio resists interpretation as systematically coordinated music and physical movement, instead reflecting the Titan's psychological development through tonal and textural processes (Example 2.5). Marked piano, it begins in D minor with a scalewise ascent and descent in the violins, embellished by chromatic neighbor tones and supported by repeated notes in the lower strings. Rising sequential statements increase tensions that erupt in a fortissimo outburst reminiscent of *Sturm und Drang* symphonies of the 1760s and '70s. In an intensified restatement, the scalewise melody acquires tremolo markings, octave doublings, and chordal support from woodwinds and brasses. Tonality then destabilizes, traversing the circle of fifths (D–G–C–F) to modulate to B-flat major, where a stepwise sequential dialogue between the bass and soprano reestablishes D minor. The agitated figuration, unstable tonality, and divided melodic exchange musically embody psychological turmoil and thus correspond in Ritorni's scenario with Prometheus thinking he must destroy his work. Equally clear parallels between music and internal motivation obtain in the number's final measures, where

---

[71]   Floros, pp. 60–61.
[72]   Smart, pp. 44–5.

Example 2.5   Beethoven *Die Geschöpfe des Prometheus*, No. 2, mm. 11–20

Example 2.5 continued.

Example 2.5 concluded.

subito piano markings and hushed woodwind chords signify a volte-face. According to Ritorni, "a higher internal voice" prevents Prometheus from destroying the creatures, and another idea occurs to him. The solution, however, remains unknown as the minor mode dissolves in a half cadence in F major, anticipating the next number.

A formal dance closes Act I, thereby fulfilling eighteenth-century ballet's choreographic expectations. The third number consequently involves little pantomime and few directions in Ritorni's scenario. Prometheus, merely indicating he has new plans, leads his creatures away, the latter action possibly coinciding with an animated coda. Thus the finale was primarily a solo for Herr Cesari, who created the title role.

The movement's stylization of the minuet's hallmark features reflects its composition late in the dance's long period of popularity (Example 2.6). Triple meter and regular four-measure phrases (divided 1+1+2) are essential in any minuet, though the tempo (allegro vivace) corresponds to the brisk pace that transformed symphonic dance movements into scherzos. Fast tempos and upbeats are nonetheless common in the German minuet, whose affect is lighter than that of its slower French counterpart.[73] Frequent accents on the second beat, likewise generically intrinsic to the minuet, produce the hemiola that results when two measures in triple meter support the dance's four-step choreography. The movement's dotted rhythms, while atypical of social minuets, often appear in familiar concert repertoire, including the third movements of Haydn's "Military" Symphony and Beethoven's immensely popular Septet. Identifying a dance type, however, scarcely determines the steps contemporary theatrical performers executed, since stage choreography differed from social practice. Indeed, the finale's angular melodic profile suggests repeated leaps as mimetic equivalents for body movements instead of the skips, half turns, and substitution steps mentioned in eighteenth-century social choreographies.[74]

A more crucial departure from dance conventions is the finale's form. Rather than observing the tight, periodic phrasing that generates the minuet's binary form and duplicating it in a similarly structured trio, the movement comprises a miniature sonata form. The exposition presents two contrasting themes, properly disposed in the tonic and dominant and connected by a modulatory transition; the first is arpeggiated and rhythmically fragmented, the second more linear and continuous. As in the overture, there is no development, and an abbreviated recapitulation omits the transition. After two statements of a new, descending melodic line possibly related to the two creatures, the coda ends with tutti authentic cadences and repeated tonic chords. The act accordingly concludes with the most formally abstract number thus far, perhaps inciting criticism of Beethoven's music as "too learned" for the dance.

Formalized dance overshadows pantomime in Act II, especially after two introductory numbers. Coordination of music and action consequently requires less attention, whereas identification of dance types and Beethoven's adherence to their conventions demand more. Act II also clarifies the ballet's description as an allegory in the playbill, the review in *Die Zeitung für die elegante Welt*, and Ritorni's scenario, which includes a subtitle, "the power of music and dance": the creatures become fully animated by interacting with gods who personify human activities and emotions, not only music and dance, but also tragedy, comedy, war, death, grief, and joy.

---

[73] Reichart, pp. 154–5.
[74] Ibid., pp. 134–7.

Example 2.6   Beethoven *Die Geschöpfe des Prometheus*, No. 3, mm. 1–12

A simple entr'acte often eludes critical notice, despite its adept illustration of straightforward stage action. Its opening four-measure maestoso doubtless accompanied the rising curtain's revelation of the gods on Mount Parnassus. Riemann likened its "radiant" key, D major, to Apollo's brilliant visage, aptly deifying its solemn alternation of unison strings and sustained chords in woodwinds, brasses, and timpani, made more resonant with fortissimo dynamics and triple stops in the violins.[75] Following a fermata, a brief andante marks the varied return of the ostinato linked with the creatures' footsteps. The playbill and review agree on the depicted action: Prometheus introduces the creatures to Apollo and his retinue. Pianissimo dynamics and regularly alternating eighth notes and rests indicate their approach is cautious but steady, and they pause every four measures, interrupting newly balanced movements twice with symmetrical, two-measure phrases. Their periodic footfall thus seems more stable than their ungainly toddling in Act I.

Ritorni's scenario for the fifth number again implies a close integration of music and stage action, although their synchronization is less detailed than in earlier pieces. Instead, an adagio and an andante quasi allegretto respectively involve actions of the gods and the creatures and emphasize pantomime and formal dance. The adagio begins with chords for the harp, an instrument Beethoven rarely employed, but utilized here to depict Ritorni's "sign from Apollo," Greek mythology's master musician, who serenaded the Olympians with his kithara, or large lyre. Apollo bids Euterpe, the Muse of lyric poetry and music, to play the instrument of her expertise, the flute, an event likewise matched with appropriate orchestration. But, as Riemann noted, the clarinet and bassoon expand the range of Euterpe's melody to three octaves,[76] anticipating their prominent concertante parts in the andante.

Ritorni also identifies Euterpe's accompanist as Amphion, the best choice among many famous Greek lyrists. Although weaker than his athletic brother, Amphion won their competition to build a protective wall around their native Thebes by playing so enchantingly that stones obeyed his command to assemble around the city. Thus Amphion alone could animate the statue-like creatures, but three legendary lyrists still assist him: Arion, a mortal poet (ca. 700 BCE) whose strumming supposedly charmed dolphins; Orpheus, whose music secured his passage through the gates of Hades and persuaded the underworld's gods to release his wife Eurydice; and Apollo himself. Riemann linked each musician's contribution to an event in the score. As Apollo's harp strikes its third chord, Amphion's accompaniment begins softly with steady pizzicato quarter notes in violins and violas. Arion and Orpheus enter simultaneously eight measures later, when cellos and basses join the upper strings. Apollo's harp arpeggios return 12 measures later.

Riemann's correlations broadly agree with Ritorni's account, but closer scrutiny supports another reading. When the low strings enter, they essentially duplicate a progression of primary chords the upper strings initially played in the tonic, B-flat major. The upper strings are marked piano in both passages, while the lower strings merely furnish weaker pianissimo reinforcement. Texture, rhythm, harmony, and dynamics soon change markedly, however, suggesting onstage counterparts: bowing replaces plucking; eighth and sixteenth notes supplant quarters; diminished seventh chords and secondary dominants proceed around the circle of fifths to a German sixth chord that reinforces the dominant; and two crescendos end with subito

---

[75] Riemann, p. 28.

[76] Ibid.

piano indications. These repeated stylistic shifts correlate better with additions of three lyrists than the single pianissimo low-string entrance Riemann advocated. Moreover, impending events complete Ritorni's scenario for the number. When the German sixth resolves, the ostinato returns as the creatures begin to "disclose signs of reason," though such glimmerings are faint, as a turn to the minor tonic and rhythmically unstable woodwind duplets indicate. And, following a cello cadenza that presages the next section's concertante writing, the creatures will advance the plot by contemplating nature's beauty and feeling human passion.

The andante quasi allegretto again illustrates Beethoven's cultivation of two principles of the *ballet d'action*. First, its pastoral idiom, a generic trait of eighteenth-century theatrical dance, aptly represents stage action as the creatures admire nature's wonders (Example 2.7). Obvious pastoralisms include solos for the adagio's three bucolic woodwinds, simple primary chords, and tonic pedal tones that simulate drones. Its expansive lyricism, foreshadowing the "Pastoral" Symphony's second movement, doubtless encouraged Robert Lach to rank it among the best works of the first half of Beethoven's creative life.[77] Second, as a formal dance it meets all the siciliano's criteria, namely a slow tempo, compound meter, regular four-measure phrases, few elisions or transitions, and gentle pastoral associations. Its choreography remains obscure, though eighteenth-century theorists often labeled it a slow gigue,[78] a faster dance entailing small hops or jumps on strong beats and skips on afterbeats, steps impractical at slower speeds. Notwithstanding its choreographic ambiguities, the number corroborates Beethoven's adherence to a specific dance type's stylistic conventions, matched perhaps by equally prosaic dancing by both creatures.

Beethoven nonetheless characteristically infused the siciliano with elements of abstract instrumental music, most notably a sonata form's clearly outlined exposition. In presenting the principal theme in the tonic, B-flat major, a solo cello plays one eight-measure period with waltz-like accompaniment and in another responds to woodwind scales. Oboe and clarinet dominate the expansive subordinate theme, alternating with flute and cello in F major, the anticipated key. And the cello regains prominence in a concluding area, where pedal tones emphasize the dominant. A transition to D-flat major intimates a development section's onset, but the new tonality is stable, supporting another periodic melody played by clarinet, bassoon, and cello, with replies from flute and harp. As in sonata form, a prolonged dominant dramatizes the tonic's return, whereupon an elaborately orchestrated principal theme initiates a recapitulation. But the exposition's remaining materials fail to reappear. Instead the principal theme's last phrase, broadened by several diminished seventh chords, prepares a coda that begins with a passage especially prescient for the "Pastoral" Symphony's slow movement (Example 2.8). The excerpt's key (B-flat major), simple diatonic progression of root position chords (vi–ii–V–I), and flowing, antiphonal woodwind lines supported by pulsating string accompaniment all foreshadow features of Beethoven's mature bucolic score before the siciliano ends with tutti chords punctuating Apollonian harp arpeggios.

―――――――――
[77]   Robert Lach, "Zur Geschichte der Beethovenschen Prometheus Ballettmusik," *Zeitschrift für Musikwissenschaft*, 3 (1921): 223.

[78]   Wye Jamison Allanbrook, "Dance as Expression in Mozart Opera" (Ph.D. diss., Stanford University, 1974), p. 97.

Example 2.7   Beethoven *Die Geschöpfe des Prometheus*, No. 5, mm. 34–41

Example 2.7 concluded.

Example 2.8   Beethoven *Die Geschöpfe des Prometheus*, No. 5, mm. 72–80

Example 2.8 concluded.

Riemann identified the sixth number as a dance for Terpsichore and the Graces, though two later analysts deemed it the moment when the creatures first show signs of awareness.[79] Floros, however, discovered an inscription ("les graces") in Beethoven's related sketches, thereby reestablishing the movement's true function in Ritorni's scenario.[80] The piece accordingly inaugurates another stage in the creatures' education as they observe the elegant comportment of four goddesses fathered by Zeus: Terpsichore, one of nine Muses, and three Graces, Aglaia (Splendor), Euphosyne (Mirth), and Thalia (Good Cheer). Thus the number, a *pas de quatre*, allows paired dancing.

Couples are essential to the movement's social dance type, the polonaise, the favorite dance of Polish aristocrats, who appropriated its folk traditions during the seventeenth century. It presumably arrived in Western Europe via Saxony toward the century's end, when Dresden functioned as Poland's capital, and spread quickly after 1763, when Austrian, Prussian, and Russian nobles acquired Polish lands.[81] Majestic and solemn, it inaugurated important society balls in Germany and Austria, displacing the French minuet, especially after the Revolution in 1789. It was often sung with moral lyrics praising human virtues or referring to lofty classical subjects—the perfect dance for educating the creatures.

The polonaise's social choreography constituted a march-like procession of couples usually begun and directed by the highest aristocrats present. Thus noble leaders reinforced the civil hierarchy, guiding lower ranking dancers through circular or serpentine patterns determined by the venue's size. French Baroque dance manuals specify the polonaise's execution to the *pas de bourée*, which entailed a bending of both knees followed by two rising steps.[82] Each movement corresponds to one beat in triple meter, with the first rising step matched by a characteristic accent on beat two. Four-measure phrases, typically divided 1+1+2, preserve metric and choreographic regularity.

Within these metric and syntactical parameters, German theorists recognized two distinct polonaises.[83] In the authentic Polish variety, full cadences begin on the second beat with a leading tone that resolves on the third, while half cadences involve flowing figuration and occur on first or third beats. German polonaises, featuring full cadences on the third beat or half cadences on the second, routinely exhibit dactylic rhythms of two sixteenth notes followed by an eighth. In practice polonaises combine properties of both types with other characteristics, including syncopation, complex ornaments, freely melodic passages of rapid figuration, repetitive chordal accompaniments, and sudden dynamic changes.

---

[79]   Riemann, p. 30; Levinson, "Le Ballet de Prométhée," p. 95; Friedrich Rust, "Ueber Salvatore Viganò's Originalscenarium zu L. v. Beethovens Ballet *Die Geschöpfe des Prometheus*," *Neue Berliner Musikzeitung*, 45 (1891): 134.

[80]   Floros, p. 54. Riemann's article contains typographical errors in numbering of the sixth and seventh movements, which Floros considers erroneous correlations between action and music.

[81]   Reichart, pp. 107–8.

[82]   Ibid., pp. 111–13.

[83]   Allanbrook, pp. 84–91.

Beethoven's polonaise largely respects these conventions (Example 2.9). Its allegro tempo exceeds the Polish prototype's speed, but accords with German custom; accents invariably emphasize beat two; an unbroken succession of four-measure phrases usually observes the standard subdivision; repeated chords accompany freely melodic passages of continuous sixteenth notes; and German dactylic rhythms invigorate the number's central section. But distinctive characteristics of the polonaise are missing. Cadences always fall on downbeats; syncopation is practically non-existent; and melodies eschew ornaments. Thus the number's conformity to specific conventions is hardly scrupulous, though its generic traits ensure its recognition as a polonaise.

The movement's structure, however, is exceedingly dance-like. A perfunctory introduction comprising tutti chords in G major presumably allowed the ballerinas to take their positions. Retaining the same key, the polonaise then unfolds as a regular ternary form, its first section presenting two statements of an eight-measure period, the second varied with added woodwind parts. Both the period's four-measure phrases cadence in the tonic. A central section likewise consists of a repeated period, though its orchestration is more uniform and the first phrase cadences in the dominant. Its eight-measure codetta, pervaded by dactylic rhythms, facilitates the fortissimo return of the number's opening phrase, now expanded by repetitions of its last two measures. Such extremely regular phrase structure and repetitive melodies suggest Terpsichore and the Graces observed conventional choreography, ensuring the creatures would comprehend the polonaise's educational message.

In extreme contrast, the seventh number rejects dance taxonomies to emulate a rhetorical model, evolving as a dialogue between passages of two distinct thematic types. The first, an *intrada* figure more solemn than the second number's introduction, reconciles well with the tempo (grave), though it is varied after two initial statements. The second encompasses three cantabile melodies exhibiting different degrees of ornamentation. Thus the seventh number anticipates a similar exchange in the celebrated central movement of Beethoven's Fourth Piano Concerto, where the orchestra's forte unison dotted rhythms alternate with the soloist's lyrical utterances.

The rhetorical mode broadly accommodates Ritorni's dramaturgy, but precise coordination of music and action remains elusive. According to his scenario, the "candidates" move about, arrive before Prometheus, recognize in him their object of thankfulness and love, prostrate themselves before him, and embrace him passionately. Beethoven's music, however, merely insinuates the creatures interact with any number of potentates, perhaps the Titan alone, but more likely other divinities as well (Example 2.10). Unison strings initiate the discourse with the *intrada* figure, associated with imposing characters such as Prometheus and the Olympians, moving from the tonic, G major, through a tonicized subdominant to a half cadence. Double reeds and horns reply, the oboes ornamenting a descent in parallel thirds. Unlike the unison *intrada* figure, the paired oboes imply an onstage duo, patently the creatures, while an authentic cadence completes classical periodicity's call-and-response pattern.

Dialogue is never absent from the piece, not even when the *intrada* figure's reduction to a quarter of its original length again prefigures the concerto's contractive processes, nor when an ornate violin cantilena supplants the oboe melody. This continuous thematic interaction invites a more nuanced though admittedly speculative reading of Ritorni. Perhaps the "candidates" move about (cantabile melodies) as they

Example 2.9   Beethoven *Die Geschöpfe des Prometheus*, No. 6, mm. 5–12

Example 2.10   Beethoven *Die Geschöpfe des Prometheus*, No. 7, mm. 1–4

approach various deities, receiving imperious responses (*intrada* figures) until they reach Prometheus. The scene's climax—recognition, prostration, and the embrace—plausibly corresponds to the score's most dramatic moment, its last three measures (Example 2.11). At this late juncture the minor mode's unexpected outbreak is intensified by the number's only fortissimo marking, violin arpeggios repeatedly traversing over two octaves, and a diminished seventh chord the rest of the orchestra reiterates incessantly in the number's pervasive dotted rhythms.

A powerful, Beethovenesque culmination is just one striking aspect of a movement whose irregular rhetorical surface and correspondingly unusual large-scale structure seemingly flaunt sonata-form conventions. An orthodox exposition presents three thematic areas in their proper keys, though the principal subject comprises two sections, one enclosing the paired oboe melody between statements of the complete *intrada* passage, another punctuating the violin cantilena with the dotted figure's quarter-length fragments. Compressing the second section's alternating materials, a sequential transition modulates to the dominant, where the subordinate theme perpetuates the dialogue. Vestigial *intrada* figures twice interrupt a slow descending scale in the oboes before the violins complete the descent, adding more filigree. And the concluding area's dominant pedal supports quasi-canonic statements of the *intrada* figure, now lacking its pompous double dotting, unlike the tutti chords disrupting them.

As in the overture and Act I finale, the development is omitted, replaced by half a measure of violin scales leading directly to the principal theme's tonic restatement. Thereafter, however, the recapitulation is anomalous, starting when another *intrada* figure tonicizes B-flat major. Then the subordinate theme's first three measures resurface, only to be succeeded by the principal theme's last four measures, still in B-flat, but quickly shifting to G minor. This recapitulative pastiche avoids reference to the exposition's remaining materials, instead culminating in the *intrada* figure's fortissimo repetitions. But precisely when the creatures and Prometheus experience their first genuinely personal interaction—a pivotal dramatic juncture marked by the climax of a correspondingly individual musical form—a communal intrusion delays their relationship's progress.

Bacchus and his bacchants enact a "heroic scene" appropriate, Ritorni asserts, for the retinue of Mars, the Roman god of War. An honored teacher of viticulture also known for inducing madness in his female followers, Bacchus (and his Greek counterpart Dionysus) usually treated mankind beneficently. He nonetheless faced persecution in his mortal mother's native Thebes until soldiers sent to arrest him instead became the first of the city's residents to worship him. Thus his reputation as an educator and affiliation with Theban soldiers respectively qualify him to instruct the creatures and lead "warlike dances." The eighth number is consequently a military march, a common eighteenth-century balletic dance that often involved carefully choreographed weapons drills, as Ritorni's scenario stipulates.

Example 2.11   Beethoven *Die Geschöpfe des Prometheus*, No. 7, mm. 36–8

Example 2.11 continued.

Example 2.11 concluded.

Multiple features confirm the number is a march (Example 2.12). An introductory timpani solo, underscoring the importance of drums in marches, establishes a martial dotted rhythm that pervades the movement. The key, D major, accommodated the period's valveless trumpets, orchestral equivalents for bugles, which join woodwinds in playing fanfares in parallel thirds. Regular two- or four-measure phrases in common time are likewise quintessential march traits, though contemporary theorists disagreed over the upbeats that begin many strains of the number.[84] Some claimed marches should begin on downbeats to avoid confusion; others believed upbeats could indicate the moment when marchers raised one leg. Indisputably unusual is the second beat's accentuation in one of the number's recurrent themes.

Associated with the tread of soldiers since Greek antiquity, marches retained their ethos in eighteenth-century music treatises.[85] As calls to communal action they unified moving bodies in accomplishing severe tasks, inspiring victory in combat or perseverance in manual labor. They excited the spirit, evoking "a certain higher, more noble joy." Bacchus' march accordingly serves two lofty purposes, directing the creatures' attention away from their attachment to Prometheus toward a larger community and attendant responsibility,[86] and ennobling their joy.

Beyond meeting generic criteria and advancing the drama, the march contains passages that define specific military modes or correspond to stage action. Its rondo form features a refrain in the tonic, episodes in contrasting keys, and a quasi-developmental section acting as a segue to a coda. The refrain displays all the march's trademarks, including the timpani solo, alternating tonic and dominant triads, brilliant woodwind and brass scoring, melodies doubled in thirds or sixths, dotted rhythms, and regular phrasing. Cast in the parallel minor, the first episode is Janissary music, a stylized rendering of fast marches played by the Ottoman sultan's guards, though it has evaded explicit identification as such.[87] It accordingly exploits unison chromatic lines for woodwinds and low strings, as in an episode in the finale of Mozart's Violin Concerto, K. 219. Timpani substitute for side drums, and Viennese Janissary music's ubiquitous cymbals and triangle are missing, but tremolos enhance the clamor. After the refrain's repetition, a second episode in the subdominant graphically represents gesture (Example 2.13). Pervaded by dotted rhythms, ascending arpeggios engender a dialogue between violins and the remaining orchestral instruments, thus imitating thrusts and parries of opponents in swordplay. Similar music accompanies Don Juan's duel with the Commendatore in Gluck's ballet, as Floros observes,[88] but identical strategies govern Mozart's better-known operatic setting of the same scene.

Following the refrain's third statement, the form evolves irregularly. Modulatory sequences emphasizing G major, A minor, D major, and E minor reach a fermata on a half cadence in B minor. Unexpectedly the tonic returns, supporting a condensed

---

[84]   Ibid., p. 100.

[85]   Ibid., pp. 99–100.

[86]   Rust, p. 143.

[87]   Floros (p. 64) describes the passage as "exotic" and "oriental"; Riemann (p. 33) likens it to a czardas.

[88]   Floros, p. 64.

Example 2.12   Beethoven *Die Geschöpfe des Prometheus*, No. 8, mm. 1–9

Example 2.12 continued.

Example 2.12 concluded.

Example 2.13   Beethoven *Die Geschöpfe des Prometheus*, No. 8, mm. 83–90

abstraction of the refrain's dotted figure, but more fermatas undermine rhythmic and tonal stability by prolonging chords that tonicize B-flat major, E minor, and A minor. Each pause undoubtedly involved pantomime, though Ritorni supplies just one clue: the creatures cannot resist impulses of glory, grasp weapons, and want to join the bacchants, events the score's features match. After the first fermata, the texture reduces to three canonic lines, one independent, the others paired, perhaps corresponding to Bacchus and the creatures. And after more fermatas, staccato chords softly alternate between winds and strings, recalling the creatures' step-like ostinato. Nondescript, however, are the coda's rapidly alternating tonic and dominant chords, embellished by a lone turn to B-flat and an augmented sixth chord.

A popular, commercial, and critical triumph, the march was transcribed for piano, quickly published, repeatedly programmed on the Augarten concert series, and praised as one of the ballet's two most successful numbers in *Die Zeitung für die elegante Welt*.[89] But the journal's critic contradicted himself, reporting that everything was "laid out too grandly for a divertissement," an assessment surely applicable to the eighth number, the longest in the ballet. From a historical perspective, however, the march confirms Beethoven could depict a "heroic scene" well before he produced his middle period's seminal works.

In the ninth number the creatures learn their infatuation with weapons has dire consequences, as Ritorni imparts. When they attempt to join the bacchants, Melpomene, the Muse of tragedy, intercedes, performing a "tragica scena" for astonished onlookers. With a dagger she demonstrates how death affects mortals, causing the creatures to shudder fearfully. Rushing to Prometheus, she reproaches him for creating miserable beings doomed to perish and threatens to punish him with death. Finally experiencing compassion, the creatures try to restrain her, but she kills the Titan with her dagger (or so it appears).

Beethoven's sketchbook contains two drafts of Melpomene's tragedy, each bearing inscriptions that again closely synchronize music with action. Differing greatly from the published version, both nonetheless closely foreshadow its style and tripartite structure. Three sections constitute a typical eighteenth-century operatic scena: an introductory adagio in E-flat major, a transitional recitative modulating from the parallel to the relative minor, and an aria in C minor. Annotations in both drafts ("la muse tragique" and "entrata") equate the adagio with Melpomene's entrance, accompanied by tutti strings with stately homophonic chords that twice crescendo from piano to forte. Then, as pulsating strings repeat dominant pedal tones, clarinets and bassoons softly play sequences of descending scales and arpeggios that end with a sudden swell to forte and a deceptive cadence. Pedal tones and soft dynamics return, but sextuplet sixteenth notes, some arpeggiated, agitate the texture. These events ostensibly correlate with Melpomene's explanation of human mortality, the creatures' terror, and the Muse drawing her dagger—the last two obviously corresponding to the dynamic outburst, deceptive cadence, and textural agitation.

---

[89]   *Letters to Beethoven*, vol. 1, p. 90; *Die Zeitung für die elegante Welt*, p. 216.

Shifting from triple meter to common time, the second section bears another *incipit* in the sketchbook, "mi presenta miseria," disclosing the passage accompanies Melpomene as she berates Prometheus for creating human misery. Her mute gestures acquire elocutionary force through the techniques of accompanied recitative. Agitated string tremolos, intensifying every harmonic change with sforzandos, support a solo oboe's alternation between declamatory repeated notes and lyrical fragments. Melpomene's admonishment concludes with a brief oboe cadenza, replete with the formulaic ending of recitatives, a downward leap from the first to the fifth scale degree. Noteworthy but invariably ignored is a solo bassoon that responds to the oboe with rising and falling thirds or descending seconds, traditional representations of sighs or tears, the latter confirmed by the sketchbook's inscription, "Prom: weint."

The ensuing allegro molto is a rage aria, a mainstay of opera seria, though its style is equally indebted to *Sturm und Drang* symphonies. Dark tonality, alla breve meter, stark unisons, syncopation, repeated notes, pregnant pauses, sudden dynamic contrasts, and unpredictable harmonies accordingly mark the outbreak of Melpomene's fury, as another sketchbook annotation confirms ("va in colera"). During a lyrical interlude, woodwinds reiterate short, scalewise descents, perhaps musical embodiments of the creatures' repeated efforts to restrain the attacker. The opening passage's varied repetition begins in the dominant but overshoots the tonic's anticipated return when the bass line relentlessly descends through a two-octave chromatic scale. After a rest, a diminuendo and fermata on a diminished seventh chord articulate the moment when Melpomene stabs Prometheus, as the sketchbook verifies ("Prometheus mort"). Melpomene thereby reenacts the harmonic coup de grace of earlier balletic and operatic murders, including the Commendatore's death in Mozart's *Don Giovanni*. An ostinato then alternates with lyrical, syncopated, and agitated phrases, implying diverse reactions from the creatures. As the number ends, however, the ostinato accompanies a single melodic line, its fragments reduced to isolated pitches as dynamics fade to pianissimo. Floros likens this dissipation to medieval hocket,[90] a time-honored means of depicting sobs, as the sketchbook's final *incipit* affirms ("les enfants pleurent"). Thus Beethoven again resorted to stock pictorialization to coordinate music with stage action.

Responding to Melpomene's tragedy, her sister Thalia, the Muse of comedy, presents a "giuocosa scena" [jocular scene] for the creatures' benefit. Revealing the murder was a sham, she holds smiling masks before their tearful faces while Pan resuscitates the "deceased" Titan. Exegetes disagree over the tenth number's relation to these events: Nottebohm, following the playbill's order of deities, claimed Terpsichore danced it; Levinson maintained it was Thalia's solo; and Riemann and Floros asserted Thalia and Pan performed it together.[91] Three sources corroborate the last alternative: a scribal copy of the score held at the Österreichische Nationalbibliothek assigns the next five numbers to dancers who performed roles other than Thalia and Pan, thus leaving the tenth movement as the only possible

---

90   Floros, p. 66.
91   Gustav Nottebohm, *Zweite Beethoveniana* (Leipzig, 1887), p. 246; Levinson, "Le Ballet de Prométhée," p. 95; Riemann, p. 111; Floros, p. 68. Floros properly objects to Riemann's translation of *giuocosa* as *komische*, though he incorrectly notes that Riemann advocates Thalia alone.

vehicle for their actions; in the sketchbook two inscriptions ("Promethe [sic] mort" and "les enfants pleurent") immediately precede the tenth number's melodic *incipits*, a proximity intimating close dramaturgical connections; and the playbill's note regarding Pan's invention of the shepherd's dance agrees with the number's designation as a pastorale in manuscript and printed sources.[92]

Eighteenth-century treatises classify the pastorale as a dance or song idealizing the Arcadian life of shepherds,[93] whose Greek ancestors worshiped the goat-like Pan. Both forms observe identical musical conventions: slurred melodies, compound duple meter, a moderate tempo between those of the faster gigue and the slower siciliano, and repetitive figures that avoid the siciliano's dotted rhythms. In practice, however, the pastorale often resembles a specific type of contredanse française, not the variety exhibiting the gavotte's half-measure upbeats, but another featuring eighth-note upbeats and regular four-measure phrases in 6/8 time.[94] Somewhat unusual is the opening theme's syncopation, which accents upward leaps as phrases end on the measure's second eighth note, though it plainly suits the prescribed social choreography of skips and hops.

In addition to its generic dance traits, the tenth number exhibits time-honored musical pastoralisms: a mellifluous oboe melody and supporting drone imitate bagpipes; lines are doubled in parallel thirds; and echoes resound between a jaunty flute solo and repeated chords in the oboes, horns, and pizzicato strings (Example 2.14). As Floros notes, the flute solo firmly links the pastorale with Pan,[95] who not only invented the pipes named for him, but also played them as sweetly as nightingales sing in spring.

Structurally Beethoven's pastorale adheres closely to sonata form. Its exposition is clearly tripartite, with the oboe melody acting as the principal theme in the tonic, C major, a triadic bassoon solo and a flute's arpeggiated response as the subordinate theme in the dominant, and the echoing panpipe tune as a concluding theme. After a transition merely consisting of a pedal point embellished by accented neighbor tones on every measure's last eighth note, the fully orchestrated oboe melody initiates the recapitulation. The subordinate theme predictably returns in the tonic, but its triads and arpeggios first are reduced to repeated chords that develop a Lydian inflection when a raised fourth scale degree clashes repeatedly with a tonic pedal. Brief panpiping concludes the number, played first by flute and oboe, then bassoons, and finally horns. Thus a sophisticated symphonic design again achieved a simple end, representing Arcadia, though Haydn, Mozart, and other eighteenth-century composers often used sonata form in their pastoral works. Indeed, Beethoven's "Pastoral" Symphony would later adopt a grander scale in three sonata-form movements.

With the pastorale's description, Ritorni's scenario is virtually complete, its final remark simply announcing that the play ends with "festive dances." The drama has

---

[92] Beethoven's autograph is lost; the scribal copy is held at the Musiksammlung, A-Wn, Cod. 16142.

[93] Allanbrook, pp. 95–6.

[94] Reichart, pp. 4, 20, 207.

[95] Floros, p. 68.

Example 2.14   Beethoven *Die Geschöpfe des Prometheus*, No. 10, mm. 1–8

likewise reached a logical conclusion: the educated, compassionate creatures are now ready to demonstrate their new faculties. A dearth of precise actions, however, scarcely means the remaining numbers lack dramaturgical significance, though they have garnered almost no critical attention. On the contrary, they contribute to the story's denouement, as previously consulted sources indicate.

The eleventh and twelfth numbers comprise one unit, the former providing a slow introduction to the latter, and both bearing related inscriptions in the scribal copy. A prefatory andante's label, "coro di Gioja," refers to Ferdinand Gioja, who portrayed Bacchus at the premiere; the introduction accordingly involves the bacchants. "Solo di Gioja" is the ensuing maestoso's designation, but the bacchants also probably participated, as contrasting episodes in Beethoven's setting imply.

Unfolding above a pedal tone on G, the eight-measure andante sustains the adjoining maestoso's dominant. Such brevity fulfills only one purpose: allowing the bacchants to take their positions. The passage nonetheless reestablishes the martial topic of the "heroic scene" (No. 8), likewise performed by Bacchus and his retinue. Trumpets and timpani repeat dotted fanfares as woodwinds and horns play a march-like canzona figure that recalls the opening of Beethoven's First Piano Concerto and foreshadows the maestoso's themes. But violins and low strings add an element lacking in the earlier "warlike dance," staccato triplets that embellish triads with largely diatonic neighbor tones. Further variation awaits the military topic in the maestoso.

The twelfth number's through-composed form entails three sections marked maestoso, adagio, and allegro. The first, a common-time march in C major, features dotted rhythms, prominent trumpets and timpani, triadic fanfares in horns and oboes, and the recurrent canzona figure. Its alternating winds and strings replicate the dueling figuration that appeared in the "heroic scene's" second episode, again suggesting factional swordplay, perhaps between Gioja and the corps or two groups of bacchants. Unprecedented in the eighth number and patently soloistic, however, is a highly mimetic violin part that repeatedly arpeggiates downward through the interval of a tenth only to leap the same distance upward to the top pitches of quadruple stops (Example 2.15). Plainly imitating Gioja's athletic choreography, the vaulting violin line nonetheless remains anchored in C major, except after a fermata on a half cadence, where D minor is abruptly tonicized. The maestoso ends with brass fanfares, a hastily inserted augmented sixth chord, and its resolution to the dominant, completing the dual thematic and harmonic process of binary form, with its implicit repetition of previous material.

Unanticipated, then, is the ensuing adagio, which contrasts sharply with the march, yet meets binary form's harmonic expectations by again modulating from tonic to dominant. An oboe makes repeated upward leaps and scalewise descents, matching the soft, chordal accompaniment's rhythm of continuous eighth-note triplets and engaging a slower bassoon in a dialogue. As in earlier numbers, cantabile woodwind solos and antiphonal exchanges signify speech or personal communication. While this wordless conversation's subject remains unknown, the double-reed dialogue strongly suggests interaction among the principals, Bacchus and the creatures, Bacchus and Prometheus, or just the creatures. The last alternative's likelihood increases when the adagio closes with florid arpeggios for the first violins, instruments previously associated with Gioja's leaps—as if a duet for the creatures concludes with a response from Bacchus.

Example 2.15   Beethoven *Die Geschöpfe des Prometheus*, No. 12, mm. 9–13

After a brief oboe cadenza ends the colloquial interlude, the allegro begins with the canzona figure, now lacking its dotted martial fanfares, heavy brass scoring, and arpeggiated swordplay. Instead horns and oboes play a lightly sprung, march-like tune in parallel thirds, loosely approximating a French bourée.[96] Tutti treatment of the canzona figure ensues, animated by forte dynamics and string tremolos. Horns and oboes then softly restate their march, now embellished by a bassoon obbligato, before a fortissimo outburst and faster tempo (mosso) inaugurate a swiftly paced coda. Thus the multi-sectional number emulates a buffo finale, replete with sudden dynamic changes in a closing stretto. If an inference derives from the reappearance of Bacchus and his military entourage, it is that an expressly martial impulse is varied and even sublimated during the eleventh and twelfth numbers. A parallel dramaturgical implication is that the creatures reacted to the earlier "warlike dance" with interest in weapons and a desire to join the bacchants. But after witnessing Melpomene's mock tragedy they ostensibly adopt a moderate perspective on heroism's martial component—a humanitarian lesson imparted, perhaps, in the adagio's dialogue, and made explicit through variation of the march tune, which ultimately loses its strongest military characteristics.

The scribal copy labels the thirteenth number a "terzettino groteschi" [small trio in grotesque style], a designation Beethoven's sketchbook explains by assigning specific passages to three anonymous dancers, two men and a woman. Angiolini's treatise defines the word "groteschi," providing a clue to their identities.[97] In the eighteenth-century balletic hierarchy, grotesque dances occupy the lowest position, beneath the heroic and comic, and typically involve peasants, cowherds, or the "common rabble" in national costume. Among Ritorni's Parnassian assembly only Pan's ugly, half-human, half-goat fauns fit this description and are the only dancers who have not yet performed, though disagreements plague later accounts of the stage action.[98]

This identification reconciles well with the number's dance type, a contredanse. Just as the grotesque dance ranked lowest in the balletic hierarchy, so the contredanse held the bottommost position among ball dances, its simple choreography allowing everyone to participate in the evening's finale regardless of social standing. The movement observes the contredanse's broad conventions with a lively tempo (allegro), duple meter, upbeats to and within phrases, and periodic subdivisions (2+2+4) already encountered in the first number (Example 2.16). But the opening melody's rhythms—namely its mixture of quarter, eighth, and sixteenth notes and placement of the longest notes at feminine cadences and the shortest on second beats—indicate the movement belongs to a particular species of contredanse française used famously to conclude Haydn's Symphony No. 88. Intrusive fermatas and octave leaps rarely occur in contredanses, however, and probably reflect Angiolini's specified choreography for grotesque dances, mostly unmeasured hops, leaps, and crude pantomime.

---

[96]   Allanbrook, pp. 104–8.

[97]   Angiolini, p. C5.

[98]   Dissenting are Levinson ("Le Ballet de Prométhée," p. 95), who considers the music so abstract that determining its programmatic function is arbitrary, and Rust (p. 153), who in falsely equating comic with grotesque chooses Thalia as the principal character.

Example 2.16   Beethoven *Die Geschöpfe des Prometheus*, No. 13, mm. 1–8

Moreover, musical pastoralisms idiomatically represent the remote forests fauns inhabited. Consistent with such rustic depictions are the folk-like opening melody, prominent woodwind parts in responding phrases, and the texture of another dance, the musette. The word musette refers to a small bagpipe, a provincial folk instrument popular at French courts during the seventeenth century, when its name was applied to sung airs that evolved first into texted dances, then purely instrumental accompaniment to choreography, and finally an abstract style detached from social, court, or theatrical performance.[99] Regardless of function, the moderately paced musette emulates the bagpipe's skirl and drone with a treble melody and pedal tone. When played on keyboard instruments incapable of sustaining drones, however, the musette's bass line often adopts the broken octaves found at the number's outset. Thus the musette's pastoral inflections enhance the contredanse as an ideal vehicle for Pan's fauns.

Their solos shape a rondo-like form revisiting structures of the first and eighth numbers, though as Riemann noted, a ternary tonal design governs eight freely ordered sections (ABA–CDE–B+Coda).[100] The tonic, D major, prevails in a twice-stated refrain (A) and an intervening episode (B) for the first male soloist. Of three ensuing episodes (CDE), the first in A major is assigned to the second male faun, the next in the tonic bears no designation, and the last in the subdominant is performed by the female soloist.

Predictably periodic, the contredanse (A) comprises an eight-measure statement, scored for strings alone and modulating to the dominant, plus a varied, fully orchestrated repetition that remains in the tonic. The first episode (B) initially preserves contredanse traits, merely exchanging the musette bass for repeated chords. But in its repeated central section, martial dotted rhythms, rushing scales, and arpeggios imply more vigorous choreography before a digression to B-flat elicits an augmented sixth chord, dominant resolution, and the ersatz refrain's return. In the next episode (C) stark unisons and sforzandos at beginnings of phrases, accented syncopation midway through or at the ends of phrases, and abrupt melodic leaps furnish ample opportunity for the grotesque dance's unmeasured body movements. A fuller texture, slightly relaxed tempo (comodo), and brass fanfares stabilize the tonic's return in a self-contained binary form (D), its first repeated period remaining squarely in D major, its second digressing to B minor. Pervading the female faun's solo (E) is a lightly articulated anapestic figure supported by the bass line's arpeggios and an inner voice's transparent Alberti figuration—features surely indicating more refined footwork than in the men's solos. After the first episode recurs, the coda accumulates orchestral layers above a tonic pedal played as repeated notes, not broken octaves. Increasing textural density culminates in a fermata, whereupon the refrain's return compensates for its earlier omission, perhaps offering a final opportunity for a *pas de trois* before rushing scales and authentic cadences close the movement.

The scribal copy allocates the next two numbers to the dancers who played the creatures, Maria Cassentini and Viganò. Both multipartite solos exploit concertante instruments and utilize variation technique, but neither assumes the form of theme and variations per se, as Paul Nettl asserts.[101] Both also contain pointedly egalitarian dances, namely another contredanse and an Austrian *Ländler*.

Four passages in as many tempos but one key, F major, comprise the fourteenth number. An introductory andante begins as strings play chords in dotted rhythms, furnishing a stately entrance for Cassentini, now portraying a fully human woman worthy to appear before the gods. Violin arpeggios supported by a dominant pedal tone then lead to a cadenza for a basset horn, an instrument Beethoven used nowhere else.

The ensuing adagio is an aristocratic minuet of the slow French variety more famously cultivated in the second movements of Beethoven's Sonata in F minor,

---

[99]   Allanbrook, pp. 133–40.

[100] Riemann, pp. 113–14.

[101] Nettl, p. 154.

Op. 2, no. 1 and Second Symphony. Its phrases expand the minuet's subdivisions proportionally (from 1+1+2 to 2+2+4), but nonetheless generate the dance's obligatory rounded binary form. The first period, a florid basset horn solo accompanied by a bass line and chordal afterbeats, is restated with modest variation by an oboe. Though not repeated, the second period satisfies tonal expectations by modulating to the dominant in its first phrase and back to the tonic for the opening melody's varied return, all while preserving the basset horn's dialogue with the oboe—perhaps signifying the female creature's new communicative abilities. In the minuet's codetta, the concertante instruments alternate rapidly until they simultaneously reach a cadential trill.

Merely a transition, the succeeding ten-measure allegro establishes duple meter as tutti strings embellish a dominant seventh chord with fanfare-like figuration. Marked allegretto, a simple contredanse angloise quickly reinstates the tonic and adopts a ternary design. In the opening section the basset horn's conventional phrases (2+2+4) initiate another conversation, and again the oboe responds by repeating the same line above slightly varied harmonies. Strings then emphasize structural closure by reiterating the oboe's last phrase in rapid sixteenth notes. In the central section the basset horn's initial call in the subdominant receives a reply from the oboe in the tonic. But another call goes unanswered, directly announcing the first section's reprise, now embellished by the violins and oboe with an obbligato line of continuous sixteenth notes that usher in an emphatic codetta. Repetitions of the contredanse's final phrase inaugurate a genuine coda, soon reaching a dramatic cadential six-four chord that portends a cadenza for the concertante instruments. Instead multiple tutti cadences close the movement.

The dance sequence in Cassentini's solo advances the dramaturgy. A stately introduction and an aristocratic minuet associated with the ancien régime are succeeded by a lively segue and a folk-like, egalitarian contredanse. Thus the female creature can dance the minuet—even the slow, serious French variety lacking upbeats—but prefers a less refined though more inclusive, conversational contredanse. Her companion will take similar actions.

Viganò's chorus and solo, as the scribal copy designates the fifteenth number, encompasses three sections, the last patently involving the corps, as its full orchestration and social dance type suggest. An introduction for strings, marked andantino in cut time, elaborates the dominant of B-flat major, doubtless as the male creature comes forward. Its steady, rhythmically sophisticated pattern of staccato chords represents progress over the unstable ostinato attending his earlier steps. But a subsequent interweaving of chromatic, quasi-canonic lines that swell from piano to forte before reaching a fermata evokes no obvious action.

Resisting dance taxonomies, the ensuing adagio would vaguely resemble the gavotte if its notated rhythmic values were doubled (Example 2.17). Upbeats would then occupy half a measure, as in the gavotte, but their dotted rhythms would remain uncharacteristic. While melodies often end idiomatically on weak beats, their underlying cadences emphasize downbeats. And few dances present an unbroken series of half cadences. Despite an attendant lack of periodic closure, the adagio's themes successfully articulate a ternary form in B-flat major. The first section consists of two statements of one phrase, played first by the violins alone, then with slight variation and a bassoon's doubling, all supported by a punctuating bass line and an inner voice's Alberti figuration. In the central passage, a clarinet traces another arching four-measure phrase and joins the bassoon in its embellished repetition, each time against the string section's background of repeated chords. Both woodwinds then restate the opening melody, but the relative minor's tonicization produces an odd, seven-measure phrase ending in a fermata. Ambiguous with respect to dance type and unconventional in its open formal design, the adagio is perhaps best considered a vehicle for Viganò's fluid choreography, as reflected in Beethoven's delicately balanced rhythms and finely spun melodies.

Example 2.17   Beethoven *Die Geschöpfe des Prometheus*, No. 15, mm. 16–20

Unlike the adagio, the concluding allegro is easily identified. Traits of several types of *Ländler*, the Austrian national dance in triple meter, appear throughout a rondo-like form in which one episode actually functions as a codetta. The refrain's quintessential "oom-pah-pah" texture comprises three strata: the bass line's emphatic downbeats; the middle register's weaker chordal afterbeats; and a treble melody exploiting an upbeat pattern used in another well-known *Ländler*, the third movement of Haydn's "Military" Symphony (Example 2.18).[102] As the number progresses, accents shift to the second beat, a common metric ploy soon leading to passages of the dance's familiar yodeling figuration.

A contrasting episode exploits another *Ländler* texture, with continuous eighth notes in the bass supporting sustained, parallel woodwind lines and culminating in true-to-form echo effects between cellos and violins, the latter doubled by flute and bassoon. The refrain's reprise, though recognizable, omits one phrase, expands another, and repeats several more. It elides with a passage recalling the polonaise's characteristic rhythms and accents, intimating another episode's advent; but repetitions of a formulaic chord progression confirm the incipient polonaise functions as the refrain's codetta. Its monotonous pattern, however, acquires urgency when fortissimo repeated notes in the strings animate sustained brass and woodwind chords, an outburst bolstered by protracted cadences, violin arpeggios, and a neighbor-tone figure that woodwinds play in parallel thirds. Had the "chorus" not yet joined Viganò, this climactic juncture would certainly have encouraged such action, for after a fermata, the opening *Ländler* reappears, played fortissimo by the tutti orchestra. Repeated authentic cadences vigorously conclude the movement.

Viganò's solo reiterates the dramaturgical message Cassentini's number imparts. The introductory ostinato's complexity verifies the male creature has progressed sufficiently to perform a courtly, gavotte-like dance. But he instead performs a folk-like *Ländler*, relegates the aristocratic polonaise to a codetta, and is joined in his nationalistic dance by the corps, now presumably his peers, a communal ending amplified in the ballet's finale.

The finale's exegetes often underscore the Titan's achievement and heroism, facets of the myth barely implicit in Ritorni's reference to "festive dances." Granted, Riemann initially asserted the sixteenth number represents both creatures as fully developed heroes, but he later claimed it concerns the pride Prometheus felt in his success.[103] Levinson concurred, maintaining it embodies the Titan's "high satisfaction of heroic pride."[104] According to Haraszti and Rust, the creatures respectively celebrate their father or, idiosyncratically, their wedding.[105] Even Floros, who predicates his observations on a broad dance typology and assiduously consults Ritorni's scenario and Beethoven's sketchbook, places Prometheus at the center of the finale, justifying his interpretation with an uncharacteristically anachronistic comparison: Viganò's later ballet on the subject, the so-called "large Prometheus" produced in Milan in 1813, ends with Hercules liberating the Titan, Zeus forgiving him, and the gods admitting him into their pantheon. A similar apotheosis, Floros argues, must have concluded the earlier ballet.[106]

---

[102] Reichart, pp. 324, 329, 156.

[103] Riemann, p. 120; Thayer, *Ludwig van Beethovens Leben*, trans. Hermann Deiters, ed. Hugo Riemann (Berlin, 1901), p. 230.

[104] Levinson, "Le Ballet de Prométhée," p. 96.

[105] Emile Haraszti, "La Cause de l'échec de Prométhée," *Collectanea historiae musicae*, 2 (1957): 234; Rust, p. 154.

[106] Floros, pp. 70–71.

Although these essentially Aeschylean readings reconcile with Beethoven's later incarnation as a Promethean hero, they diverge from eighteenth-century conceptions of the myth and Viganò's first rendering of it. In closer agreement with balletic convention and the unfolding dramaturgy are Nettl's assertion that the finale is a "big dance ensemble" and an oft-noted correlation linking the two creatures with the principal theme's duality, manifested in its renowned bass line and equally famous treble melody.[107] Both astute observations nonetheless overlook two crucial issues: the selected dance type's dramaturgical significance and Beethoven's adherence to its conventions.

Example 2.18   Beethoven *Die Geschöpfe des Prometheus*, No. 15, mm. 39–47

---

[107]   Nettl, p. 154.

Example 2.18 concluded.

As previously discussed, the finale's principal theme is universally recognized as a contredanse. Less widely noted, however, is that it epitomizes a specific type of contredanse that developed as the English country-dance spread throughout Europe during the Enlightenment, adopting distinct French, German, and Austrian guises.[108] Known as the *Englische* in Vienna, where it enjoyed tremendous popularity beginning in the 1790s,[109] the Austrian variety exhibits traits readily apparent at

---

[108] Reichart, p. 246.
[109] Ibid., pp. 251–5.

the finale's outset (Example 2.4c above), including simple duple meter, mandatory upbeats, cadences often occurring after the downbeat, and phrases of four or eight strong beats, which precisely accommodate the eight-step choreographic figures prescribed in eighteenth-century dance manuals. Likewise obvious is an emulation of social dance's quintessential three-part texture, comprising two treble parts (one melodic, the other accompanimental) and a bass line, as in a minimal dance orchestra of two violins and a bass instrument. Thus Beethoven's music closely observes contemporary Viennese social dance practices.

The contredanse's choreography and position in the eighteenth-century dance hierarchy are dramaturgically significant. In German-speaking lands, a contredanse invariably ended social balls, allowing everyone, perhaps as many as 40 couples, to participate.[110] Dancers formed two long lines, men facing women, and executed the first set of figures following a lead couple. During obligatory repetitions, however, couples changed positions and other dancers assumed leadership. Such egalitarian choreography often caused masters and servants to exchange roles in social settings, thus fostering a "democratic atmosphere" temporarily free of class distinctions. The contredanse accordingly joined the *Ländler* in the "low style" of eighteenth-century dance, as opposed to the higher minuet, sarabande, and gavotte or the middle-ground bourée and gigue. Thus Viganò's choreography for a "democratic" finale probably involved couples from the entire company, with the creatures acting as the lead couple and Prometheus, the gods, Graces, Muses, bacchants, and even Pan's lowly fauns following them. The dynamic of the ballet's ending is consequently reversed: the creatures are not so much accepted by the gods as they become the leaders of a new, humanitarian order that embraces beings of all ranks.

Viganò's coupled choreography finds conspicuous parallels in Beethoven's music, which comprises a largely self-contained rondo and the previously discussed passage recalling the overture's allegro. The rondo's refrain, often dubbed the "Prometheus theme," is a model of conventional binary form. Two repeated periods, each symmetrically constructed of two, four-measure phrases, observe the standard tonal scheme, the first modulating from the tonic, E-flat major, to the dominant, the second reversing the process. A fermata punctuating the second period—doubtless matching lost choreography—is the only irregularity in a perfectly structured social dance, presumably led by the creatures, as the refrain's treble-bass polarity suggests.

Another dualism informs the first episode. Centered squarely in the dominant, a fortissimo dialogue between descending scales, played by unison violins and flutes, and chordal replies from horns and low woodwinds preserves the contredanse's weak-beat cadences. Tutti scoring, loud dynamics, and contrasting registers suggest the alternation occurs between unidentified groups of Parnassians. The episode nonetheless soon reverts to a treble-dominated texture notable for a violin tune that evokes the stylized fiddling of many of Haydn's folk-like melodies, another indication of the finale's "low style." A short transition's dominant pedal anticipates the refrain's return, varied by a second violin part embellishing the fifth scale degree, slightly altered wind writing, and modest melodic ornamentation.

---

[110]   Ibid., pp. 95, 228.

The second episode in G major, published as the eleventh of the Twelve Contredanses, WoO 14, likewise embraces musical dualism. Two freely contrapuntal melodies overlap, the violins repeating a gradual ascent, the bass line tracing a long inverted arch. Features of both lines recall the tenth number, Pan's pastorale: accented syncopation destabilizes the violins, the bass line's ties obscure bar lines, and the fourth scale degree is often raised, starting in the violins but growing more insistent in subordinate woodwind parts. The rhythmic irregularities and modal exoticism invite Pan and his fauns to join the creatures. Otherwise the episode observes balletic orthodoxy, its simple ternary form consisting of two eight-measure periods, each enclosed in repeat signs, and a heavily varied restatement of the first. A sequential transition then prepares the refrain's third appearance, which again displays varied part writing.

A third episode, presenting another dialogue in the tonic, again offers clues regarding the dancers' identities. Clarinets, horns, and timpani initiate the discourse with dotted fanfares, recalling the "heroic scene" enacted by Bacchus and his militant followers. Strings and flutes answer with arpeggios and broken scales in octaves, figuration dominating the entire episode as brasses and timpani add an insistently reiterated pedal point. The unison textures and percussive pedal tone plainly evoke the Janissary style of an episode Gioja and the bacchants performed in the eighth number. After the violins play one last scale, the refrain again recurs with slight variation, its closing phrase notably altered by a harmonic sequence that veers toward F major, G minor, and A-flat major before an authentic cadence elides with the second part of the finale.

Like an opera buffa, the ballet concludes with a fast-paced, multi-sectioned coda (allegro molto). A variant of the overture's principal theme first provides the subject for a fugato whose culminating tutti presentation cadences emphatically in unison arpeggios. Next the finale's contredanse returns in a varied guise preserving the melody's essential contour, but not its rhythms. Another tutti passage exploits syncopation and abrupt dynamic contrasts until a sustained pedal tone precipitates a concluding presto whose thematic materials are nondescript compared to the allegro's cyclical recurrences: the strings, soon joined by the woodwinds, merely play sweeping, rhythmically uniform, largely diatonic scales, reinforced by sustained octaves in the brasses. This tumult subsides when most of the orchestra falls silent, leaving clarinets and horns to prolong simple primary chords, perhaps recalling earlier pastoral numbers in an idyll that nonetheless abruptly ends with tutti tonic chords and a martial timpani flourish.

The finale's choreographic and musical dualities clearly indicate the creatures occupy the center of attention, not Prometheus. And rightly so, since they are the ballet's genuinely eponymous characters, and the dancers who portrayed them, Cassentini and Viganò, were the company's leading artists. Prometheus may dominate Act I, fleeing a storm, awakening the creatures with fire, attempting to communicate with them, and threatening their destruction. But after presenting the "candidates" before the gods at the beginning of Act II, he entrusts other deities with their education and remains passive: the creatures recognize him; Melpomene berates and "murders" him; and Pan revives him. Thus Prometheus is a creator who relies on external powers to complete the animation of two lifeless statues, a well-established eighteenth-century representation of the Titan that contrasts with his romantic conception as an autonomous, unrepentant rebel. That Prometheus created or animated statues ranks among the legend's oldest motifs, dating to its origins in Hesiod, who claimed the Titan molded men from clay.[111] But this theme achieved remarkable popularity with Enlightenment philosophers, mythographers, and playwrights whose attitudes were succinctly expressed by Bernard Le Bovyer de Fontenelle: "in reality he is nothing but a capable sculptor."[112]

Likewise attesting to the ballet's eighteenth-century affinities is its preservation of important traits of the era's principal dance genres, the divertissement and *ballet d'action*. Viganò chose the period's most familiar dance types—contredanse, minuet, siciliano, polonaise, march, pastorale, musette, bourée, gavotte, and *Ländler*—and Beethoven usually observed their stylistic conventions rigorously. Moreover, an uninterrupted succession of "festive dances" extends from the moment Thalia reveals the Titan's "murder" is a sham in the eleventh number to the ballet's conclusion, a sequence comprising a typical eighteenth-century divertissement, capped with French court ballet's quintessential massed contredanse. The individual dance types and concluding series, however, transcend purely decorative or formalistic purposes to articulate a coherent plot and advance dramaturgy in accordance with the *ballet d'action*'s principles. Social dances and their choreographies often have meaning within the storyline: Prometheus first invites the creatures to participate in a contredanse; the Graces educate them with a polonaise; Bacchus' march beckons them to join the community; and both creatures favor egalitarian over aristocratic dances in their solos. Perhaps only two pastoral dances remain largely decorative: a siciliano portrays the creatures naïvely admiring nature's wonders, a cliché of the myth's Enlightenment treatments, and a pastorale offers a foray into a "low" but inclusive style. And as Beethoven's sketchbook frequently divulges, stage action and body motions closely correlate with musical events in numerous pantomimic passages, most notably in depicting the creatures' first halting steps, the menaces Prometheus directs toward them when they fail to understand him, their animation by four lyrists, their interest in weapons, and above all in Melpomene's "tragica scena." To serve such purposes, Beethoven departed from formulaic structures for dance music, infusing his score with harmonic unorthodoxies, through-composed passages, instrumental recitatives, sonata-form elements, anomalous constructs, and even stock figuration. Thus the ballet perpetuates Noverre's legacy, "rendering the gestures of dancers intelligible" and "fixing their movements in time and tone."

Finally, *Die Geschöpfe des Prometheus* is layered with allegory, a mainstay of French court dance since its inception in the seventeenth century. Its allegorical strata, however, not only hearken back to the Enlightenment, but also anticipate romanticism. Locally, the ballet's climax is allegorical: when the creatures witness the Titan's "murder" and feel compassion, they learn to generalize from a "paternal" relationship and empathize with the entire human race. Comprehensively, the ballet is an allegory of aristocratic patronage: just as Parnassian deities animate the creatures through the arts, so Empress Marie Therese revived Viennese ballet after

---

[111]   Hesiod, *Theogony*, p. 26.
[112]   Bernard Le Bovyer de Fontenelle, *De l'origine des fables (1724)*, ed. J.R. Carrée (Paris, 1932), pp. 29–30.

the blight it suffered under Joseph II. And a third allegorical layer accrued beginning in October 1802, when Beethoven confessed in his Heiligenstadt Testament that deafness had tempted him to consider suicide, a destiny he had repudiated because his art had held him back; he could not leave the world without producing all that he felt was within him.[113] Like Prometheus, he was willing to endure a harsh fate in order to bestow the gifts of genius on mankind. With the "Eroica" Symphony's incorporation of the theme from the ballet's finale, this third level of allegory achieved wide dissemination among musicians, critics, and the public throughout the nineteenth century and became an accepted tenet of Beethoven historiography. The ballet's humanitarian message, musical ambition, and indirect association with the image of the artist as outcast accordingly represent a dawning romantic tradition of interpreting the Prometheus myth in music.

---

[113] The Heiligenstadt Testament is sensitively translated in Solomon, pp. 151–4.

Chapter 3

Three Settings of Goethe's Transgressive Ode

More than any other author, Goethe established distinctly romantic perspectives on Prometheus. His ode replaced the Enlightenment's benefactor of an Arcadian mankind with a modern rebel who endured unjust persecution in the solitude of creative genius. Goethe achieved this metamorphosis not only by depicting an impenitent revolutionary and autonomous creator, but also by rejecting earlier poetic conventions governing stanzaic structure, line length, syntax, and vocabulary. The ode's daring subject and formal traits exerted an immediate and lasting influence. For Goethe's contemporaries it embodied the *Sturm und Drang* movement,[1] while later writers, especially Shelley, Coleridge, Browning, and Bridges, interpreted its indictment of authoritarianism as the source of human suffering in new versions of the legend or critical essays. And three lieder composers—Reichardt, Schubert, and Wolf—matched its thematic and stylistic audacities by violating generic norms and subverting tonal conventions.

Investigating these songs requires an account of the ode's unorthodox content and style, facilitated here by speech act theory, a branch of the philosophy of language. The ode's early reception likewise illuminates its revolutionary traits, though Goethe's contemporaries differed over whether his Prometheus rebelled against religious, political, literary, or moral authority. They nonetheless agreed Goethe's Titan personified transgression, a subject Michel Foucault elucidated in writings on politics, jurisprudence, literature, and sexuality. Foucault's ideology provides a context for analyzing the role transgression played in each composer's life, declamatory vocal styles blurring generic distinctions between the lied and opera, relationships between textual and musical forms, and specific stylistic features, especially striking introductory gestures, discursive harmony, the treatment of dissonance, and linear procedures that eschew Schenkerian principles.

The ode's seven stanzas observe a tripartite temporal design (Table 3.1). Set in the present, stanzas I and II condemn Zeus and the Olympians; stanzas III through VI narrate past events, beginning with the Titan's childhood; and stanza VII outlines future actions of Prometheus and mankind. David Wellbery likens this threefold schema to a juridical prosecution comprising an accusation, the witness's interrogation, and a call for the verdict, an analogy consistent with Goethe's early legal training.[2] Naturally influencing musical form, these divisions also chronicle

---

[1]   Regarding the ode's early reception, see pp. 99–101 below.

[2]   David E. Wellbery, *The Specular Moment: Goethe's Early Lyric and the Beginnings of Romanticism* (Stanford, 1996), p. 292.

the Titan's growth from childhood to maturity,[3] a personal development obviously correlating with humanity's progress toward freedom from tyranny, with each stanza advancing this parallel evolution.

Table 3.1   Goethe's Ode: The Text and a Translation

1 Bedecke deinen Himmel, Zeus, mit Wolkendunst und übe, dem Knaben gleich, der Disteln köpft, 5 an Eichen dich und Bergeshöhn; mußt mir meine Erde doch lassen stehn, und meine Hütte, die du nicht gebaut, und meinen Herd, 10 um dessen Glut du mich beneidest.	Cover thy heaven, Zeus, with veils of cloud and, like a boy who lops off thistle heads, smite oaks and mountaintops; my earth, however, must remain mine, and my hut, which you did not build, and my hearth, whose glow makes you envy me.
12 Ich kenne nichts Ärmeres unter der Sonn' als euch, Götter! Ihr nähret kümmerlich 15 von Opfersteuern und Gebetshauch eure Majestät, und darbtet, wären nicht Kinder und Bettler 20 hoffnungsvolle Toren.	I know nothing poorer under the sun than you, gods! You wretchedly nourish your majesty on the levy of sacrifice and the breath of prayer, and would starve, were not children and beggars hopeful fools.
21 Da ich ein Kind war, nicht wußte wo aus noch ein, kehrt' ich mein verirrtes Auge zur Sonne, als wenn drüber wär' 25 ein Ohr, zu hören meine Klage, ein Herz wie mein's, sich des Bedrängten zu erbarmen.	When I was a child, not knowing where to turn, I raised my mistaken eye toward the sun, as if above there were an ear to hear my lament, a heart like mine to have compassion for a sufferer.
28 Wer half mir wider der Titanen Übermut? 30 Wer rettete vom Tode mich, von Sklaverei? Hast du nicht alles selbst vollendet, heilig glühend Herz? Und glühtest jung und gut, 35 betrogen, Rettungsdank dem Schlafenden da droben?	Who helped me against the Titans' arrogance? Who rescued me from death, from slavery? Have you not accomplished everything yourself, sacred, glowing heart? And did you not glow youthfully and well, though betrayed, offering thanks to the sleeper above?

---

[3]   The ode receives a Freudian interpretation in Carl Pietzcker, *Trauma, Wunsch und Abwehr: Psychoanalytische Studien zu Goethe, Jean Paul, Brecht, zur Atomliteratur und zur literarischen Form* (Würzburg, 1985), pp. 65–94.

37 Ich dich ehren? Wofür?	I honor you? Why?
Hast du die Schmerzen gelindert	Have you ever lightened the pains
je des Beladenen?	of the one so burdened?
40 Hast du die Tränen gestillet	Have you ever stilled the tears
je des Geängsteten?	of the one so fearful?
Hat nicht mich zum Manne geschmiedet	Was I not forged into a man
die allmächtige Zeit	by almighty time
und das ewige Schicksal,	and eternal destiny,
45 meine Herrn und deine?	my lords and yours?
46 Wähntest du etwa,	Did you imagine
ich sollte das Leben hassen,	I should hate life,
in Wüsten fliehen,	flee into the desert,
weil nicht alle	because not all
50 Blütenträume reiften?	blossoming dreams ripened?
51 Hier sitz' ich, forme Menschen	Here I sit, forming men
nach meinem Bilde,	in my image,
ein Geschlecht, das mir gleich sei,	a race, like myself,
zu leiden, zu weinen,	to suffer, to wail,
55 zu genießen und zu freuen sich,	to rejoice and to be happy,
und dein nicht zu achten,	and not to honor you,
wie ich!	like me!

Stanza I begins with a command, a speech act employing characteristic imperative syntax and conjugation, but here lacking a necessary element: the speaker's volition. Prometheus is scarcely bidding Zeus to create a storm and smite mountains and oaks with his fearsome thunderbolts. The Titan is instead goading Zeus to do his worst, which will be ineffective, a futility underscored by comparing the Olympian's impending actions with those of a child. Thus Prometheus disarms a threat, liberating himself from authority with a "parodied command."[4]

Prometheus ends the stanza by claiming the earth for himself and relegating Zeus to the clouded heavens. This proclamation of ownership, a second speech act, derives illocutionary power by referring to the myth's events. Prometheus, not Zeus, built the first hut, a skill he ultimately teaches men. The hearth inside the hut accordingly belongs to his earthly realm, as transparent assonance affirms (Erde, Herd). And the hearth's glow recalls his original defiant act—stealing heavenly fire, which Zeus could not prevent. Hence Prometheus successfully appropriates his realm, just as he prevailed in obtaining the forbidden, divine spark. Furthermore, the hearth's glow rekindles in stanza IV when Prometheus asks if his glowing heart has not accomplished everything itself. Inverted double assonance (Herd-Glut, glühende Herz) reinforces this significant interstanzaic connection: the same stolen fire glows in the hearth's independent realm and the Titan's self-sufficient heart.

---

4   Wellbery, p. 295.

Stanza II denounces the gods as the poorest beings under the sun, a speech act brazenly inverting the cosmological hierarchy, yet—like most exclamations—requiring elaboration.[5] Prometheus, previously reserving the earth as his and conceding heaven entirely to Zeus, now restricts the gods to a smaller domain between the earth and sun. His ensuing declaration justifies the new limits: religious belief, as manifested in sacrifice and prayer, originates in hope, as opposed to fear engendered by threats of force as in stanza I.[6] But those who invest hope in the gods, namely children and beggars, worship beings as childlike and impoverished as themselves, a claim reinforced by the materiality of the stanza's pervasive nutritional metaphor: without their only nourishment—the hope of fools—the gods would starve. Overtly condemning exploitive relations between the deities and mankind, stanza II supports the ode's interpretation as a rebellion against religious authority. But it also emphasizes one of the myth's essential facets, expounded since Aeschylean times: false hope leads men astray, a warning usually embodied in Epimetheus, the Titan's brother, whose impulsive actions invariably proved cause for regret. How Prometheus recognized and rejected false hope is revealed as the ode unfolds.

Constituting one syntactical unit, stanza III is a narration, as the opening adverbial phrase and past tense indicate. The vocabulary more precisely identifies the stanza as a lament, a speech act obtaining performative impact when sufferers address implicit or explicit auditors.[7] During childhood Prometheus lacked orientation, a form of suffering doubtless afflicting the second stanza's foolish children. He consequently turned his eye toward the sun, Zeus' previously circumscribed realm, seeking someone like himself. This anthropomorphic process, which the Enlightenment's comparative mythologists considered a developmental stage in many world religions, is manifested materially and spiritually.[8] Prometheus conceives a corporeal divinity with an ear to hear his lament and a heart like his own, capable of showing mercy toward suffering. But because the Titan's eye was mistaken, there was no auditor to emulate, a perception strengthened by the conditional conjunction, and the heart he sought was actually his, as stanza IV discloses. Thus stanza III corroborates the ode's elucidation as a revolt against artistic authority, with Prometheus representing Goethe freeing himself from the Enlightenment's literary constraints, a process of self-actualization he famously confirmed in his autobiography.[9]

Stanzas IV through VI form a single unit comprising one speech act, an incantation, and sharing a common subject, the recollection of past suffering as a means of achieving self-awareness. An incantation accumulates illocutionary force through repetitive formulas and intonation patterns, criteria the three stanzas meet by presenting ten essentially rhetorical questions that trace a large-scale intonational

---

[5]   Regarding properly performed speech acts, including exclamations, see John R. Searle, *Speech Acts: An Essay in the Philosophy of Language* (Cambridge, 1969), pp. 22–41.

[6]   Wellbery, p. 311.

[7]   Regarding performative impact, see Searle, pp. 63–4.

[8]   Wellbery, p. 316.

[9]   Goethe, *Aus meinem Leben: Dichtung und Wahrheit*, ed. Klaus-Detlef Müller (Frankfurt, 1987), p. 691.

arc.[10] Stanza IV, a self-interrogation, starts with two questions beginning with the nominative pronoun "who" and eliciting the resounding answer, "no one," or, more pointedly, "not Zeus." It proceeds with a negative construction demanding an affirmative response and concludes with an inversion, a positive construction requiring a negative answer. Replies accordingly trace a pattern of intensification (negative, negative, affirmative) followed by abatement (negative).

Stanza V breaks the scheme as two short questions shift the burden of response from Prometheus to Zeus. In Wellbery's juridical model, this disruption represents a prosecutor anticipating the defense's objections, an apt analogy since Prometheus soon indicts Zeus. The rest of stanza V and all of stanza VI duplicate the fourth stanza's intonational pattern: two queries—direct reproaches instead of anonymous, rhetorical questions—compel negative answers; a negative formulation again obliges an affirmative response; and a positive construction yields a negative reply.

The patently well-crafted incantation also transforms Prometheus from child to man, recounting past suffering that induced him to cultivate inner resources. Completely unaided in earlier struggles, his sacred glowing heart, emblem of the stolen, divine spark, accomplished everything itself, even when deceived into thanking Zeus for salvation. This epiphany allowed him to mature: his afflictions— the pain of one so burdened, the tears of one so fearful—were neither lightened nor stilled by Zeus, but instead—in due course of almighty time and all-powerful destiny—forged Prometheus into a man. The appositely chosen word "geschmiedet" not only resonates with the ode's glowing hearth and heart, but also recalls the occupation of Hephaestus—the Olympian smithy and son of Hera alone—another allusion to the Titan's independence from Zeus.[11]

Leaving childhood's deception behind, having come of age, Prometheus ridicules Zeus for believing that suffering would make him hate life or withdraw to the desert. His mockery's sarcasm, underscored by the monstrous compound words "Blütenträume" and "Knabenmorgen,"[12] raises a question: What did Prometheus do rather than hate life or flee to the desert? The final stanza provides the answer.

Stanza VII establishes a bold declaration's authority through long-recognized parallels with a passage from Genesis.[13] Seated—replicating time-honored depictions of working craftsmen, but defying protocol when in the presence of eighteenth-century ecclesiastical or court officials—Prometheus forms men in his image, a self-referential act reversing the direction of anthropomorphization in stanza III, before the incantation began. But beyond enhancing the ode's symmetry, the conclusion describes the new race: mankind will suffer, rejoice, and, most importantly, not honor Zeus. The terse final line stipulates the new order's members, like Prometheus, will be free to duplicate his process of auto-realization, to become independent creators.

---

[10]   Wellbery, pp. 318–20.

[11]   Athena sprang from Zeus' head fully formed; Hera, jealous of his independent procreativity, attempted to duplicate it, but Hephaestus was deformed.

[12]   Karl Otto Conrady, "Johann Wolfgang von Goethe—*Prometheus*," in Benno von Wiese (ed.), *Die deutsche Lyrik: Form und Geschichte* (2 vols, Düsseldorf, 1959), vol. 1, pp. 217–18.

[13]   Ibid. In German the passage reads, "Und Gott sprach: Lasst uns Menschen machen, ein Bild, das uns gleich sei."

This autonomy, symbolizing an emancipation of artistic creativity in general and Goethe's genius in particular, embodies the fundamental difference between the myth's romantic representations and the Enlightenment's concept of imitation, whereby Prometheus merely reproduced divine actions by animating dormant creatures who paid him homage, as in eighteenth-century divertissements.

The ode's tripartite temporal scheme, rhetorical structures, narrative strategies, and interstanzaic allusions reveal Goethe's cohesive view of the legend as a vehicle for self-realization. Its structural and thematic coherencies, however, contrast sharply with an irregular poetic surface exhibiting unequal stanza and line lengths, various numbers of syntactical units per stanza, enjambments, little rhyme, and novel words. Such unorthodoxies have threefold significance: they sometimes reinforce the trifurcated design, rhetorical structure, or attributes of speech acts; they preoccupied critics for generations; and they challenged phrasing and cadential organization in musical settings.

Critical tradition maintains the ode's irregularities produce an "expressive immediacy" integral to *Sturm und Drang* aesthetics.[14] Most obviously, four stanzaic line lengths lack any pattern (11–9–7–9–9–5–7). Wellbery nonetheless detects symmetry in the ode's 1778 rendering, where stanza I, line 8 is divided between "Hütte" and "die."[15] Stanza I accordingly comprises 12 lines, not 11, with two syntactical units respectively encompassing five and seven lines, totals duplicated in stanzas VI and VII. Moreover, the symmetry among outer stanzas enhances the temporal scheme, separating the initial denunciation from the ensuing narration, while stanza VI functions as both an ending to the incantation and a transition to the final declaration. Internal stanzas, however, disclose no comparable pattern.

Equally asymmetrical line lengths range from two to ten syllables. Within this compass, lines most commonly contain six syllables, though counts from four through nine pervade the ode.[16] Of three anomalous tallies, two mark important rhetorical junctures: three- and two-syllable lines respectively begin the incantation and end the ode. Ten syllables appear in line 8, except in the 1778 edition, where the relative clause occupies its own line, perhaps simply articulating grammatical structure or emphasizing the independence of Prometheus' realm. In stanza V lines of six syllables alternate with variously longer lines, faintly underscoring the incantation's repetitive quality.[17]

The number of syntactical units per stanza varies less than the number and length of lines, but differences remain striking. Stanzas III, VI, and VII consist of one unit, I and II of two, IV of four, and V of five. Larger totals coincide with the incantation's onset and unfolding, further illuminating rhetorical structure. Enjambments account for discrepant tallies of lines and syntactical units within stanzas, though frequent correspondences between the endings of poetic lines and subordinate clauses mitigate the effect of one line continuing into the next.[18] Nevertheless, enjambments

---

[14]   Wellbery, p. 314.

[15]   Ibid., pp. 312–14.

[16]   Six-syllable lines occur 14 times; four, five, and eight syllables appear nine times each; seven lines contain seven syllables; and six lines comprise nine syllables.

[17]   Shorter alternations inaugurate stanzas I and VII.

[18]   Purposeful emphasis achieved by segregating three consecutive nouns in lines 15–17, for example, contrasts with the conventional enjambment in lines 18–20.

frequently start or conclude syntactical units, or alternatively, span entire units, increasing momentum as stanzas begin or end. Their duple appearance midway through stanza III consequently attracts notice, animating the narration's flow.

That the ode eschews rhyme is no exaggeration, with isolated instances of exact rhyme scattered among four stanzas.[19] Assonance, plentiful in the first three stanzas, soon disappears and is often weakened by natural and umlauted vowels or merely created by standard suffixes.[20] Accordingly more conspicuous, then, are several strong assonances, especially the previously mentioned pairing of "Herz" and "Herd."

Strained syntax likewise generates linguistic unorthodoxies. In stanza I, for example, the verb's separation from its reflexive pronoun (übe dich) delays construing the sentence as a command, while the placement of direct objects (Erde, Hütte, Herd, Glut) before and after their attendant compound verb (lassen stehn) produces an obstinate enumerative emphasis. Other convolutions reverse anticipated parallel word order. In stanza III the conjunction (als wenn) initially fails to elicit inverted word order, but later succeeds, as it normally should.[21] Similar reversals disturb stanza IV, where pronouns and prepositions exchange places (mir wider, vom mich), and stanza V, where interrogatives twice observe standard order (Hast du), whereas the final invocation does not (Hat … die allmächtige Zeit). The latter instance plainly heightens the rhetoric, but the pattern's disruption epitomizes the text's instability.

Finally, the ode expands the eighteenth-century German lexicon with colorful or extraordinary words. Verbs assume nominative forms (Bedrängten, Beladenen, Geängsteten), a routine linguistic occurrence. More evocative are compound nouns that unite readily associated words (Wolkendünst, Bergeshöhn, and Rettungsdank, literally cloud-haze, mountain-heights, and salvation-thanks). Others, however, make unusual connections, including "Opfersteuern" [sacrifice-tax] and "Gebetshauch" [prayer-breath], while still more outrageously breach poetic decorum, particularly "Knabenmorgen" [youth-morning] and "Blütenträume" [bloom-dreams], the latter made even more impudent by umlauts. Two nouns shun customary descriptors: tears are stilled, not dried, creating fractured assonance between "gestillet" and "gelindert"; and the Titan's heart glows rather than beats, action appropriate in a fiery Promethean context.

The ode's rebellious themes and poetic unorthodoxies quickly unleashed scandal in Goethe's circle and achieved public infamy a decade after its completion in 1774. For ten years its custodian, the novelist and philosopher F.H. Jacobi, shared it with colleagues to prove he was close to Goethe, by then considered the German Shakespeare.[22] In 1775 Jacobi corresponded with Georg Foster, who read the ode and simply stated, "I feel Goethe is right."[23] Likewise in 1775 another Goethe intimate,

---

[19]   The syllable "-ich," merely involving pronouns and standard adverbial forms, ends four lines in stanzas II, IV, and VII. The syllable "-ut" ends three lines in stanzas I and IV. Strict rhyme thus occurs in proximity only twice, in stanzas IV and VII.

[20]   Lines 2–3 and lines 10–11 exhibit paired assonances, a tendency likewise evident in lines 21–3, and, with altered word order, lines 25–7.

[21]   The infinitives appear in different places in the parallel construction: "Eine Ohr *zu hören* meine Klage," but "Ein Herz…sich des Bedrängten *zu erbarmen*."

[22]   Nicholas Boyle, *Goethe: The Poet and the Age* (2 vols, Oxford, 1991-), vol. 1, p. 188.

[23]   Hans Blumenberg, *Work on Myth*, trans. Robert M. Wallace (Cambridge, Mass., 1990), p. 407.

Heinrich Leopold Wagner, lampooned the ode in *Prometheus, Deukalion und seine Rezensenten*, a defense of Goethe's novel, *Die Leiden des jungen Werthers*. Wagner's satire casts Goethe as Prometheus and Werther as Deucalion, the Titan's son. An especially farcical passage—which the narrator slyly judges a misprint to be glossed over—describes Deucalion's heart as "filled with chatter of glowing rapture," a travesty on two keywords in the ode, heart and glow.[24] Predictably, rapture is induced by hearing Mignon's famous song from *Werther* in the company of "F."—Fritz Jacobi.

More seriously, Jacobi permitted G.E. Lessing to read the ode in 1780, shortly before the renowned critic and dramatist died. Lessing admitted "its viewpoint [was his] own," ostensibly alluding to rebellion against religious authority.[25] Jacobi, however, misrepresented Lessing's avowal in a dispute with the philosopher Moses Mendelssohn. In publicly exchanged letters Jacobi claimed Lessing admired the poem's "viewpoint" because it coincided with Spinoza's pantheism. Mendelssohn, whose passionate religious opinions were undoubtedly threatened by Lessing's endorsement, replied: "One who can lose his religion because of bad verses must certainly have little to lose."[26] The ode's unorthodox language probably elicited Mendelssohn's gibe regarding "bad verses," since he judged the ode's content "adventurous."[27] Jacobi countered, noting the ode "was directed against any Providence in very strong language," and deeming it "the genuine, living spirit of antiquity, newly embodied in form and content."[28] To defend his convictions, Jacobi published the ode in 1785 without Goethe's consent, foiling censors by printing it on a detachable insert within a larger volume. Goethe's protest exacerbated the controversy, enhancing the poem's revolutionary reputation.

After the scandal linked its radical content and literary style, the ode suffered temporary neglect. But as Goethe's works became readily available early in the nineteenth century, *Prometheus* was recognized as "an exceptional expression" of his "rebellious pre-revolutionary tendencies."[29] The ode's eminent critics included Heinrich Heine, who widely publicized the debate over Spinoza, Karl Marx, who emphasized its obvious political implications, and Friedrich Gundolf, who reflected Nietzsche's influence in dubbing Goethe's Titan an *Übermensch*.[30] As late as 1922 Georg Brandes hyperbolically claimed it was "the greatest revolutionary poem of all time."[31] Goethe's autobiography, however, best evoked its original incendiary impact:

---

[24]   The satire, published simultaneously in Frankfurt, Berlin, and Düsseldorf in 1775, is reprinted as Heinrich Leopold Wagner, *Prometheus, Deukalion und seine Rezensenten*, in August Sauer (ed.), *Stürmer und Dränger*, Zweiter Teil, *Lenz und Wagner* (Berlin, [1883]), p. 372.

[25]   Franz Saran, *Goethes Mahomet und Prometheus* (Halle, 1914), p. 68.

[26]   Moses Mendelssohn, "An die Freunde Lessings, (Berlin, 1786)," in Heinrich Scholz (ed.), *Die Hauptschriften zum Pantheismusstreit zwischen Jacobi und Mendelssohn* (Berlin, 1916), p. 299.

[27]   Ibid.

[28]   F.H. Jacobi, *Werke*, ed. Friedrich Roth and Friedrich Köppen (6 vols, Darmstadt, 1976), vol. 4, pt. 2, p. 215.

[29]   Saran, pp. 72–8.

[30]   Braemer, pp. 326–34.

[31]   Georg Brandes, *Goethe*, 2nd edn (Berlin, 1922), p. 85.

Prometheus was the priming powder for an explosion that revealed and brought into discussion the most secret relations of estimable men: relations, unknown to those men themselves, slumbering in an otherwise highly enlightened society.[32]

Goethe thus considered the ode an agent that illuminated suppressed human relations, a catalyst activating a latent revolutionary discourse whose animation—like the ode's controversial theme, audacious style, and clandestine publication—violated a "highly enlightened society's" norms. Goethe's *Prometheus* accordingly articulates different modes of transgression, a topic explored most probingly by Michel Foucault.

Transgression pervades Foucault's critical thought, from his earliest writings to his final interviews, regardless of the issue involved. Corroborating this preoccupation are monographs on madness, science and society, the penal system, and sexuality,[33] plus numerous essays on aesthetics, ethics, and criticism's obligations.[34] But Foucault most explicitly addressed the subject in "A Preface to Transgression," an early essay foreshadowing later work on sexuality's history.[35] Collectively these writings scarcely comprise a cohesive theory of transgression, though they articulate recurrent and consistent principles applicable to Goethe's ode and its musical settings.

Foucault defines transgression as "an action which involves the limit, that narrow range of a line where it displays the flash of its passage, but perhaps also its entire trajectory, even its origin."[36] Schubert, Wolf, and to a lesser degree, Reichardt devised introductory gestures that meet Foucault's conditions, as later analysis demonstrates.[37]

Equally vital to Foucault's concept of transgression is that it "incessantly crosses and recrosses a line which closes up behind it in a wave of extremely short duration, and thus is made to return ... to the horizon of the uncrossable."[38] It accordingly eschews merely dichotomous relationships: "transgression then, is not related to the limit as black is to white, the prohibited to the lawful, the outside to the inside, or as the open area of a building to its enclosed spaces."[39] Rather, it consists of "a permanent

---

32   Goethe, *Dichtung und Wahrheit*, quoted in Blumenberg, *Work on Myth*, p. 413.

33   *Madness and Civilization*, trans. Richard Howard (New York, 1965); *The Order of Things: An Archaeology of the Human Sciences*, trans. unidentified (New York, 1966); *Discipline and Punish: The Birth of the Prison*, trans. Alan Sheridan (New York, 1975); and *The History of Sexuality: An Introduction*, trans. Robert Hurley (Harmondsworth, 1976).

34   See especially "The Order of Discourse," trans. Ian McLeod, in Robert Young (ed.), *Untying the Text: A Post-Structuralist Reader* (London, 1981), pp. 48–78; "Truth and Power," trans. Colin Gordon, in Colin Gordon (ed.), *Power/Knowledge: Selected Interviews and Other Writings, 1972–1977* (Brighton, 1984), pp. 32–50; and "The Ethic of Care for the Self as a Practice of Freedom," trans. J.D. Gauthier, in James Bernauer and David Rasmussen (eds), *The Final Foucault* (Cambridge, Mass., 1988), pp. 1–20.

35   Michel Foucault, "A Preface to Transgression," in Donald F. Bouchard (ed.), *Language, Counter-Memory, Practice: Selected Essays and Interviews*, trans. Donald F. Bouchard and Sherry Simon (Ithaca, 1977), pp. 29–52.

36   Ibid., pp. 33–4.

37   Foucault's influential definition is discussed in Moya Lloyd and Andrew Thacker, "Introduction: Strategies of Transgression," in *The Impact of Michel Foucault on the Social Sciences and Humanities* (New York, 1997), pp. 1–9.

38   Foucault, "A Preface to Transgression," p. 35.

39   Ibid.

re-activation of the rules."[40] Transgression's continuity, Foucault often declared, is essential to "the practice of liberty" and actions triggering political rebellion.[41] Foucault's convictions thus intersect with central thoughts of Goethe's ode.

Foucault's third stipulation posits that transgression must be "situated ... in uncertainties which are immediately upset so that thought is ineffectual as soon as it attempts to seize them."[42] Characterizations of this "complex and unstable" context recur throughout Foucault's writings and the secondary literature.[43] In the three lieder, repeated violations and reinstatements of ambiguous generic and tonal contexts produce instability.

For Foucault the "experience of the limit" is realized in language that is "discursive (even when it involves a narrative)."[44] The resulting discontinuity, typically affecting small linguistic units in an unbroken discourse,[45] again has clear musical equivalents in discursive harmonies, interrupted tonal processes, and fragmented phrases.

Finally, one of Foucault's ideological corollaries pertains to the ode's incantation. The truest form of discourse, "which inspired respect and terror, and to which one had to submit because it ruled, was the one pronounced ... according to the required ritual."[46] Hence ritual discourse's imposed limits, like those of any discourse, are simultaneously "restricting and enabling,"[47] and function "as a generative form of power rather than in a merely repressive or dominating fashion."[48] This "generative" power is in turn the means whereby "a human being turns him- or herself into a subject,"[49] an act "an external authority figure" nonetheless typically mediates.[50] Ultimately, however, "a rigorous language ... will not reveal the secret of man's natural being, nor will it express the serenity of anthropological truths, but rather, it will say that he exists without god."[51]

While the final quotation concerns sexuality's history, it and the entire corollary unequivocally resonate in Goethe's ode, which engages with metaphysical transgression, poetic language's limits, and an incantation's ritualistic discourse. Through this discourse, Prometheus performs an act of self-formation, mediated by an external authority, Zeus, and ending with his negation of the gods' existence. Features of the lieder, particularly sonorous evocations of an incantation, illustrate Foucault's theories equally well.

---

40   Foucault, "The Order of Discourse," p. 61.
41   See Foucault, "The Ethic of Care for the Self," p. 87; *Discipline and Punish*, p. 83.
42   Foucault, "A Preface to Transgression," p. 34.
43   See, for example, Foucault, "The Order of Discourse," p. 60; Jon Simons, *Foucault and the Political* (London, 1995), p. 69.
44   Foucault, "A Preface to Transgression," pp. 51, 39.
45   Foucault, "The Order of Discourse," p. 69.
46   Ibid., p. 54.
47   Simons, p. 69.
48   Lloyd and Thacker, p. 3.
49   Paul Rabinow, introduction to *The Foucault Reader* (New York, 1984), p. 10.
50   Ibid.
51   Foucault, "A Preface to Transgression," p. 30.

Reichardt

Johann Friedrich Reichardt (1752–1809) is routinely judged a conservative lieder composer, an appraisal his work often verifies. Of almost 1,500 songs based on texts by 125 poets, many perfectly suited domestic music making during the *Goethezeit*, rarely challenging his intended amateur audience.[52] The best known, already sung in German schools by 1800, remain in music curricula today.[53] But before Schubert's birth in 1797, Reichardt's songs transcended the fashionable continuo lied's syllabic text setting, regular strophic form, skeletal accompaniment, and predictable correspondence between textual end rhyme and musical cadence. Indeed, his mature songs gravitate between two poles. The *Lieder im Volkston* still reflect ideals of the First Berlin Lieder School, composers of the previous generation who cultivated singable melodies, cursory yet fully notated accompaniments, and folk-like poetry and music. His odes and declamations, however, are "bedeutende Gesänge" [meaningful vocal pieces], as Reichardt named them.[54]

A prolific music journalist, Reichardt expounded his aesthetics in "To Young People: Encouragement toward Pure and Proper Singing," an essay published in 1777. Stipulating a song's ambitious purpose was "to make a poem's given content more significant and expressive through its musical setting,"[55] he conceded some poetic genres posed unique problems. "High odes," for example, required composers to foster "unity of feeling if the impression of the whole is to be strikingly penetrating."[56] Reichardt's observation admittedly concerned devising one melody for all of an ode's stanzas, a "most difficult task" unrelated to his *Prometheus*. But in claiming new territory for the lied—enhancing expressive poetic content through a unified musical setting—he hastened the advent of the genre's centrality during the romantic era.

Reichardt's liberal politics and progressive literary tendencies likewise deserve attention because they have Promethean parallels. After visiting France in 1792, he developed permanent revolutionary sympathies, which he published pseudonymously as "J. Frei," an amalgamation forming the word "free" from initials and letters obviously drawn from his given names and surname.[57] His employer, Friedrich Wilhelm II of Prussia, surmised his identity and promptly dismissed him without pension, thus familiarizing Reichardt with transgression and punishment. He recovered from this scandal as director of the salt mines in Halle beginning in 1796, when his estate in nearby Giebichenstein became known as "the hostel of the romantics," so named because young writers and philosophers, including

---

52   Walter Salmen, *Johann Friedrich Reichardt: Komponist, Schriftsteller, Kapellmeister und Verwaltungsbeamter der Goethezeit* (Freiburg, 1963), p. 296.

53   Walter Salmen, "Reichardt, Johann Friedrich," in *The New Grove Dictionary of Music*, vol. 21, p. 137.

54   Johann Friedrich Reichardt, "Ueber Klopstocks komponirte Oden," *Musikalisches Kunstmagazin*, 1 (1782): 22.

55   Reichardt, "An die Jugend: Aufmunterung zum reinen und richtigen Gesang," *Ephemeriden der Menschheit*, 1/11 (1777): 36.

56   Reichardt, "Ueber Klopstocks komponirte Oden," p. 62.

57   Reichardt's views appeared in his epistolary collection, *Vertraute Briefe über Frankreich* (Berlin, 1792).

Goethe, paid visits until 1806, when Napoleon's army pillaged it.[58] Giebichenstein accordingly provided a forum for republican intellectuals who doubtless shared the revolutionary sentiments of Goethe's ode.

Reichardt developed close though turbulent relations with Goethe during the 1780s. Their earliest creative contact, however, dates from 1772, when Corona Schröter, one of Goethe's favorite singers, brought his poems to Reichardt's attention.[59] And like many young Germans, Reichardt read *Werther*, the source of several lieder, in 1774.[60] They finally met ten years later, when Goethe visited the Harz Mountains.[61] By 1786 Reichardt had ingratiated himself with Weimar Classicism's triumvirate, Goethe, Schiller, and Herder, but the latter two rejected his camaraderie.[62] Reichardt nonetheless became Goethe's friend and musical advisor, a role formally recognized in 1789, when Goethe commissioned Reichardt to write music for *Claudine von Villa Bella*, inaugurating a series of theatrical collaborations.

Goethe acknowledged Reichardt "had done well by him" with *Claudine*,[63] noted his settings of poems from *Wilhelm Meisters Lehrjahre* were "full of grace and meaning,"[64] and recognized him as "the first to make my lyrical works known to the general public through music, in a serious and steady manner."[65] In 1795, however, Reichardt's request to publish reports on Weimar's political activities alienated Goethe and Schiller.[66] Total estrangement ensued in 1796 after Reichardt criticized *Die Hörer*, a reactionary periodical both Weimar luminaries edited.[67] Civil relations resumed a year later, but Carl Friedrich Zelter became Goethe's musical advisor, and Goethe seldom answered Reichardt's persistent correspondence.[68]

Both men nonetheless held similar views on the lied. In the *Berlinische musikalische Zeitung* Reichardt declared, "the most accomplished poetic verse structure and rhythm attain their highest power and effectiveness only through the adjoining musical rhythm."[69] Goethe's later observation regarding Zelter's lieder echoes Reichardt's attitude: "A poem is merely the naked essence, which,

---

[58]   Concerning activities at Giebichenstein, see Dietrich Fischer-Dieskau, *"Weil nicht alle Blütenträume reiften": Johann Friedrich Reichardt, Hofkapellmeister dreier Preußenkönige, Porträt und Selbstporträt* (Stuttgart, 1992), pp. 208–25.

[59]   Walter Salmen, foreword to *Goethes Lieder, Oden, Balladen und Romanzen* (Munich, 1970), p. [i].

[60]   Fischer-Dieskau, *"Weil nicht alle Blütenträume reiften,"* p. 412.

[61]   Salmen, *Johann Friedrich Reichardt*, p. 57.

[62]   Regarding the objections of Schiller and Karoline Herder, who often spoke for her husband, see Salmen, *Johann Friedrich Reichardt*, pp. 50–51, 83.

[63]   Ibid., p. 67.

[64]   Goethe, *Sämtliche Werke nach Epochen seines Schaffens*, ed. Karl Richter et al. (21 vols, Munich, 1985-), vol. 8, p. 145.

[65]   Salmen, foreword to *Goethes Lieder*, p. [i].

[66]   Salmen, *Johann Friedrich Reichardt*, pp. 83–4.

[67]   Ibid.

[68]   See Max Hecker (ed.), "Die Briefe Johann Friedrich Reichardts an Goethe aus dem Goethe- und Schiller-Archiv," *Jahrbuch der Goethe-Gesellschaft*, 11 (1925): 203–29.

[69]   Reichardt, [untitled editorial], *Berlinische musikalische Zeitung*, 1 (1805): 13.

clothed only with musical fullness, becomes complete."[70] Few of Goethe's poems challenge this aesthetic more than *Prometheus*, perhaps explaining why Reichardt set it at the end of his career.

Reichardt published his *Prometheus* in *Goethes Lieder, Oden, Balladen und Romanzen*, the second installment in a three-volume collection devoted to Goethe's works completed between 1802 and 1811.[71] He sent Goethe copies of every volume, repeatedly inquiring if they had been accepted before receiving a reply.[72] The collection included songs, odes, ballads, romances, and "meaningful vocal pieces" of a relatively new kind: the *Deklamationsstück*. Featuring through-composed forms, improvisatory rhythms, declamatory vocal writing, recitative-like accompaniment, and characteristic motives, declamation pieces enjoyed popularity in private venues around 1800 before making inroads in concert halls.[73] Although few in number, Reichardt's declamation pieces attest to his originality and preoccupation with enhancing textual meaning and rhetoric.

Contemporaries often admired Reichardt's declamatory skills. After hearing him perform at Giebichenstein, the poet Adam Oehlenschläger declared, "he read well; he declaimed *Saint Anthony's Sermon to the Fishes* quite splendidly."[74] Reichardt himself claimed Prince Lobkowitz, one of Beethoven's patrons, listened attentively as he recited entire acts of Schiller's *Wilhelm Tell*.[75] The painter Franz Gereis depicted Reichardt "sitting under a tree, reading to his daughter Luise."[76] And Elisabeth Stägemann, Reichardt's compatriot from Königsberg, asserted, "he declaimed beautifully and properly, but just a bit too strongly."[77]

Excessive rhetorical strength likewise concerned Reichardt, who once informed Goethe that when he set Schlegel's verses, his "strictest possible observance" of meter precluded traditionally accepted performance practices involving "shorter or longer note durations, melodic additions, and overly strong declamation."[78] Reichardt also critiqued other performers' abilities. Karoline Jagemann, star of the Weimar stage, had a "sense and feeling for high declamation," but her equally renowned colleague August Iffland "falsely declaimed."[79] Reichardt's exacting performance standards and

---

[70] See Salmen, *Johann Friedrich Reichardt*, p. 300.

[71] See Reichardt's letter of 29 July 1802 in Hecker, p. 216.

[72] See Reichardt's letters of 1 August 1809, 21 December 1809, and 28 July 1810 in Hecker, pp. 231–4.

[73] Irmgard Weithase, *Anschauungen über das Wesen der Sprechkunst von 1775–1825* (Berlin, 1930), pp. 124–54.

[74] Adam Gottlieb Oehlenschläger, *Meine Lebens-Erinnerungen* (2 vols, Leipzig, 1850), vol. 2, p. 19.

[75] Reichardt, *Vertraute Briefe geschrieben auf einer Reise nach Wien und den oesterreichischen Staaten zu Ende des Jahres 1808 und zu Anfang 1809*, ed. Gustav Gugitz (2 vols, Munich, 1915), vol. 1, p. 391.

[76] Ulrich Thieme, Felix Becker, et al. (eds), *Allgemeines Lexikon der Bildenden Künstler von der Antike bis zur Gegenwart* (37 vols, Leipzig, 1920), vol. 13, p. 190.

[77] Johanna Elisabeth von Stägemann, *Erinnerungen für edle Frauen* (Leipzig, 1858), p. 209.

[78] Hecker, p. 209.

[79] Ibid., pp. 208, 212.

preference for lyrics of highest literary quality helped transform the eighteenth-century domestic lied into the romantic art song, as his *Prometheus* clearly illustrates.

Reichardt scrupulously observed the text's structure, temporal scheme, and rhetoric, as multiple stylistic features affirm, beginning with texture. Stanzas I and II, condemning the gods, exploit one prosaic type of recitative: sustained keyboard chords support an arpeggiated vocal line that occasionally fills melodic gaps with non-harmonic tones.[80] Stanza III, the narration's onset, is an arioso in chorale-like, homophonic style. Stanzas IV though VI, where wide leaps and lively dotted rhythms respectively animate the vocal and keyboard parts, comprise different varieties of recitative, thus forming one unit, the incantation. The chorale-like texture returns in stanza VII, though dotted rhythms and a faster tempo enliven the closing proclamation. Texture thus strengthens textual parallelisms regarding mode of discourse and meaning. Recitative is reserved for addressing the gods in the opening condemnation and interrogatory incantation, whereas homophony coincides with the Titan's actions, whether in the past or future (stanzas III, VII). More importantly, homophony emphasizes the correlation between his original constitutive act—turning his eye toward the sun to conceive the gods—and his autonomously creative act—forming men in his image.

Metric and tonal changes reinforce congruencies of poetic structure and musical texture. (Example 3.1 broadly summarizes the song's harmonic content, though linear processes, the Schenker graph's primary focus, are discussed separately.) The condemnation, set in common time, modulates in stanza I from the tonic, B-flat major, to the dominant, where it remains for stanza II. Adopting triple meter, the narration (stanza III) shifts to F minor, as a new key signature indicates, before modulating to A-flat major. The incantation reverts to common time, traversing ephemeral tonalities in stanzas IV (G and A minor, F major, D minor) and V (D and E-flat minor), before settling in D-flat major for stanza VI, peregrinations rendering a key signature superfluous. The tonic, its key signature, and triple meter return for the final declaration (stanza VII).

Cadential structure and the vocal line's rests articulate syntactical units within stanzas. In stanza I, for example, the first cadence marks the end of the first sentence, and rests punctuate the vocal line twice, first separating the two commands, then isolating the proposed action of Zeus from its object (lines 1–2, 3–4, 5). Cadential rhythms, likewise underscoring textual structure, distinguish between conclusions of sentences and stanzas. As the first sentence ends, the voice and keyboard reach the tonic simultaneously, the final chord is reiterated, and the voice continues after a quarter rest. Stanzas I and II, however, close with two unaccompanied pitches in the vocal part and two chords separated by a quarter rest. Stanzaic cadences thus last five or more beats.

---

[80]   Providing no tempo indication, Reichardt marked stanzas I and II "Kräftig deklamirt" [powerfully declaimed].

Example 3.1   Voice Leading in Reichardt's *Prometheus*

Fastidious attention to rhetoric produces large- and small-scale results. Irregular phrases consistently reflect textual asymmetry, as the opening accusation illustrates: stanza I entails three phrases, six, two, and five measures long; stanza II comprises two phrases, five and three measures long. Similarly uneven phrases prevail throughout the lied. Detailed text setting likewise enhances poetic structure and meaning. Textural gradation accentuates the interrogative pattern's disruption at the beginning of stanza V, where tremolos—not sustained chords—accompany the short questions that shift the burden of response to Zeus. As stanza V ends, the vocal line's rest separates "meine Herrn" from "und deine," segregating the realms of Prometheus and Zeus and suggesting time and destiny will treat them differently. But no pause separates the ode's last two lines, intensifying the conclusion's abruptness and stressing that neither Prometheus nor humanity will honor Zeus, a declaration emboldened by the singer uttering both lines without accompaniment.

Thus far Reichardt's setting embodies his aesthetics: music enhances the ode's expressive content, observing limits imposed by stanzaic structure, temporal-narrative design, and rhetorical detail. It nonetheless abounds with transgressive elements, particularly unorthodox harmonies and daring dissonances. The lied admittedly commences not with a brilliant, Foucaultian flash revealing the trajectory of the whole, but rather with two features of recurrent importance (Example 3.2). First, a tonic pedal underpins the initial phrase, generating dissonance with fully diminished and dominant seventh chords that accumulate above it. Throughout the setting, levels of dissonance exceed contemporary norms, especially for lieder, and accordingly equate with tonal transgression, as elaborated presently. Second, the phrase's lone non-diatonic pitch, G-flat, develops a meaningful history during the song. In stanza I it produces non-functional dissonance, simply acting as a neighbor to F in a static harmonic context. But in stanza II, the G-flat becomes functional, tonicizing the subdominant as the seventh above a diminished triad and pungently embellishing the word "Ärmeres." Throughout stanzas V and VI it becomes the third, seventh, and root of diatonic chords in D-flat major, though its weightiest occurrence—as the bass of a German sixth chord—reinstates F, the dominant, before the tonic's return. In stanza VII it reassumes its neighboring role to F, but it acquires its own triad, undoubtedly reflecting the tonal power it accrued as the lied progressed. The pitch's "composing-out" thus corresponds to Foucault's notion of a limit's transgression revealing the trajectory of the whole.

Example 3.2   Reichardt *Prometheus*, mm. 1–6

Meeting another of Foucault's criteria for transgression, Reichardt's setting incessantly crosses limits of two kinds. Generically, declamation pieces normally consist exclusively of recitatives that vary in dramatic intensity, whereas Reichardt's recitatives alternate with lyrical, homorhythmic arioso, repeatedly crossing limits that define heightened speech and pure song. Harmonically, new keys are established and instantly obscured. In the first of many examples, the short second phrase cadences when a secondary dominant tonicizes F major (Example 3.3). Immediately following the F-major triad, however, a major seventh chord appears with its root, B-flat, in the bass, an ambiguous sonority intimating either a return to an enigmatic tonic, B-flat, or a continuation in the dominant with a peculiar subdominant seventh chord, the latter soon corroborated. Similar tactics govern the next cadence, where F major is confirmed as the new tonic; but an ensuing diminished seventh chord again tonicizes B-flat, inducing a resolution in the minor mode. And when F minor achieves tonic status at the first cadence in stanza II, two more diminished seventh chords respectively reinforce the new dominant (C major) and tonicize G—a rapid succession not only undermining F minor, but also creating a cross relation between the keyboard's A-flat and the voice's A-natural. Reichardt's setting thus crosses the tonic-dominant boundary three times in stanzas I and II, always violating new tonal limits the moment they are circumscribed. Comparable strategies play small roles in the homophony of stanzas III and VII, but the incantation deploys them so pervasively and in such brisk succession that they create the uncertain context in which Foucault maintains transgression occurs.

Example 3.3   Reichardt *Prometheus*, mm. 7–9

Mode is a primary means of destabilizing the lied's tonality, globally and locally. As noted, it obscures the new key as stanza II cadences, when the prosaic dominant, F major, is supplanted by its parallel minor. Quickly shrouded by diminished seventh chords, F minor reemerges as the principal tonality of stanza III, a slightly unusual secondary key in the original tonic, B-flat major, well suited to the Titan's lament, a topos identified by the text and matched by dissonant suspensions and retardations. An ensuing modulation to A-flat major, however, is anomalous, though it prepares D-flat major, the incantation's only other stable key. D-flat in turn compounds large-scale modal ambiguity, since the tonic's third scale degree, D-natural, achieves tonic status only briefly as stanza V begins.

Localized modal vagary thoroughly pervades the incantation. As stanza IV commences, a diminished supertonic triad implies G minor as a tonic, but the cadence is in G major. The ensuing phrase reverses the process, anticipating a cadence in A major with the vocal line's F-sharp, though A minor soon arrives. A major nonetheless resurfaces as stanza IV concludes, functioning temporarily as a dominant. In stanza V the first phrase's ostensible goal is E-flat major, but the cadence establishes the parallel minor. Two modal uncertainties in stanza VII cloud an otherwise transparent B-flat major: the "composing-out" of G-flat and textual allusions to suffering and crying require an appropriation of the parallel minor's lowered submediant triad; and the previously contested third scale degree generates additional friction in the song's last four measures, where rapid juxtapositions of D, D-flat, and another D-natural are harsher because the D-flat appears in the vocal line while the accompaniment is silent. Thus a relentless contest between major and minor establishes a nebulous harmonic background consistent with Foucault's precept of transgression occurring in an unstable context.

Other harmonic procedures foil tonal expectations. For example, regular resolutions of augmented sixth chords to attendant dominants conclude stanzas IV and VI, the second underscoring the audacious compound noun, "Blütenträume." Midway through stanza V, however, a sonority heard as a German sixth chord in D minor is spelled and resolved as a dominant seventh in E-flat minor, which eludes tonal confirmation and instead facilitates a modulation to D-flat major. Deflecting a routine harmonic progression, the unorthodox resolution illustrates Foucault's conceptualization of transgressive discourse as a discursive language. A more brazen interruption disrupts stanza IV (Example 3.4). Following an arrival in A minor rather than A major, an abruptly interpolated dominant seventh chord with a root on C becomes an augmented triad, intensifying the intrusion and emphasizing the crucial words "heilig" and "glühend." Its resolution to F major on the word "Herz" reinforces assonance with the word "Herd" in stanza II, when F major last functioned as a stable tonic. After the cadence, the initial A-minor triad returns in major mode with an added seventh and resolves to D minor, the initial goal before the minor mode thwarted earlier expectations.

Example 3.4   Reichardt *Prometheus*, mm. 42–5

The incantation partially realizes Foucault's final criterion for transgression, ritualism. In stanza IV the accompaniment answers every question by reiterating chords in dotted rhythms, thus satisfying the requirement of repetition. The vocal line's arc also follows the text's intonational pattern, ascending from G to A between the first two phrase endings, arpeggiating up to C in the third, and rising to D before plummeting a seventh in the fourth. And while stanzas V and VI fail to duplicate this threefold intensification and final release, they reveal close linear and harmonic connections, joining other stanzas in fulfilling distinct linear functions within the whole of Reichardt's setting (Example 3.1).

Despite its harmonic unorthodoxies, Reichardt's *Prometheus* observes Schenkerian principles, that is, its fundamental tonal movements project the tonic triad, with the bass line's arpeggiation from tonic to dominant supporting a stepwise descent from the fifth through the first scale degrees. It even begins with an ascent to the *Hauptton*, F, a quintessential Schenkerian gesture. Several atypical strategies nonetheless reflect its unusual tonal surface.

Individual stanzas initially perform discrete, straightforward linear functions. In stanza I the bass arpeggiates from tonic to dominant, the latter elaborated by an upper neighbor and its own dominant, while the soprano ascends to the *Hauptton*. Stanza II confirms the new tonic, F, with the bass arpeggiating to C, which likewise acquires a dominant, and the soprano sustaining the *Hauptton*.

Unusual operations transpire in stanza III, where F again arpeggiates, but in the minor mode, to an A-flat elaborated by further arpeggiation. The A-flat supports the ascending soprano line, which arpeggiates (F–A-flat–C) and moves by step to E-flat, the fourth scale degree, marking the onset of the *Urlinie*'s descent, an important event reinforced by the fact that E-flat is the vocal line's highest pitch in the entire lied. The E-flat proceeds to D-flat, however, necessitating the *Urlinie*'s eventual return to D-natural to restore the original tonic's major mode.

Redressing earlier elaboration of A-flat, stanza IV reinstates A-natural as the dominant's proper arpeggiation. A rigorously stepwise descent through a complete octave, twice interrupted by octave displacement, conceals the bass line's arpeggiation of A-natural, which balances similar treatment of A-flat. Thus A-flat functions retrospectively as a chromatic neighbor to A-natural, though it later assumes another role. The *Urlinie*'s descent also resumes in stanza IV, replacing the errant D-flat with D-natural, an event obscured by a voice exchange.

Thus far stanzas perform relatively discrete linear functions, but stanzas V and VI reveal closer ties. Stanza V consolidates previous events, elaborating the dominant with both A-natural and A-flat in the bass line. The A-flat is not a neighbor tone, however, but the dominant of D-flat, which achieves stability in stanza VI before an augmented sixth chord reestablishes the true dominant, F. Third-related elaborations of the dominant accordingly connect both stanzas. Meanwhile, the *Urlinie* descends from the third to the second scale degree, C, mediated by a chromatic passing tone, D-flat. Camouflaged by a voice exchange, the C will return to the *Urlinie*'s register in stanza VII.

Predictably, the final stanza affirms the tonic in the bass line, first with a lower neighbor, then a triadic arpeggiation. Likewise unsurprisingly, the *Urlinie* descends from C to B-flat in the appropriate register.

While linear analysis demonstrates Reichardt's *Prometheus* largely observes tonal conventions, it is scarcely conservative. Its third relations, foreshadowing romantic practice, are especially adventurous in the context of the lied, often judged a conservative genre during the nineteenth century's first decade, before Schubert composed his earliest masterpieces. Additional unorthodoxies, particularly generic and modal ambiguity, irregular phrases, and discursive harmonies that undermine keys the moment they are established, match Goethe's transgressive subject and literary style. Such traits, however, never compromise the ode's stanzaic structure, temporal scheme, or rhetorical detail, which Reichardt delineated through variations in texture, meter, tonality, and cadential structure, thereby attaining his goal of enhancing a poem's expressive content through music.

Reichardt's aesthetics undoubtedly appealed to Schubert, who found models for several songs in Reichardt's 1804 collection, *Lieder der Liebe und der Einsamkeit*.[81] Whether he was acquainted with the 1809 volume of *Goethe-Lieder* containing *Prometheus*, however, remains unknown. Features of Schubert's setting nonetheless strongly indicate he was.

Schubert

Franz Schubert's first Promethean encounter decisively influenced his career, as was the case with Beethoven. In 1816 he composed a lost cantata on the subject to honor Heinrich Josef von Watteroth, a political science professor at the University of Vienna who frequently entertained Schubert's friends. Philipp Dräxler, a Watteroth pupil, wrote the libretto, and the 19-year-old Schubert received his first commission. His diary entry for 17 June 1816 boasts, "Today I composed for money for the first time."[82] Moreover, some of the cantata's performers would affect Schubert's early professional activities. Leopold Sonnleithner, one of the choristers and an accomplished music theorist and composer, later promoted Schubert's songs and arranged another reading of the cantata on 8 January 1819 to impress members of the venerable Gesellschaft der Musikfreunde.[83] Another participant, Franz Schlechta, praised the cantata in a poem published in the *Wiener Allgemeine Theaterzeitung* on 27 September 1817, the first time Schubert's name appeared in a periodical.[84] The work's success probably encouraged Schubert to pursue freelance opportunities rather than resume teaching at his father's suburban school in the autumn of 1816.[85]

Recollections of the cantata's debut indicate it expounded romantic views of Prometheus. Dräxler's libretto, recounting the Titan's "tragic fate and its cause,"[86] included a chorus sung by "the pupils of Prometheus," an overt tribute to Watteroth, who expressed liberal political and religious opinions in his classroom despite the repressive atmosphere of Metternich's Vienna, a topic addressed shortly.[87] And the cantata purportedly ended with rousing calls for liberty, grounds for restricting performances to private venues that were monitored, but not censored.[88] The lost cantata thus articulated revolutionary issues within Schubert's circle.

---

[81] Kenneth S. Whitton, *Schubert and Goethe: The Unseen Bond* (Portland, 1999), p. 98.

[82] See Otto Erich Deutsch, *Schubert: A Documentary Biography*, trans. Eric Blom (London, 1946), p. 65.

[83] Ibid., p. 112.

[84] Ibid., pp. 68–9.

[85] See, among others, Elizabeth Norman McKay, *Franz Schubert: A Biography* (Oxford, 1996), p. 65.

[86] Leopold Sonnleithner, "Appeal for the *Prometheus Cantata*," in Otto Erich Deutsch (ed.), *Schubert: Memoirs by his Friends*, trans. Rosamond Ley and John Nowell (London, 1958), p. 443.

[87] Ibid., p. 445.

[88] George R. Marek, *Schubert* (New York, 1985), p. 72.

Schubert remained interested in the cantata and Prometheus throughout his short life. Scheduling another performance in 1820, he abandoned the project after unsuccessful rehearsals.[89] Likewise unfulfilled were plans he made with the singing teacher Josef Frühwald for several performances of the score in Lower Austria.[90] Schubert corroborated his enduring fascination with the myth by listing Beethoven's Promethean overture as the first of "many great pieces by great masters" in a letter dating from the early 1820s, and by attending a reading of Aeschylus' play in February 1828 during a respite from the illness that killed him nine months later.[91] But most importantly, between the cantata's premiere and the noted events—in October 1819—he set Goethe's ode, by which time he had moved from the suburbs to the inner city, residing first with Franz Schober, the hedonistic leader of a *Bildungkreis* [education circle] who promoted fashionable intellectual and artistic issues, then with Johann Mayrhofer, a poet employed in the book censor's office.

Freed from teaching duties and surrounded by artistic friends, Schubert pursued public and professional musical opportunities, rising from relative obscurity to the brink of a promising career. But his contact with young intellectuals had ominous consequences: he was implicated in seditious activities. During and after the Napoleonic Wars, Vienna essentially became a police state under Emperor Francis I, whose patriarchal demeanor nonetheless endeared him to his subjects.[92] Francis shrewdly allocated authority to suppress republicanism to ruthless ministers, beginning with Count Johann Anton Pergen, who advocated restricting the press in 1793, and ending with Prince Clemens Metternich, who dominated foreign and domestic policies for 40 years after his appointment in 1809.[93] Metternich stifled liberal religion and politics through widespread surveillance, often directed at intellectuals. His office monitored the press, mail, public speech, and printed music, while his agents infiltrated universities, schools, and youth groups. Police brutality was uncommon, but Viennese subjects lived under threats of arrest, losing employment, and observing inconvenient curfews.

Schubert directly experienced Metternich's oppression. His *Bildungkreis*, though absorbed in aesthetics, was investigated for subversion beginning in 1815. Police harassed several of his friends, and he was advised to cease visiting them at the Stadtkonvikt, his alma mater.[94] From 1817 to 1818, Schubert was active in the Unsinns-Gesellschaft [Nonsense Society], whose members expressed political dissatisfaction in satirical plays and private newsletters.[95] Schubert also intended to join the Ludlamshöhle, an artistic fraternity that forbade political discussions during sardonically conceived meetings.

---

[89]   Deutsch, *Schubert: A Documentary Biography*, p. 132.

[90]   Ibid., p. 165.

[91]   Ibid., pp. 265, 730.

[92]   Raymond Erickson, "Vienna in its European Context," in Raymond Erickson (ed.), *Schubert's Vienna* (New Haven, 1997), pp. 16–23.

[93]   Metternich's career is comprehensively assessed in Donald E. Emerson, *Metternich and the Political Police: Security and Subversion in the Habsburg Monarchy, 1813–1830* (The Hague, 1968).

[94]   McKay, pp. 54–5.

[95]   Rita Steblin, *Babette und Therese Kunz: Neue Forschungen zum Freundeskreis um Franz Schubert und Leopold Kupelwieser* (Vienna, 1996), pp. 1–2, 56.

Before he became a member, however, the Ludlamshöhle was denounced for suspected ties to India, speculations that proved groundless after its papers were confiscated, the homes of its members searched, and a prominent member, the poet Franz Grillparzer, interrogated.[96] But worst of all was Schubert's arrest in March 1820 after police found him at the home of Johann Christoph Senn, a member of the *Bildungkreis*, known pantheist, and agitator for Tyrolean independence from Austria.[97] Just five months earlier, Schubert composed his *Prometheus* amid political repression.

The ode was scarcely Schubert's first encounter with Goethe's poetry. Indeed, between 1814 and 1816 he produced nearly 50 of the 80 Goethe settings completed during his unparalleled career as a lieder composer. They never met, although in 1816 Josef Spaun, Schubert's classmate at the Stadtkonvikt and longtime mentor, persuaded the composer to send copies of 16 *Goethe-Lieder* to the author. Goethe declined to acknowledge the songs' proposed dedication, neglected to record the gift in his diary,[98] and returned the songs without comment. In June 1825 Schubert again dedicated three songs to Goethe and dispatched copies. Failing to respond, Goethe at least noted the package's arrival in his diary, perhaps signifying his awareness of Schubert's burgeoning reputation during the intervening decade.[99]

Schubert's *Prometheus*, like Reichardt's, is a declamation piece comprising recitative interspersed with lyrical episodes. Generic bonds, however, inadequately explain their "striking similarities," which Schubertians attribute to the influence of Reichardt's 1809 edition of *Goethe-Lieder*.[100] These commentators nonetheless consistently avoid mentioning correspondences that are both numerous and specific, but are often dislocated with respect to Goethe's text.

Affinities are obvious from the outset. In each lied the vocalist's first phrase unfolds over a pedal tone that generates dissonance with overlying chords. Schubert, however, adopts this strategy for two lines, not five, and utilizes only a dominant seventh chord instead of pairing it with a diminished seventh as Reichardt had. Both composers likewise obscure their initial modulations with subdominant major seventh chords, Reichardt in line 8, Schubert already in line 3. Augmented dominant seventh chords produce a textual connection between the lieder, underscoring the word "glühend" in Reichardt's setting and "Glut" in Schubert's. Both songs also contain chorale-like homophony, used for the Titan's narration by Reichardt, but for his derision of the impoverished gods by Schubert. Moreover, the tonality of both chorales is, unexpectedly, the parallel minor of a previously implied major key. Augmented sixth chords resolve irregularly, once in Reichardt's version, emphasizing the word "Tränen," and twice in Schubert's rendition, simply compounding harmonic ambiguity rather than intensifying specific words. A final

---

[96] Lucia Porhansl, "Auf Schuberts Spuren in der 'Ludlamshöhle,'" *Schubert durch die Brille*, 7 (1992): 52–78.

[97] Deutsch, *Schubert: A Documentary Biography*, pp. 128–30.

[98] Ibid., pp. 56–7.

[99] Whitton, pp. 139–47.

[100] Marjorie Wing Hirsch, *Schubert's Dramatic Lieder* (Cambridge, 1993), p. 24; Dietrich Fischer-Dieskau, *Schubert's Songs: A Biographical Study*, trans. Kenneth S. Whitton (New York, 1978), pp. 130–31; McKay, p. 50.

precise resemblance involves multiple insertions of lowered submediant triads in otherwise diatonic settings of stanza VII, in lines 53–4 of Reichardt's setting and lines 54–6 of Schubert's.

Table 3.2   Episodic Structure of Schubert's *Prometheus*, D. 674

Stanza	Episode's Features	Markings
Introduction	Characteristic dotted motive Octaves, then chords	[Kräftig]
I	Recitative, tremolos, dotted motive	= Introduction
IIa, lines 12–13	Recitative, sustained chords	
IIb, lines 14–20	Parodied lament in chorale style Equivalent to Reichardt's arioso	Etwas langsamer
III	Melodic vocal line Downbeats and afterbeats in accompaniment	Alla breve
IVa, lines 28–33	Recitative, sustained chords	Recit.
IVb, lines 34–6	Accompaniment recalls stanza III, but vocal line is declamatory	
Va, lines 37–41	Recitativo accompagnato	Geschwinder
Vb, lines 42–5	Homorhythmic texture Vocal line doubles inner voice	
VI	Recitative, sustained chords Bass on measure's weak beats	Etwas langsamer
VII	Martial, dotted rhythms Homophonic texture	Kräftig

In addition to the foregoing details, both settings exhibit broad similarities. They heavily exploit diminished seventh chords and dotted rhythms, though these features rarely occupy analogous places in the text, and they initially share the same key signature. Despite specific and general likenesses, however, Schubert's rendering is far more elaborate, subdividing three of Goethe's stanzas and cultivating greater variety regarding types of recitative and degrees of lyricism (Table 3.2).

Recitative takes three forms: agitated tremolos, found in only four measures of Reichardt's setting, dominate stanza I, yielding occasionally to dotted figures; secco recitative's sustained chords prevail in stanzas IIa, IVa, and VI; and *recitativo accompagnato*, involving the keyboard's restless octaves and trills, is unique to stanza Va. Lyricism likewise assumes various guises. Stanza IIb, a chorale, features upward leaps and stepwise descents in the vocal line. The voice traces stepwise and triadic patterns in stanza III, where the accompanist's hands alternate between octave downbeats and chordal afterbeats, a texture supporting vocal declamation in stanza IVb. In stanza Vb the voice merely adds repeated notes as it doubles an inner line in the homophonic accompaniment. And dotted rhythms animate stanza VII, suggesting a martial character consistent with the closing key, C major, a tonality associated with triumph in several Schubert lieder.[101]

The number and variety of episodes, resulting partly from Schubert's stanzaic subdivisions, have elicited mixed criticism. Maurice Brown asserts "the episodic structure of *Prometheus* is not wholly successful since inevitably it leads to a disjointed effect."[102] Jack Stein concurs, deeming Schubert's approach "only partially successful" because the music "dilates" the ode's "highly concentrated language."[103] Elizabeth McKay, however, believes the "magnificent setting" stretches the genre to "new dramatic expressiveness," a sentiment Kenneth Whitton echoes in characterizing the song as a "heaven storming lied."[104] Neither detractors nor advocates, however, analyze *Prometheus* in detail, an enterprise that illuminates Schubert's attitudes toward individual lines of text and his especially sensitive realization of the incantation's rhetoric.

Schubert's setting sometimes differs from Reichardt's regarding stanzaic divisions and affects. Most conspicuously, Schubert's rendition unites stanza I and the first two lines of stanza II with a continuous harmonic progression that passes from the subdominant of E-flat major at the end of stanza I, through a six-four chord in stanza II, line 1, to an augmented sixth chord and half cadence in the ensuing line. Confirming this unique elision is an immediate shift from recitative in the connected lines to chorale style in the rest of stanza II. The link suggests Prometheus knows nothing more impoverished than the gods (IIa) because they exact tribute through fear (I) instead of deriving power from foolish hope (IIb), a reading concordant with a denunciation of Metternich's regime, which maintained authority through intimidation.

But a transparent political allegory's facile detection diminishes a stanzaic bond that is based on more than mere contiguity. Indeed, stanza IIa represents a culmination of all previous events: the accompaniment makes its first shift from tremolos and characteristic motives to sustained chords, thereby directing attention toward the vocal line; the voice reaches E-flat above the bass staff, its highest pitch thus far; and the half cadence that concludes the Titan's declaration concerning divine poverty completes a harmonic process initiated midway through stanza I, where Prometheus asserts the earth, the hut he built independently, the hearth, and its glow must remain

101   E.G. Porter, *Schubert's Song Technique* (London, 1961), p. 38.
102   Maurice J.E. Brown, *Schubert Songs* (Seattle, 1969), p. 18.
103   Jack Stein, *Poem and Music in the German Lied* (Cambridge, Mass., 1971), pp. 65–6.
104   McKay, p. 94; Whitton, p. 230.

within his realm.[105] The gods' poverty thus equates with their lack of terrestrial authority, particularly over the Titan's creative labors. Schubert's elision accordingly reinforces artistic autonomy, a cardinal trait of the myth's romantic treatments.

The rest of stanza II likewise elucidates Schubert's textual insights. A four-part chorale exhibits a lament's standard features, namely prominent suspensions, a repetitive bass line consisting mostly of upward leaps followed by stepwise descents, and funereal keys, B-flat minor at the outset, then D minor.[106] Schubert's setting thus reveals a close parallel in Reichardt's, where stanza III uses the same texture and tonal relationship to preceding material—the newly established dominant's parallel minor. But while Reichardt's lament genuinely reflects the Titan's sorrowful childhood, Schubert's chorale scarcely expresses sympathy for gods who would starve without the sacrifices and prayers of hopeful fools. It instead seethes with irony, intensifying the protagonist's mockery of his Olympian oppressors. Irony, typically associated with Schumann's lieder, is surely within Schubert's expressive range, especially in his late songs. His setting of stanza IIb, however, verifies his mastery of sarcasm much earlier in his career.

Stanza III emphasizes the discrepancy between the Titan's power and divine destitution. Although his narration of earlier afflictions begins mournfully in D minor, it modulates to F major as the stanza's second line concludes, remaining in the brighter key until stanza IV begins. Moreover, the vocal line's gracious curves and higher tessitura, plus the faster alla breve meter and the accompaniment's simple alternation between downbeats and afterbeats, suggest childhood's burdens were light, or at least not lamentable. The almost untroubled setting of stanza III perhaps indicates Schubert's Prometheus knows that turning his eye toward the heavens to constitute the gods was actually his means of self-realization.

Displaying extremely diverse styles, textures, and tonalities, stanzas IV through VI nonetheless articulate the rhetorical pattern of two questions demanding positive answers, a third constructed negatively but requiring a positive response, and a fourth that inverts the third (AABC). In stanza IV the first two queries are set as secco recitative, with sustained chords supporting vocal declamation. The third retains the declamatory vocal style, but the homorhythmic accompaniment's harmonies move faster, in quarter and eighth notes. And in the fourth the accompaniment's alternating downbeats and afterbeats recall stanza III, though the vocal line is angular, not curved.

Stanzas V and VI generate a similar pattern through textural and textual manipulations. Stanza V begins regularly as two short questions ("I honor you? Why?") anticipate a longer interrogative asking if Zeus ever lightened the Titan's pain. Schubert then repeats both short questions before a second longer query. Each grouping of three inquiries constitutes a single unit that cadences when a dominant ninth chord resolves deceptively to a lowered submediant, the first such progression ending on a C-flat major triad, the second a half step higher. Both groupings nonetheless share one texture: a declamatory vocal line outlines the sequential harmonies, while the accompaniment,

---

[105]   Cast entirely in E-flat major, the passage tonicizes the subdominant, dominant, submediant, and again the subdominant before cadencing with a six-four chord, augmented sixth, and dominant.

[106]   Regarding these key associations, see John Reed, *The Schubert Song Companion* (Manchester, 1985), pp. 492, 486.

steadily alternating between eighth notes and dotted quarters, emulates an orchestra with dense chords and clashing pedal and neighbor tones. Thus the two groupings articulate the rhetorical structure's first two divisions (AA). In the third question's essentially homorhythmic setting (B) the chordal accompaniment moves in quarter notes and the vocal line merely doubles an inner voice, likewise recalling their homophonic analogues in stanza IV. And the fourth interrogative (C) also approximates its counterpart's texture, but rather than alternating between downbeats and afterbeats, the accompaniment is divided between sustained chords in the right hand and octaves on the measure's second and fourth beats in the left. The rhetorical sequence accordingly remains intact in both quadripartite groups: two opening inquiries are set as similar types of recitative, the third in homorhythmic style, and the fourth reverting to recitative and an accompaniment whose bass line features eighth notes separated by rests.

Stanza VII comprises a discrete section defined by its repetitive martial rhythms, largely triadic vocal writing, and tonality, a conspicuously transparent C major colored only by the previously noted turn toward A-flat, the lowered submediant. Schubert, again taking a meaningful textual liberty, repeats the two concluding lines ("Not to respect you, like me!"), thereby emphasizing the crux of the Promethean revolt: a free humanity will achieve fulfillment without divine aid, an assertion underscored by the incursion of A-flat in the prevailing diatonic context.

Schubert's *Prometheus* observes most major rhetorical divisions in Goethe's text. Stanzas I and II challenge large-scale rhetoric, however, since both condemn the gods and thus form one textual unit based on a parallelism between two sources of authority, fear and foolish hope. Schubert's segregation of stanza IIb nonetheless amplifies the Titan's mockery of impoverished gods in a "parodied" chorale. Otherwise the lied respects rhetorical functions, dividing into a relatively lighthearted narrative (stanza III), an effective realization of the incantation's structure (stanzas IV through VI), and a finale distinguished by tonality and figuration. Previous criticism has ignored the lied's coherent design, focusing instead on its admittedly unusual harmonies. Alfred Einstein, for example, mentioned the "extraordinary harmonic progression" that accompanies "Hat mich nicht zum Manne geschmiedet."[107] Brown, who disdained the "episodic" structure's "disjointed effect," nonetheless described the treatment of the two ensuing lines, both concerned with the power of time and fate, as "the boldest and most revolutionary harmonic writing in all of Schubert's lieder."[108] And Dietrich Fischer-Dieskau claimed the central stanzas' chromaticism "explored the dramatic limit of the lied," foreshadowing McKay's comparable assessment.[109] As allusions to "revolutionary content" and generic "limits" suggest, harmonies that exceed early nineteenth-century tonal practice constitute the setting's primary mode of transgression.

A bold opening gesture illustrates Foucault's transgressive theories, revealing a fundamental aspect of the entire setting, namely that tonal norms scarcely apply (Example 3.5). Rather than establishing the key before the singer enters, the piano outlines a triad in bare octaves and then switches to five-part chords, a pattern occurring twice. The first statement involves three major triads: stark octaves imply

---

[107] Alfred Einstein, *Schubert: A Musical Portrait* (New York, 1951), p. 120.
[108] Brown, p. 18.
[109] Dietrich Fischer-Dieskau, *Schubert's Songs*, pp. 130–31.

B-flat major as a tonic, but A-flat and E-flat major chords produce an unmistakable plagal effect in E-flat. In neither key, however, is the progression truly viable. If construed in B-flat, the second chord on A-flat is not diatonic, nor does conventional tonicization prepare the arrival on E-flat. If interpreted in E-flat, every chord is diatonic, but the order is non-functional or retrogressive (V–IV–I, not IV–V–I or I–IV–V). Moreover, ensuing phrases confirm neither key.

Example 3.5   Schubert *Prometheus*, mm. 1–6

Departing from its model, the second statement involves major and minor chords. More octaves maintain E-flat major as a provisional tonic, but their A-natural annuls fleeting tonal stability. D-major and G-minor triads then articulate an authentic cadence in G minor, where lines 1–5 unfold. Retrospectively the second statement's harmonies function conventionally in G minor (VI–V–i), though the sequence governing both statements is tonal, not real, and hence slightly unpredictable. (The first ends a fifth below its starting point, the second a sixth.) Ambiguous, unpredictable harmonic syntax, however, is but one means whereby the introduction foreshadows events throughout the lied. It also prefigures subsequently important tonalities: E-flat major resurfaces in stanza I, B-flat major in stanza IIb, D in stanza III, where it acquires minor coloring, and A-flat major in stanza VII, as noted.

Of comparable schemes that permeate Schubert's song, one is noteworthy because Wolf also deploys it heavily and it embodies Foucault's second principle by defining limits only to cross them. Augmented sixth chords often imply keys by resolving to attendant dominants, which fail to lead convincingly to anticipated tonics three times. In the first instance, found midway through stanza I, a French sixth chord resolves conventionally to a six-four chord in the well-established key of G minor (mit Eichen). The six-four chord twice moves to the dominant and finally proceeds to the tonic (Bergeshöhn), but the arrival is weak, not only because the bass line arpeggiates downward through fifth, third, and first scale degrees instead of leaping directly from dominant to tonic, but also because the root-position chord falls on the measure's second beat, not the downbeat. Though long-awaited, the G-minor chord immediately moves to a secondary dominant tonicizing E-flat major, a sudden modulation serving two purposes: it foils harmonic expectations, thus preserving the introduction's strategy, and separates heavenly and earthly realms, set respectively in G minor (lines 1–5) and E-flat major (lines 6–11).

A German sixth chord receives more unusual treatment as stanza IIa ends, though it initially proceeds to a B-flat major triad, its expected dominant in E-flat. In stanza IIb, however, B-flat becomes the tonic, negating the German sixth's traditional role, and the mode unexpectedly changes to minor for the lament. Similarly, stanza V concludes with an Italian sixth chord's resolution to a G-sharp major triad, but stanza VI begins in G-sharp minor. Here, however, G-sharp is not the tonic, but rather the submediant in the short-lived key of B major. Employing comparable tactics but lacking an augmented sixth chord, a passage in stanza III prolongs the dominant of F major for five measures. But after the long-awaited resolution, the tonic triad immediately behaves as a new dominant until it regains tonic status.

Harmonic unorthodoxies often emphasize specific words or phrases in Reichardt's setting, with "heilig glühend Herz" and "Blütenträume" furnishing prime examples. Schubert, however, typically places thwarted resolutions at formal or textual junctures, separating stanzas or the realms of Zeus and Prometheus. Only in stanza III does the dominant's delayed resolution coincide with a pivotal word, "Klage" [lament]. Elsewhere Schubert's setting avoids madrigalesque "painting" of individual words.

Instability engendered by discursive discourse—the third of Foucault's precepts—is obvious in Schubert's introduction, as already noted. In the first three stanzas, however, tonality is basically stable. Stanzas I and IIa respectively unfold in G minor and E-flat major, a duality clouded only by a brief tonicization of F major (lines 3–4) and the previously mentioned French sixth chord's unconvincing resolution. Stanza IIb, moving freely among B-flat, G, and D minor, exploits neo-Baroque, common-chord modulations that are occasionally modal, but never jarring. And stanza III, which modulates conventionally from D minor to F major, is disturbed only by an abrupt tonicization of G minor.

Tonal stability dissolves in the incantation, where Schubert's daring harmonies match Goethe's poetic audacities. Sequences regulate stanzas IV and V. In the former, tonal centers initially change every two measures, with D, E, and F-sharp minor each implied by a diminished seventh chord, a secondary dominant (V/V), and dominant triad. Thereafter six-four and diminished seventh chords harmonize an ascending chromatic bass line, whose eventual collapse in an angular descent prepares a German sixth chord as the stanza closes.

In stanza V a new sequential pattern and another chromatic bass ascent rely on deceptively resolved dominant ninth chords to define three minor keys—E-flat, E, and F—in just 12 measures. The stanza's conclusion, dubbed "extraordinary" and "revolutionary" by Einstein and Brown, truly deserves such descriptors (Example 3.6). Featuring chromatic bass descents and another sequence, the excerpt actually conceals a framework of rising parallel thirds found on downbeats in the outermost voices. Across barlines, dominant sevenths resolve to new tonics, alluding to B, C, and C-sharp minor. If these chords provide transient orientation in an extremely unstable context, they identify others as diminished seventh chords on seventh scale degrees (one spelled enharmonically) and minor supertonic triads in second inversion that act as passing chords between the diminished sevenths. Crowned by an augmented sixth progression, the nearly atonal passage merits Brown's description as "the boldest and most revolutionary harmonic writing in all of Schubert's lieder," offering a worthy counterpart to "the greatest revolutionary poem of all time."

Example 3.6   Schubert *Prometheus*, mm. 78–82

Stanza VI relieves chromatic intensity, but nonetheless perpetuates discursive tendencies as Prometheus inquires whether Zeus expected him to hate life and flee into exile. Supporting the voice's repeated stepwise descents and upward leaps, the piano's mysterious, sustained harmonies imply four keys—D-sharp, E, and B minor, then G major—before establishing C major in stanza VII. Marked pianissimo, the enigmatic passage contrasts sharply with the stolid tonality and fortissimo dynamics of the Titan's final vow to form an independent race. Thus discursive and lucid tonal languages distinguish the actions Zeus expected from those Prometheus ultimately takes.

Schubert's setting also meets an efficacious incantation's repetitive and intonational requirements. Sequences in stanzas IV and V satisfy both conditions, reiterating material at successively higher pitch levels. But even when stanza VI abandons sequences, the voice makes two almost entirely stepwise descents from B to D-sharp and expands the range slightly in a third.

Finally, Schubert's *Prometheus* flouts Schenkerian principles, most obviously by beginning and ending in different keys (Example 3.7). Moreover, no dominant prepares any key adequately enough to fulfill the bass line's obligatory arpeggiation. Indeed, the score's strongest dominant in stanza III prepares F major, which relates to the opening gesture's B-flat but achieves little prominence elsewhere. Nor does a systematic scalewise descent link the segmented soprano lines that cohere intermittently throughout the song. Schubert's rejection of linear paradigms nonetheless fails to qualify as another manifestation of the Promethean revolt, since his dramatic lieder often start and finish in different keys and even some lyrical songs subvert Schenkerian norms.[110]

Example 3.7   Voice Leading in Schubert's *Prometheus*

---

[110]   Hirsch (p. 86) lists 12 Schubert songs with open tonal structures. See also Lawrence Kramer, "The Schubert Lied: Romantic Form and Romantic Consciousness," in Walter Frisch (ed.), *Schubert: Critical and Analytical Studies* (Lincoln, 1986), pp. 200–234.

Schubert and Reichardt share several perspectives on the Prometheus myth, notwithstanding its special importance in inaugurating the younger composer's career. Both men's experience with political oppression doubtless informed their approaches to Goethe's ode, and both devised musical equivalents for its revolutionary poetic language. Features of Schubert's lied suggest he knew Reichardt's intimately, though their renditions differ significantly. Reichardt scrupulously observes the text's large-scale temporal and rhetorical divisions; Schubert manipulates texture and tonality, eliding the first two stanzas and subdividing others. Reichardt's chorale conveys the Titan's suffering, whereas Schubert's mocks divine penury. Schubert, exploiting such differences to emphasize Promethean independence, equates the gods' poverty with their lack of terrestrial authority, treats the Titan's childhood less mournfully to underscore artistic autonomy, and repeats his final vow. Reichardt typically stresses individual words with unorthodox harmonies, while Schubert delineates textual junctures. Reichardt's chromaticism, bold enough in the context of pre-Schubertian lieder, pales before Schubert's extravagant use of altered chords and several essentially atonal passages. And unlike Reichardt, Schubert avoided long-range linear procedures associated with Schenkerian theory. In these latter respects, Schubert has more in common with Wolf, who developed a unique method of emphasizing individual words without resorting to "word painting," cultivated extreme chromaticism, and usually disdained Schenkerian techniques.

Wolf

Hugo Wolf's fame rests on over 300 songs with lyrics of the highest literary quality, a large corpus dating mostly from between 1877, when chronic strife with the Vienna Conservatory's faculty prompted his expulsion, and 1897, when the mental illness that hastened his death at age 42 first manifested itself. Wolf accordingly joined Strauss, Mahler, Zemlinsky, Schoenberg, and Berg in a last generation of romantic composers of German lieder whose members developed individual variants of a similar, highly chromatic style. Wolf, however, is more often dubbed "the Wagner of the lied," an apt sobriquet because his songs not only epitomize post-Wagnerian tonal practice, but also share broad affinities with Wagnerian music dramas, namely declamatory vocal writing, freely contrapuntal textures, and occasionally mimetic figures reminiscent of leitmotifs. Enhancing the nickname's suitability is that when Wagner visited Vienna in 1878, he assessed some of Wolf's student works and recommended he pursue a compositional career.[111]

Wolf heeded Wagner's advice, though without formal credentials, his vocation took several odd turns before proving viable. Upon leaving the Conservatory, he reluctantly returned to his native Windischgraz, a bilingual village in lower Styria where Slavs outnumbered Germanophiles like Wolf. Ill-suited to provincial life, he resettled in Vienna, earning meager income as a music master to children of family friends, moving from one boarding house to another, and composing songs

---

[111]   Romain Rolland, *Musicians of To-Day*, trans. Mary Blaiklock (Freeport, 1969), pp. 172–6.

to ambitious texts by Lenau, Heine, Eichendorff, and Goethe. Dire financial straits compelled him to return to Windischgraz in 1881, but after a stint as a Salzburg chorus master and a sparsely documented period of military conscription, he resided permanently in Vienna, beginning in 1883.[112]

Two events of this period illuminate Wolf's Wagnerism. In 1879, between his Styrian sojourns, Wolf had an infamous encounter with Brahms, who reportedly agreed to examine several of Wolf's scores, commented on them, and advised him to study counterpoint with Gustav Nottebohm.[113] Offended, Wolf never pursued lessons beyond inquiring about the pedagogue's fee, but the incident reinforced his Wagnerian stance. Soon after establishing permanent residence in Vienna, he wrote reviews for the *Wiener Salonblatt*, supporting progressive Wagnerites and deriding conservatives, especially Brahms.[114] He thereby alienated Vienna's most powerful critic, Eduard Hanslick, who championed Brahms and advocated the anti-Wagnerian, formalist concept of absolute music in the prestigious *Neue freie Presse*. Although Wolf made a formidable enemy, he ultimately prospered in Vienna, thanks to select admirers who performed and promoted his music in private and public venues.

Wolf abandoned journalism in 1887 to concentrate exclusively on composition. Fitfully productive during the previous decade, he enjoyed an astonishingly prolific nine-year period, completing over 200 songs to texts by Eichendorff, Mörike, Goethe, Geibel, and Heyse. These large, poet-based collections are not song cycles per se, because they do not chronicle one central character's experiences, as in Schubert's *Winterreise*, nor does recurrent music unify separate songs, as in Schumann's *Dichterliebe*. Indeed, their length and use of different voice types of both genders preclude performances of entire collections, except under extraordinary circumstances. Careful groupings of songs are nonetheless evident within collections, including the *Lieder nach Gedichten von Johann Wolfgang Goethe*. *Prometheus* appears at the end of the collection with two songs on mythological subjects, *Ganymed* and *Grenzen der Menschheit*, thus balancing three Harper's songs from *Wilhelm Meisters Lehrjahre* that inaugurate the collection. Both framing trilogies address divine authority's problematic nature: the Harper holds heavenly powers responsible for human suffering, while the mythological protagonists contemplate rebellion, pantheism, and resignation to mankind's insignificance before God.[115]

That Wolf set all six poems was itself a critical act, since he studiously avoided texts which he felt had already received convincing treatment from other composers.[116] He accordingly thought Schubert's famous settings of the same poems

---

[112]   Regarding Wolf's military service, see Frank Walker, *Hugo Wolf: A Biography* (New York, 1952), pp. 126–7.

[113]   Brahms described the encounter for his biographer, Max Kalbeck, who placed the event in 1881 or 1882. See Max Kalbeck, *Johannes Brahms* (4 vols, Vienna, 1912), vol. 3, pp. 410–12.

[114]   See selected reviews in *The Music Criticism of Hugo Wolf*, trans. Henry Pleasants (New York, 1979), pp. 23–9, 56–61, 100–102, 147–50, 153–5, 184–7, 195–7, 249–50, 253–5, and 271–3.

[115]   Lawrence Kramer, "Hugo Wolf: Subjectivity in the Fin-de-Siècle Lied," in Rufus Hallmark (ed.), *German Lieder in the Nineteenth Century* (New York, 1996), pp. 200–201.

[116]   Mosco Carner, *Hugo Wolf Songs* (London, 1982), p. 35.

were unsuccessful, as he expressly stated in a letter of 22 December 1890, almost two years after finishing *Prometheus* on 2 January 1889, in response to praise from his close friend Emil Kauffmann:

> What you have written ... about *Prometheus* and *Ganymed* deeply delighted me. I am also of the opinion that Schubert did not succeed with ... these two poems and that these great poems had to await the post-Wagnerian era before they could be set to music in a truly Goethean spirit.[117]

Paul Müller, founder of Berlin's Hugo Wolf Gesellschaft, likewise told Wolf his Goethe collection's last three songs superseded Schubert's renditions. Wolf found himself in agreement, believing Schubert had not understood Goethe.[118] Testimony from Wolf and his contemporaries thus dictates that post-Wagnerian criteria inform an analysis of his *Prometheus*. Declamation, recurrent motives shaping the song's large-scale form, intense chromaticism, and the accompaniment's function accordingly assume special importance in illuminating his representation of the myth.

Wolf, like Reichardt, was known for declaiming poetry, though contemporary accounts typically favor general impressions over specific details. He read "in purest Styrian dialect," as Müller noted, but he "brought out the inner expression with such sensitivity, that only a completely foolish person could have taken offense from this superficiality."[119] As playwright Hermann Bahr declared, when Wolf spoke, the words "assumed a prodigious truth, they became corporeal things: indeed, we felt as though his body had suddenly become an incarnation of the words."[120] Significantly, Wolf's recitations of poems usually preceded their performances as lieder, confirming his desire for auditors to understand the texts and perceive his songs as musical realizations of poems. His declamatory methods brightly illuminate facets of Goethe's ode.

Immediately striking is the vocal line's proclivity for repeated notes. Following a protracted instrumental prelude, the singer intones ten syllables on one pitch, D, before dropping an octave for the second line's last two syllables. The sum of ten is exceeded twice: 12 reiterations of D-flat accompany all-powerful time forging Prometheus into a man in stanza V, conceivably an appropriate musical depiction of a long process; as stanza VII begins, 11 consecutive E-naturals balance repetition in stanza I, perhaps reflecting the Titan's obstinacy in declaring he will remain seated, forming men in his image, in defiance of Zeus. Vitiating interpretations of repeated notes as equivalents for textual images, however, is their preponderance throughout the setting. In addition to the three specified tallies, totals of four to eight repetitions occur 16 times, affecting a third of the ode's lines. Wolf's reiterations are even more obvious when compared with the practices of Reichardt and Schubert,

---

[117]   Hugo Wolf, *Briefe an Emil Kauffmann*, ed. Edmund von Hellmer (Berlin, 1903), p. 25; quoted and translated in Susan Youens, *Hugo Wolf: The Vocal Music* (Princeton, 1992), p. 335.

[118]   Paul Müller, "Erinnerungen an Hugo Wolf," *Die Musik*, 2/3 (1903): 36.

[119]   Ibid., *Die Musik*, 2/2 (1903): 429.

[120]   Hermann Bahr, preface to *Gesammelte Aufsätze über Hugo Wolf*, ed. Hugo Wolf-Verein in Wien (Berlin, 1898), pp. x–xi.

who respectively employed only six and seven repetitions just once each. Repetition accordingly seems more an integral part of Wolf's declamatory style than a response to poetic imagery.

Wolf's keen interest in contemporary Viennese theatrical technique explains his text setting. While he lived in the city, its leading actors included Josef Kainz and Alexander Moissi, who based their stylized yet highly expressive form of recitation on exaggerated pitch inflections. Like many contemporaries, they emphasized crucial words by pronouncing them on higher pitches within a lower prevailing context, used different registers to distinguish between adjacent phrases, and intensified climaxes through gradual ascents in pitch—unlike modern actors who typically exploit variations in speed and volume. Early recordings of Kainz and Moissi performing Goethe's *Prometheus* suggest Wolf adopted theatrical mannerisms in his song, as Edward Kravitt has effectively demonstrated.[121]

Thespian delivery certainly helps account for Wolf's three longest strings of repeated notes. The 11 opening reiterations of D immediately precede a phrase that rises chromatically from A to B-flat and B-natural before it leaps downward to D, replicating the first phrase's ending. Wolf thereby distinguishes between the two commands in stanza I: Prometheus goads Zeus to produce a storm with inflexible, high-pitched intonation, but urges him to strike the mountaintops and oaks with lower, more modulated inflections. Two types of recitation thus differentiate heavenly and earthly realms, and godlike and childlike actions. The 12 D-flats in stanza V initiate a slow chromatic ascent to E-natural, an augmented second higher, marking a climax in consecutive accusations against Zeus. Fulfilling the same role, the 11 E-naturals inaugurating stanza VII furnish the starting point for a line that ends on D, a major ninth higher, though in this case frequent leaps interrupt essentially scalewise motion.

Wolf generally observes theatrical practice throughout the lied, setting keywords with higher pitches and distinguishing successive phrases with pitch stratification. The latter tactic conspicuously governs the beginning of stanza IV, where the singer intones lines 28–9 on D and lines 30–31 on E-flat, with octave descents again concluding both phrases. Melodic contours normally reconcile with exaggerated yet idiomatic inflections. Rare exceptions occur in stanza V at parallel junctures in questions regarding whether anyone ever lightened the Titan's burdens or stilled his tears (Example 3.8). The vocal line is awkward, not only because weak final syllables of "gelindert" and "gestillet" occupy the highest points in both phrases, but also because these climaxes are approached by large upward leaps, producing accents that seem incongruous with normal inflection.

Wolf's rhythms are likewise well considered, though the ode's irregular meter prompted several idiosyncrasies and infelicities. Predictably, the spoken language's unaccented words and syllables routinely appear on the measure's weak beats. Many of Goethe's lines, for example, begin with unstressed syllables or weak words such as articles, relative pronouns, and conjunctions; corresponding musical phrases appropriately start with anacruses. Observing this time-honored practice, Reichardt,

---

[121]   Edward F. Kravitt, "The Influence of Theatrical Declamation upon Composers of the Late Romantic Lied," *Acta musicologica*, 34/1–2 (1962): 22–7.

Schubert, and Wolf make similar choices regarding anacruses, with one exception that illuminates Wolf's reading of the text. In the phrase "die du nicht gebaut," Reichardt and Schubert place the relative pronoun "die" [which] on the beat, setting it and the next three syllables with equal notes to cause the strong syllable "-baut" to fall on the downbeat. Wolf, however, sets "die" as an anacrusis and "du" [you, meaning Zeus] with a longer note on the downbeat, thereby personalizing and intensifying the Titan's accusation.

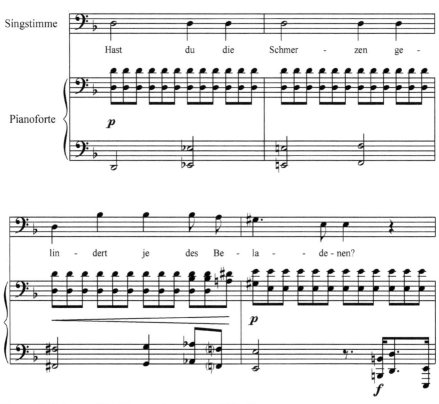

Example 3.8   Wolf *Prometheus*, mm. 137–40

Further rhythmic comparisons reveal Wolf's insights into the dynamics of power in the relationship between Prometheus and Zeus. In stanza I Reichardt and Schubert again use four equal notes for "mußt mir meine" to situate "Erde" on the downbeat, whereas Wolf prolongs "mußt" [must] to emphasize the imperative nature of the Titan's command that the earth remain his. Through similar manipulations in the next line, Reichardt and Schubert avoid stressing "doch," which thus simply means "but." (But you must leave my earth to me.) Wolf conversely stresses "doch," which then reports a fact contrary to expectations. (Despite your preconceptions, you must leave my earth to me.) The subtle difference is important: Wolf heightens the adversarial conflict; Reichardt and Schubert merely observe rhetorical detail. In stanza VII the opening line's respective treatments confirm that Wolf's nuanced declamation sharpens the clash between opponents. Schubert and Reichardt emphasize "sitz" [sit] rather than "Hier" [here], while Wolf's lengthening of "Hier" underscores Prometheus' claim upon the earth as the site of his rebellion.

Sometimes, however, Wolf's rhythmic decisions are ineffective. Three emphases of the conjunction "und" [and] delay the utterance of more vital words, and throughout stanzas IV and V, Wolf repeatedly prolongs "Hast" [have] instead of "du" [you], a peculiar pattern that depersonalizes the Titan's accusations, though its regularity is an essential trait of the incantation comprising stanzas IV–VI. Wolf occasionally corrects such problems midway through phrases with syncopation, a distinctive characteristic of his vocal lines rarely cultivated by Reichardt and Schubert, but often by Schumann.[122] In such passages weak words or syllables are lengthened, allowing their strong successors to occupy downbeats. Often adjustments entail several syllables or words, as in stanza II, where syncopated treatment of the adverb "als" [as] and the pronoun "euch" [you] causes "Götter" [gods] to fall on a downbeat (Example 3.9a). Syncopation frequently highlights especially strong words, with Wolf's setting of "Zeus" affording the first and one of the best of 15 examples (Example 3.9b). Reichardt and Schubert more typically place important words on beats or emphasize them with unusual harmonies.

Example 3.9a   Wolf *Prometheus*, mm. 56–8

Example 3.9b   Wolf *Prometheus*, mm. 23–6

Detailed consideration of Wolf's declamatory style yields two important observations. First, and surprisingly, *Prometheus* weakly illustrates a strictly Wagnerian type of declamation. Ubiquitous repeated notes are basically foreign to Wagnerian *Versmelodie*, which admittedly derives from the imitation of speech, but is ultimately grounded in melodic contours shaped by the internal rhyme scheme known as *Stabreim* [root rhyme]. Nor is widespread syncopation typical of vocal lines in Wagner's music dramas. And

---

[122]   Regarding the Schumannesque comparison, see Rita Egger, *Die Deklamationsrhythmik Hugo Wolfs in historischer Sicht* (Tutzing, 1963), pp. 25–39.

very few pitches last several beats, scarcely matching the infamously long tones that require Wagner's stentorian voices. Wolf's setting instead heavily exploits conventions of spoken theater. Second, Wolf's detailed attention to individual words and lines suggests the ode's large-scale rhetorical structure may be articulated with less clarity than Reichardt and Schubert achieved, as further analysis indicates.

Extensive musical repetition creates a broad, six-part formal design represented schematically as Introduction[A]+ABA'C + Coda[A] (Table 3.3). All the recurrent material appears in the piano introduction, which consists of two parts. The first, as critics universally agree, depicts Zeus' impending thunderstorm with tremolos, a descending chromatic bass line, an ascending triadic soprano line, and chords that erupt in dotted rhythms at the ascent's climax.[123] The second comprises bare octaves that rise and fall chromatically, often embellish strong beats with trills and double-dotted notes, and yield to chords on the fourth beats of most measures. Both accompany the declamation of stanza I, where the tremolos explicitly evoke the storm (stanza Ia) and the bare octaves support the command for Zeus to strike mountaintops (stanza Ib). New material (stanza Ic) appropriately separates heavenly and earthly domains: slowly

Table 3.3   Episodic Structure of Wolf's Prometheus

Stanza	Episode's Features	Markings
A		
Introduction 1	Tremolos, then dotted chords Upper voice arpeggiates Inner voices sustain pedal points Bass descends chromatically	Groß, kraftvoll und gemessen
Introduction 2	Scalewise octaves, trills Chordal punctuation	
A		
Ia, lines 1–2	= Introduction 1, recitative	
Ib, lines 3–5	= Introduction 2, recitative	
Ic, lines 6–11	Sustained chords alternate with ascending scalewise octaves in dotted rhythms, recitative	
B		III, line 24,
II–III	Lyrical lament, scalewise vocal line Appoggiaturas in upper voice Chromatic bass ascends, descends	mit immer gesteigerterm Ausdruck, piano codetta, immer beschleunigend

---

[123]   Rolland, p. 192; Walker, p. 250; Eric Sams, *The Songs of Hugo Wolf* (London, 1983), p. 15; Kramer, "Hugo Wolf," p. 200.

A′   Tempo wie zu Anfang

IVa, lines 28–31	= Stanza Ia
IVb, lines 32–6	Recitative
	Soprano line ascends,
	descends chromatically,
	then changes to neighbor tones
	Sustained chords, then tremolos
Va, line 37	= Stanza Ic

C

Vb, lines 38–45	Vocal line's repeated notes	
VI	make gradual diatonic ascent,	
	interrupted by leaps	VI, line 50,
	Chromatic bass ascends	von da ab etwas breiter
	Repeated octaves in left hand	

Coda^A   kräftig

VII	Recitative	line 56, Erstes Zeitmaß
	Homophonic chords	
	Bass descends chromatically,	
	ascends more diatonically	
	Introduction returns briefly	

---

moving chords alternate with faster ascending scales that retain the earlier octaves and dotted rhythms. Wolf accordingly observes the first stanza's rhetorical subdivisions.

The next two stanzas, however, form one unit (B) and thus fail to distinguish the Titan's acerbic indictment of impoverished gods (stanza II) from the narration of his childhood (stanza III). Both stanzas recall the laments Reichardt and Schubert employed. A lyrical vocal line makes repeated scalewise descents only to leap upward and begin again, as in Schubert's setting of the same passage. The accompaniment's bass line traverses extended chromatic scales as the right hand enters on appoggiaturas that resolve to further dissonances against the moving bass. A lament may viably represent divine poverty, as Schubert's depiction of the Titan's mockery demonstrates. But continuing with identical music as Prometheus narrates his sorrows scarcely differentiates between sarcasm and sincerity. Wolf consequently missed an opportunity to strengthen his portrayal of Prometheus and articulate the ode's large-scale rhetoric.

Stanzas IV through VI raise similar issues. The introduction's storm returns, first in the tonic, D minor, then a semitone higher (stanza IVa). New material then disrupts a sequential pattern that could have intensified the Titan's repetitive questioning of Zeus (stanza IVb). Instead, however, vocal recitation continues against an accompaniment that shifts from a chromatic soprano line harmonized with sustained chords to incessant alternating pitches supported by tremolos. After the introduction's second section recurs (stanza Va), the remainder of stanza V and all of stanza VI combine to produce one large section (C). Its slightly more melodic vocal line, featuring ascending diatonic scales interrupted by descending arpeggios, contrasts with the bass line's strictly scalewise motion and the right hand's repeated notes.

Wolf's stanzaic manipulations compromise the ode's rhetorical design and semantic meaning. In both earlier songs, the incantation is a discrete formal section whose pattern of positively and negatively formulated questions (AABC, AABC) is realized through Reichardt's changes in vocal tessitura in stanza IV and Schubert's textural variations in stanzas IV–VI. Wolf's rendition begins promisingly by treating the first two questions sequentially (AA, stanza IVa). But it consolidates the two succeeding queries (BC, stanza IVb) and attaches the intrusive questions of stanza Va to the previous section. The four remaining questions comprise one unit (AABC, stanzas Vb–VI), suggesting the incantation's large-scale rhetoric, so faithfully observed by Reichardt and Schubert, eluded Wolf or held little appeal for him.

Wolf's setting likewise negates meaning in several lines of stanzas IV–VI. The storm's return in stanza IV initially seems appropriate, reflecting a shift from the narration of the Titan's past to further accusations against Zeus. But the ensuing questions chronicle the growth of Prometheus from a boy who sought comfort from someone like himself into a man capable of forming an independent race. Imposing the Olympian's music on this self-actualizing process again strengthens Zeus and weakens Prometheus. Stanza VII propagates the same tendency. While it functions as a separate formal section distinguished by homorhythmic chords and a bass line that descends chromatically but rises in largely diatonic fashion, it also reprises the introduction's tremolos and eruptive dotted chords, a resurgence coinciding with "Dein" and persisting until the song's conclusion. Referring to Zeus, "Dein" [your] precipitates another outburst of the Olympian's storm precisely when Prometheus should achieve his greatest triumph. A figurative storm cloud thus hangs over the entire setting. No musical motive necessarily evokes just one textual association. Indeed, Wagnerian leitmotifs, Wolf's prime models, behave much more flexibly than Hans von Wolzogen's popular labels for them suggest. In Wolf's lied, however, recurrent material overshadows the Promethean persona's emergence and development, regardless of the tempestuous music's potential for semantic variation. The Titan's character is consequently less clearly defined than that of Zeus.

In precisely this sense Wolf's setting meets Foucault's first criterion for transgressive discourse: the opening gesture reveals the path the entire work will take as Zeus dominates Prometheus. But the introductory measures acquire force not through mere restatement, but through two tonal processes shaping the song's form. First, the initial tonic returns periodically, despite the astonishing chromaticism of intervening passages. Before digressing to remote, ambiguously defined keys, a stable D minor begins and ends three formal sections (Introduction; A, stanza I; A', stanza IV), inaugurates a fourth (C, stanza Vb), and concludes the lied (stanza VII, lines 55–7). Second, the opening gesture's bass line descends chromatically from D to G-sharp, a pitch influencing the song's tonal trajectory. G-sharp and D immediately alternate in the bass six times in five measures, and G-sharp twice furnishes starting points for bare octaves as they rise and fall chromatically in the introduction's second section. As the introduction ends, G-sharp discharges its force, acting as a dissonance above a dominant triad instead of the customary seventh, G-natural. But it quickly rises to A, the fifth scale degree, which leaps downward to D for an authentic cadence in the tonic. Identical events transpire when the introduction's material returns in stanzas I and IV. A different use of G-sharp likewise corroborates the pitch's importance in the lied as a whole (Example 3.10). In the last five measures, a relatively conventional diatonic chord progression—a rarity in the score—reinstates D minor, though the key is destabilized by a chord spelled as a dominant seventh in third inversion in E-flat major. The dominant seventh, however, is actually a German sixth chord, with G-sharp spelled enharmonically as A-flat. An interpolated diminished seventh chord spells the pitch correctly before the German sixth, now spread across a whole measure in bare octaves, announces the final cadence. The conflict between D and G-sharp, initiated at the lied's outset but resolved only in its final moments, verifies the opening gesture's potency throughout the score.

Example 3.10   Wolf *Prometheus*, mm. 170–74

Augmented sixth chords and their irregular resolutions underscore crucial words or delineate important textual junctures in settings by Reichardt and Schubert. Wolf's rendition employs the distinctive sonorities so profusely, however, that they not only define tonal limits that are crossed and recrossed, but also contribute to the uncertain context of transgressive discourse. Even in Wolf's extremely chromatic tonal language, augmented sixth chords still supply reliable syntactical markers, defining dominants in otherwise impenetrable successions of altered chords. The beginning of stanza Ib, where Wolf separates heavenly and earthly realms, furnishes a prime example (Example 3.11).

Example 3.11   Wolf *Prometheus*, mm. 39–46

The excerpt begins on a unison B-flat, itself a deceptive resolution of a prolonged dominant in D minor. Next, an augmented sixth chord reaches its implicit objective, an E-major triad, although the chord's eponymous interval appears in inner voices, thereby producing an unorthodox inversion typical of Wolf's voice leading. Taken as a dominant, the E-major triad proposes A as a new tonic, a customary goal in D minor. But it instead changes mode, creating a pungent cross relation between the voice and piano, and returns to B-flat. Similar localized tritone substitutions, to borrow Schenker's term for a large-scale tonal manipulation, occur throughout the lied, exacerbating harmonic unpredictability. A second, properly inverted augmented sixth chord then leads to a C-major triad, suggesting F as another new tonic. C, however, inaugurates a sequential statement of the four preceding measures that ends on D, which is no longer the tonic, but a dominant that resolves deceptively to E-flat. Thus Wolf's harmonies define goals only to generate others, crossing old limits and establishing new ones in uncertain contexts. The passage's linear structure is nonetheless coherent: the bass line makes a scalewise ascent from B-flat to E-flat, despite tritone interpolations.

As previous allusions suggest, ubiquitous chromatic bass lines severely destabilize Wolf's harmonic discourse, since the bass line generally defines or clarifies harmonic goals in earlier tonal music rather than obscuring them. Stanza II provides a quintessential example of a chromatic bass line engendering instability (Example 3.12). At the stanza's outset, the largely chromatic bass-line descent includes two whole steps on either side of A. Above, the voice and the right hand form an A-major triad, embellished by B-flat, an unprepared appoggiatura. If listeners construe succeeding chords by filtering out dissonances in the same way, the whole passage can be heard in A minor, as closer analysis indicates.

Example 3.12   Wolf *Prometheus*, mm. 55–61

When the A-major triad adopts the minor mode, it is no longer a dominant, but its new function remains unclear. The next chord, embellished by an appoggiatura and passing tones, is a dominant seventh on B, though its all-important third, D-sharp, arrives after the bass has moved to A, when the chord above has already become a diminished seventh rooted on the postponed D-sharp. The dominant and diminished seventh chords should elicit an E-minor triad, which is vaguely perceivable when the bass proceeds to G. Thwarting the construal of E minor as the progression's goal, however, are the vocal line's appropriation of a suspended pitch, C, from the accompaniment's right hand, and its descent to B just as the right hand's E moves to D-sharp. Ambiguity escalates on the word "als," where the voice and right hand produce another dominant seventh on B, in conflict with the bass line's sustained G. The seventh chord is nonetheless redefined clearly when the bass reaches F-sharp. Thus the bass line's non-chromatic segment connects two dominant seventh chords with roots on B, and the intervening chords are merely passing sonorities.

When the bass line reaches F-natural, the previous chord's A and D-sharp linger respectively in the vocal line and listeners' ears, defining an augmented sixth chord that resolves to E. (Again auditors must retain the singer's G-sharp longer than the notation indicates.) The progression is briefly and retrospectively viable in A minor, comprising a first-inversion tonic triad above the bass line's C, a tonicization of the dominant, E, prolonged as the bass passes from B to F-sharp, an augmented sixth chord on F-natural, and a half cadence on E. Wolf's practices—localized "tritone substitutions," spelling, inverting, and resolving augmented sixth chords irregularly, and obscuring harmonic intelligibility with dissonance—create a rarefied harmonic context of post-Wagnerian uncertainty and instability that accords perfectly with Foucault's theories.

Repetitive and intonational schemes that ensure an incantation's efficacy and satisfy Foucault's last transgressive condition, while totally absent from Wolf's fractured setting of stanzas IV and Va, are partially realized in stanzas Vb and VI. Of four questions (AABC), the first two articulate a previously noted sequence, presenting the same material at two pitch levels, and hence initiate a pattern. The third query thwarts strict sequential expectations, but its vocal line continues to climb, and its increasingly animated accompaniment replaces brief outbursts of dotted rhythms with longer eruptions of arpeggiated triplets. In the fourth question (stanza VI), the initially lower vocal tessitura declines further, and the accompaniment, though active almost until the incantation concludes, ultimately substitutes sustained pitches for triplets. Voice and piano accordingly approximate the three-stage intensification and release of Goethe's textual arc.

Finally, Wolf's rejection of Schenkerian linear norms seems predictable. His contempt for orthodoxy precipitated his expulsion from the Vienna Conservatory, he resented Brahms's advice regarding counterpoint lessons, and he was a devoted Wagnerite. His works thus typically disclose elaborate Schenkerian middle grounds, but not fundamental background structures. Wolf's tonal procedures nonetheless greatly differ from those of Schubert. As previously outlined, Schubert's setting initially obscures any sense of one key, temporarily stabilizes tonality, indulges in discursive, essentially atonal harmony, and ends in a foreign key. In Wolf's version, however, D minor is clearly defined at the outset, returns periodically, and reinforces the conclusion (Example 3.13). Moreover, the dominant anticipates every tonic recurrence, suggesting a semblance of conventional tonal relations that surprisingly embody Schenker's broadest principles: one of the dominant's many bass arpeggiations supports a vaguely perceivable descent in the soprano line, which begins on the third scale degree, passes to the second as stanza III begins, and reaches the tonic through a voice exchange spanning stanzas VI and VII.

Example 3.13   Voice Leading in Wolf's *Prometheus*

Nevertheless, Wolf's pervasive surface chromaticism and fractured registration effectively conceal the song's broad linear structures. Dominants, for example, rarely receive conventional tonicization or resolve directly to the tonic, but instead usually participate in the bass line's ongoing chromatic ascents and descents, as stanza II illustrates (Example 3.12). Framed by tonic-dominant progressions, the excerpt otherwise features parallel chromatic voices moving at slightly different rates. The fifth scale degree's intervening occurrences in the bass line (mm. 56, 61) function as passing tones in protracted descents and ascents, not true dominants. Chromatic parallelism admittedly elaborates the dominant as the stanza ends. But an E-major triad (m. 58) is difficult to perceive as a secondary dominant of A, since it serves primarily as a fulcrum in the bass line's almost entirely chromatic arc, and ten extremely chromatic measures separate it from the true dominant. No other passage approaches even this suspect degree of conventional tonal relations, suggesting orthodox linearity played a limited role in Wolf's progressive agenda. In the sense that Wolf probably regarded his unconventional linear techniques as departures from traditional methods, they may be considered elements of transgressive discourse in his *Prometheus*.

Wolf's ardent Wagnerism, encouraged by early contact with Wagner himself, developed into a virulent critical orientation and still colors assessments of his life's work. But his opinion that the ode needed to await the post-Wagnerian era to be set in Goethe's spirit—as Schubert's "unsuccessful" attempt purportedly demonstrated—requires cautious evaluation. Wolf undeniably surpassed his predecessors in achieving a grand, quasi-Wagnerian scale, and his stormy figuration and violent eruptions convincingly reflect Zeus' power and the Titan's volatility. But other Wagnerian affinities are weak. The declamatory styles of both composers, for example, derive from principles of speech, but otherwise differ substantially. Wolf's ubiquitous repeated notes, use of relative pitch to emphasize individual words or differentiate phrases, and idiosyncratically deployed syncopation, though occasionally found in Wagner's operas, contrast sharply with Wagner's more characteristically supple lines. Wolf's declamation nevertheless heightens the conflict between Prometheus and Zeus, intensifying the Titan's accusations through melodic inflections and rhythmic emphases.

Notwithstanding Wolf's egotism, his treatment of large-scale rhetoric indicates he, not Schubert, misunderstood Goethe's text: the homogeneous setting of stanzas II and III fails to distinguish between parodied and sincere laments, and Zeus' recurrent music overshadows pivotal moments in the Titan's evolution into an independent creator, especially the ode's defiant conclusion. Moreover, the song's large-scale formal repetition hardly resembles Wagner's leitmotivic technique, with its intricate web of through-composed relationships, though this utter dissimilarity has not stifled comparisons between Zeus' storm and passages of ascending scales with Wotanesque analogues in Wagner's *Ring*.[124] A genuinely post-Wagnerian trait of Wolf's *Prometheus*, however, is its densely chromatic harmony, which exploits augmented sixth chords, tritone relations, chromatic bass lines, and obscuring dissonances to destabilize tonality. Prometheus scarcely emerges as an unequivocal champion in Wolf's lied, but he incontestably rebels with intensity unmatched in the settings of Reichardt and Schubert. In doing so, Wolf's Titan defines transgression not as "a site beyond limits, but work on them."

Goethe's *Prometheus* and its three settings have generally elicited similar critical responses. The ode's numerous exegetes have focused primarily on its theme of metaphysical rebellion and its revolutionary language's "expressive immediacy," usually overlooking its temporal, narrative, and rhetorical coherencies. Musical commentators have likewise typically emphasized broad characterization or local harmonic details while neglecting comprehensive formal design. Each song's structure is nonetheless important because it illuminates aesthetic decisions and facets of the myth that drew each composer's attention.

---

[124]   Carner, p. 39; Sams, p. 20.

Reichardt, cultivating tonal, metric, and textural contrasts, preserved the ode's temporal, narrative, and rhetorical organization, thereby making "the given content of a poem more significant and expressive through its musical setting." Within a lucid framework, he underscored crucial or audacious words with harmonies exceeding the early nineteenth-century lied's conservative generic context. Schubert probably modeled his setting on his predecessor's, as numerous "striking similarities" illustrate. But he also amplified Reichardt's formal and harmonic gestures and manipulated Goethe's text to develop central points. The gods are impoverished, for example, because they lack terrestrial authority, not because they exact tribute from children and beggars through fear and foolish hope, as Schubert's stanzaic fusion indicates. Within stanzas, Schubert inserted formal subdivisions, adopted specific affects, and repeated individual lines, mocking the gods with an ironic lament, reducing the burdens of the Titan's childhood, realizing the incantation's complex rhetoric, and underscoring creative autonomy. Wolf's claims regarding Schubert's misinterpretation of Goethe and the ode's need to await the post-Wagnerian era may reflect his progressive critical stance. But Wolf actually distorted Goethe's meaning in a six-part form that fails to differentiate between sincere and sarcastic laments and grants Zeus supremacy over Prometheus. Wolf apparently took keener interest in escalating the conflict between the two principals, as his accentuation of particular words with specifically theatrical declamatory practices often affirms.

All three lieder share two common traits: vocal declamation and extravagant harmonies. The first differs noticeably among settings: Reichardt observes the ode's detailed rhetoric, placing rests and differentiating cadences at the ends of lines and stanzas; Schubert predictably embraces greater lyricism; and Wolf's theatrical recitative exploits repeated notes, lengthened pitches, and stylized inflections. The second is evident in modal ambiguity, irregularly resolved augmented sixth chords, pervasive dissonance, interrupted tonal processes, and sequences. Such harmonic content embodies Foucault's theories of transgression, which offer criteria for analyzing introductory gestures that forecast trajectories in every song, the arousal and denial of listeners' expectations as equivalents to establishing and violating limits, ambiguous tonal contexts as cognates for discursive language, and an incantation's repetitive and intonational requirements.

Reichardt, Schubert, and Wolf thus matched the audacious thematic and literary audacities of Goethe's ode, an incarnation of the *Sturm und Drang* revolt and the chief harbinger of a new, romantic approach to Prometheus that elevated suffering, defiance, and triumph in creative solitude over eighteenth-century notions of the Titan as the benefactor of a mankind awakened from idyllic naïveté. Suffering, defiance, and triumph resonate in the legend's later nineteenth-century representations, attesting to Goethe's potent influence.

Chapter 4

Toward a Philosophy of History: Liszt's Prometheus Music

In 1848 Franz Liszt renounced his unprecedented career as a virtuoso pianist to become "kapellmeister in extraordinary service" at the Weimar court in provincial eastern Germany.[1] His patron, Grand Duke Carl Alexander, charged him with restoring the city's status during the German Enlightenment, when its citizens included Goethe, Schiller, Wieland, and Herder. Annual progress toward this goal began in August 1849, when the Thuringian hamlet's lavish celebration of the centennial of Goethe's birth garnered national attention. The following summer another festival acknowledged Herder's philosophical and literary contributions to the Golden Age of Weimar Classicism. Liszt composed music for both occasions. For the Goethe Jubilee, he provided a stately march to accompany a civic procession and an overture to the play *Torquato Tasso*. In 1850 he received one of his Weimar tenure's most demanding commissions: he was to write incidental music for Herder's *Der entfesselte Prometheus*, a set of 13 mythological scenes produced as a play with costumes, scenery, and limited stage action (Figure 4.1).

The works associated with both festivals engrossed Liszt for decades. In 1856 he published greatly revised versions of the overtures to Goethe's play and Herder's scenes as symphonic poems, a new genre intended to establish his reputation as an orchestral composer. Eight choruses that originally punctuated Herder's scenes required adaptation for concert performance, a task occupying Liszt from 1856 to 1861, when C.F. Kahnt published the first printed score, and again from the late 1860s to 1876, when Kahnt issued a revised edition. Surviving polemic criticism in ongoing campaigns between progressive and conservative musical factions, the choruses ultimately became staples on the programs of the Allgemeiner deutscher Musikverein, a leading nineteenth-century concert society.

Despite the attention Liszt showered on his Promethean incidental music, it is not especially well known today. It nonetheless deserves attention because it raises issues that deeply interested Liszt and his contemporaries. First, the scenes illustrate the central tenet of Herder's philosophy of history, *Humanität*, its fulfillment in an organic national group, and its transformation into a universal state—a process reflected in Liszt's music, especially the choruses. Second, the symphonic poem participates in the contemporary dialectics of sonata form, infusing abstract, absolute music with extramusical, programmatic meaning, as demonstrated by the application of semantic theory, an analytical mode productively adopted in recent studies of

---

[1]   The memorandum concerning Liszt's appointment is reprinted in Lina Ramann, *Franz Liszt als Künstler und Mensch* (3 vols, Leipzig, 1880–94), vol. 2, p. 197.

other Lisztian compositions. And third, Liszt's reactions to Herder's scenes, as documented by his correspondence and decision to replace them with another text, illuminate his insights into the Prometheus myth.

„Der entfeffelte Prometheus"
von G. v. Herder, Mufik von Dr. F. Lifzt

Am Vorabend der Herderfeier aufgeführt 1850

Deutfches Nationaltheater   Phot. Fr. Baltl

Figure 4.1   Franz Xaver Vältl, The Staging of Herder's *Der entfesselte Prometheus*

Johann Gottfried Herder (1744–1803), one of the German Enlightenment's preeminent philosophers, critics, folklorists, and linguists, received formal schooling only because a Russian army surgeon sponsored his education in exchange for the precocious teenager's translation of a medical treatise, an opportunity beyond the means of his father, a weaver. As a theology student in Königsberg, Herder encountered two teachers who directly influenced his intellectual development. Emmanuel Kant's lectures on natural science and geography inspired Herder's later cultivation of organic models and interest in the physical environment, factors shaping his concept of *Humanität*.[2] Johann Georg Hamann, a mystic and, like Herder, a pietist, intensified his pupil's hostility toward the French Enlightenment, an attitude likewise affecting his views of culture and nation.

From 1764 to 1775 Herder worked as a preacher, first in Riga, a self-governing liberal city, then at the Bückeburg court. During this productive period he wrote seminal essays on German literature, art, and folklore, earning national repute as a scholar. He was accordingly nominated for a post at the University of Göttingen, but

---

    [2]   Robert Reinhold Ergang, *Herder and the Foundations of German Nationalism* (New York, 1931), pp. 37–8.

during protracted negotiations, Goethe secured Herder's employment as the Weimar court's chief pastor, preacher, and superintendent of the ecclesiastical department.

Under the reign of Anna Amalia and Carl August, the Weimar court fostered liberal politics and an atmosphere of dynamic intellectualism. Their policies of religious tolerance, freedom of the press, and educational reform promoted their subjects' material welfare, while their patronage of Wieland, Goethe, Herder, and later, Schiller ushered in the age known as Weimar Classicism.[3] Herder flourished in this milieu, but distanced himself from Goethe and Schiller, largely because of differences in aesthetics, though Herder's irascibility doubtless exacerbated tensions. Such distractions scarcely impeded Herder from developing his theory of historical evolution—his most influential contribution to the history of ideas—in his best-known treatises, the *Ideen zur Philosophie der Geschichte der Menschheit* (1784–91) and the *Briefe zu Beförderung der Humanität* (1793–7).[4] Comparably influential during and after his lifetime were his investigations of language, as formulated in his *Abhandlung über den Ursprung der Sprache* (1772) and *Vom Geist der Ebräischen Poesie* (1782–3). All three issues—aesthetics, historical evolution, and language—are integral to an understanding of Herder's conception of myth and the Prometheus legend.

The doctrine that pervaded Herder's philosophy of history was *Humanität*, a term eluding precise definition. Referring to neither mankind (the human population at any point in history) nor humaneness (unconditional love for mankind),[5] it instead embodied humanity's ultimate goal, achieved only through conscious developmental processes.[6] As a dynamic agent compelling mankind to strive for progress and perfection,[7] it occupied the central position in Herder's social philosophy: "In all states, in all societies, man … could aim at nothing better than *Humanität*, whatever ideas he may have formed of it."[8] Herder thus affirmed his relativism, acknowledging different societies could form diverse notions of *Humanität*.

Indeed, the "fullest development and most complete expression of man's peculiar virtues and talents," as Herder once formulated his principle, lie in the group, not the individual.[9] Moreover, the ideal group for realizing mankind's potential is the nation,[10] an "integral and indestructible unit" that allows the group to express its "characteristic traits" and achieve its "fullest possibilities."[11] The nation is likewise the most natural group, providing it results from each group's unique circumstances, not an external force's imposition, as in traditional governments.[12]

---

[3]   F.M. Barnard, *Herder's Social and Political Thought* (Oxford, 1965), p. 4.

[4]   Ibid., pp. 109–27.

[5]   Johann Gottfried Herder, *Herders Sämmtliche Werke* [henceforward: HSW], ed. Bernhard Suphan (33 vols, Berlin, 1877–1913), vol. 17, p. 137.

[6]   HSW, vol. 13, p. 196; vol. 17, p. 138.

[7]   HSW, vol. 5, p. 98; vol. 8, p. 230; vol. 14, p. 205; vol. 15, p. 263; vol. 16, p. 567; vol. 17, p. 27.

[8]   HSW, vol. 14, p. 208.

[9]   HSW, vol. 1, p. 366; vol. 8, p. 194; vol. 11, p. 238; vol. 13, pp. 159, 343, 346; vol. 14, pp. 83–4.

[10]   HSW, vol. 5, pp. 425, 502–9; vol. 9, pp. 350–52; vol. 14, p. 227.

[11]   HSW, vol. 5, p. 502; see also HSW, vol. 1, p. 366; vol. 8, p. 194; vol. 9, p. 238.

[12]   Ergang, p. 247; Barnard, p. xviii.

Herder's appeal to a natural paradigm reflects a mode of organicist thought that pervaded eighteenth-century arts and letters, owing largely to the burgeoning prestige of the natural sciences, especially biology.[13] Herder's application of organic theories to nations accordingly has ample precedents in Rousseau's "natural theology" and Justus Möser's writings.[14] But unlike Rousseau, who maintained culture's corruption of mankind's "primitive" condition could be remedied only by promoting the individual's innate talents, Herder argued "national plants" and "national animals" obeyed the same evolutionary laws as other organisms.[15] They could therefore "change from bad to good, from good to better and best, from best to less good, from less good to bad, ... each growing, producing buds, blossoming, and withering."[16] Most significantly, in describing societies as groups of mutually connected and closely interacting organisms, Herder replaced the French Enlightenment's mechanistic construct of a world comprised of dynastic states with one consisting of "organic" nations, each distinguished by self-determined "characteristic traits."[17]

Nature, however, offered Herder more than metaphorical language and archetypes for social development: it was the primary differentiating factor in human evolution. As Herder repeatedly maintained, man was "no independent substance," but was "connected with and changed by every element of nature."[18] Mountains and oceans, for example, "determined national borders" and "altered the whole current of culture,"[19] ultimately deciding "the inclinations and often the destiny of nationalities."[20] Nature exerted this power, Herder explained, by inciting man to acquire knowledge, with each environment posing problems and prompting unique solutions that shaped an indigenous population's perception of its world.[21]

Essential though nature was to Herder's philosophy of history, it constituted merely one aspect of a broader concept, *Klima*. Translated literally as climate, the term encompasses many elements involved in a culture's formation,[22] two of which directly concern Herder's views of nation, myth, and the Prometheus legend. *Bildung* [education] patently affects mankind's development, as Herder observed: "men are formed only by education, instruction, and permanent example."[23] It also helps define national characteristics, with Chinese and Hebrew traditions of rote memorization providing historically ineffective models.[24] Similar misgivings about

---

[13]   Barnard, p. xviii.

[14]   Regarding parallels between Herder and Rousseau, see Hans M. Wolff, "Der junge Herder und die Entwicklungsidee Rousseaus," *Publications of the Modern Language Association of America*, 57 (1942): 753–839. Regarding Möser's writings as precedents for Herder's organicism, see Barnard, p. 24.

[15]   HSW, vol. 13, p. 384 (animals); vol. 14, p. 8 (plants).

[16]   HSW, vol. 1, pp. 151–2.

[17]   HSW, vol. 14, pp. 83–4.

[18]   HSW, vol. 13, p. 399.

[19]   HSW, vol. 14, p. 92; vol. 13, pp. 37–42; vol. 14, pp. 32, 47.

[20]   HSW, vol. 5, p. 527.

[21]   HSW, vol. 13, pp. 37–42; vol. 14, pp. 32, 47.

[22]   HSW, vol. 13, pp. 253–61.

[23]   HSW, vol. 14, p. 34.

[24]   HSW, vol. 14, pp. 10, 67–76; see also vol. 5, p. 439.

German education informed Herder's deferral of "direct democracy" and "majority rule" as viable governmental methods until higher standards prevailed.[25]

Language, another facet of *Klima*, defined "the basic unit of any social or political organization," expressed characteristic traits,[26] and supplied the vehicle for gaining a clear understanding of "the world in which [man] lives, his employment and relations, and their means and purposes."[27] Herder again chided Germans for not recognizing a uniform national language "as the organ of social activity and cooperation, as the bond of social classes, as a means for their integration."[28] Transcending the scope of earlier linguistic reformers who merely sought to purge foreign accretions from the written language, adopt one provincial dialect as a national standard, or reconcile grammar with French linguistic theories,[29] Herder advocated German-language instruction in all schools and subjects, including the Latin-dominated sciences, policies he implemented in Bückeburg and Weimar.[30] Of marginal relevance to *Der entfesselte Prometheus*, Herder's ideas on language decisively shaped his nineteenth-century reputation, influencing Humboldt's educational reforms in Prussia, Fichte's patriotic *Reden an die deutsche Nation*, and Hegel's predication of statehood on an identity of language and nation.

Herder's linguistic philosophy spawned an equally momentous corollary: folk songs and poems—the "archives of a nationality," "imprints of the national soul," and "living voice of nationalities, nay, even of humanity itself"—should form the basis of national literatures.[31] In Germany this notion was so innovative Herder needed to coin new terms (*Volkslied*, *Volkspoesie*, and others) for expressing a nation's unity with its characteristic literature.[32] Urging his compatriots to collect, publish, and study folk poems, he set an example with his *Stimmen der Völker in Liedern* (1778–9), the first such anthology in Germany.[33] Containing only 20 selections, it profoundly influenced German romanticism and inspired similar work throughout Eastern Europe and Scandinavia.[34]

The synthesis of language, literature, and nation also incited political activism. Herder never produced a coherent nationalist doctrine, but he occasionally addressed German unity's overwhelming obstacles, including the Holy Roman Empire's

---

[25]   HSW, vol. 17, pp. 96, 127; vol. 18, pp. 331–2.

[26]   HSW, vol. 1, p. 1; see also vol. 1, pp. 167, 272; vol. 2, p. 19; vol. 5, pp. 123–34. Herder's views are discussed in J.H. Hayes, "Contribution of Herder to the Doctrine of Nationalism," *American Historical Review*, 32 (1927): 720.

[27]   HSW, vol. 17, p. 2.

[28]   HSW, vol. 16, p. 607; vol. 18, p. 384.

[29]   Ergang, pp. 140–45.

[30]   HSW, vol. 1, p. 7. Regarding Herder's local policies, see Ergang, p. 166.

[31]   The three phrases are respectively drawn from HSW, vol. 9, p. 532; vol. 3, p. 29; vol. 24, p. 266.

[32]   Joseph Edward Wackernell, "Das deutsche Volkslied," *Acta Germanica*, 7 (1911): 305. See also HSW, vol. 5, pp. 164, 174; vol. 1, p. 266; vol. 39, p. 263; vol. 25, p. 129.

[33]   HSW, vol. 9, p. 526.

[34]   Ergang, pp. 260–62. See also Jan Máchal, "Die böhmische Literatur," Friedrich Riedl, "Die ungarische Literatur," and Emil Setälä, "Die finnische Literatur," all in Paul Hinneberg (ed.), *Die osteuropäischen Literaturen und die slawischen Sprachen* (Berlin, 1908), pp. 190, 284–5, 320.

disintegration during the Thirty Years War, class divisions, restrictions on political organizations and free speech, and rampant "Gaulomania," whereby the aristocracy and bourgeoisie embraced French culture.[35] For Herder these impediments thwarted not only Germany's unification, but also the achievement of the nation's fullest potential, its *Humanität*.[36] He accordingly praised those who promoted "the unity of the territories of Germany through writings, manufactures, and institutions," partly because they would "facilitate the cooperation and mutual recognition of ... diverse powers," but more importantly because they would "bind the provinces of Germany with spiritual and hence with the strongest ties."[37]

Of more concrete political impact, however, were Herder's calls for a single national capital, an academy to foster national awareness, and harmony between Protestants and Catholics, who should "work together for the common good, as members of one nationality and speech."[38] Herder thus became known as an ardent German nationalist, "the father of the fatherland," "the only truly genuine German," and "an original German mind."[39] His image and ideas exerted tremendous influence well into the nineteenth century, inspiring political autonomy's advocates in Germany, the Slavic lands, Russia, *Risorgimento* Italy, and—most notably with respect to Liszt's life and music—Hungary, where patriots mounted ill-fated campaigns for independence from Austria during the late 1840s.[40]

Notwithstanding his reputation, overtly political comments, and far-reaching influence, Herder ultimately embraced universalism over nationalism. Politics served only to advance the development of a nation's culture, the "flower of its existence."[41] Distinct national cultures were, in turn, components within the whole of human civilization, as Herder pointedly declared: "the multifarious variety ... on our earth is astonishing; but even more astonishing is the unity that pervades this inconceivable variety."[42] He propounded his cultural ideal—diverse national groups within a unified humanity—in criticizing the French Enlightenment's cosmopolitanism:

---

[35]   Barnard, p. 62.

[36]   HSW, vol. 23, pp. 160–61; see also, vol. 18, p. 115.

[37]   HSW, vol. 17, p. 26.

[38]   Regarding Herder's calls for one capital, an academy, and religious tolerance, see HSW, vol. 1, pp. 141, 249, 290; vol. 16, pp. 600–16; vol. 11, p. 204.

[39]   Heinrich Düntzer and Ferdinand Gottfried von Herder (eds), *Von und an Herder: Ungedruckte Briefe aus Herders Nachlass* (2 vols, Leipzig, 1861–2), vol. 1, pp. 130, 159; Düntzer and F.G. von Herder (eds), *Aus Herders Nachlass* (3 vols, Frankfurt, 1856–7), vol. 2, p. 330; Arthur Jonetz, *Über Herders nationale Gesinnung* (Brieg, 1895), p. 3.

[40]   Ergang, pp. 249–60; Barnard, pp. 36, 105. Herder's comments regarding Slavic lands and Hungary appear in HSW, vol. 14, pp. 280, 269. Regarding his influence in Russia, see Rolf Schierenberg, *Der politische Herder: Ein Staatswissenschaftlicher Versuch* (Graz, 1932), pp. 65–92. Giuseppe Mazzini acknowledged his debt to Herder in "On the Genius and Tendency of the Writings of Thomas Carlyle," in *Life and Writings of Joseph Mazzini* (6 vols, London, 1891), vol. 4, p. 57.

[41]   HSW, vol. 14, p. 147.

[42]   HSW, vol. 13, p. 25.

The wise men of the *Aufklärung* apparently do not consider that man can and must be modified in a thousand different ways according to the earth's structure, ... but that under the husk, changed so variously, the same essence of nature and happiness always can be—and in accordance with human expectations, always must be—preserved.[43]

Herder's universalism thus opposes a narrow form of nationalism that emerged midway through the nineteenth century, when earlier democratic-revolutionary campaigns yielded to conservative or reactionary movements promoting self-centered, closed societies. It resounded in the internationalism of only a few writers, Giuseppe Mazzini in Italy, Jules Michelet in France, and Adam Mickiewicz in Poland.[44] Universalism is nonetheless paramount in Herder's approach to Prometheus, as are the principles of *Humanität*, organicism, *Klima*, and *Bildung*.

Der entfesselte Prometheus suffers gross neglect, even among Herder scholars, who invariably consider it weak when invoking aesthetic criteria of drama. Maurice Tresch deems it a pale imitation of Aeschylus; Amand Treutler complains it is neither good drama nor effective satire; and Robert T. Clark contends the "uniformly pedestrian" play lacks "qualities that distinguish poetry from scholarship."[45] But Herder never intended it to be judged by such standards, as he disclosed in a letter to fellow German nationalist J.W.L. Gleim:

> These scenes should not compete with Aeschylus; they are not called a drama. For who could rob this mighty poet of Melpomene's club and hurl it forth with his power? And who in our time would even venture to portray ... Prometheus as Aeschylus represents him?[46]

The answer to these rhetorical questions was Goethe, whose ode depicts an Aeschylean Titan.[47] Such pointed interrogatives fittingly appeared in Herder's *Adrastea*, a journal that published *Der entfesselte Prometheus*, prefaced by the letter to Gleim, in 1802.

Aptly named for the Greek goddess of historical destiny, the *Adrastea* was a pulpit from which Herder reviewed the eighteenth century, expounded his philosophy of history, and criticized the aesthetics of Goethe and Schiller. Herder objected chiefly to Goethe's reactionary sentiments, expressed through ever-growing veneration of the ancien régime and articulated explicitly in the drama *Palaeophron und Neoterpe*.[48] But more integral to an understanding of the scenes is that Herder's relativism fundamentally opposed Goethe's increasingly pronounced devotion to Greek art as an absolute aesthetic ideal and Schiller's reflective neo-Hellenism, both of which

---

[43] HSW, vol. 5, p. 558.

[44] Hans Kohn, "Nationalism," in *Dictionary of the History of Ideas*, ed. Philip P. Wiener (5 vols, New York, 1973), vol. 3, p. 328.

[45] Maurice Tresch, "Prométhée et sa race, Satan, Caïn et Faust dans la poésie," *Programme, Ecole industrielle et commerciale de Luxembourg* (Luxembourg, 1908–9), p. 29, quoted in Trousson, vol. 1, p. 277; Amand Treutler, *Herders dramatische Dichtungen* (Stuttgart, 1915), p. 95; Robert T. Clark, *Herder: His Life and Thought* (Berkeley, 1955), p. 428.

[46] HSW, vol. 28, p. 329.

[47] See Chapter 3, pp. 93–8.

[48] Herder's play *Aeon und Aeonis* blatantly satirizes Goethe's drama. See HSW, vol. 28, pp. 247–63.

deprived myth of material significance, reducing it to a literary corpus that was to be appreciated only for its aesthetic worth.

In sharpest contrast, Herder considered myths keys to the basic structure of human consciousness, the spontaneous outgrowth of human thought, and not merely well-crafted stories.[49] General truths could be perceived by analyzing mythological ideas, images, and characters, as he argued in his influential essay *Vom neueren Gebrauch der Mythologie*.[50] Crucial to Herder's ideology is that myth possessed a moral force, a tangible power capable of granting his era a new poetic, subjective vision of the world and life.[51] Myths consequently transcended poetics to acquire material significance; they were not the mere aesthetic objects Goethe and Schiller admired. Herder thus intended *Der entfesselte Prometheus* not for theatrical production, but rather as a vehicle for criticizing Weimar's luminaries and reaffirming myth's essential role in his philosophy of history. A synopsis of the scenes facilitates an appraisal of their primary themes, which emphatically reinforce Herder's ideals (Table 4.1).[52]

Table 4.1   A Synopsis of Herder's *Der entfesselte Prometheus*, 13 Mythological Scenes

Scene	Action
1	Prometheus, bound to a cliff, contemplates his deed, awaiting one greater still.
2	Prometheus rejects the Oceanids' complaints regarding human intrusion on the seas.
3	Prometheus, addressing Oceanus, the Oceanids, and Tritons (heralds of Oceanus), foresees a Golden Age: after further struggle, mankind will alter the undersea realm's borders.
4	Prometheus takes pride in the preceding events.
5	Prometheus rejects the Dryads' complaints regarding human intrusion in their realm, the forests. Prometheus asks Gaea, the earth mother, to give mankind patience. Gaea refers to Hercules rescuing Theseus, again protesting human incursion in divine realms.
6	Prometheus hails humanity's founding upon fraternal principles.
7	Ceres, goddess of the harvest, recounts lessons she has taught mankind. Prometheus and a Chorus of Reapers praise Ceres for teaching mankind to bear their burdens.
8	A Chorus of Vintners praises Bacchus as the giver of happiness and the king of hope. Prometheus chastises Bacchus for giving mankind false hope.

---

[49]   HSW, vol. 32, pp. 68–9, 82–4.
[50]   HSW, vol. 1, p. 427.
[51]   HSW, vol. 1, p. 93.
[52]   All translated quotations of Herder's scenes derive from *Der entfesselte Prometheus, Scenen, 1802*, HSW, vol. 28, pp. 330–52.

9   Hermes, messenger of Olympus, leads a veiled figure to Prometheus, who rejects
         Pandora, endowed by the gods with false arts.

10   Prometheus awaits the hour of his destiny.
         After an earthquake opens a fissure in the cliff, a Chorus of Subterranean Voices
         narrates the victorious battle of Alcides (Hercules) against Cerberus.

11   Hercules frees Prometheus.
         A Chorus of Invisible Spirits praises Themis, a Titan identified with divine justice.

12   Themis absolves Prometheus of stealing fire from the heavens.
         Hercules recognizes the worth of perseverance.

13   Athena bids a Chorus of Muses to praise Prometheus as mankind's benefactor.

Humanität, Herder's chief doctrine, pervades the scenes, appropriately achieving clearest expression in the finale. Athena, goddess of wisdom, bids the Muses to "sing truthfully of the work of Prometheus" in attaining "pure humanity." They comply, declaring "humanity is that of heaven which blooms on earth, which men raise high to the gods, their most blessed, holiest gift."

Again a dynamic agent, *Humanität* achieves results only in due course of time. In scene 3, for example, the Oceanids predict "the Golden Age will appear on our rising tides." Prometheus concedes it will do so, but "only after a long, wild fight." He accordingly asks his mother Gaea to give mankind patience in scene 5 and requests Ceres, goddess of nature, teach men perseverance in scene 7. Hercules recognizes perseverance in scene 12 as both the means whereby Prometheus endured punishment and "the great and difficult duty of the earth dwellers." Mankind's progress toward fulfilling this task is manifested in human encroachments on three divine realms: Oceanids protest intrusions on the seas in scene 2; Dryads lament incursions in sacred forests in scene 3; and Ceres denounces the underworld's violation by Hercules in scenes 5 and 6. The goal of such progress, as Prometheus already explained in scene 1, is that "reason would flourish on earth."

Thus the scenes reiterate Herder's interpretation of the myth's basic meaning, as articulated in his *Briefe zu Beförderung der Humanität*:

> Through storm and waves, over cliffs and deserts, I came to where Prometheus, the old friend of humanity, sat … and he spoke: "… I knew what I had given men with my gift. … With light, which I fetched for them from Olympus, they had everything. Idle creatures, so long as they went in twilight, have now finally found the resource that lay within them: reason."[53]

Clearly Herder conceptualized reason as a balance of fully developed faculties acquired through historical struggle, not the innate, all-powerful force that inspired the French Enlightenment.

Achieving *Humanität* is the national group's duty in Herder's global philosophy, but universalism eclipses nationalism in his later works, including *Der entfesselte Prometheus*. The objective's attainment, however, is still the function of a group, not

---

53   HSW, vol. 17, p. 112.

an individual, as Herder invariably indicates by referring to *Menschheit* [mankind], *Volk* [people or nation], *Geschlecht* [race], or *Gesellschaft* [society]. Indeed, mortals appear as groups of reapers and vintners, but individuals are absent, with two exceptions. As Prometheus learns in scene 5, Alcides (the name Hercules uses until he earns immortality) will soon rescue his friend Theseus from the underworld. Prometheus rejoices, for he has long awaited this "greatest deed," the founding of humanity on fraternal principles, an attitude his ensuing monologue succinctly formulates: "On this cornerstone I form my race, on friendship and brotherhood."

A fraternal group, though not a nation, still requires characteristic traits. Beyond patience and perseverance, bravery is indispensable, since "men venture much" in seeking to develop, to "grow and wither like cedars and flowers," as Ceres observes in scene 5. Men must also eschew deceit, as Prometheus demonstrates in scene 9 by rejecting Pandora's "sweet power to beguile." And like a nation, the fraternity of mankind is a natural condition that force cannot impose: in scene 9 Prometheus fears "tyrants will trample upon the peaceful industrious people, subdue them, and make them serfs of the sod." But in scene 13 his anxiety proves unfounded when Themis, goddess of justice, denounces the Olympians for taking power "through force and cruel savage law."

Der entfesselte Prometheus matches Herder's philosophical writings in cultivating natural models. Organic metaphors permeate the scenes, as Ceres illustrated by equating mankind's development with the growth and withering of cedars and flowers. Further examples occur in scene 3, where Prometheus claims men will populate the waves like "fish in countless schools," and in scene 5, where he predicts his race will transform "mire, cliffs, and wilderness" into "a garden." Scene 11 fulfills his prophecy when an olive tree, the emblem of Athena's wisdom, sprouts from the rock where he was chained, signifying his deliverance and his people's victory. Finally, fruit symbolizes the harvest mankind will reap after attaining full development (scene 3), the product of foresight and diligence (scene 7), and human wisdom and love, gifts mankind offers Prometheus as thanks for his work (scene 13).

Furnishing more than linguistic images, nature again affects human development, thus reinforcing a vital precept of *Klima*. In scene 3 Prometheus notes the Oceanids benefit mankind with gifts of rain and sun, despite their protests against human intrusion on the seas. Reapers thank Ceres in scene 7 for "wonderful seedlings, the richness of harvests, and refreshing bread." And in scene 8 Bacchus calls his grape vine "the stem of life that laboriously supports mortals," but Prometheus fears wine will induce confusion, madness, rage, sensual pleasure, quarreling, and "most dangerous of all, false hope." Boons or vices, nature's gifts influence humanity's moral evolution.

Herder's scenes likewise emphasize *Bildung*, another essential aspect of *Klima*. As noted, mankind learned perseverance from Ceres, who in scene 7 relates she also "taught [men] to sow and grow precious seed, weaning them of blood and roaming." To strengthen the new agrarian society, Ceres revealed how to mark the seasons and build houses, while Gaea tutored men in animal husbandry, as Prometheus observes in scene 5. Thus the highly allegorical scenes unambiguously impart Herder's message: "men are formed only by education, instruction, and permanent example."

Language and literature, a nation's foremost characteristic traits, are lesser concerns amid pervasive universalism. Indeed, the scenes do not directly address language, literature, or nationalism per se, though they allude to German political unity. In scene

3 Prometheus predicts men will "change the borders" of Oceanus' kingdom, rejoining "what was once divided." Although Herder never advocated the Holy Roman Empire's restoration, he urged German provinces to form an alliance with one capital, establish a patriotic academy, and end religious factionalism. The topic resurfaces in scene 12, wherein mankind—embodied in a multi-generational "tribe" of Perseus—unites in admiring the eternal youth and bravery of the newly deified Hercules.

An emphasis of universalism over nationalism accords with the ersatz drama's completion late in Herder's life, when he promoted mankind's unity within diverse nations. Scene 3, devoted largely to the subject, begins as Oceanus claims the sea as his "untouchable, sacred realm." Prometheus retorts: "In the earth's wide realms, everything belongs to everyone. Above, below, rules the same law: 'Whatever lives and works, works one for another.'" Moreover, as the Titan warns, the sea once divided men but will ultimately unite them, with Oceanus serving as "the peace maker between all peoples." Prometheus concludes by predicting the seas will become "a bond among all the world's nations," a decree inciting the Oceanids and Tritons to proclaim that common interests and freedom now rule where winds blew and waves roared, brotherhood prevails where reefs shook, and compassion triumphs where depths engulfed and storms destroyed. Herder was no utopian, but his universalism never flagged, even when couched in heavy allegory.

Herder's altruism doubtless appealed to Liszt's humanitarianism. Attending Saint-Simonian meetings in Paris during the 1830s, he supported the movement's Christian socialist doctrine, which resembled Herder's philosophy. The group's leader, Claude Henri de Rouvroy, promoted education for the lower classes, advocated a peaceful global culture, and charged artists with guiding social reform. Liszt consequently adopted the lifelong maxim, "Génie oblige."[54]

More strongly influencing Liszt's humanitarian development were the visionary principles of the Abbé Félicité de Lamennais, who heralded the July Revolution of 1830 as the "dawn of a universal republic" that would establish religious, philosophical, and scientific unity throughout Europe.[55] Meeting Lamennais in April 1834, Liszt praised the universalist sentiments of his *Paroles d'un croyant* and paid two more visits that year, while the abbé was completing his *Esquisse d'une philosophie*. One of the tract's axioms, that "the aim of art is the perfectioning of beings whose progress it expresses,"[56] resonated in Liszt's essay, *De l'avenir de la musique d'église* (1834):

> Come, then, thou glorious time, when art will unfold and complete itself in all its forms, soaring to the highest perfection, and, like a bond of fraternity, unite humanity in enchanting wonders.[57]

Liszt's convictions, obviously concordant with Herder's precepts, had practical applications. He performed humanitarian acts throughout his virtuoso career, visiting

---

54   Paul Merrick, *Revolution and Religion in the Music of Liszt* (Cambridge, 1987), p. 5; see also Eleanor Perényi, *Liszt: The Artist as Romantic Hero* (Boston, 1974), p. 101.

55   Félicité Robert de Lamennais, *Correspondance générale: Textes réunis, classés et annotés*, ed. Louis Le Guillou (9 vols, Paris, 1971–88), vol. 6, p. 752.

56   Lamennais, *Esquisse d'une philosophie* (4 vols, Paris, 1840–46), vol. 3, p. 112.

57   Ramann, *Franz Liszt*, vol. 1, p. 247.

prisons, hospitals, and asylums in response to Saint-Simonianism and playing benefit concerts that provided financial relief for striking workers in Lyons, flood survivors in Hungary, and victims of a fire in Hamburg.[58]

Liszt openly admired Herder's humanitarianism and universalism in the preface he published with *Prometheus*, the revised symphonic poem, in 1856. Beyond praising Herder as "the apostle of humanity," he subscribed to Herder's doctrine of progressive cultural evolution by recognizing "creative activity and the necessity of development" as "the loftiest destinies that the human spirit can achieve."[59] Liszt also mentioned "a liberator who will raise the long-tortured captive to other worldly regions" and "the accomplishment of the work of mercy"—references to events in the scenes, namely the Titan's emancipation by Hercules and humanity's foundation on fraternal principles.[60] Liszt's inclusion of perseverance among the myth's salient themes likewise confirms his close engagement with Herder's philosophy of history.

Liszt's music also reflects Herder's ideals. His choral settings intensify textual references to the doctrine of *Humanität* and its attendant precepts, including human progress in formerly divine realms, the necessity of struggle, Arcadian life's idealized virtues, universalism, victory in peace, freedom, and brotherhood, and to more specific incidents in the scenes, including the rescue of Theseus and the Titan's liberation. Such wide-ranging sentiments naturally required an equally expansive musical vocabulary that encompasses laments, chorales, marches, pastoral episodes, and operatic interludes, to name only several musical topics supporting Derek Watson's assessment of the choruses as Liszt's "most important large-scale secular choral work."[61] Likewise justifying Watson's appraisal are the choruses' length, formal complexity, and massive performing forces comprising a narrator, vocal soloists, full orchestra, and large choir. In the symphonic poem Liszt utilized comparably vivid topics or quoted passages from the choruses, imbuing an abstract sonata form with a materiality congruent with Herder's conception of myth as a moral force, a tangible power capable of transforming an era's self-perceptions.

Music intended to meet such ambitious agendas typically resists conventional structural analysis based on formal, motivic, or linear processes. Indeed, the complexities of reconciling distinctive, nontraditional forms with their expressive content—a task Liszt's mature music frequently imposes—have responded most effectively to semantic analysis, as important studies of his piano and orchestral works attest.[62] Such methodology recognizes three broad formal categories: enumerative forms comprising discrete, successive sections (for example, ABCBA, or arch form);

---

[58]   See Alan Walker, *Franz Liszt* (3 vols, New York, 1983–96), vol. 1, pp. 245, 253–5, 290–91, 368–9; vol. 2, pp. 390–91.

[59]   Franz Liszt, preface to *Prométhée, Poème symphonique* (Leipzig, 1856), p. 2.

[60]   Ibid.

[61]   Derek Watson, *Liszt* (New York, 1989), pp. 291–2.

[62]   Márta Grabócz, *Morphologie des œuvres pour piano de Liszt: Influence du programme sur l'évolution des formes* (Budapest, 1986); Constantin Floros, "Die Faust-Symphonie von Franz Liszt: Eine semantische Analyse," in Heinz Klaus Metzger and Rainer Riehn (eds), *Franz Liszt, Musik-Konzepte: Die Reihe über Komponisten*, vol. 12 (Munich, 1980), pp. 42–87; Keith T. Johns, *The Symphonic Poems of Franz Liszt*, ed. Michael Saffle, Franz Liszt Studies Series, no. 3 (Stuyvesant, NY, 1997).

evolutionary forms exploiting variation technique or thematic transformation; and "forms of renewed balance" involving syntheses of sonata, variation, and cyclical principles.[63] Every chorus belongs to the first category.

Liszt explained enumerative form in the preface to his *Album d'un voyageur* (composed 1837–8), a "suite of pieces which, confining themselves within no special framework, take successively the most appropriate rhythms, movements, and figures to express the reverie, the passion, the thought which inspired them."[64] Moreover, sequential repetition often subdivides discrete sections, articulating "fields of action" that intensify or diminish an affect, alternately called a topos or intonation.[65] Determining affects is usually secure in vocal music, where a passage's text, expressive marking, and figuration engender strong correlations. A survey of topoi in the choruses not only reveals a comprehensive sequence with an equivalent in Herder's ideology, but also illuminates the symphonic poem's quotation of several choral themes.

In the first chorus the Oceanids utter a lament, "Woe to you, Prometheus," four times. After each of the first three statements, they sing a stanza, first condemning human intrusion on the seas, next expressing fear of the bodies of drowned mortals, and finally holding Prometheus responsible for such sorrows. During multiple revisions, Liszt discarded the last stanza and added an introduction, a transition between the two retained stanzas, and a coda, which all share motivic connections, thus producing an enumerative form represented schematically as i–A–tⁱ–A–cⁱ. The resulting symmetry was consciously cultivated, as Liszt informed Johann Herbeck, who conducted the choruses' Viennese premiere in 1860:

> In my work, I strove after the ideal of Antiquity, which should be represented not as an archaic skeleton, but instead fashioned in a manner both lively and self-animated. André Chenier's lovely verse, "Let us make new thoughts from antique verses," was my principle—and pointed me toward musical plasticity and symmetry.[66]

Inspired by antique ideals, symmetry influenced the forms of several choruses and the symphonic poem.

Marked *allegro agitato*, the introduction establishes the lament as the primary topos (Example 4.1). Persistent calls of "Weh," marked *klagend* [plaintively], begin on painful dissonances and feature madrigalesque sighs of descending minor seconds. Rising sequentially through a diminished triad's pitches, these cries culminate in a long melismatic descent in staggered parallel sixths that finally confirms the tonic, A minor, 22 measures into the movement. The accompaniment entails string tremolos and *colla parte* woodwind writing, both preceded by a solo horn's chromatic ascent in half notes (D-sharp–E–F), a simple motive whose recurrence in the sixth chorus provides rudimentary unity within the score.

---

[63]   Grabócz, p. 15.

[64]   Franz Liszt, preface to *Album d'un voyageur* (Vienna, 1842).

[65]   See Theodor W. Adorno, "Verfremdetes Hauptwerk: Zur *Missa Solemnis*," in *Musikalische Schriften*, ed. Rolf Tiedemann (6 vols, Frankfurt, 1978–84), vol. 4, p. 161.

[66]   Ludwig Herbeck, *Johann Herbeck: Ein Lebensbild von seinem Söhne Ludwig* (Vienna, 1885), Briefwechsel, pp. 21–2.

No. 1. CHOR der OCEANIDEN
(Frauenchor__Sopran u. Alt.)

Example 4.1   Liszt *Chöre zu Herder's* Entfesseltem Prometheus, No. 1, mm. 1–18

Both stanzas retain the introduction's texture, though added layers intensify the lament as the primary topos. The flutes articulate stanzaic climaxes with rapidly ascending chromatic scales in parallel thirds, stock figuration drawn from operatic storms to underscore textual references to disturbed seas. Likewise borrowed from opera are recitative-like unison vocal parts featuring repeated notes and monotonously alternating minor thirds. Upper strings incessantly repeat rising five-note scales set to a dactylic rhythm of two sixteenth notes and an eighth, recalling the introduction's sequential ascent through a diminished triad before climbing in semitones. Hypnotic figuration, repetitive rhythms, and sequences have analogues in Alberich's curse scene in *Das Rheingold*, a parallel reinforced in the transition, where repetitions of dissonant chords as quarter-note triplets correspond to syncopated figures that pervade Wagner's accompaniment. Indeed, a curse looms behind the Oceanids' complaints, as their accusation against Prometheus in the omitted third stanza implies.

Each of the coda's 15 statements of the chorus's opening line, "Woe to you, Prometheus," exhibits varied harmony, part writing, and length. This epilogue unfolds over the bass line's repeated descending chromatic scales, a cliché of Baroque laments epitomized by "When I am laid in earth" from Purcell's *Dido and Aeneas*. Linking discrete formal sections and reinforcing overall symmetry are recurrences of the transition's quarter-note triplets and the opening chromatic horn call, whose retrograde inversion notably initiates the bass line's final descent. The opening movement accordingly embodies three somber intonations: lament, storm, and curse, the first intensified in the coda. All three reappear in later choruses, but their juxtaposition with different topoi intimates another dramatic trajectory that eventually dispels the morose lament.

The second chorus, unlike the first, features extreme textual contrasts. Tritons, heralds of Oceanus, initially invoke peace, but soon juxtapose bolder sentiments: fierce winds, roaring waves, threatening cliffs, and terrifying depths respectively yield to fellowship, freedom, brotherhood, and compassion. Responding enthusiastically, the Oceanids hail Prometheus, adorn him with jewels, and foresee a Golden Age. Everyone then praises the indivisible sea and open air as heaven's gifts, events Liszt supplemented with further exaltations of Prometheus.

Liszt masterfully imposed an arch form on Herder's lyrics (A–B–^AC–B–A).[67] The prefatory invocation of peace and the Titan's final tribute receive nearly identical settings (A), as do the second section's juxtapositions of nautical images and human virtues and the fourth section's acclamations of sea and air (B). Enhancing the palindromic design is that much of the second section's material appears in reverse order in the fourth. The central section initially recalls the introduction, but is otherwise unique (^AC). Passages meticulously alternate between the tonic, F major, and remote keys, matching formal rigor.

Diverse textual elements predictably elicit various musical topoi. The introduction and coda exemplify Liszt's frequent use of a specific pastoral topos that mirrors peace, harmony, and nature's stasis with rippling figuration.[68] In this case, undulating arpeggios provide sonorous equivalents for textual references to waves, an effect enhanced by hierarchical metric pulsations stressing downbeats

---

[67]   See Paul A. Bertagnolli, "A Newly Discovered Source for Franz Liszt's *Chöre zu Herder's* Entfesseltem Prometheus," *Journal of Musicology*, 19/1 (Winter 2002): 157–9.
[68]   Grabócz, p. 94.

in common time. The fifth scale degree's emphasis and the major mode likewise accord with a pastoral intonation.

The second and fourth sections depict storms, pastoral imagery of a totally different kind. They accordingly illustrate Liszt's frequent adoption of an *appassionato* topos epitomized by *Orage* from the first book of the *Années de pèlerinage* and portions of *Les Préludes*. Lisztian tempests usually exhibit several textural layers distinguished by register, direction of linear movement (contrary or oblique), and intermittent martial fanfares in dotted rhythms, as is abundantly true here. Scales often trace wide melodic arcs before ending in thick chords, an ideal scheme for reflecting juxtapositions of turbulent nautical images and humanity's fellowship, freedom, brotherhood, and compassion, which receive hymn-like settings. Such figuration derives more from Liszt's virtuosic piano works—in turn indebted to Paganini— than from familiar orchestral storms in Beethoven's Sixth Symphony and Rossini's overtures, though all exploit now stereotyped clichés, including diminished seventh chords, repeated notes, and chromatic scales. Liszt's storms typically symbolize struggle or heroic combat, as is consistent with textual references to humane values prevailing over nature's adversities.

The central section's prophecy regarding a Golden Age's arrival is cast as a bel canto interlude for soprano and alto soloists with choral interjections (Example 4.2). Lacking *parlante* elements that normally infiltrate Liszt's operatic topics, the scena—replete with finely spun, heavily ornamented melodies, regular periodic phrasing, and an intricate barcarolle accompaniment—duplicates the reverie Liszt's *Liebestraum* evokes. Remote from pastoral allusions, the interlude appropriately emulates opera, a cultivated vocal art, to match textual references to an utterly human subject—mankind's progress toward development.

Example 4.2   Liszt *Chöre zu Herder's* Entfesseltem Prometheus, No. 2, mm. 93–6

Intrusive fanfares herald the return of stormy seas, though previous material varies conspicuously: depictions of nature's turbulence lead not to fraternal hymns, but to march-like proclamations concerning heavenly gifts of sea and air. Liszt, like Mahler, often used minor-mode marches to represent macabre, ceremonial subjects. But the present example, a rare Lisztian march in a major key, implies victory over struggle, like the finale of Beethoven's Fifth Symphony. The second chorus's episodic sequence thus articulates Herder's concept of progress: two pastoral states—natural tranquility, then impassioned struggle—yield to an operatically human reverie; renewed struggle prompts a triumphant march, which elicits a concluding pastoral peroration in homage to Prometheus. The next three choruses replay this sequence on a larger scale.

Dryads, nymphs who inhabit and protect forests, sing another lament in the third chorus. After renewing the Oceanids' cries of "Woe to you, Prometheus," they bewail their realm's desecration. An alto soloist then recalls better days, before the gods abandoned their forest altars. The nymphs conclude with a dire prediction: no tree, no Dryad will be spared. Liszt's enumerative form comprises different music for each of the four expressed sentiments, a restatement of the opening lament before the alto solo, and an orchestral codetta related to the prophecy (A–B–A–C–D–c^D).

The lament (A) reproduces an eighteenth- and early nineteenth-century operatic intonation known as *ombra*, meaning dark or shadowy.[69] Typically this affect involves monotonous chanting of homophonic "chordal melodies," rendered here as divisi soprano and alto parts consisting exclusively of repeated parallel thirds. The resulting stasis is scarcely disturbed by pointed declamatory rhythms, another convention of the *ombra* topos Liszt observed with a *pesante* marking and numerous accents. Intensifying the dark hue are the key (C-sharp minor), ominous timpani rolls, muted horn doublings of the voices, and suspensions and retardations that embellish staggered, ascending parallel thirds in the low woodwinds. Two sequential statements—one in the dominant,

---

[69]   Ibid., p. 75.

another in the tonic—end as upper woodwinds and strings anticipate a phrase from the alto solo (C), a motivic link Liszt added just before publication.

In the second section (B) a curse supplants the lament, as in the first chorus. Unison declamation and incessant syncopated chords accompany textual references to the forest's defilement, a declining state with an obvious musical analogue: a largely chromatic bass line descends an octave, reaching its lowest point in the entire chorus when the opening lament recurs in abbreviated form. No anticipation of the ensuing alto solo, however, marks this juncture.

Recitative, a speaking personage's musical embodiment, acquires genuinely *parlante* attributes in the alto solo (C, Example 4.3). Her protest against desecration of hallowed altars displays numerous musical symbols of mourning: the vocal line emphasizes tritones, the harshest intervals; the English horn, the quintessential instrument of Baroque funeral cantatas, doubles the voice, assisted by flutes and violas; and diminished seventh chords, emblems of bereavement or fatal struggle, disrupt her phrases, intensified by their fortississimo dynamics and expressive marking (*äusserst scharf*, extremely sharply). The Dryads answer with repetitive phrases of decreasing length, a disintegrative process ending in further cries of woe.

Example 4.3   Liszt *Chöre zu Herder's* Entfesseltem Prometheus, No. 3, mm. 43–9

Dedicated Lisztians know the alto solo recurs cyclically throughout the symphonic poem. Rarely noticed, however, is another quotation of the ensuing section (D) as part of the orchestral work's principal theme. Both passages will therefore help determine affects in wordless contexts. Similarities between the fourth section and the second chorus's turbulent passages suggest the return of an *appassionato* topos, but Herder's text offers a more precise clue: the Dryads, knowing they will not be spared, are anxious about their fate (Example 4.4). Confirming their agitation is a new tempo (*più mosso, agitato*), an obstinate neighbor tone above a dominant pedal, declamatory vocal parts that repeatedly descend in parallel thirds before converging on unisons, and the clash of major seconds as divisi sopranos and altos arrive on the tonic from half steps above and below. Agitation in the face of destiny is, of course, a response the Dryads share with Prometheus.

Example 4.4   Liszt *Chöre zu Herder's* Entfesseltem Prometheus, No. 3, mm. 82–9

The codetta dissipates earlier turmoil with a gradual *ritardando*, softer dynamics, slower neighbor tones, and a plagal effect implied by the dominant's lower neighbors. Thus the first and third choruses present similar comprehensive topical sequences involving various aspects of laments. But the Dryads react to human intrusion more dramatically than the Oceanids: their lament becomes a curse, returns to its original state, acquires humanly communicative power in a solo recitative, and expends itself in resigned agitation.

Although easily the longest, the fourth chorus is the simplest in terms of lyrics, topoi, and form. Its highly repetitive text expresses three thoughts: reapers thank Ceres for seedlings, fertile crops, and invigorating bread; they sowed seeds while a lark warbled and saw them sprout while a nightingale sang; but their own love songs accompanied them home. Perfectly suiting a pastoral intonation, Herder's delightful Arcadian images inspired some of the most vividly rustic music in Liszt's entire *œuvre*. Indeed, the movement exploits just one other affect, the waltz. Textual transparency and limited topical content engendered formal simplicity: three large choral sections are respectively devoted to praising Ceres, the planting and sprouting of seeds, and the reapers' love songs, the third a variation of the second. The orchestra supplies an introduction, a transition between the first two choral sections, and a long coda (i–A^i–t–B_1–B_2–c^{i+B}).

The introduction establishes a pastoral topos through myriad significations recognized since the Renaissance (Example 4.5).[70] Horns and bassoons sustain drones, initially playing octaves and fifths but eventually adding the tonic triad's third. Unequivocally defining the key of A major, static tonic and dominant chords observe one repetitive rhythmic pattern, a common musical pastoralism, but their duple note values contradict the triple meter signature, a discrepancy resolved when infectious waltz rhythms supplant the hemiola pattern. Another rudimentary motive enters, embellishing the fifth scale degree with an upper neighbor tone. The dominant then arpeggiates upward to the leading tone, which successively acquires a lower neighbor and reinstates the opening pitch. This neighbor-tone figure is scored for English horn and oboe, quintessential pastoral instruments soon joined by the equally bucolic flute and clarinet. After six repetitions the figure begins a dialogue with a broken scale that traverses wide melodic arcs played by alternating flutes. Pentatonic English horn and bassoon solos conclude the introduction.

No. 4. CHOR der SCHNITTER
(Gemischter Chor — Sopran _ Alt _ Tenor _ Bass)

Example 4.5		Liszt *Chöre zu Herder's* Entfesseltem Prometheus, No. 4, mm. 1–21

---

[70]		Ibid., p. 63.

The first choral section (A^i) is merely an expanded trope of the introduction. As the orchestra repeats previous material with fuller scoring, voices add static chords or arpeggios doubled in thirds. Antiphonal echoes among the choir's divided sections correspond to alternating orchestral solos.

In the transition (t) flutes, oboes, and violins imitate birdcalls, prefiguring imminent textual references. Their chirping nonetheless provides more than a colorful evocation of nature: its continuous eighth-note duplets suspend the prevailing hemiola pattern, thus initiating dance rhythms that ultimately pervade the texture. Moreover, incrementally smaller rhythmic values convert the duplets into a trill that becomes a pedal tone in the upper register, in contrast to earlier bass drones.

The next two sections (B_1–B_2) abjure nature's stasis to depict human bodies in motion, adeptly reflecting the text's shift from honoring Ceres to the reapers' physical activities. Motoric associations initially derive from a repetitive rhythm (four eighth notes followed by a quarter) that mimics a guitar's strumming, a simulation increasingly elaborate pizzicato string figuration enhances. Gradually, however, waltz rhythms suffuse the accompaniment, furnishing musical counterparts to muscular motions. The waltz attains its greatest vigor when the reapers mention their love songs, thus reaching the movement's climax when the most human sentiment completely eclipses natural imagery.

Reprising the introduction's motives, the coda (c^{i+B}) begins as the neighbor-tone figure and the broken scale alternate, played respectively by tutti winds and strings. The strumming rhythm and pizzicato figuration briefly return and then join the broken scale, which ends the chorus in a solo clarinet's dissipating murmurs.

The fourth movement's naïveté belies a sophisticated structural process Liszt commonly employed in variation forms, whereby increases in textural density produce subdivisions within sections. Such "structural crecendi" entail incremental additions of thematic and accompanimental layers and varied scoring of themes.[71] Typical procedures include melodic doublings, shifts of register, gradually thicker accompaniments, and fragmentation of textural components.

All the preceding characteristics appear throughout the fourth chorus, but are best illustrated by the strumming figure's treatment. Only oboes play its first two statements, with pizzicato violins doubling primary pitches. Then flutes, bassoons, and two solo violins present the melody as clarinets add arpeggios and horns sustain drones. Two horns next play the figure, allowing the strings to engage in all manner of pizzicato figuration, harmonics, and fragmented arpeggios. The strumming achieves its most elaborate guise when hocket, a medieval technique, distributes its pitches among several instruments, one of which sounds while another is silent.

Comparable schemes generate climaxes in and among the chorus's sections. The number of layers and their internal activity increase steadily in the introduction and three subdivisions of the first formal section before thinning slightly in a fourth (i–A^i). Following the lightly scored transition, escalation resumes in both ensuing sections (B_1–B_2). But a reduction temporarily interrupts progressive increases, making renewed drive toward the movement's climax—the waltz rhythm's sovereignty—even more emphatic. The coda dwindles steadily toward its final three measures, played by one clarinet.

---

[71] Ibid., p. 128.

The fourth chorus marks a crossroads in the overall sequence of movements, dispelling earlier darkness, agitation, and turbulence. Somber topoi recur only in the sixth movement, where heroism quickly overcomes them. The movement's beguiling charms also explain its success during Liszt's lifetime. Even when much of his music aroused polemic strife, it was encored frequently, programmed independently in important venues throughout Germany and in Budapest, Rome, and London, and published separately in full and vocal scores and arrangements for women's chorus, piano four-hands, and solo piano. The latter version is the only number of the original incidental score currently available in a modern edition, except the symphonic poem.

In the fifth chorus vintners wish Bacchus joy just as he gives them happiness. They then exalt patience, a virtue the earth taught them, and offer thanks for wine, a heavenly gift that invigorates hope and warms life. Liszt aptly used only men's voices and accordingly omitted Herder's concluding personification of hope as a feminine counselor, comforter, and source of courage.[72]

Liszt's setting, a drinking song, so closely emulates models in Schubert's part songs and German romantic operas that the composer once chided conductors not to allow "the entire chorus to reek of beer and the beer hall."[73] Its enumerative form comprises an introduction, two closely related sections based on repeated lyrics, and a coda (i–A_1–A_2–c). While the introduction embodies a topos not yet encountered in the choruses, remaining sections recall familiar intonations, converting the drinking song into a heroic march.

The introduction's tempo (allegro con brio), triple meter, and pervasive staccato and pizzicato markings imply a scherzo's light character, a topos confirmed by diatonic harmonies, spirited fanfares heralding Bacchus' arrival, and—in one manuscript source—autograph instructions to conduct the passage in one beat per measure (Example 4.6). Unadulterated scherzos are rare among Liszt's works, which

Example 4.6   Liszt *Chöre zu Herder's* Entfesseltem Prometheus, No. 5, mm. 36–9

---

[72]   Feminine nouns (*Rathgeberinn, Trösterinn, Besänftigerinn,* and *Mutherweckerinn*) agree with the gender of hope (*Hoffnung*).

[73]   See Bertagnolli, p. 157.

typically distort dance elements, as numerous Mephistophelean pieces illustrate. Pure scherzos, however, invariably represent liberty or liberation, as in the *Dante Sonata*'s exposition, where a lively concluding theme affords relief from a long section marked *lamentoso*. *Scherzando* qualities thus suit Herder's portrayal of vintners freed from life's cares by Bacchus.

Recitative inaugurates the first main section (A_1) as pizzicato chords punctuate unison parts of four soloists. Successively longer phrases introduce deep chromatic inflections and four-part writing, now doubled by low woodwinds, horns, and upper strings. But when the *Männerquartett* glorifies invigorating hope, triadic fanfares, repetitive common-time rhythms, and a new tempo (allegro moderato) establish the march as the prevailing topos. Thereafter continuous textual repetition elicits steady alternation between tonic and dominant triads embellished occasionally by chromatic chords. Textural accumulations of repeated chords, arpeggios, and neighbor-tone figures nonetheless produce variety, as in the fourth chorus. Climaxes mark the beginning and end of the second section (A_2), first when the men's chorus initiates a dialogue with the soloists, then as a tutti orchestra, regular alternation between strong and weak pulses, equally repetitive harmonies, and timpani rolls all evoke the actions of marching (Example 4.7). In the context of a men's chorus, a martial character is explicit.

Example 4.7   Liszt *Chöre zu Herder's* Entfesseltem Prometheus, No. 5, mm. 148–52

An accelerando ushers in the coda, where further tribute to Bacchus renews the introduction's sentiments and thus demands a musical complement. Liszt's revisions transformed several perfunctory tutti chords into an integral conclusion whose ternary rhythmic subdivisions recall the introduction's triple meter and abrupt modulation from D major (the tonic) to F balances the introduction's downward shift from C to A. Reinforcing the previous section's militarism are triadic brass fanfares designated for offstage performance in manuscript sources, but not published scores. A final presto saturates the orchestral texture with fanfares and draws the quartet and chorus into their only unisons. The faster tempo, ubiquitous fanfares, and unified performing forces suggest victory or heroism, as in several symphonic poems, most obviously *Les Préludes*, *Festklänge*, and *Hunnenschlacht*.[74]

The fifth movement thus completes a large unit that begins with the third chorus's lament, continues with the fourth movement's pastorale, and ends in martial triumph. As previously noted, a comparable sequence spans the first two choruses, where a lament precedes a juxtaposition of pastoral and martial topoi. The last three choruses also form a unit, reprising the lament and heroic victory, but exchanging the pastorale for a new topos, the hymn.

Arcadian images of field and vineyard vanish when Prometheus realizes his fateful hour has arrived, believing he hears the rustling wings of an eagle, his daily tormentor. Instead an earthquake's rumbling splits the rocks where he is chained. Subterranean voices emanate from the fissure, renewing cries of "Weh" previously uttered by Oceanids and Dryads. As invisible male choristers then impart, the holy realm of the dead is disturbed, Medusa's shadowy form has fled, the imprisoned are rising up, and Cerberus, the three-headed dog guarding the gates of hell, howls and dies, graphic events inspiring some of the score's most dramatic music.

Liszt's setting of Herder's vivid text divides into four sections, none overtly related (ABCD), but some linked with other movements. In the first, suspensions and retardations embellish descending parallel sixths, recalling procedures in the first chorus's melismatic lament and the third movement's staggered ascent in parallel thirds. As in both earlier choruses, tremolos are pervasive, though they involve repeated notes, not alternating pitches. Strengthening connections with earlier movements is that the initial cries of "Weh" are set to inversions of the first chorus's opening motive, namely the horn's chromatic ascent in half notes (D-sharp–E–F), now beginning on the enharmonically spelled pitch (E-flat–D–D-flat). In the theater, this section furnished purely instrumental accompaniment as the earth rumbled and the rock split. In concert performances, however, the narrator explains the action as the music unfolds, producing melodramatic declamation likewise adopted in the seventh chorus.

The second section reinstates the third movement's shadowy *ombra* topos, matching textual references to death's realm and Medusa's specter. Unison voices repeat pitches as low winds and strings play a funereal chromatic basso ostinato that meanders monotonously between G, the nominal tonic, and E-flat. The passage's sequential structure, with one statement followed by another a major third higher, anticipates the ensuing section's longer series of tertian harmonies.

To portray the apocalyptic resurrection of the underworld's prisoners, Liszt cultivated a *furioso* topos he often used to represent storms (Example 4.8). The new tempo (*più mosso*) supports this intonation, but another marking, *rasselnd* [rattling], implies the prisoners are clanking their chains. Additional features create one of the

---

[74]   Johns, pp. 54–60.

entire score's most dramatic moments: triadic fanfares evoke the sounding of the last trump; precipitous leaps animate formerly static vocal parts; triadic roots extend the previous section's series of plummeting thirds (B–E-flat–C–G-sharp–E); and low strings imitate the barking of Cerberus with grace-note figures, recalling the hound's depiction in the Ballet of the Furies from Gluck's *Orfeo ed Euridice*.

Example 4.8   Liszt *Chöre zu Herder's* Entfesseltem Prometheus, No. 6, mm. 37–44

Regrettably, Liszt revised the passage for publication, interrupting its climax with the narrator's announcement that Hercules has prevailed in his subterranean combat. Thereafter the purely instrumental fourth section exploits heroic music's banalities, including homorhythmic orchestral parts, repeated tonic triads in the parallel major key, continuous dotted rhythms with martial overtones, an incessant pedal point, heavy accents, and the score's loudest dynamics (fortississimo). The concluding bombast nonetheless breaks the pattern that occurs following the second and fifth movements, when laments return after other topics have been established.

In the penultimate movement invisible beings praise Themis, the benevolent goddess of justice. Offering guidance when foresight errs and delusions lead mankind astray, she humbles the prideful, but raises the lowly; all the earth's people, deeply bowed, pray to her, casting away arrogance. Herder's lyrics inspired a lovely, hymn-like setting that exemplifies one of several distinct *religioso* intonations common in Liszt's works.[75] The hymn, however, is just one of three sections whose statement and repetition in order blends strophic and through-composed forms (ABC–ABC).

During the Herder Festival offstage woodwinds softly played a cantabile version of the sixth chorus's Herculean music, a fitting prelude to the utterances of invisible voices likewise emanating from offstage. But Liszt's concert adaptation was equally ingenious: in a radiant E major muted divisi strings arpeggiate primary harmonies in sixteenth-note duplets, furnishing a transparent background for a solo violin's presentation of the cantabile Hercules motive (Example 4.9). This diaphanous texture—appropriately evoking a heavenly subject—transforms the crude, militaristic depiction of the power of Hercules into a solemn paean to Themis, thereby subjugating force to justice in musico-dramatic terms. Prior to publication Liszt again added melodramatic declamation for the narrator, who relates an olive tree, a sign of Athena's blessing, now sprouts from the Titan's cliff.

Example 4.9   Liszt *Chöre zu Herder's* Entfesseltem Prometheus, No. 7, mm. 1–4

In the second section (B) paired male soloists sing unison *parlante* recitative, again an emulation of a speaking personage and hence a suitable representation of specifically human thoughts, errant foresight and self-delusion. Reflecting these ominous allusions are sequential

---

75   Grabócz, p. 41.

forays into darker, remote keys, D and F minor. The sparse accompaniment consists not of recitative's quintessential chordal interjections, but rather of *colla parte* woodwind doublings, and, in the strings, chromatic scales that move against the voices in contrary motion. Each phrase culminates in an overtly operatic gesture, the familiar Wagnerian melodic turn.

The hymn itself (C) epitomizes a *religioso* style famously illustrated by *Sposalizio*, the opening movement in the second book of Liszt's *Années de pèlerinage*.[76] Beneath singing diatonic melodies in major keys (in this case, the tonic, E major) arpeggios typically evoke bells or the harp, here making its second and final appearance in all eight choruses (Example 4.10). Enhancing the hymnodic topos are the movement's

Example 4.10   Liszt *Chöre zu Herder's* Entfesseltem Prometheus, No. 7, mm. 26–37

---

76   Ibid.

quasi-strophic design and plagal cadences, though the section's most striking harmonies comprise a series of secondary dominants leading to the major submediant (C-sharp major) and their bold juxtapositions with the lowered submediant (C major), tertian tonal gestures the chorus's ending amplifies. The hymn also facilitates the symphonic poem's analysis, functioning as its subordinate theme.

All three sections recur in order, the first bearing a choral trope regarding Themis' treatment of the prideful and lowly, the second again suiting the human action of bowing to Themis, and the third preserving the *religioso* character so well matched to offering a deity prayers. The final phrase expands the third section's tertian gesture into a remarkable series of descending thirds (C-sharp–A–F-sharp–D–B-flat), finishing a tritone away from the tonic. Reinstating E major, a codetta fortifies the *religioso* intonation with plagal cadences and more harp arpeggios.

Hymn-like attributes also pervade the finale, though variants evoke secular, not religious connotations. A chorus of Muses decrees, "humanity is that of heaven which blooms on earth, that which men raise high to the gods; it is mankind's most gracious, most sacred gift." Liszt supplemented Herder's acclamations with repeated statements of "Hail Prometheus, Hail humanity." The text accordingly indicates an apotheosis, a standard category for endings of Liszt's multi-movement works, notably the *Faust* and *Dante Symphonies*. Consistent with this signification are the tempo marking (*andante solenn*) and a triumphant, *grandioso* character produced by unison or strictly homorhythmic vocal parts, massively orchestrated brass and woodwind chorales, and military heroism's dotted fanfares.

The form again encompasses four sections, the last a variation of the third ($A–B–C_1–C_2$). In the first, unison winds play a series of descending thirds that notably recurs—at pitch in D-flat major—as the subject of the symphonic poem's developmental fugue (Example 4.11). Repeated twice by the full chorus, the thirds acquire precise textual associations: humanity is heaven's earthly blossom, a gift worthy of the gods. Dotted tutti orchestral chords answer every phrase, establishing the movement's heroic topos.

Sung first by the chorus and then by four soloists, the second section's four-part chorale modulates to E major, the key of the preceding movement's *religioso* hymn. Hence tonality correlates with Herder's text: the seventh movement praises Themis as humanity's guide, while the eighth lauds humanity as mankind's sacred gift. The orchestra's uninterrupted sequences of the first section's descending thirds, played above pedal points consisting of repeated triplets, reinforce connections with human virtues.

In the remaining sections the repeated triplets move to the upper strings and the descending thirds govern the bass line, generating bold harmonic progressions. Unison choristers and soloists hail Prometheus and humanity with declamatory dotted rhythms. After a rising chromatic scale disrupts the bass line, all voices erupt in five-part chords for the fourth section's exaltations as the orchestra doubles every part in a grandiose chorale.

All eight movements present a comprehensive topical sequence that articulates a central tenet of Herder's philosophy of history, namely, humanity's fullest development necessarily entails persistent struggle (Table 4.2). The first two choruses outline fundamental events in nascent form: a lament, tinged with elements of storm, recitative, and curse (chorus 1) leads to a pastorale inflected with a specifically

Example 4.11   Liszt *Chöre zu Herder's* Entfesseltem Prometheus, No. 8, mm. 4–8

human reverie and an incipient victory march (chorus 2). A similar cycle is writ large in the next three movements: another lament—intensified by *ombra* coloring, another curse, and resigned agitation (chorus 3)—again yields to a rustic pastorale imbued with expressly human dance characteristics (chorus 4); and liberation resurfaces in a scherzo and a fully evolved victory march (chorus 5). A final curse is then broken by a furious apocalypse and Herculean heroism (chorus 6), which assumes a cantabile guise in preparing a third human vocalization (*recitativo*), a *religioso* hymn (chorus 7), and an apotheosis both grandiose and triumphant (chorus 8). Thus Liszt exploited multiple series of topoi to represent humanity's threefold effort to achieve fulfillment, with successive attempts culminating in increasingly pronounced heroism. Global architecture also gains reinforcement from recurrent motives, tonal emphasis of intertextuality, and persistent sequences of descending thirds and staggered parallel sixths or thirds.

The intonational sequence and each number's striking features validate the assessment of the choruses as Liszt's "most important large-scale secular choral work." But they are also crucial for analyzing *Prometheus*, the symphonic poem, which quotes several choral themes and thus offers starting points for semiotic interpretations of events in its otherwise largely abstract sonata form. These referents confirm the orchestral work again propagates Herder's ideals.

As a young virtuoso Liszt boldly confronted sonata-form conventions in the Italian book of his *Années de pèlerinage* (1837). The book's finale, entitled *Après une lecture du Dante* after Victor Hugo's poem and alluding to the *Divine Comedy*, bears another inscription, *Fantasia quasi Sonata*, referring to Beethoven's Op. 27 sonatas, which are both designated *Sonata quasi una fantasia*. Liszt's pointed inversion signifies he conceived his *Dante Sonata* not as a classical structure imbued with elements of fantasy, but rather as a freer, improvisatory form infused with the multi-movement sonata's motivic, formal, and cyclical properties.

Table 4.2   The Topical Sequence in Liszt's Choruses

Chorus 1	Chorus 3	Chorus 6
Lament	Lament	Lament
Storm		
Recitative	*Ombra* recitative	
Curse	Curse	Curse
	Agitation	*Furioso*
		Heroic
Chorus 2	**Chorus 4**	**Chorus 7**
Pastorale	Pastorale	Heroic becomes Divine
Peace – Storm		*Recitativo*
Bel canto reverie	Dance (Waltz – Love)	*Religioso* hymn
	Chorus 5	**Chorus 8**
	Scherzo, Liberation	*Grandioso*, Triumphant
March	Victory march	Apotheosis

Such innovations and attendant structural unorthodoxies, also found in the sonata forms of Liszt's contemporaries, are, according to semantic theorists, the result of "the confrontation of inherited constructions with new contents or intonations,"[77] or the attempt "to reconcile emphatically expressive gestures derived from French romanticism with the thematic-motivic legacy of classicism."[78] Liszt, as noted, had disclosed intentions to portray similar "reveries, passions, and thoughts" with appropriate "rhythms, movements, and figures" in his preface to the *Album d'un voyageur*, the precursor to the *Années de pèlerinage*.

Liszt preserved the same approach in his later orchestral music. As he maintained in an essay on Berlioz's *Harold en Italie* (1855), "the poeticizing symphonist sets himself the task of rendering ... an image existing distinctly in his mind, a series of states of the soul which unambiguously and precisely lie in his consciousness."[79] But the Weimar symphonic poems are not mere configurations of diverse topoi supported by titles, poetic ideas, or explicit programs, nor are they simply musical illustrations of literary prefaces. Instead, symphonic and "poeticizing" principles assume equal roles in determining each score's unique structural features. Liszt's orchestral works consequently observe classical formal precepts more assiduously than his earlier piano pieces. Thus their motivic saturation achieves Beethovenesque density; thematic transformation links separate formal sections; and prefaces elucidate flexible expressive content. Liszt thereby sought to ennoble program music, which

---

[77]   Ibid., p. 25.

[78]   Carl Dahlhaus, "Liszts *Bergsymphonie* und die Idee der symphonischen Dichtung," *Jahrbuch des staatlichen Instituts für Musikforschung*, 1975 (1976): 97.

[79]   Franz Liszt, "Berlioz und seine *Harold-Symphonie*," in *Gesammelte Schriften von Franz Liszt*, ed. Lina Ramann (6 vols, Leipzig, 1880–83), vol. 4, p. 50.

he considered the goal of music's historical development, to raise it from a low, descriptive genre to an elevated, poetic-philosophical enterprise.[80]

Two more factors undoubtedly stimulated Liszt's engagement with sonata form. First, Liszt's imagination apparently fused various types of classicism. The Weimar Classicism of Goethe and Schiller elicited unmatched structural rigor in the *Faust Symphony* and the symphonic poem, *Die Ideale*. And classical antiquity, as already mentioned, prompted Liszt to imbue his incidental music with "plasticity and symmetry." Scarcely coincidental, then, is that of all the symphonic poems, the two based on classical subjects, *Orpheus* and *Prometheus*, exhibit the most straightforward sonata forms. Second, while Liszt rarely harbored reactionary compositional attitudes, he was probably influenced by the burgeoning contemporary Beethoven literature, which recognized an opposition of "heroic" and "cantabile-elegiac" themes as an emergent topos readily apparent in the symphonic poems.[81] Both factors decisively shaped the structure of *Prometheus* (Table 4.3).

Table 4.3   Formal Divisions in Liszt's Symphonic Poem

Introduction		**Recapitulation**	
Allegro energico ed agitato assai		Tempo primo	
12	Quartal harmonies, *Prometheus* motive	8	Quartal harmonies, *Prometheus* motive
9	Maestoso (un poco ritenuto il tempo)		
5	[accelerando]	5	[accelerando]
21	Andante recitativo espressivo molto	19	Andante (recitative)
Exposition			
Allegro molto appassionato		Allegro molto appassionato	
1st theme area		1st theme area	
14	1st theme proper	14	1st theme proper
8	Duplet pedal	8	Duplet pedal
8	Chromatic scales in bass	8	Chromatic scales in bass
6	*Prometheus* motive, trills, chords		
Transition		Transition	
13	Sequential transition figure		
5	*Prometheus* motive exchange	3	*Prometheus* motive exchange
14	1st theme, recitativo melody alternate		
13	Ritenuto il tempo (quasi recitativo)	13	Sustained octaves on A
2nd theme area		2nd theme area	
31	a tempo, Themis melody (3)	19	Stretto, più animato, Themis melody (2)
Development		**Coda**	
Allegro moderato			

---

[80]   Ibid., pp. 44–7.
[81]   Dahlhaus, "Liszts *Bergsymphonie*," p. 98.

16	Exposition 1	14	Fugue subject augmented
8	Episode 1	7	Pedal on E, Part 1
10	Exposition 2, poco a poco accelerando	7	Pedal on E, Part 2
	il tempo sin' al Allegro agitato assai	12	[Prestissimo]
3	Episode 2	19	Reprise of Themis melody
16	Exposition 3	8	Fugue subject, *Prometheus*
7	Stretto 1		motive alternate
7	Strettto 2, with 1st theme		Poco a poco sempre più
3	1st theme continues		stringendo sin' al fine
		16	*Prometheus* motive varied
		12	Fugue subject in sequence
		4	Exchange of scales
		12	*Prometheus* motive augmented
		9	Fanfares, tonic chords

Comprising five sections, the lucid sonata form encloses the exposition, development, and abbreviated recapitulation between a substantial introduction and lengthy coda. Noteworthy structural irregularities include the introduction's division into four passages that recur throughout the form, a fugal development section whose subject is unrelated to other motives, and a multipartite coda juxtaposing themes from other sections.

Tonality likewise reconciles reasonably well with sonata-form precepts at mid nineteenth century. The tonic, A minor, is defined by the introduction's dominant emphasis and confirmed in the exposition's principal theme area. After a transition, the subordinate theme appears in D-flat major, the enharmonically spelled raised mediant, and re-emerges in the recapitulation in A major. The development begins in D-flat, passes through many keys usually related by fifths, and anticipates the tonic's return with a prolonged pedal tone on F, the dominant's upper neighbor. The rest of the score is anchored in the tonic or its parallel major.

In greater detail, Liszt infused the form with recurrences of five motives or themes that establish connections between discrete sections and presage or recall important structural events (Example 4.12a–e): (a) the introduction's opening quartal harmonies, repeated vigorously by the tutti orchestra and embellished with a neighbor tone, recur in every formal section and in conjunction with all salient motives except the subordinate theme; (b) the introduction's *recitativo* passage, borrowed from the third chorus's alto solo, appears in every section except the coda; (c) the principal theme's initial gesture, comprised of arpeggios that descend rapidly in sixteenth-note duplets and are embellished with nearest chromatic neighbors, returns at the end of the transition, in the developmental fugue's stretto, above the ensuing pedal point, and in the recapitulation; (d) the subordinate theme, a quotation of the seventh chorus's hymn to Themis, and (e) the fugue's subject, extracted from the eighth chorus's bass line, helps articulate the score's cyclical form by adopting transformed guises in the coda.

Example 4.12a   Liszt *Prometheus*, mm. 1–6

Example 4.12b   Liszt *Prometheus*, mm. 27–36

Example 4.12c   Liszt *Prometheus*, mm. 48–9

Example 4.12d   Liszt *Prometheus*, mm. 129–37

Example 4.12e   Liszt *Prometheus*, mm. 161–3

The score's formal divisions, tonal contrasts, and motivic recurrences engender a dialectic between two extremely differentiated ideas—the principal theme's sixteenth-note duplets and the hymn to Themis—with the quartal harmonies, *recitativo* melody, and fugue subject consigned to anticipating, recalling, and mediating between the two primary themes. Liszt acknowledged this dialectic in his preface, asserting the myth elicits a series of opposing reactions: "strongly held beliefs and their utter negation; symbolism that secretly appeals to the imagination, but is read with the most opinionated instincts; and the most bitter sorrows juxtaposed with the sweetest presentiments." He then summarized the contrasting affects as "Malheur et Gloire!"—Misery and Glory.[82]

Binary oppositions, though plainly essential to Liszt's aesthetics of sonata form, are not merely structural in nature. Affirmation and negation, imagination and instinct, sorrow and sweetness, misery and glory—all illuminate musical events, or so Liszt believed in furnishing a preface as a guide to semantic meaning. Indeed, individual formal sections relate to Liszt's dichotomies in unique ways, exhibiting specific affects yet contributing to a large-scale topical sequence that again conveys Herder's doctrine of *Humanität*.

The symphonic poem's first 12 measures are justifiably famous. Above timpani rolls, two quartal harmonies accumulate in the brasses (F–B–E–A, then F-sharp–B–E–A) before the full orchestra repeats them with added neighbor tones. Quartal sonorities impart various semantic meanings in several Lisztian compositions, symbolizing a curse in the *Malédiction Concerto*, the suffering of Jesus and Mary in the fourth movement of the *Via Crucis*, and satanic negation in the distorted dance elements of the second *Mephisto Waltz*.[83] Herder's scenes, however, furnish a more precise dramatic context, since the repeated quartal harmonies originally served as an entr'acte that accompanied the raising of the curtain, and thus preceded the stage action. In an ensuing monologue Prometheus explains patience had eased his pain and lightened his burden, notes his persistent complaints had loosened his shackles, and declares he now awaits humanity's greatest deed. The quartal harmonies consequently lack any direct reference to a curse and relate better to suffering (Liszt's "malheur") and divine

[82]   Liszt, preface to *Prométhée*, p. 2.
[83]   István Szelény, "Der unbekannte Liszt," in Klara Hamburger (ed.), *Franz Liszt: Beiträge von ungarischen Autoren* (Budapest, 1978), pp. 284–5; Dieter Torkowitz, "Innovation und Tradition, zur Genesis eines Quartenakkords: Über Liszt's *Prometheus* Akkord," *Die Musikforschung*, 33/3 (1980): 291–302.

authority's negation. Indeed, they allude to an event omitted from the monologue, one that occurred before the curtain rose.

An explanation consistent with Herder's drama is that Prometheus defies Zeus before the stage action begins, just as the quartal sonorities challenge conventional analysis.[84] As "harmonic audacities" that eschew nineteenth-century tonal paradigms, they "perfectly symbolize revolt," and thus participate in the transgressive discourse cultivated in Beethoven's overture and the settings of Goethe's ode. Structuralist accounts naturally posit narrower frameworks for the quartal harmonies, either detecting prescient examples of Schoenberg's "emancipation of dissonance, denied the force of their resolution," or reordering and supplementing their pitches in a series of thirds (F–A–C–E–G–B) that governs the entire score's structure.[85] Such perspectives nonetheless fail to integrate the quartal motive's structural and programmatic roles, a task requiring study of the introduction's remaining sections.

Marked *grave*, the introduction's second section comprises sustained brass chords linked by ascending and descending chromatic scales in the strings. The marking and figuration recall eighteenth-century opera's sinister yet majestic *ombra* topos, epitomized by music associated in Mozart's *Don Giovanni* with the Commendatore's statue.[86] (Liszt's preface mentions the dedication of a statue of Herder during the Festival, but the music obviously alludes to Zeus.) Moreover, such passages usually anticipate recitative in Liszt's music, as occurs here. Reinforcing the ominous intonation are chords whose roots descend precipitously in thirds (C minor, A-flat minor, E major, and C-sharp minor) before rising arpeggios outline a diminished seventh chord on G-sharp, the nearest the introduction has come thus far to defining the tonic.

When the diminished seventh chord's arpeggios reach their highest point, a premonition of the sonata form's principal theme interrupts them. Upper strings descend through the same chord in sixteenth-note duplets as low winds and strings double primary pitches in eighths. In the exposition the descending duplets are marked *allegro molto appassionato*, a designation suiting fully developed material. But the brief outburst in the introduction fulfills two purposes: interrupting a climax, and initiating disintegrative processes the ensuing recitative amplifies.

The introduction's conclusion quotes the third chorus's alto solo, a lament over abandoned altars, lost dreams, and neglected customs. Against insistently repeated diminished seventh chords on G-sharp, the declamatory melody disintegrates: phrases grow shorter, dynamics softer, rhythms slower, and the range lower, until an unaccompanied bass line's chromatic descent arrives on F, the introduction's starting point.

These liquefacient techniques, illustrated in Liszt's works by *parlante* passages in the Sonata in B minor and *La notte*, encapsulate a dissipative process occurring throughout the introduction. The boldest gesture—the quartal revolt—yields to an ominous but weaker *grave* section whose climax is foiled by a nascent *appassionato*

---

[84]   Walker (vol. 2, p. 324) considers the chords "harmonic deviations" that "cannot be explained according to academic theory."

[85]   Torkowitz, p. 293; see also Carl Dahlhaus, "Zur Kritik des aesthetischen Urteils: Über Liszts *Prometheus*," *Die Musikforschung*, 23/4 (1978): 411–19.

[86]   Grabócz, pp. 75, 136.

outburst. Incremental decreases in intensity continue in the recitative. All the introduction's parts thus reflect the "malheur" in Liszt's affective dichotomy, though misery ostensibly subsides in a lament.

Just as the introduction's sections combine to present various guises of one topos, so they constitute one structural unit. Voice leading scarcely observes Schenkerian principles, but is continuous (Example 4.13a). The chromatic bass line, passing from F to F-sharp during the initial quartal harmonies, reaches G as the *grave* section begins. All voices then arpeggiate upward and acquire largely chromatic neighbor tones until they form the diminished seventh chord on G-sharp, which descending arpeggiation and diatonic passing tones elaborate during the *appassionato* outburst and recitative. As the recitative ends the bass line passes chromatically from G-sharp back through F and finally to E, the impending exposition's dominant. The quartal harmonies thus function as an unstable pre-dominant sonority, with the diminished seventh chord substituting for the dominant until the introduction's final moments.

Example 4.13a   Voice Leading in the Introduction to Liszt's *Prometheus*

Example 4.13b   Voice Leading in the Recapitulation of Liszt's *Prometheus*

Corroborating the preceding analysis is a similar process that transpires when the quartal harmonies announce the recapitulation (Example 4.13b). Here the bass line's pitches are reversed, descending from F-sharp to F, and support an enharmonically spelled German sixth chord and its attendant six-four chord in B-flat minor, a semitone above the tonic. Through a voice exchange, however, the bass line descends chromatically to G-sharp, again the root of a diminished seventh chord that instigates an *appassionato* outburst. After the recitative once more elaborates the diminished seventh chord, the enharmonically spelled G-sharp descends chromatically to E, duplicating the introduction's events. Hence the quartal harmonies again initiate dominant preparation.

As the exposition begins, the diminished seventh chord acquires E as a root to form a genuine dominant, extended by an added ninth. But the tonic triad remains unstable as the principal theme unfolds, appearing only in second inversion. Even when the tonic pitch finally occupies the bass line, it supports a seventh and merely acts as a passing tone that returns to the persistent G-sharp. Harmonic instability numbers among many traits defining the principal theme's agitated *appassionato* topos, which perfectly evokes the idiom of eighteenth-century *Sturm und Drang* symphonies, albeit with nineteenth-century orchestral techniques. The theme exhibits the style's cardinal features, including minor mode, intense chromaticism, unison thematic presentation, short phrases, syncopation, repeated notes, and lean accompaniment.

Agitation persists in the principal theme's second discrete section, in which the sixteenth-note duplets lose arpeggiated contours to become neighbor tones that tenaciously reinforce stable pedal tones, first on the dominant, then the tonic. The rumbling pedal tones support an unmistakable quotation from the third chorus, recalling the moment when the anxious Dryads confront their fateful destiny. Additional dotted fanfares, played by trumpets, flutes, and the fife-like piccolo, establish an explicitly martial tone that alludes to conflict or, in Promethean contexts, defiance of Olympian rule.

The thunderous squall becomes a full-fledged storm in the principal theme's penultimate section. As woodwinds and brasses sustain diminished seventh chords, unison strings repeat wave-like chromatic ascents and descents, explicitly illustrating a comment in Liszt's preface: "the fundamental thought of this truthful fable lends itself only to a tempestuous, flashing interpretation." In another sense, however, the passage is nondescript because it refers to no recurrent motive and thus initiates a dissipative process that continues in the first theme's conclusion, the bridge to the subordinate theme, and the recitative's recurrence. Its structural function accordingly matches its stormy intonation, which typically signifies struggle or transition in Liszt's music, as the second chorus illustrated.

As the chromatic scales yield to even less distinctive trills and repeated notes, the quartal motive returns, alternating between brasses and strings. But its neighbor tone is now a whole step, not a semitone, and its final descending fourth contracts or expands in successive statements. Thus the originally defiant gesture grows malleable, perhaps simply anticipating further imminent changes, but just as plausibly suggesting an abatement of the rebellion embodied in the quartal harmonies, as ensuing motivic treatment confirms.

The transition meets several criteria for an "ideal type" in structuralist analytical models.[87] It is modulatory, exploiting sequential repetition of a figure derived from the quartal motive to move from E minor, through the parallel major, to F major. Moreover, its syntax is loosely constructed, juxtaposing the motive's variants with arpeggios embellished by nearest neighbor tones, and thereby distinguishing itself from contiguous sections that focus largely on one figure. Thematically dependent material, however, is atypical of an "ideal" transition, and thus warrants attention. The transition subjects the motive to the Beethovenesque technique of foreshortening. Originally comprising seven notes in the introduction and preserving its length as the principal theme concludes, the motive contracts to its last five pitches, then four, and finally two, inviting interpretation as the Promethean revolt's further dissolution, notwithstanding fortissimo dynamics. A sudden resurgence of the recitative's phrases, alternating with fragments of the first theme proper, verifies the principal theme area expires in disintegration.

As a *dolente* marking affirms, the recitative's return restores a unified topos, the lament. But instead of providing equilibrium, the lament escalates instability, dividing four-measure phrases in half, adding suspensions to already dissonant diminished seventh chords, gradually eliminating textural strata, and adopting a slower tempo and final *ritenuto*. Hence all the introduction's motives, even its *appassionato* duplets, disintegrate, as though their inherent power weakens through fragmentation, juxtaposition, and foreshortening. "Utter negation" and "bitter sorrows"—the "malheur" of Liszt's preface—accordingly dissipate in the transition and recitative.

Liszt's contrasting intonation—"gloire"—is manifested in the subordinate theme, a quotation of the seventh chorus's hymn. Again invoking the *religioso* topos linked with praising Themis as humanity's guide, the theme counterbalances all preceding material, featuring the major mode (transposed from E in the chorus to D-flat), largely diatonic harmony, long-breathed periodic phrases, a cantabile melody accompanied by string arpeggios that imitate the harp (an instrument used in the chorus but not the symphonic poem), and a *dolce* marking Liszt often associated with *religioso* topics,

---

[87]   Dahlhaus, "Liszts *Bergsymphonie*," p. 109.

as in *La Chapelle de Guillaume Tell* and *Harmonies du soir*.[88] The intonation likewise typically connotes redemption and thus aptly suits the subject of Prometheus, who is ultimately freed from his shackles and hailed as mankind's champion.[89]

But beyond specifying semantic meaning, the hymn reverses all previous disintegrative procedures, growing in intensity in three consecutive statements. The first assigns the melody to cellos and a solo horn, the harp-like arpeggios to violas, sustained chords to violins and woodwinds, and pizzicato downbeats to basses. In the second, an oboe and the first violins double the melody, and the basses are marked *arco*. And in the expansive third presentation, the melody appears in divisi violins, two horns, and tutti woodwinds, the arpeggios become emphatic repeated notes, and the timpani reinforce the basses. Despite these escalations, Liszt preserved the *religioso* character with unchanging piano dynamics, numerous *dolce* markings, and instructions for the timpanist to use soft mallets, thereby reserving further thematic amplification for the recapitulation and coda.

Dissent over the development section's programmatic meaning is predictable since its abstract fugue by nature resists semantic analysis. Moreover, the fugue subject relates to no other motive, precluding identifications based on internal references. Lina Ramann, Liszt's authorized biographer, revealed the composer inscribed the name of Prometheus' brother, Epimetheus, above the fugue's onset in an archival copy of the published score. Epimetheus, Ramann explained, endowed mankind with hindsight, and the fugue accordingly symbolizes conservatism, whereas Prometheus, whose name means foresight, personifies "eternal living progress."[90]

Peter Raabe, the first curator of Weimar's Liszt-Museum, rejected Ramann's assessment because Liszt's preface never mentions Epimetheus.[91] Raabe instead claimed the fugue represents human industry, a view consistent with the fact that its subject quotes the eighth chorus's main theme, whose lyrics praise *Humanität* as mankind's greatest gift. Both interpretations nonetheless obscure fugal writing's normal role as a sign of struggle or transition in Liszt's music, as passages in *Hunnenschlacht* and the *Purgatorio* of the *Dante Symphony* illustrate.[92] Indeed, as an emblem of mankind's struggle toward progress, the fugue reconciles perfectly with Herder's philosophy and the symphonic poem's ensuing events.

Recapitulations challenge semantic analysis, as early exegetes of Beethoven's symphonies discovered. Their orderly repetition of the exposition's events, even if varied, often seems little more than "the mere playing out of a musical form," an inevitable result of using sonata principles.[93] The programs advanced by Ramann and Raabe nonetheless accord reasonably well with broad structural events. If the fugue represents conservatism, then it would necessarily elicit further defiance (quartal

---

[88]   Regarding Liszt's use of *dolce* markings, see Grabócz, pp. 69–70, 140.

[89]   Merrick, pp. 274–5.

[90]   Ramann, *Franz Liszt*, vol. 2, Heft 2, p. 152. The score bears the number L 1835 in the catalogue of the Herzogin Anna Amalia Bibliothek in Weimar. Liszt's annotation appears on p. 32.

[91]   Peter Raabe, *Franz Liszt*, supplemented by Felix Raabe (2 vols, Tutzing, 1968), vol. 2, p. 100.

[92]   Watson, p. 188.

[93]   Scott Burnham, *Beethoven Hero* (Princeton, 1995), p. 18.

motives) and "malheur" (principal theme, recitative), which a stronger resurgence of "gloire" (subordinate theme) would vanquish. A depiction of human industry implies a twofold process: in the exposition Prometheus experiences "malheur" and "gloire," states mankind must duplicate after a contrapuntal struggle.

Both accounts, however, overlook the most obvious dissimilarity between the exposition and recapitulation, namely the subordinate theme's transposition from D-flat to A major. Better explaining this difference is a "dramaturgy of tonalities" that frequently informs Liszt's large-scale works, reconciles "immanent contrasts" between the exposition's *appassionato* and *religioso* topoi, and likewise applies to the fugal struggle.[94] In the exposition the principal theme's unstable key, A minor, contrasts with the subordinate theme's unwavering D-flat major, also the fugue's main tonality. The recapitulation must accordingly assimilate both primary keys, an obligation the subordinate theme's restatement in A major deftly fulfills: A predictably remains the first scale degree, while D-flat is respelled as the third, C-sharp. Thus the subordinate theme absorbs the D-flat of the exposition and development, just as "gloire" prevails in the recapitulation and coda. Enhancing this tonal-semantic scheme is the subordinate theme's renewed intensification, a process begun in the exposition. Marked *stretto, più animato*, the Themis melody initially recurs in the horn, bassoon, and first violins as the other strings play repeated notes in triplets. The second time upper woodwinds join the violins, now two octaves higher.

Nevertheless questioning the necessity of a complete recapitulation, Liszt authorized an optional cut. If observed, it omits the entire principal theme area from the recapitulation, leaving only the truncated introduction and the subordinate theme intact, and thereby vastly diminishing the potency of the "malheur." Whether Liszt introduced the cut to reconcile semantic content with sonata form's exigencies remains open to question, but the symphonic poem's length—approximately 13 minutes—scarcely requires reduction, suggesting he was more interested in an attenuation of "malheur."

Liszt's preface reveals the coda's foreseeable goal: to depict, in contrast to all preceding material, "the infallible awareness of an innate grandeur and future deliverance, tacit faith in a liberator who will raise the long-suffering captive to celestial regions where he stole the luminous spark ... and finally, when the great day arrives, the accomplishment of the merciful deed." In a literal scenario Prometheus triumphs through the heroic act of his liberator, Hercules. Thus the coda discharges its duty—recasting earlier material in a style that divulges its "innate grandeur"— by cultivating a heroic-*grandioso* topos involving new motivic treatments and combinations, plus prosaic figuration such as military fanfares.

The coda starts with brasses repeating the augmented fugue subject's first five pitches. Rising sequential statements strengthen, progressing from unisons to lines that are initially doubled in thirds, then harmonized with full triads. Valorizing struggle, these procedures immediately recur in condensed form above a dominant pedal, with strings and woodwinds restoring the fugue subject's original rhythmic values. As the pedal tone persists, strings and woodwinds execute nondescript scales

---

[94]   Grabócz, p. 111.

in triplets, thus highlighting the quartal motive's return, now lacking its melodic contour and played as repeated notes in brass fanfares.

Further development of the fugue subject culminates in the coda's defining moment, the subordinate theme's reprise. Instead of the exposition's *dolce* markings, the hymn appears with fortissimo dynamics, first in violins and trumpets, then in tutti woodwinds and high brasses. Melodic turns, borrowed from the exposition's climactic third statement, embellish its upward leaps. Vigorously supporting the theme's first phrase are more of the fugue subject's descending thirds in the horns, repeated triplets in the woodwinds, and full chords in the trombones and tuba; its second phrase gains timpani rolls, triple stops on the offbeats in the upper strings, and alternating arpeggios and sextuplet neighbor tones in the lower strings. The hymn's transformation into a heroically triumphant march could scarcely be more explicit.

Thereafter the quartal motive dominates the coda, regaining its melodic profile and acquiring heroic overtones. It initiates antiphonal exchanges with the fugue subject; its neighbor tone expands from a semitone into a whole step, as the major key dictates; and its augmented rhythms enhance the *grandioso* intonation just before the onset of concluding fanfares. This potent emblem of "malheur" accordingly experiences sufficient variation to be assimilated by the heroic topos. Glory supplants all forms of misery.

Like the choruses, the symphonic poem articulates a central tenet of Herder's philosophy of history—mankind can achieve its highest goal, *Humanität*, only through repeated struggle—as manifested in a dynamic process whereby various representations of misery gradually yield to increasingly stronger depictions of latent glory. In five sections reproducing sonata form's "inherited constructions," the score's "emphatically expressive gestures" replay a conflict between two opposing affects. The introduction's quartal harmonies—embodiments of authority's negation and the Titan's revolt—and its sinister *ombra* intonation collapse in an impassioned outburst and fractured lament, events the exposition duplicates on a larger scale in a *Sturm und Drang* principal theme, a tempestuous transition, the malleable quartal motive's disintegration, and the lament's fragmentation. Three statements of the subordinate theme, a hymn to justice, reverse the dissolution, preparing a fugue related to humanity's progress, perhaps pitted against conservatism. The recapitulation, scarcely a "playing-out of a musical form," allows the subordinate theme's "gloire" to absorb the principal theme's "malheur," ushering in a heroic coda that portrays the myth's themes—innate grandeur, deliverance, and mercy—by valorizing the fugal struggle, transforming the hymn into a victorious march, and combining the quartal revolt with triumphant fanfares. Thus the wordless symphonic poem conveys Herder's precepts as unequivocally as the choruses.

Quite surprising then, are Liszt's initial rejection of Herder's text and immediate interest in replacing it. In late April or early May 1850, upon learning the Festival committee intended to produce the scenes,[95] he promptly expressed dissatisfaction in a letter of May 13 to Franz Dingelstedt, a Munich theater director enlisted to deliver a prologue for the occasion:

---

[95]   As of 24 April 1850, the Festival's program was undetermined. See *Franz Liszts Briefe*, comp. and ed. La Mara [Marie Lipsius] (8 vols, Leipzig, 1893–1905), vol. 8, p. 63.

In my opinion, this prologue should relate more to Weimar, to its past and future, than to Herder, for whose anniversary ... a theatrical celebration scarcely seems desirable. The performance of an oratorio in the cathedral is obviously more appropriate to commemorate a court preacher, general superintendent, and high consistorial councilor.[96]

Two months later, finding Dingelstedt in agreement,[97] Liszt asked him for "another connecting text" to replace the scenes in concert performances of the choruses.[98]

Several factors may explain Liszt's aversion to Herder's play. First, on practical grounds, retaining the scenes would have restricted performances of the choruses to theatrical venues. Second, Liszt, a liberal Catholic, doubtless shared little sympathy for Herder's stern pietism, as references to the philosopher's three clerical vocations indicate. But Liszt's concern with Herder's reputation also implies he probably wanted to distance himself from Herder's nationalism, which defined his nineteenth-century reputation, often to the exclusion of his universalism. Indeed, nationalism repeatedly surfaced during the Festival in the Herder monument's pointed inscription, "Erected by Germans of All Lands,"[99] and two ceremonial speeches. Adolf Schöll, the Festival's chairman, disclosed an explicitly nationalistic agenda at the statue's unveiling:

This noble memorial teaches that we Germans still have luminaries who, despite outwardly bitter barriers, hold us together in a steadfast unity of feeling, in a deeply spiritual unanimity of intent.[100]

A stirring exhortation from Gottfried Stichling, Herder's grandson, verified the Festival's patriotic undercurrents: "Give us what we should be allowed to have, a German fatherland!"[101] Such narrow, politically charged interpretations of Herder's vaunted nationalism doubtless struck Liszt as hollow, an assessment supported by new attitudes he adopted during the late 1840s.

As a virtuoso, Liszt had espoused the ideals of Lamennais and even set one of his revolutionary texts, *Les Forgerons*, while touring Iberia in 1845.[102] But three years later, as Weimar's kapellmeister, Liszt limited his participation in the revolutions of 1848 to visiting Viennese troops, sheltering Wagner when he fled Dresden, and composing two commemorative works: the *Arbeiterchor*, supporting Parisian workers, thousands of whom died during riots in June; and *Hungaria*, a cantata honoring his homeland's new, short-lived independence.[103] He nonetheless deferred publishing the *Arbeiterchor* until "a more suitable time," while *Hungaria* remained

---

[96] Ibid., vol. 8, p. 66.

[97] *Briefe hervorragender Zeitgenossen an Franz Liszt*, comp. and ed. La Mara (3 vols, Leipzig, 1895–1904), vol. 1, p. 137.

[98] *Franz Liszts Briefe*, vol. 8, p. 69.

[99] Franz Liszt, *Sämtliche Schriften*, ed. Detlef Altenburg, vol. 4, *Lohengrin et Tannhäuser de Richard Wagner*, ed. Rainer Kleinertz (Wiesbaden, 1989), pp. 14–15.

[100] Schöll's comments are quoted in Rudolph Haym, *Herder* (2 vols, Berlin, 1954), vol. 2, p. 823.

[101] Adelheid von Schorn, *Das nachklassische Weimar* (2 vols, Weimar, 1912), vol. 2, p. 291.

[102] Merrick, p. 4.

[103] Ibid., p. 30.

in manuscript until 1961.[104] After Hungary's crushing military defeat in 1849, Liszt became disillusioned with political revolution's failure "to bring peace to a world in which the individual would be treated justly by society."[105] Musically he responded not with protest songs or patriotic anthems, but with two threnodies: the *Funérailles* for piano, and a preliminary version of *Héroïde funèbre*, a symphonic poem later published with a preface denouncing war and its carnages. German nationalism thus probably held little appeal for Liszt during the Festival.

Finally, the connecting text the critic Richard Pohl supplied in 1857 for concert performances of the choruses departs from Herder's scenes by altering two of the Titan's important attributes, suggesting Liszt had different notions of Prometheus. Herder's Titan twice admits his defiance of Zeus waned during his long punishment: "Always greater and quieter became my courage," he declares in scene 1, "hardly do I still scorn the god who flung me here; happily thinking of my work, I forget him." In scene 11 Prometheus admits his "heart grew quiet and happier" while contemplating his rescue by Hercules. Conversely, in Pohl's opening prologue Prometheus is "the high-minded son of Gaea, not frightened by the wrath of the gods." He "humbles himself not; to the gods his hatred remains."[106] Recalling Aeschylus and especially Goethe, Pohl's narrative adopts the romantic view of Prometheus, the rebel whose defiance never abated.

Pohl's text also promulgates the Titan's quintessentially romantic image as an independent creator. Its opening lines disclose Prometheus is enchained "where no human voice is ever heard, nor where eyes ever behold [him], languishing motionless."[107] Herder's Prometheus, however, was rarely alone during his imprisonment: "the air and sea spoke to him," bringing news of humanity, and "figures of many kinds visited [him], sometimes criticizing, cursing, even damning [him], sometimes hoping and anticipating." As the hour of his destiny approaches, however, dramatic exigencies require conversations with many callers in both the scenes and the connecting text.

Pohl's depiction of an autonomous creator who relentlessly opposes authority when faced with persecution doubtless attracted Liszt, whose career followed a similar path fraught with comparable adversities. As a virtuoso pianist, his detractors accused him of superficiality and charlatanism; his tenure as kapellmeister ended with his premature resignation in 1857, when the Grand Duke's fiscal conservatism and favoritism toward spoken drama thwarted his ambitions to complete new, challenging works and promote contemporary music as a conductor and critic; and his avant-garde compositions elicited virulent partisan criticism long after he left Weimar to enter a Roman monastery's seclusion in 1861. Indeed, five years earlier he had published his symphonic poem, *Tasso*, whose preface enumerates hardships the controversial sixteenth-century poet endured at the Ferrara court, thus offering an obvious and sobering parallel to his own situation.

---

[104]   Hedwig Weilguny, *Das Liszthaus in Weimar* (Weimar, 1968), p. 31.

[105]   Fanny Lewald, *Zwölf Bilder nach dem Leben: Erinnerungen* (Berlin, 1888), p. 341.

[106]   Richard Pohl, *Chöre zu Herder's* Entfesselter Prometheus, *Musik von Franz Liszt, Verbindende Dichtung von Richard Pohl* (Leipzig, 1861), pp. 9–11.

[107]   Ibid., p. 9.

Notwithstanding sympathies Liszt very likely held for Pohl's romantic accretions to the scenes, he clearly espoused the fundamental tenet of Herder's philosophy of history. Mankind can achieve its ultimate condition—a state of freely self-determined *Humanität*—only through continuous struggle, a message articulated by repetitive topical sequences in Liszt's choruses and symphonic poem. While this progressive view is scarcely a uniquely romantic perspective on Prometheus, it certainly reflects the era's philosophical, literary, and political idealism, whereby human freedom held the potential for revealing human nature's innermost secrets. Precisely in this sense, the fundamental thought of Herder's scenes and Liszt's incidental music departs from eighteenth-century depictions of Prometheus, as one final comparison illustrates.

During the Enlightenment, myth was considered a body of literature that conveyed the underlying rationality of its collective authors, and Prometheus often simply awakened human reason, typically by animating previously inert creatures who then naïvely admired nature's wonders. Pastoralism likewise surfaces in Herder's scenes as reapers and vintners respectively thank Ceres and Bacchus for agrarian life's bounties. But in both cases homage shifts away from antiquity's gods to specifically human virtues: the reapers revel in love, while the vintners extol patience and invigorating hope. Liszt emphasized each shift, changing from a pervasive hemiola rhythm to a waltz as the reapers celebrate love, and transforming a drinking song into a heroic march as the vintners praise hope. Thus humanity's progressive virtues occupy central positions in Herder's scenes and Liszt's music, a shared ideology justifying the assessment of both as genuinely romantic representations of the Prometheus myth.

Chapter 5

The French Prometheus

The Prometheus myth achieved tremendous popularity in France much later in the nineteenth century than in German-speaking lands, a delay three factors explain. First, the fusion of Prometheus and Napoleon that appealed to writers and composers during revolutionary upheavals became unattractive in France after Napoleonic idealism collapsed. Indeed, except for Ferdinando Paër's Italian-language cantata, *Prometeo al Caucaso*, completed in Paris during the 1810s, composers produced no other musical renditions during the succeeding imperial, republican, and royalist periods until 1849, when Fromental Halévy published his large-scale cantata.[1] Second, critical and popular reactions to romantic theatrical excess precipitated a flurry of new translations of classical dramas during the 1840s, reinforcing an earlier neoclassicism that suffused paintings of Jacques Louis David (1748–1825) and other emulators of Renaissance models. And third, even after neo-Hellenism regained artistic potency, Prometheus endured lingering neglect because Aeschylus was considered inferior to the other great Athenian playwrights, Sophocles and Euripides.[2] The situation changed by the late 1840s, when new Aeschylean translations demonstrated his supposed literary coarseness was a virtue, not a flaw. His *Prometheus Bound* subsequently inspired nine musical settings, all completed between 1849 and 1900.[3]

Four of these versions raise unique, extraordinarily diverse issues of importance in French culture while preserving the myth's traditional humanism, whereby mankind progresses toward enlightened freedom. Halévy's cantata reflects burgeoning neo-Hellenism by using quarter tones, intervals found in the music and theory of ancient Greece. Another cantata by Camille Saint-Saëns glorifies his nation's emergence as an industrial power. An unpublished score by Augusta Holmès offers a perspective on the Franco-Prussian War. And Fauré's *tragédie lyrique*, designed for a giant amphitheater in Béziers, articulates Languedoc's regional identity and honors populist theatrical traditions.

The librettos of these four compositions also verify changes in literary tastes during the nineteenth century. Neoclassical reactions against romanticism

---

[1]   Paër's cantata plausibly dates from after 1812, when he succeeded Spontini at the Théâtre Italien.

[2]   Léon Halévy, *La Grèce tragique: Chefs-d'œuvre d'Eschyle, de Sophocle et d'Euripide traduits en vers* (3 vols, Paris, 1849), vol. 1, pp. v–viii; Howard Lee Nostrand, *Le Théâtre antique et à l'antique en France de 1840 à 1900* (Paris, 1934), p. 52.

[3]   The total includes cantatas by Halévy (1849), Camille Saint-Saëns (1867), Georges Bizet (1867, lost), Jules Massenet (1867, lost), Peter Benoit (1867), Augusta Holmès (1871), André Messager (1877), Georges Matthias (1882), and Gabriel Fauré's *tragédie lyrique* (1900).

prompted simpler styles; the Parnassians laced refined language with antique references; and the Symbolists exploited mythic ambiguities in mixtures of poetry and prose. All four works likewise contain harmonic unorthodoxies, including radically modal writing, atonal counterpoint, and the aforementioned quarter tones. But unlike Germanic composers who employed unconventional harmonies to represent the Promethean revolt, their French peers devised new sounds to evoke classical antiquity's exoticism. And three scores raise the specter of Wagnerism, a crucial topic for composers, poets, and critics in *fin-de-siècle* France.

Halévy

Jacques-François-Fromental Halévy (1799–1862) is today best remembered for his masterpiece, *La Juive*, a grand opera whose long, acclaimed run at the Opéra began in 1835. But during his lifetime and much of the nineteenth century, the native Parisian achieved renown in three additional fields: his highly successful *opéras comiques* received unequivocal praise from the normally sarcastic Heinrich Heine and the equally redoubtable Eduard Hanslick;[4] he obtained increasingly prestigious appointments at the Paris Conservatoire, first as professor of harmony and accompaniment (1827), then counterpoint and fugue (1833), and finally composition (1840); and after his induction into the Académie des beaux arts in 1836, he served as its vice president beginning in 1844 and was elected secretary for life a decade later.

Halévy's professorial and academic duties entailed public lectures that frequently allude to Greek culture, reflecting his family's intellectual background, his brother Léon's professional success in translating Greek drama, and strong predilections for the Prometheus myth. In an address entitled "Les Arts et l'industrie," he corroborated his belief in society's education through art, noting Pericles sought "to charm and instruct the Athenians" by commissioning a statue from Phidias, a sculptor who could "render art accessible to the masses."[5] The foreword to his *Leçons de lecture musicale* (1850) discloses another Promethean affinity: music serves "a significant purpose for the progress of civilization and human society; singing in particular functions as a harmonious rhythm that unites the world's prayers."[6] Halévy thus espoused the myth's notion of mankind achieving progress through unity, echoing the humanitarian message that resounds in Beethoven's ballet and Liszt's incidental music.

Léon, a prominent Saint-Simonian, conveyed similar views in the foreword to his first volume of dramatic translations, naming the theater as Greek antiquity's "greatest, most advanced expression of the ideas of renewal and progress."[7] And in his preface to *Prométhée enchaîné [Prometheus Bound]* he underscored the Titan's

---

4   Heinrich Heine, *Werke und Briefe*, ed. Hans Kaufmann (10 vols, Berlin, 1962), vol. 6, p. 472; Eduard Hanslick, *Aus dem Opernleben der Gegenwart* (Berlin, 1884), pp. 173, 176.
5   Fromental Halévy, *Souvenirs et portraits* (Paris, 1861), p. 313.
6   Fromental Halévy, preface to *Leçons de lecture musicale* (Paris, 1850), n.p.
7   Léon Halévy, *La Grèce tragique*, vol. 1, p. xxiii.

"deep and generous compassion for the miseries of humanity, his lively sympathy for and faith in its progress, and its free and glorious destinies."[8]

Receptive to the subject though both brothers were, they did not collaborate until 1847, when two events elicited their cantata. First, Léon completed several translations, including *Prométhée enchaîné*; and second, one of Fromental's colleagues, mathematics professor Alexandre-Joseph-Hidulphe Vincent, published a monograph on ancient Greek music. Both events represented broad trends that already boasted distinctive histories and would continue to shape nineteenth-century French culture.

Over 600 French plays (either translations of original Greek and Roman dramas or modernizations of them) and over 500 literary or historical works never intended for the stage date from between 1840 and 1900.[9] This vast corpus attests not only to an unprecedented and unmatched florescence of French neo-Hellenism, but also to new approaches to literary antiquity. Earlier writers typically adapted Athenian tragedy to suit contemporary stage practices. Enlightenment playwrights, including Racine, Voltaire, and Crébillon, cultivated homogeneous verse forms and poetic meters in the stylized declamation of their classical adaptations. The *Philosophes*, likewise embracing a contemporary perspective, valued myths primarily as allegories whose exegesis revealed the underlying rationality of their creators.[10]

Neoclassical subjects inspired few plays during the Revolutionary and Napoleonic eras, when current events provided models for heroic stage action,[11] and were equally unappealing when romanticism finally arrived in France in the 1830s. Rare exceptions such as the *Caligula* of Alexandre Dumas *père* still indulged prevailing tastes, exploiting vehement passions, an agitated acting style, and extraneous references to contemporary events. Already by the late 1830s Stendhal, Jules Janin, and Sainte-Beuve were calling for a return to antiquity, "to ennobled nature, to that type of beauty which reproduces the lines of statuary."[12]

Neo-Hellenism's fortunes reached a turning point on 22 April 1843, when the Théâtre Français presented François Ponsard's *Lucrèce*. Audiences reacted to the drama's sordid plot: the title heroine commits suicide after exhorting her father and husband to avenge her rape by the Roman emperor Sextus, whose dynasty falls when he further indulges his oppressive passions. Critics, in contrast, noticed its intentionally archaic language, simple, well-defined action, and use of Athenian tragedy's monologues and choruses. In short, they recognized "a spirit as opposed as possible to that of the preceding generation."[13] So great

---

[8]   Ibid., p. 7.

[9]   Nostrand, p. 1 (Nostrand [pp. 189–315] comments on all 600); Henri Peyre, *Bibliographie critique de l'hellénisme en France de 1843 à 1870* (New Haven, 1932), pp. 83–215.

[10]   Frank Manuel discusses the "new allegorism" in *The Eighteenth Century Confronts the Gods* (Cambridge, Mass., 1959), pp. 129–48, 245–82.

[11]   Nostrand, p. 12.

[12]   Charles Augustin Sainte-Beuve, *Portraits contemporains, nouvelle édition* (3 vols, Paris, 1847), vol. 3, pp. 419–20.

[13]   André Le Breton, *Le Théâtre romantique* (Paris, 1927), p. 222.

was the popular and critical success of *Lucrèce* that within a year of its debut it inspired three reprints, a sequel, and three parodies.[14] The next year the Théâtre Français mounted a genuine Greek tragedy, the *Antigone* of Sophocles, in a verse translation by Paul Meurice and Auguste Vacquerie and in imitation of ancient Greek productions. A spectacular triumph, *Antigone* ensured the lasting viability of neoclassical drama on Parisian stages and precipitated an outpouring of original plays and translations.[15]

Léon distanced himself from numerous writers who profited from neoclassicism's popularity by furnishing an uncritical public with pedestrian prose translations of antique dramas and histories. In the preface to his *La Grèce tragique*, he quoted speculations of his mentor Abel-François Villemain (1790–1870), the founder of comparative literature in France: "The true manner of imitating Greek tragedy would be to translate it with an impassioned exactitude, to be transported by the imagination ... into all the impressions that are inspired, and to find naïve and beautiful words to express them."[16] Léon then pointedly noted, "a translation in prose, however faithful, however impassioned, however happily it may be inspired, would scarcely realize the wish expressed ... by M. Villemain."[17] A translator's duty, Léon argued, was to reproduce all the original text's verse forms and thereby distinguish between declamatory utterances of individual characters and lyrical passages for the chorus, a practice earlier translators had either avoided altogether or observed inconsistently in flexibly molded declamatory passages. Though falling short of his goal, Léon set standards most of his contemporaries simply disregarded and few matched for over 20 years.[18] His *Prométhée enchaîné* accordingly features lyric metrical translations of excerpts others rendered in prose, including the Titan's opening monologue, his ensuing dialogue with Oceanus, Io's anguished speeches, and the play's apocalyptic ending.

Léon's fidelity to Aeschylus, reflecting the epoch's new zeal for classical antiquity, was transferred to Fromental's cantata (Table 5.1). Of the libretto's 147 lines, 72 directly quote Léon's translation, 19 vary slightly, and nine paraphrase stage directions. Only 47 added lines provide text for several of the cantata's lyrical numbers, most notably the Titan's air (No. 4), much of the Chorus of Oceanids and an attached recitative (No. 5), and the finale (No. 6). Otherwise the libretto illustrates Léon's "impassioned exactitude" with a restrained vocabulary, clear syntax, and largely appropriate verse and line structures. It thus comprises a worthy addition to the enormous total of neoclassical stage works written in France beginning at mid century.

---

[14]   Nostrand, p. 198.

[15]   Peyre, pp. 21–5.

[16]   Abel-François Villemain, *Cours de littérature française: Tableaux de la littérature française aux XVIII* siècle* (Paris, 1828–9), p. 352, quoted in Léon Halévy, *La Grèce tragique*, vol. 1, p. xviii.

[17]   Léon Halévy, *La Grèce tragique*, vol. 1, p. xix.

[18]   Nostrand, p. 205. Some passages in stichomythic meter eluded Halévy's "impassioned exactitude."

Table 5.1   Léon Halévy's Libretto after Aeschylus

Cantata Number	Scene and Lines in Aeschylus	Textual Variants	Action
Overture			
No. 1, Introduction			
Récitatif: La Force, Vulcain	i, 1–8, 17–20	12, 1v	Force compels Vulcan to imprison Prometheus.
No. 2			
Air: Vulcain	i, 25–36	12, 0v	Vulcan reflects on the Titan's isolation.
No. 3			
Duo: La Force, Vulcain	i, 43, 62–9, 73–100	37, 6v	Force urges Vulcan to work quickly; Vulcan pities Prometheus.
No. 4			
Strophe: Prométhée			
Récitatif Andantino Récit.	ii, 109–14 ii, 115, 119 ii, 137–8, 143–6	23, 12v	Prometheus invokes the elements to witness Olympian injustice.
Pastorale: Orchestre			
No. 5			
Chœur des Océanides 1ers Sop., 2ds Sop.	iii, 147–8, 153–4, 161–2, 449–50, 457–8	24, 5v, 7a	Oceanids console Prometheus, lament his torments, and wish him happy dreams.
Récitatif: Prométhée	iii, 157–8	8, 2v, 6a	Prometheus remains chained, despite his gift to humanity.
Récitatif: Une Océanide	v, 436–7	8, 2v, 6a	His torment is a harbinger of his victory.
Chœur: 1ers Sop., 2ds Sop., Ténors, Basses		4r, 1a	The Titan's triumph is near.

No. 6			
Hymne: Prométhée Chœur	iv, 369, iii, 275–6	22, 3v 19a	Prometheus is acclaimed as a martyr and creator. He will deliver humanity to a new day of equality.

Textual variants in column 3 indicate the total number of lines in Léon's libretto, and the numbers of lines he varied (v), added (a), or repeated (r) from the previous number.

The second broad cultural trend that prompted the brothers to collaborate was escalating scholarly and popular interest in archaeology, a science barely emerging from its infancy in the 1840s. Indeed, the study of ancient European cultures had remained largely anecdotal since the time of Pausanius, a Roman whose account of his travels in Greece during the second century CE furnished scholars with information on Hellenic monuments for 1,600 years.[19] Early in the eighteenth century, however, French academicians began systematic investigations of ancient ruins, inspired by earlier writings of the naturalist Nicolas de Fabri and the physician Jacques Spon, who revived the term archaeology itself.[20] Beyond attaining scholarly standards that still withstand scrutiny today, eighteenth-century archaeologists mounted large-scale excavations, starting at Herculaneum in 1719 and at Pompeii in 1784. Commercially motivated excavators capitalized on public enthusiasm for their projects, initiating vogues for archaeology after major discoveries, such as Jean-François Champollion's decoding of hieroglyphics in 1822, which inspired pseudo-Egyptian fashions and jewelry.[21] Excavations culminated in the establishment of the Ecole française d'Athènes, the first state-sponsored institute devoted to research on antiquity's civilizations. The school opened in 1846, precisely when Léon was engrossed in his translations and only a year before Fromental mounted rehearsals of his cantata.

Archaeological activity reawakened interest in ancient Greek music, a subject whose study had followed a course similar to that of its parent discipline. Just as the Roman traveler Pausanius had provided the bulk of information on Greek monuments, so the Roman mathematician and philosopher Boethius (ca. 480–524 CE) had transmitted the body of Greek music theory to the Latin world. His *De institutione musica* remained the principal treatise on the subject throughout the Middle Ages, but after it was twice published in Venice late in the fifteenth century, Renaissance theorists, who had begun deciphering original Greek texts, realized Boethius and others had consulted Alexandrian writers active during the second century CE, not

---

[19]   O. Charles-Picard, "Classical Greece," in Gilbert Charles-Picard (ed.), *Larousse Encyclopedia of Archaeology*, trans. Anne Ward (New York, 1972), p. 267.

[20]   Gilbert Charles-Picard, "What is Archaeology?" in *Larousse Encyclopedia of Archaeology*, p. 14.

[21]   Ibid., p. 16.

primary sources.[22] By 1558 Gioseffo Zarlino had benefited from his predecessors' work, but still justifiably declared antiquity's authors could provide nothing but "confusion of mind" regarding the order, number, and names of the modes.[23] Little had changed 200 years later, when Johann Nikolaus Forkel, Johann Josef Fux, and Friedrich Wilhelm Marpurg respectively described the system of Greek *genera* as a "dark subject," "the chaos of antiquity," and a *Zankapfel*, a word translated literally as "apple of discord," but more idiomatically as "bone of contention."[24] As late as 1838 Raphael Georg Kiesewetter could still claim, "the theory of ancient Greek music is by no means generally understood."[25] But by the mid nineteenth century, musical paleographers, stimulated by recent archaeological findings, developed a new awareness of antiquity's surviving musical fragments and rediscovered Greek music theory's roots.

Among many distinguished contributors to the field of Greek music was Alexandre Vincent, a mathematics professor at the Sorbonne and prolific essayist on archaeology and Hellenic philology. His magnum opus was a 600-page monograph containing the first modern French translations of two anonymous Greek treatises (the second the only text then known regarding details of rhythmic notation in antique sources), several fragments, a thirteenth-century harmonic treatise by Georgios Pachymeres, and copious commentary.[26] Vincent formalized his study on 18 December 1840, when he and the organologist Jean-Joseph-Auguste Bottée de Toulmon demonstrated at the Académie an instrument of their own design intended to reproduce every interval and mode of ancient Greek music. The instrument, much simpler than the archicembalo Nicola Vicentino had devised nearly three centuries earlier, could generate scales, but not play actual compositions. Vincent's expertise in calculus and acoustic logarithms nonetheless allowed him to achieve unprecedented accuracy in dividing intervals according to specifications in Greek theoretical writings. The institute's members declined to judge the instrument's merits, asking instead for a report on the Greek texts that had inspired its construction. Vincent offered preliminary findings five months later, staking his claim to the topic when the German scholar Frederick Bellermann began to translate the same anonymous treatises. Vincent's monograph appeared in 1847, with the Académie's approval.

Vincent's commentary outlines Greek music theory's familiar precepts, as codified definitively in the fourth century BCE by Aristoxenus, who conceived pitch as a continuum susceptible to limitless varieties of subdivisions. Thus an infinite number of microtonal intervals was theoretically possible, but only one, the enharmonic

---

[22]   Claude V. Palisca, "Introductory Notes on the Historiography of the Greek Modes," *Journal of Musicology*, 3/3 (1984): 222.

[23]   Gioseffo Zarlino, *Le istitutioni harmoniche* (Ridgewood, NJ: 1966), p. 367.

[24]   Johann Nikolaus Forkel, *Allgemeine Geschichte der Musik* (Graz, 1967), pp. 51–2; Johann Joseph Fux, *Gradus ad Parnassum: A Facsimile of the 1725 Edition* (New York, 1966), p. 221; Friedrich Wilhelm Marpurg, *Kritische Einleitung in die Geschichte und Lehrsätze der alten und neuen Musik* (Berlin, 1759), p. 120.

[25]   Raphael Georg Kiesewetter, *History of the Modern Music of Western Europe*, trans. Robert Müller (New York, 1973), p. 269.

[26]   Alexandre-Joseph-Hidulphe Vincent, *Notice sur divers manuscrits grecs relatifs à la musique, Comprenant une traduction française et des commentaires* (Paris, 1847).

diesis or quarter tone, appeared in any of the three tetrachords constituting the basis of Greek music and theory: within the compass of a perfect fourth and in descending order, the diatonic tetrachord consisted of two modern whole tones followed by a semitone, the chromatic of a minor third followed by two semitones, and the enharmonic of a major third followed by two quarter tones. Tetrachords combined to form and "shade" *tonoi*, larger scale-like modes bearing well-known ethnic names that reflect their use in regions of ancient Greece, such as Lydian, Phrygian, and Dorian. Each *tonus* could begin on any pitch, thereby offering tonal options nineteenth-century composers lacked, as Vincent passionately observed:

> We cannot leave this subject without ... noticing the immense advantage the ancients had over us and found in ... their modes. What a fertile source of variety, and a means ... of imparting to a melody this or that character! Indeed, without even speaking of the enharmonic genus (a genus so expressive that we lack it entirely), we moderns recognize only two finals, those of the major and minor modes, whereas the ancients could establish theirs on every scale degree. ... This study will not perhaps be finished unless one of our most capable composers (if I am permitted to name M. Halévy, who has demonstrated the possibility of reproducing and appreciating the intervals of the enharmonic genus) may succeed in realizing the vow we have made to see revived in our theater this genus so full of pathos.[27]

Halévy helped Vincent keep his vow in the cantata's fifth number, the Chorus of Oceanids, for women's chorus and orchestra. The movement entails three contrasting formal sections, the first varied upon immediate repetition (AA'BC). Consoling Prometheus, the Oceanids lament his torments (A) and, as they pity him, a cloud of tears swells in their eyes (A'). After common time shifts to triple meter, they urge him to "close his eyes momentarily" so he may experience "happy dreams of joyous days" (B). When common time returns, the Oceanids invite "his brothers in misery" to charm him with sweet words and mingle their tears with his sorrows (C).

Quarter tones occur four times throughout the form: in the orchestral introduction, in brief instrumental segues following the first section (A) and its variation (A'), and at several phrase endings in the final section (C). In the first three cases they appear in purely orchestral passages and consequently pose no threat to vocal intonation. They are always assigned to string instruments, which typically execute microtones more easily and accurately than woodwinds or brasses. Their likewise straightforward notation involves small diagonal strokes on the stems of conventional flat signs (Example 5.1a–b). Such accidentals invariably fall between two pairs of pitches, E and F, and B-flat and B-natural, in a tonal context otherwise adhering to nineteenth-century norms for D minor, with occasional modalisms that intensify the antique coloring. The movement thus employs two conjunct enharmonic tetrachords, each encompassing a major third and two quarter tones, and illustrates the genus Vincent described as "full of pathos" (Example 5.2).

---

[27]   Ibid., p. 101; see also Vincent, "De la musique dans la tragédie grecque à l'occasion de la représentation d'Antigone," *Journal general de l'instruction publique*, 69 (1844): 759.

Example 5.1a–b Halévy *Prométhée enchaîné, Scènes d'après Eschyle*, No. 5, mm.
        4–9, 35–40

Vincent's characterization accords not only with the Oceanids' expression of sympathy, but also with twentieth-century perspectives on the ethical nature of Greek modes. As relatively recent investigations have shown, a mode with a final on D was known as the Mixolydian *tonus* to Cleonides and Ptolemy, who derived their theories from Aristoxenus.[28] Plato and Aristotle likewise reached a rare consensus regarding the Mixolydian mode's ethos, the former ascribing to it a "lamentable character," the latter noting it "makes men sad and grave."[29] Their opinions thus plainly agree with the Oceanids' mournful sentiments. But like many nineteenth-century scholars, Vincent was unaware of relevant writings and apparently accepted traditional Boethian names of the modes.[30] He accordingly identified the chorus's enharmonically "shaded" *tonus* as the Dorian mode in his monograph and cited its time-honored characterization from Plato's *Republic* as a "noble and virile

---

[28]   Claude V. Palisca, "Theory, Theorists," in Stanley Sadie (ed.), *The New Grove Dictionary of Music and Musicians* (20 vols, London, 1980), vol. 18, p. 743.

[29]   Vincent's "caractère lamentable" reconciles with descriptions in Plato's *Republic* (3.398–9) and Aristotle's *Politics* (8.1340a).

[30]   See Calvin M. Bower's transcription of Boethius's modal matrix in "The Modes of Boethius," *Journal of Musicology*, 3/3 (1984): 261.

harmony."[31] His errant identification is nonetheless compatible with the cantata's subject, since Prometheus is undeniably a "noble and virile" figure.

Example 5.2   Conjunct Enharmonic Tetrachords in Halévy's *Chœur des Océanides*

Ethical typologies scarcely influenced the cantata's reception. Originally scheduled for 18 April 1847, the premiere was canceled because the quarter tones posed severe technical difficulties.[32] Nearly two years later, on 18 March 1849, the rescheduled debut aroused great anticipation after the *Revue et gazette musicale* published the cantata's libretto.[33] One anonymous reviewer deemed the effect of the quarter tones "highly original," while another thought their "garbled combinations" produced "muddy effects."[34] Hector Berlioz, rarely impressed with Halévy's operatic successes, admitted the "episodic and quite short use" of the intervals engendered "a type of wailing whose strangeness was perfectly motivated by and connected with the sad tone of the quite lovely chorus in which it is introduced."[35] He nonetheless doubted Halévy's "modest attempt" could "recreate the effect ... quarter tones could produce in Greek music," though he granted the issue could be resolved only by sending "musicians truly given to philosophical impartiality to a place where Greek musical practice has been preserved," namely the convents of Mount Athos, where he believed quarter tones survived in the liturgy. An anonymous, less objective critic for *La France musicale*, however, insisted Halévy had wasted an opportunity to rise to the subject's "poetic heights" and had instead presented "a grotesque musical outline reminiscent of the Greeks."[36] Although he begrudgingly noted various passages in the cantata had enchanted "a few musical amateurs," he also observed the Chorus of Oceanids had met with "complete silence."

Vincent had anticipated mixed criticism, conceding modern music's infusion with Hellenic modal variety would require "a great deal of good taste, even more of

---

31   Vincent, *Notice*, p. 83.
32   "Nouvelles," *Revue et gazette musicale de Paris*, 14/16 (1847): 135.
33   Léon Halévy, "*Prométhée enchaîné: Scènes d'après Eschyle*," *Revue et gazette musicale de Paris*, 16/11 (1849): 85.
34   Ruth Jordan, *Fromental Halévy: His Life & Music (1799–1862)* (London, 1994), p. 203.
35   Hector Berlioz, "5ᵉ Séance de la Société des concerts," *Revue et gazette musicale de Paris*, 16/12 (1849): 92–5.
36   "Société des Concerts du Conservatoire, 5ᵉ Séance: *Prométhée enchaîné* par MM. Halévy," *La France musicale*, Numéro 12 (1849): 89–90.

knowledge, and above all freedom from prejudice."[37] J.-L.-M. Lecomte, writing for the *Revue et gazette musicale*, agreed, but sounded an optimistic note:

> We know … with what indifference, or rather with what bias, musicians in general, preoccupied exclusively with modern harmonic music, … will receive … antiquity's music. … But in reviving an element of forgotten effect, … who knows what singular impulse M. Halévy's effort could give to the art's future? Guided by M. Vincent's scientific observations, the great composer could rediscover the colossal expressive means about which history has bequeathed us the most fabulous accounts.[38]

Halévy perhaps fell short of realizing Lecomte's hyperbolic exhortation, and his score had only one nineteenth-century successor in using quarter tones, a cantata Jean-Jacques Débillemont composed in 1863.[39] But the Halévy brothers incontestably succeeded in encapsulating a moment in French cultural history, when theatrical neoclassicism and archaeology captured the public imagination and reviving antiquity's glories became a paramount concern in the arts and letters.

Other features of their collaborative effort also warrant attention, since they either reflect romantic views of Prometheus or are of intrinsic musical interest. The cantata's overture, wielding "truly Lisztian force,"[40] provides material for several ensuing vocal numbers (Example 5.3a–d). Its slow introduction begins as a plaintive solo clarinet outlines primary triads in the tonic, C minor, and makes a long scalewise descent in the score's pervasive dotted rhythms (5.3a). After more woodwinds briefly join the clarinet in parallel sixth chords,

Example 5.3a   Halévy *Prométhée enchaîné, Scènes d'après Eschyle*, Overture, mm. 1–12

---

[37]   Vincent, *Notice*, p. 102.

[38]   J.-L.-M. Lecomte, "Archéologie: Manuscrits relatifs à la musique des grecs anciennes publiés par l'institut avec une traduction française et des annotations de M. Vincent," *Revue et gazette musicale de Paris*, 14 (1847): 279.

[39]   Frank Reinisch, "Französische Vierteltonmusik in der Mitte des 19. Jahrhunderts," *Die Musikforschung*, 37 (1984): 121–2.

[40]   Hugh Macdonald, "Halévy, Fromental," in Stanley Sadie and John Tyrrell (eds), *The New Grove Dictionary of Music and Musicians*, vol. 10, p. 690.

a livelier tempo marks an ambitious sonata form's onset. The exposition entails three keys, a quintessential strategy in nineteenth-century sonata forms, though Halévy's choices are distinctive. Cast in C minor, the principal theme (5.3b) alternates between scalewise ascents in vigorous dotted rhythms and cascades of descending triplets, all played by tutti strings.

Example 5.3b   Halévy *Prométhée enchaîné, Scènes d'après Eschyle*, Overture, mm. 13–30

Following an oboe's scherzo-like solo in E-flat major, the principal theme concludes in the tonic as the full orchestra repeats the dotted rhythms and triplets. The lyrical subordinate theme (5.3c), another clarinet solo supported by transparent pizzicato and tremolo figuration in divisi violins and violas, unfolds at a slower tempo in C-flat major, reflecting Halévy's penchant for keys involving many flats.[41] And in A-flat major, a third below the tonic rather than the conventional third above, the closing theme (5.3d) restores the original tempo as violins arpeggiate a single rhythmic figure against a background of muted strings. After the full orchestra confirms A-flat major in an animated episode, the development section first exploits the lyrical subordinate theme, then the oboe's scherzo-like solo. In both cases thematic fragments pass antiphonally among orchestral sections or solo instruments. The recapitulation presents all three themes in order with C as the tonic, though the subordinate and closing subjects adopt the parallel major. Recalling A-flat, the coda assumes the manner of Meyerbeer, repeating a simple rhythmic figure to a steady crescendo, before the principal theme's reprise in C minor.

Example 5.3c   Halévy *Prométhée enchaîné, Scènes d'après Eschyle*, Overture, mm. 85–90

Example 5.3d   Halévy *Prométhée enchaîné, Scènes d'après Eschyle*, Overture, mm. 104–7

41   Ibid.

Like an operatic *introduzione*, the first number recalls portions of the overture, namely the introduction's clarinet solo and parallel sixth chords and the exposition's principal theme, until the soloists enter. Vulcan (bass), the Olympian blacksmith, shackles Prometheus (tenor) to a cliff, fulfilling a role the allegorical character Force (tenor) pointedly describes as servile. The dialogue is set as simple recitative, with Halévy's typically supple declamation interrupted by tremolos or sustained chords in the strings and occasional tutti outbursts of the overture's dotted rhythms and cascading triplets. In the second number, a short air in F minor, Vulcan emphasizes the Titan's isolation far from voices dear to him, unaided by mortals, including his future liberator (Hercules). Nondescript vocal lines, consisting largely of repeated notes within stepwise descents, match prosaic string accompaniment, whose nearly unbroken pattern of a downbeat followed by three afterbeats varies only when woodwinds sustain several diminished seventh and dominant ninth chords.

Again set in F minor, the third movement is much more engaging. Force, urging Vulcan to work relentlessly, inspects the Titan's bonds to verify their strength. In a resentful reply Vulcan sympathizes with Prometheus, but Force claims the punishment fits the crime. A vehement recurrence of the overture's principal theme gradually subsides as both characters bicker in an operatic *recitativo accompagnato* interspersed with characteristic motives that intensify the conflict, including the bass line's repetitive ascending scales and insistent neighbor-tone figures in inner voices. A tutti orchestral reminiscence of the overture's cascading triplets concludes the duet.

In extreme contrast, the fourth movement affords Prometheus a moment of lyrical repose. He summons the four elements to witness the evils the gods perpetrated with Force's aid, dispelling earlier dark keys with a radiant E major. His invocation again emulates simple recitative, though distinctive instruments sustain accompanimental chords: flutes in their lowest register, paired flutes and clarinets, and four valved horns (*cors à pistons*), whose use Halévy pioneered.[42] Throughout the attendant strophe the horns repeat a rising triadic figure in parallel thirds, maintaining a rhythm of a triplet followed by two quarter notes. Against this gentle background, Prometheus vows to conceal his tears and shameful bondage despite his earlier cries, which had disturbed a realm of eternal silence. When a soaring violin melody culminates in flurries of tremolos, he speculates the sound represents the beating wings of a vulture, his daily tormentor, in another brief recitative. The ensuing instrumental number, however, is scarcely ominous, comprising a pastorale replete with double-reed solos, drones for five solo cellos, harp arpeggios, and tinges of the Aeolian mode, the natural form of A minor. Such bucolic music aptly prepares the arrival of the nymph-like Oceanids, who then sing the "ravishing" fifth number,[43] as described above.

In one last animated *recitativo accompagnato* Prometheus observes he remains imprisoned, despite endowing mortals with the supreme gift of fire—the Olympian heritage, source of the arts, and glory of the world. The Oceanids reply, "his torment is his victory," a sentiment the full chorus and orchestra develop in a decidedly martial finale, replete with an introductory march cadence, dotted fanfares, triadic figuration, and brassy orchestration. An interlude for tenors and basses, balancing

---

[42]   Ibid.
[43]   Léon Halévy, *F. Halévy: Sa vie et ses œuvres* (Paris, 1863), p. 47.

earlier reliance on women's voices in the Chorus of Oceanids, supplies contrast with reiterated triplets and reduced scoring for the strings.

The finale's lyrics reflect typically romantic views of Prometheus:

Every martyr of a new faith
Has his vulture and his crag
Until the day when god summons him
And makes a throne of his pyre!
Toward equality the day advances;
The fallen giant will be reborn.
And when deliverance comes,
With a cry of love and hope
The entire world will salute him.

Prometheus, a martyr suffering in isolation, leads mankind toward deliverance, whereupon his beneficiaries honor him. Suffering and isolation, largely neglected during the Enlightenment, number among the myth's primary nineteenth-century themes. The interlude for men's voices likewise illustrates a romantic topos, extolling the Promethean flame as a fertile power that will produce an earthly bond and inspire creators to unite humanity's arms and hearts. Halévy's cantata thus concludes by depicting artists as creators capable of transforming society, a favorite romantic reading of the legend.

Halévy's success was essentially a phenomenon of the July Monarchy. *Le Dilettante d'Avignon*, his first great triumph, began its long run in 1829, months before Louis Philippe accepted the crown, and other principal operas flourished under the Citizen King's regime. But after Louis Philippe's mismanaged domestic and foreign policies precipitated the Revolution of 1848, Halévy's compositions foundered. New stage works attracted only modest critical and public interest after 1850, when he visited the exiled Louis Philippe in London while preparing an ill-conceived musical treatment of *The Tempest*. This inattention may reflect Halévy's declining compositional powers, but it also indicates he more adeptly captured the Orléanist period's prevailing attitudes, as when his *Les Mousquetaires de la reine* capitalized on the Dumas novel's extraordinary popularity. The same was certainly true of his *Prométhée enchaîné*, which scarcely garnered popular or critical acclaim, but indisputably reflected the era's rejection of romanticism in favor of theatrical neoclassicism and its preoccupation with recent archaeological discoveries. Following Charles-Louis Napoléon's unexpected landslide victory in the elections of 1848, however, a new political era required a new musical spokesman. Halévy's young pupil, Camille Saint-Saëns, accepted the challenge, again using the Prometheus myth to voice the Second Empire's foremost issues.

Saint-Saëns

The prodigious feats of Camille Saint-Saëns (1835–1921) so astonished Orléanist Paris that critics, patrons, and audiences compared him to Mozart and Mendelssohn.[44] He began piano lessons with his overly protective mother at age three, started composing before his fourth birthday, and soon after performed a Beethoven violin sonata in a private salon. Saint-Saëns subsequently studied piano with Camille Stamaty, a pupil of the celebrated virtuoso Friedrich Kalkbrenner, and composition with the iconoclastic Pierre Maleden, whose rejection of the Conservatoire's strict curriculum in favor of an intuitive system indebted to the German theorist Gottfried Weber anticipated his pupil's later status as an outsider in Parisian musical circles.[45] He gave his formal debut at age ten, entered François Benoist's organ class at the Conservatoire two years later, and won the coveted *première prix* after three years of study. By then he had enrolled in the composition classes of Fromental Halévy, whom he remembered as a self-absorbed, inattentive teacher.[46]

Like many prodigies, Saint-Saëns experienced setbacks in making the transition to a successful adult career. Although he won two competitions sponsored by the progressive Société Sainte-Cécile, the award that would have conferred an imprimatur on his compositional vocation—the Prix de Rome—eluded him twice, partly because of his age. In 1852 the judges considered him too young and unseasoned to live in Italy for the three-year term of study incumbent on the victor;[47] and in 1863 he was almost three years older than any previous winner.[48] That he was by then the protégé of Berlioz, himself a maverick in Paris's musical community, scarcely helped his cause.

The event that "threw him into the limelight," as composer Alfred Bruneau later recalled, was another contest held in association with the Exposition universelle of 1867.[49] Amid inventions and technological displays, a cantata would be performed in the newly constructed Palais de l'Industrie. An imperial commission's notices, published in the *Moniteur universel* on 13 March and 6 April 1867, solicited librettos pertaining to the Exposition and emphasizing France's industrial progress during the 15 years since the Second Empire's founding. The commission also set 5 June as the deadline for submitting musical settings of a prize-winning text.[50] Controversy again plagued Saint-Saëns, but he triumphed in a *succès de scandale*.

Some 222 authors met the commission's deadline of 10 April.[51] Seventeen judges, including the poet Théophile Gautier, awarded 1,000 francs to the young

---

[44]   Brian Rees, *Camille Saint-Saëns: A Life* (London, 1999), p. 33.

[45]   Camille Saint-Saëns, *Musical Memories*, trans. Edwin Gile Rich (Boston, 1919), pp. 11–12.

[46]   Ibid., pp. 18–19.

[47]   Stephen Studd, *Saint-Saëns: A Critical Biography* (London, 1999), p. 29.

[48]   Rees, p. 121.

[49]   Alfred Bruneau, *La Musique française* (Paris, 1901), p. 3.

[50]   See the reprinted document in Oscar Comettant, *La Musique, les musiciens et les instruments de musique chez les différents peuples du monde, Ouvrage enrichi de texts musicaux, orné de 150 dessins d'instruments rares et curieux, Archives complètes de tous les documents qui se rattachent à l'Exposition internationale de 1867* (Paris, 1869), p. 27.

[51]   Ibid., p. 25.

Romain Cornut *fils*, whose father, a locally renowned literary scholar, had forced both his sons to submit librettos.[52] Cornut's *Les Noces de Prométhée* [*The Wedding of Prometheus*] narrates the Titan's rescue from "terrible suffering on frightful crags" by Humanity, a "beneficent spirit." Their marriage inaugurates an era of "justice, peace, and unity."[53] Ranking the naïve allegory "among the feeblest efforts of the French muse," a correspondent for the London *Times* ridiculed the French belief that prizes could elicit works of literary merit.[54]

Notwithstanding such criticism, over 100 composers entered the competition.[55] A panel of judges comprising some of Paris's most powerful musicians nonetheless considered only 11 cantatas quite good, three excellent, and just one—that of Saint-Saëns—perfect.[56] Still humiliated by the debacle over the Prix de Rome, Saint-Saëns had almost not participated.[57] But encouraged by the spectacular reception of Pablo de Sarasate's performance of his First Violin Concerto on 4 April 1867, he set Cornut's text, barely meeting the commission's deadline. Fearing age might again disqualify him, Saint-Saëns disguised his entry by using an unfamiliar type of English manuscript paper, though he never sent it to Britain to have it postmarked, as legend often relates.[58]

His subterfuge only incited further intrigue. One judge, Emile Paladilhe, thought the paper came from Germany, asserted Richard Wagner had composed the mysterious submission, and claimed his colleagues were "disagreeably surprised" to learn otherwise.[59] Later the judges confessed their belief stemmed from advanced brass writing consistent with modern German practice, dubious reasoning that overlooked two extended choral fugues—passages with few counterparts in Wagner's music and certainly none among the compositions known in Paris during the 1860s.[60] The episode nevertheless illustrates an emergent preoccupation of French composers, poets, and critics throughout the rest of the nineteenth century: Wagnerism.

Wagner's reputation had burgeoned after the Société Sainte-Cécile presented the overture to *Tannhäuser* in 1850, when Gautier and Gérard de Nerval inaugurated a distinguished critical tradition of espousing Wagner's ideology in the French press.[61] Debate over Wagner's revolutionary theories of culture, drama, and opera raged throughout the 1850s, culminating in contentious concerts in 1858 and 1860 and the scandalous Parisian premiere of *Tannhäuser* in 1861. The latter elicited a famous review by Charles Baudelaire, who attracted many young artists to Wagner's

---

[52] "The Great French Exhibition," *The Times*, 6 May 1867, p. 10.

[53] Romain Cornut, *Les Noces de Prométhée, Cantate pour solos, chœurs et orchestre* (Paris, [1867]), p. 14.

[54] "The Great French Exposition," p. 10.

[55] Secondary sources impart various totals, but the imperial commission (Comettant, p. 40) recorded 102 contestants.

[56] See Georges Bizet, *Lettres à un ami (1865–1871)*, ed. Edmond Galabert (Paris, 1909), p. 117.

[57] Saint-Saëns, pp. 35–49.

[58] Georges Servières, *La Musique française moderne* (Paris, 1897), pp. 295–6.

[59] Mina Curtiss, *Bizet and his World* (New York, 1958), p. 198.

[60] Comettant, p. 40.

[61] Gerald D. Turbow, "Art and Politics: Wagnerism in France," in David C. Large and William Weber (eds), *Wagnerism in European Culture and Politics* (Ithaca, 1984), pp. 137–8.

radicalism, including August de Gasperini and his acolyte Léon Leroy, whose short-lived periodical, *L'Esprit nouveau*, incurred the wrath of the Second Empire's censors by promulgating Wagner's subversive agenda of disseminating art to the masses. The withdrawal of the journal's license in June 1867 ended a six-month run a week after the deadline for submitting the cantata.[62]

Saint-Saëns had not directly linked his score with Wagnerian radicalism. He had nonetheless implied it embodied the revolutionary agenda championed in *L'Esprit nouveau* by inscribing the title page with Victor Hugo's maxim, "La musique est dans tout, un hymne sort du monde" [Music is in everything, a hymn emanating from the world].[63] The citation doubtless alarmed the judges because Hugo, known as the scourge of the Second Empire, remained in Belgian exile after siding against Louis Napoléon in the 1851 coup d'état that transformed the Second Republic into the Second Empire. Despite the offending epigram, tinged with elements of the Promethean revolt, the adjudicators made a unanimous choice.

Upon learning the winner's identity, however, the judges withheld the prize, then apparently set at 5,000 francs,[64] and canceled the cantata's performance on 1 July, offering two excuses: its supposedly delicate scoring would be lost in the cavernous Palais de l'Industrie, and its specified 25-minute duration was actually too long to introduce a protracted ceremony for announcing numerous awards.[65] Saint-Saëns lodged a protest with the Exposition's general commissioner, one Monsieur F. Le Play, demanding that the competition's ordinances be observed by making all necessary resources available for the performance.[66] But Le Play contended an imperial commission was not obliged to honor the music committee's rules, leaving Saint-Saëns few options. He accordingly wrote to the editors of *Le Figaro*, who rallied readers to his cause by asserting he "had the right to the highest respect as a man, a prize winner, and a long-esteemed artist."[67] Hippolyte Prévost, reporting for *La France*, echoed his complaints.[68] Faced with public opposition, the committee begrudgingly awarded Saint-Saëns 2,500 francs, but refused to sponsor the cantata's premiere.

Saint-Saëns supplemented his winnings with his own funds to produce his score in an unlikely venue, the Cirque de l'Imperatrice. Performed amid circus equipment on 1 September 1867, the cantata drew a "small, but select" audience "animated by the most benevolent attitudes," as Emile Mathieu de Monter noted in the *Revue et gazette musicale*.[69] The critic nonetheless condemned the libretto's academic rhetoric and scarce opportunities for musical treatment, and while he praised the music as "a mosaic carved and assembled with exquisite care, taste, and sentiment," he objected to difficulties created by "writing no more than six measures in the same tonality and

---

[62]   Ibid., p. 153.

[63]   Comettant, p. 48. The quotation is from the third book of Hugo's *Consolations*. See Saint-Saëns, pp. 26–34.

[64]   Comettant, pp. 27, 46.

[65]   See a statement by an Exposition official, one P. Ramon, in Jean Bonnerot, *Saint-Saëns: Sa vie et sa œuvre* (Paris, 1922), p. 47.

[66]   Ibid., pp. 48–50.

[67]   Ibid., p. 48.

[68]   Rees, p. 135.

[69]   Emile Mathieu de Monter, "Festival pour l'exécution de la cantate couronnée au Concours international de composition musical," *Revue et gazette musicale de Paris*, 34/36 (1867): 285.

… rhythm." His final assessment: *Les Noces de Prométhée* "would remain a radiant date in the lives of its authors," but was "neither a revelation nor still less an artistic event." Oscar Comettant, in assembling documents related to the Exposition's musical activities, partly agreed, deeming the occasion "a fine success," not only for Saint-Saëns, but also "for France, which emerged victorious in a universal and most serious musical struggle."[70] The nation thus received credit for the composer's achievements, despite the conduct of Exposition officials.

The French state redressed previous failings after Saint-Saëns founded the patriotic Société nationale de musique during the Third Republic's first decade, when the cantata inaugurated the Grand Salle de Trocadero to open the Exposition of 1878. Most reviewers focused on the hall's acoustics and size (it accommodated over 4,800 spectators).[71] An anonymous critic for the *Revue et gazette musicale*, however, rephrased Monter's remarks, applauding Saint-Saëns for lending "movement and variety to a score whose text seemed so little suited" to musical treatment. Its finale, "a fine chorus in the form of a march, with harps, especially made an impression."[72] Hanslick, Vienna's foremost critic and an honorary judge of the earlier competition, remained unconvinced, numbering the cantata among the poor successes of 1867.[73] A correspondent for the *New York Times*, though awed by the Trocadero, deemed the score "scientific, but not particularly melodious," despite "some striking passages."[74] The cantata's description as "scientific" unquestionably refers to its fugues, which Georges Bizet, the competition's favored entrant and chagrined loser, considered the reason for Saint-Saëns's victory. But it also alludes to the cantata's original purpose: celebrating the Second Empire's industrial accomplishments.

France's economy during the nineteenth century, once considered "retarded" or "stagnant" compared to its English and German counterparts, actually experienced steady growth for six decades, from 1810 to 1870.[75] Admittedly, no area of France underwent the heavy industrialization that transformed Lancashire, the English Midlands, and the Ruhr Valley into sprawling factory zones, nor did the French population's modest 45 percent increase match astounding respective rates in England and Germany, 350 and 250 percent.[76] But a stable rate of growth in France's non-centralized population, the industrial sector's significant expansion and modernization, and radical changes in production techniques within largely artisanal fields ensured the viability of regional markets, allowed a tripling of per capita physical production scarcely distinguishable

---

[70] Comettant, p. 41.

[71] See, for example, an anonymous notice, "Les Concerts de l'Exposition," *Revue et gazette musicale de Paris*, 45/17 (1878): 131–2.

[72] "Nouvelle musicales de l'Exposition," *Revue et gazette musicale de Paris*, 45/23 (1878): 180.

[73] Originally published in the *Neue freie Presse*, Hanslick's essay was translated as "Dr. Hanslick on the Music of the Paris Exposition," *Dwight's Journal of Music*, 38/9 (1878): 273–4.

[74] See the article's reprint, "Music in Paris," *Dwight's Journal of Music*, 38/7 (1878): 264.

[75] William H. Sewall, Jr., *Work and Revolution in France: The Language of Labor from the Old Regime to 1848* (Cambridge, 1980), pp. 146–7, 302.

[76] Patrick O'Brien and Caglar Keyder, *Economic Growth in Britain and France (1780–1914): Two Paths to the Twentieth Century* (London, 1978), pp. 149, 151; J.H. Clapham, *The Economic Development of France and Germany (1815–1914)* (Cambridge, 1966), p. 278.

from or even higher than the rate in Britain, and minimized demand for standard goods of nominal quality, the factory system's chief commodities.[77]

The British Exposition of 1862 nonetheless shocked French manufacturers, highlighting 75 years of technological advances in steam-driven mechanics, the adoption of Bessemer converters and the Siemens furnace, which caused Britain's annual steel production to rise from 14,000 to 111,000 tons between 1851 and 1862, and the virtual completion of Europe's most developed railroad system.[78] French industries struggled to match such gains, achieving significant growth during the Second Empire. Annual coal production, for example, had risen from under 900,000 tons after the Congress of Vienna to over 5,000,000 in 1847,[79] but after the pits opened at l'Escarpelle and Pas de Calais during the 1850s, yields increased to 13,000,000 tons between 1852 and 1869.[80] After converting from older, smaller charcoal furnaces to modern coal fuel, French Bessemer steel production rose from 600,000 tons in 1846 to 1,400,000 tons in 1869, soon excelled British standards by refining the Bessemer process, and ultimately forced England to import France's cheaper, higher-quality steel products.[81] The newly pressed steel stimulated French railroad construction, which lagged far behind England, Germany, and Belgium during the July Monarchy,[82] when Louis Philippe's administration fostered a fearsome bureaucracy among 40 rival companies. Louis Napoléon, however, reconsolidated the industry: 2,000 miles of railroad lines were completed between 1848 and 1852, all the trunk lines were finished by 1860, and the system as it was known until World War II was essentially in place by 1870.

Despite a gradual shift from agrarian to industrial economics, France remained peerless in producing high-quality goods that required specialized labor.[83] Strict standards maintained Europe's highest grades of wool, cotton, and silk, even when the textile industry adopted mass production's techniques.[84] More typically, however, cloth manufacture occurred in small "spinning sheds," where many new mechanical devices rapidly proliferated, including cotton spinning machines, steam-driven power looms, flying shuttles, and Joseph-Marie Jacquard's revolutionary looms for weaving figure fabrics—all of which were developed with governmental subsidies,[85] an advantage English and American inventors rarely enjoyed. Strong rural economies permitted small farms to continue to produce western Europe's finest wheat, the temperate zone's purest beet sugar, and dairy and viticulture products for which regions of France are still famous, notwithstanding the advent of technological innovations such as simple threshing machines. At the opposite end of the spectrum, the market for luxury items flourished, again by observing rigorous criteria while

---

[77]   Sewall, pp. 145, 151–3; O'Brien and Keyder, pp. 146–7.

[78]   Clapham, pp. 140, 236, 242–3.

[79]   Ibid., p. 57.

[80]   Ibid., p. 232.

[81]   Clapham, pp. 235–6; Percy A. Sanguinette, "Tools and Machinery for the Manufacture of Iron and Steel," in Hodgson Pratt (ed.), *Modern Industries: A Series of Reports on Industry and Manufactures as Represented in the Paris Exhibition in 1867* (London, 1868), p. 71.

[82]   Clapham, pp. 140–41, 150.

[83]   Sewall, p. 153.

[84]   Sewall, p. 153; Clapham, p. 26.

[85]   Clapham, p. 55.

employing new technologies.[86] Limoges thrived as the porcelain industry's hub, Saint Etienne dominated the field of fashion accessories, and the mainstays of industrial Paris remained fine furniture, tapestries, and jewelry.[87] Advances in the chemical industry, likewise centered in small Parisian shops, prompted new techniques for making soap and candles, a new method for refining India rubber, and the daguerreotype process's invention.[88]

All these marvels and more were proudly featured at the Exposition of 1867. Miners from Blanzy displayed implements they used to produce over 5,500,000 kilograms of coal annually.[89] Their fuel stoked France's largest iron mill, the Cruesot Works, sponsors of a "magnificent show" of a complete steelmaking process that yielded 110,000 tons of metal per year, most notably a single 30-ton piece of forged iron, the largest at the Exposition.[90] New steel from Charente won the gold medal, a manifestation of French metallurgical prowess attributable to Berard's reduction of oxidizable trace minerals that the British Siemens furnace introduced in Bessemer steel fabrication. French Bessemer steel products available for public scrutiny included large marine crankshafts, locomotive components (wheels, axles, rails, electromagnetic brakes that exploited innovations in manufacturing galvanic batteries and India rubber, and even entire engines, some of which had been designed for Britain's Great Eastern Railway), and the largest Bessemer structure yet built—a new bridge on the Quai d'Orsay connecting the Exhibition grounds on the Champ de Mars with the opposite side of the Seine.[91] Among light industrial presentations were a large horizontal engine capable of ventilating the enormous Palais de l'Industrie, another engine utilizing side valves rather than customary external sheaves or straps, an innovative lathe exploiting as yet somewhat unreliable rack and pinion technology, and drilling and pumping machines employed in building railroad tunnels through the Apennines.[92]

Magnificent French artisanal displays matched their impressive industrial counterparts. Textile manufacturers demonstrated recent advances: power looms equipped with electrical detectors immediately issued warnings if threads broke, flaws appeared, or the machinery "became deranged," permitting one worker to supervise several machines; Jacquard's loom techniques were applied to decorative paper, a flourishing craft in French markets for fine articles; and a Lyonnaise machine transfixed spectators by simultaneously weaving and cutting two pieces of chenille, thus producing two and a half yards per minute, or 1,500 meters daily, even while achieving unprecedented quality.[93] Automated shoemaking reduced the time for cutting, punching, binding, and shaping tanned leather into finished products to

---

[86]   Ibid., p. 69.
[87]   Sewall, p. 153.
[88]   Clapham, p. 69.
[89]   E. Dentu and Pierre Petit (eds), *L'Exposition universelle de 1867 illustrée* (2 vols, Paris, 1867), vol. 1, p. 85.
[90]   John Randall, "Iron, China, and Ceramic Work," in *Modern Industries*, p. 71.
[91]   Frederick A.P. Barnard, *Paris Universal Exposition, 1867: Report on Machinery and Process of the Industrial Arts* (New York, 1869), pp. 272, 293.
[92]   Ibid., pp. 71, 151–2.
[93]   Barnard, pp. 258, 267; Dentu and Petit, vol. 1, p. 99.

under two hours.[94] Agricultural yields likewise increased, most notably as a result of numerous steam-powered machines for planting and harvesting various crops, including seed-drills and the modern combine's ancestors,[95] and F.J.V. Minchin's patented enhancements of the diffusion process for extracting sugar from beets, used by an agriculturist named Desprez to win the gold medal for his harvest near Capelle.[96] Displays of Parisian luxury items were tremendously popular, especially the jewelry of 132 gold and silver merchants, which revealed "almost priceless value, the greatest variety and elegance of design, combined with the finest workmanship."[97] Conceding French dominance in the porcelain division, British commentators were particularly intrigued by large plaques decorated with landscapes that had been transferred from daguerreotypes.[98] Likewise virtually unrivaled were Parisian photography, lithography, engraving, and labor-intensive trades such as the making of buttons, artificial flowers, and high-grade leather.[99] Thus the progress of French industry, whether of the heavy or the cottage variety, supplies an appropriate context for evaluating Cornut's libretto and Saint-Saëns's music.

Cornut's text begins as a narrator reviews the myth's familiar background. On frightful crags at the ends of the ancient universe, an immortal vulture tortures an immortal victim: thus Prometheus expiates his pious and sublime theft of fire from an ethereal palace. But the Titan's flame acquires topical symbolic meaning as the narrative proceeds: fire signifies the arts and industry, produces genius, and regenerates "our fading race." Prometheus accordingly epitomizes the archetypal inventor; the products of his genius are clearly the Second Empire's technological innovations; and the "fading race" is patently France emerging from a period of revolution and industrial complacency to assume a leading role in Europe's economy. Humanity clarifies the already transparent allegory in a monologue, announcing the hour of the Titan's deliverance has struck; she will marry him "under the beautiful sky of France," in a "palace that stands erect," attended by people "in their royal pomp." The French palace obviously equates with the Palais de l'Industrie, while the guests in "their royal pomp" doubtless represent Louis Napoléon and his court.

Prometheus confirms this explication after a chorus extols triumphant peace and liberty. "What sovereign power," he asks, "has vanquished the wrath of the cruel, jealous gods?" His rhetorical question receives no verbal response, but his eyes behold stately porticos, and purple silken robes—indisputable tokens of royal patronage—cover his naked limbs. After the chorus repeats its accolades, Humanity and Prometheus designate their wedding as the dawn of a new day when justice, peace, unity, and fraternity will prevail, thereby articulating a quintessentially Promethean theme that the chorus echoes. Cornut's libretto consequently embodies an allegory of France in the Industrial Age: Prometheus represents the prototypical inventor, his

---

[94] Barnard, p. 253.

[95] Dentu and Petit, vol. 1, p. 103.

[96] Ibid., vol. 1, p. 27.

[97] P.A. Rasmussen, "Gold and Silver Work," in *Modern Industries*, p. 23.

[98] Thomas Kirkby, "Pottery and Porcelain," in *Modern Industries*, pp. 13–16.

[99] Seventy-nine such industries are anonymously catalogued in *Documents from the Archives nationales relating to the Exposition universelle de 1867 à Paris* (Paris, [1966]), n.p.

flame technology, and Humanity a society whose latent creativity becomes manifest in tangible industrial products, with an obligatory tribute to the Second Empire's court.

Portions of Saint-Saëns's through-composed score likewise articulate the Exhibition's agenda. In a short instrumental introduction, tenor trombones, alto saxophones, and chromatic trumpets play an arching melody punctuated by chords in the violins and harp (Example 5.4), novel instrumentation presumably leading the judges to believe Wagner devised it, though he never used saxophones.[100] Monter more astutely observed that the arching melody's Dorian mode evoked the atmosphere of ancient Greece: "The antique drama is thus set with a great verisimilitude of accent and color. It is one of the score's best passages."[101] Moreover, the traditional major mode emerges during the opening narration and ensuing orchestral interlude, thereby reflecting a transition from antiquity to modern times, when the Titan's union with Humanity will usher in a Golden Age. In 1910 Saint-Saëns recalled this passage's success, noting he "could not prevent himself from smiling" when he encountered "someone astonished by a few notes written in the first mode of plainchant" at the outset of Debussy's opera, *Pelléas et Melisande*, since his cantata had exploited the mode "more fully, a long time ago."[102]

Example 5.4   Saint-Saëns *Les Noces de Prométhée*, Introduction, mm. 1–20

[100]   See the letter the judges published in *Le Moniteur* on 12 June 1867, reprinted in Comettant, p. 40.

[101]   Monter, p. 286.

[102]   See Saint-Saëns's letter of 16 January 1910 in "Saint-Saëns et Romain Rolland: Lettres inédites publiées par Jean Bonnerot," *Revue de musicologie*, 39/40 (1957): 198.

Two choral fugues also suited the occasion. Fugal passages often represent struggle or transition in nineteenth-century program music, as the development section in Liszt's *Prometheus* illustrated. Some fugues more specifically depict humanity striving toward enlightenment, as is again the case in Liszt's symphonic poem and, most famously, the double fugue in the finale of Beethoven's Ninth Symphony, which juxtaposes two strikingly Promethean excerpts from Schiller's ode. In the first, all men enter the sanctuary of joy—the brilliant spark of the gods—intoxicated with fire; in the second, millions receive the creator's embrace and kiss. On a less exalted but equally vigorous scale, both of Saint-Saëns's fugues promote the myth's humanism. In the first, following Humanity's monologue, triumph, victory, peace and liberty signify the arrival of mankind's day of glory in a conventional fugal exposition, with a cappella vocal entries alternating between the subject's tonic and dominant statements (Example 5.5a). In the second, marking the end of the Titan's soliloquy, the first fugue's transposed restatement acquires a supporting bass line of continuous eighth notes played initially by bassoon and contrabassoon, then by low strings (Example 5.5b). The fugues' overt humanitarianism would have plainly corresponded to French industrial progress had the cantata's premiere occurred at the Palais de l'Industrie, where surrounding exhibits would have corroborated the dawn of a new technological age. And animated fugal rhythms, especially the motoric eighth notes in the second, would have equated with the sounds emanating from ongoing demonstrations of engines and machines. By indulging this metaphor of fugue as machine one degree further, the second fugue may be construed as a mimetic representation of French industrial activities underlying the nation's progressive humanitarianism.

The cantata's remaining sections derive from contemporary French opera, as Monter again perceived.[103] A broad ternary design informs an opening monologue for the narrator, a tenor, who outlines the myth's background in simple recitative. Vocal lines mirror the French language's rhythms and intonation with repeated notes and shallow intervals, reflecting rigorous methods of text setting advocated at the Conservatoire, while the orchestra harmonizes modal fragments from the introduction. But when the narrator reveals the Promethean flame signifies the arts and industry, his arching phrases outline a new key, E-flat major, and upper strings and woodwinds play cascading arpeggios doubled in thirds. The monologue's return to modal recitative suits the grave subject of the Titan's suffering.

Humanity's oration comprises an operatic scena for a lyric soprano. In an accompanied recitative she announces the Titan's deliverance, betraying her excitement over their imminent wedding with animated vocal lines incorporating jagged leaps. The orchestra repeatedly inserts two characteristic motives, one a syncopated figure played by double reeds, the other an outburst of brass fanfares. In the ensuing aria Humanity contemplates the palace where her wedding will occur, her love for Prometheus, and the impending ceremony's royal pomp. Harp arpeggios, woodwind duplets, and more fanfares reinforce her triadic melody, embellished by typically Wagnerian turns. At the aria's climax the chorus acclaims triumph and victory before initiating the first fugue. The sequence of recitative, aria, and chorus thus respects a convention of Italian and French opera of the first half of the nineteenth century.

---

[103]   Monter, p. 285.

Example 5.5a   Saint-Saëns *Les Noces de Prométhée*, First Choral Fugue, mm. 16–33

Example 5.5a concluded.

Example 5.5b   Saint-Saëns *Les Noces de Prométhée*, Second Choral Fugue, mm. 17–34

Example 5.5b concluded.

A comparable design governs the soliloquy for Prometheus, a baritone, except an instrumental prelude reprises the introduction's Dorian melody, now appearing in the bass line and adopting the major mode. Scored for bassoon, contrabassoon, and tenor trombone, the melody supports tremolos in the second violins and arpeggios played by three flutes and divisi first violins. This passage and others like it probably afforded the judges an excuse to cancel the cantata's performance in the Palais de l'Industrie, where the cavernous acoustics would have supposedly ruined such delicate effects.[104] After a piquant modulation to B-flat major, Prometheus initiates his scena with accompanied recitative, questioning the identity of the beneficent spirit who frees him from his chains, the nature of the sovereign power who vanquishes divine wrath, and the destination of zephyrs that transport him through the air, the latter evoked by the rippling arpeggios of four harps. A march-like aria in B-flat major, an idiomatic key for the accompanying wind instruments, suits the Titan's visions of stately porticos and his new imperial attire of purple silken robes. Choral interjections of triumph and victory anticipate the second fugue.

Finally, all nineteenth-century pseudo-operas require love duets. In the cantata's longest self-contained section, Humanity and Prometheus consider their wedding a catalyst for a new era of justice, unity, and fraternity. Against pulsating triplets in the double reeds, they sing long-breathed phrases, initially in octaves, then in canon, ascending triadically and descending in scales as the tonality twice shifts between B-flat and B major. During the last harmonic fluctuation the chorus repeats the soloists' final thoughts as the bass line descends from B, past B-flat, to A, the cantata's dominant. After A resolves to D, the concluding chorus begins with free counterpoint and ends with a homophonic march that "brought down the house," as *The Times* correspondent noted.

Saint-Saëns overcame the competition's intrigues to enjoy success with audiences and some critics, an achievement, like others that established his reputation during the late 1860s, realized as the Second Empire flourished. He nonetheless fulfilled his potential as "one of the most prominent composers of the day" not during Louis Napoléon's prosperous reign, but rather during a new epoch that began in 1870 with a dark chapter in French history. Neither the cantata's auditors nor the Exhibition's visitors could have suspected the Empire would crumble during the Franco-Prussian War, interrupting long-term industrial progress and economic stability. As Saint-Saëns casually remarked, "the Empire fell, and Victor Hugo came back to Paris," inaugurating a new political and cultural era in France.[105] As a founding member and the first vice president of the Société nationale de musique, Saint-Saëns assumed a leading role in French musical life under a new regime administered by Adolphe Thiers. With its rallying cry of "Ars Gallica," the Société promoted serious works by French composers, partly to resist a devastatingly victorious and newly unified Germany's imperialist policies. The Société's agenda benefited one of the new era's great patriots, Augusta Holmès, who responded to the war in another Promethean cantata.

---

[104]   Rees, pp. 135–6.
[105]   Saint-Saëns, p. 28.

Holmès

Like Saint-Saëns, Augusta Holmès (1847–1903) was a child prodigy raised by an indulgent single parent.[106] Born in Paris, she grew up in Versailles under the watchful care of her father, a British cavalry officer of Irish heritage and independent finances, after her mother died in 1858.[107] Major Charles William Scott Dalkeith Holmes indulged literary ambitions, writing a travelogue in 1841 and assembling a personal library of 2,000 volumes.[108] Augusta evinced similar talents, learning four languages by age 12 and soon writing lyrics for her songs, though her greatest aptitude was for music.

As Holmès once reminded her equally literary uncle Alfred de Vigny, she studied with four local teachers.[109] She began piano lessons with one Mademoiselle Pyronnet before her thirteenth birthday, soon outshining her teacher's older pupils.[110] Harmony and counterpoint instruction with Henri Lambert, chief organist at the cathedral in Versailles, decisively influenced her compositional career.[111] Famed clarinetist and military bandmaster Hyacinthe Klosé tutored her in instrumentation, though her first orchestral works date from her early twenties. And Guillot de Sainbris, founder of a local choral society, trained her distinctive contralto voice. In his salon's heady atmosphere, she encountered the Second Empire's leading artistic personalities, including composers such as Gounod, Thomas, and Saint-Saëns,[112] who quickly spread word of her precocity throughout Parisian salon society.

Accounts of Holmès's early salon performances typically emphasized her physical attractiveness, unique (*étrange*) vocal timbre, and beguiling effect on audiences, especially men. Such objectification often influenced perceptions of nineteenth-century virtuosos, whether male or female, as countless descriptions of Liszt illustrate.[113] But the process is singularly fascinating in the case of Holmès, who successfully transformed herself from a siren of the salon into a composer of orchestral works and operas recognized for their striking "virility."[114] As discussed shortly, this metamorphosis first became evident in choral works written after her twentieth birthday, including *Prométhée*, an unfinished cantata.

During the 1860s Holmès developed a reputation based largely on performances of her songs.[115] According to the novelist Henri Gauthier-Villars, "her voice was the

---

[106]   The eccentricities of Augusta's parents are discussed in Nancy Sarah Theeman, "The Life and Songs of Augusta Holmès" (Ph.D. diss., University of Maryland, 1983), p. 7.

[107]   Ingeborg Feilhauer, "Augusta Holmès und die Französische Revolution," *Musica*, 43/2 (1989): 138.

[108]   Gérard Gefen, *Augusta Holmès, l'outrancière* (Paris, 1987), p. 35.

[109]   Gefen, p. 61; Feilhauer, p. 138.

[110]   See Holmès's account of the *concours* in Ernest Dupuy, *Alfred de Vigny: Ses amitiés, son rôle littéraire* (2 vols, Paris, 1912), vol. 2, p. 376.

[111]   René Pichard du Page, *Une Musicienne versaillaise: Augusta Holmès* (Paris, 1921), p. 20.

[112]   Gefen, p. 53.

[113]   See Walker, *Franz Liszt*, vol. 1, pp. 87, 229, 344, 377, 381.

[114]   Jann Pasler, "The Ironies of Gender, or Virility and Politics in the Music of Augusta Holmès," *Women & Music: A Journal of Gender and Culture*, 2 (1998): 1–25.

[115]   Jean Bernac, "Interview with Mademoiselle Augusta Holmès," *The Strand Musical Magazine*, 5 (1897): 136.

most natural of many talents with which a fairy had endowed an exceptional being in its cradle, a gift that completed the seduction she invariably achieved in performance."[116] The poet Auguste Villiers de L'Isle-Adam likewise described the teenage Augusta as "so beautiful beneath her halo of golden hair that she gave the impression of a fairy-tale creature."[117] Women also noticed her physical attractiveness. British composer Ethel Smyth remembered a soiree in Versailles when Augusta sang "with worshippers grouped at her feet," vying to light her cigarettes.[118] Madame Alphonse Daudet considered her "capable of walking among the statues on the *grand allée* of the *Tapis vert* [a park in Versailles] without compromising her elegant allure and classic beauty,"[119] a comparison that acquired palpable form. The painter Henri Regnault, later Augusta's close friend, was dissatisfied with his banal depiction of Thetis in a tableau he planned to enter in the Prix de Rome competition of 1866. After hearing Augusta sing, Regnault exclaimed, "This is a goddess, this is a Valkyrie!" He then altered his canvas, substituting Augusta's face for that of Thetis—a concrete appropriation of her physical appearance reducing her role from composer to muse.[120]

Holmès assumed an altogether different persona during the 1870s, seeking public performances, cultivating larger genres, and expressing fervently patriotic reactions to the Franco-Prussian War in her music. She wrote a particularly nationalistic song entitled *Vengeance!* soon after German shells bombarded Paris in December 1870, but her transformation began in earnest on 1 August 1871 with the first performance of any of her compositions in an important public venue.[121] The *Chœur nuptiale*, presented during the Festival populaire du Châtelet with vocal soloists, 50 choristers, and full orchestra, prompted an anonymous critic to recognize her talent as "one of the rarest and most powerful that awaits us in a not too distant future."[122]

The power of her scores again garnered critical attention a year later, on 3 August 1872, when Holmès helped inaugurate a concert series at the royal chapel in Versailles, a venue necessarily abandoned while the town served as the seat of the Prussian imperial government. For the occasion Holmès composed settings of the hymn *Ave Maria* and the psalm *In exitu Israël*, the latter disclosing "a very great power of inspiration" and "a rare knowledge of modern music's resources," as two anonymous reviewers independently noted.[123] The psalm's topical conclusion, as another unidentified journalist declared, was

---

[116]   See the quotation in Pichard du Page, p. 14.

[117]   Auguste Villiers de l'Isle Adam, *Chez les pasants* (Paris, 1890), p. 64.

[118]   Ethel Smyth, *A Final Burning of Boats* (London, 1928), p. 128.

[119]   Madame Alphonse Daudet, *Souvenirs autour d'un groupe litteraire* (Paris, 1910), pp. 195–6.

[120]   André Theuriet relates the anecdote in *Le Journal de Tristan: Impressions et souvenirs* (Paris, 1884), pp. 81–4.

[121]   In 1867 Jules Pasdeloup presented Holmès's *Chanson de la caravane* at the Hôtel-de-Ville. An unidentified critic marked the occasion as "the beginning of a glorious career" in one of numerous articles collected at the Bibliothèque nationale in the *Recueil d'articles de journaux sur Augusta Holmès* (F-Pc 4° B391). Most of these articles bear only a date; others also identify the journal; few credit an author.

[122]   *Théâtres et beaux-arts*, October 1871. Notices also appeared in *Le Figaro*, 17 October 1871, and the *Gazette de Paris*, October 1871. The *Recueil* contains all three articles.

[123]   The unidentified notices are dated 3 and 9 August 1872 (*Recueil*).

"a triumphant song of deliverance" that audience members "showered with applause," doubtless equating Israel's emancipation with the Prussian army's recent withdrawal from Versailles.[124] When the newly founded Société nationale de musique encored *In exitu Israël* on 7 December 1872, it still produced a "magisterial effect" in the more intimate Salle Pleyel, despite the orchestra's replacement with piano and organ.[125]

As the 1870s progressed, Holmès completed her evolution from seductive prodigy to powerful composer in large-scale works articulating struggles of oppressed peoples. *Lutèce*, a dramatic symphony with voices (1872), narrates a Gallic couple's courage in war. Vindictive gods persecute the title characters in *Les Argonautes*, another dramatic symphony for soloists, chorus, and orchestra (1880). Two symphonic poems, *Irlande* (1882) and *Pologne* (1883), plead for political freedom in subjugated countries. And *Ludus pro patria*, a symphonic ode for choirs and orchestra (1888), and the *Ode triomphale*, celebrating the Revolution's centennial (1889), return to French subjects. Regardless of their diverse nationalistic settings, these works appealed to French sentiments in the wake of the Franco-Prussian War, earning Holmès a reputation as "the most ardent, most impassioned, and most enthusiastic of French women."[126] Her adoption of French citizenship and the addition of the *accent grave* to her name in 1872, when she reached the legal age for naturalization, verified her patriotism.[127]

Several factors effected Holmès's self-transformation. First, she matched heroic subjects with bold compositional gestures, mixing "cries of war with songs of love," graceful cantilenas with the "excessive fracas" of brass instruments, and "calls of liberty" with "passionate eroticism"—all "virile" traits her contemporaries associated with Wagner.[128] Second, she participated in *Le Parnasse contemporain*, a dynamic literary movement that emerged during the 1860s. And third, she reacted to the Franco-Prussian War, voicing the collective response of her compatriots and her sentiments as a woman. All three factors form a nexus in *Prométhée*, a cantata begun in 1871, precisely when Holmès left the salon to forge her new public identity.

As "Wagnerians of the first hour," Holmès and her father heard Jules Pasdeloup conduct excerpts from Wagner's operas at the Cirque Napoléon during the late 1860s.[129] So enthusiastic was their reaction that Major Holmes organized Wagner concerts from 1867 onward.[130] They also traveled to Munich in 1869 for the premiere of *Das Rheingold*, a trip arranged by Emile Ollivier, Augusta's close friend, first minister in Louis Napoléon's imperial government, and the brother-in-law of Cosima Liszt von Bülow, Franz Liszt's eldest daughter and Wagner's soon-to-be wife.[131] On 27 August,

---

[124]   *Liberté*, August 1872 (*Recueil*).

[125]   *Liberté*, 7 December 1872 (*Recueil*).

[126]   Ryno [pseud.], "Augusta Holmès, Profil," *Gil Blas*, 22 October 1885; quoted in Pasler, p. 8.

[127]   The date ranges from 1872 to 1874 in secondary sources: Theeman, p. 58; Gefen, p. 123; Bernac, p. 136.

[128]   The quoted phrases are from Eugène de Solonière, *La Femme compositeur* (Paris, 1895), p. 14; for illuminating analysis of how such traits were perceived as Wagnerian, see Pasler, pp. 2–3, 9–10.

[129]   Solonière, p. 14; see also Pichard du Page, p. 26.

[130]   Gefen, p. 109.

[131]   Ibid., p. 99.

at the general rehearsal, Augusta sat next to Liszt, who had already judged her music "noble and vigorous" after receiving a packet of her scores from Ollivier in 1868.[132] Four days later Augusta and her father conversed at length with Wagner and were invited to Tribschen, the home overlooking Lake Lucerne where he and Cosima then lived.[133] On 7 September they visited Tribschen, a sojourn Augusta later recalled in three different interviews.[134] Although her accounts vary in detail, they all impart that she performed Erda's scene from *Das Rheingold* for Wagner, who requested some of her own compositions. She obliged by singing several songs that Wagner praised, but he also suggested she moderate her intense admiration for his work and avoid belonging to any particular school.[135] Thus the visit was a great triumph: Holmès met two composers she greatly esteemed and received Wagner's encouragement to cultivate a personal musical style, which immediately developed in the *Chœur nuptiale* and *In exitu Israël*.

Momentous events nonetheless temporarily prevented Holmès from capitalizing on her successful pilgrimage. Her father died on 19 December 1869, whereupon she vanished from Parisian salons. The following April Henri Cazalis asked Stéphane Mallarmé if he had heard from her, fearing she was "lost to him."[136] As late as September 1870 Cosima wrote to Augusta, inquiring if she was in Ireland,[137] a question close to the mark: Augusta evidently visited England to settle her father's estate, which earned over 20,000 francs annually and guaranteed her financial security for the foreseeable future.[138] But the true reason for her disappearance was that early in 1870 she gave birth to the first of her five children, all fathered by Catulle Mendès, a writer married to Gautier's daughter, Judith.[139]

After Mendès and Holmès met in 1868, they lived openly as a couple in their apartment on the rue Mansart for 17 years.[140] Their children, born between 1870 and 1881, were nonetheless raised secretively by a nurse and never appeared in public with their mother. Indeed, only several close friends knew of them, and Mendès retained their custody when he and Holmès separated in 1885. The relationship influenced her life, her career, and her *Prométhée*, in which a man and a woman take comfort in knowing that the Titan's flame protects their sleeping children from war's perils, an autobiographical reference awaiting detailed consideration. More broadly, Mendès and Holmès shared three interests that shaped their artistic work: Wagnerism, the Parnassian movement, and involvement in the Franco-Prussian War.

During the mid-1860s Mendès had published *La Revue fantaisiste*, a short-lived Wagnerian journal, and for years afterward promoted Wagner among a circle of young

[132] Pichard du Page, p. 28.

[133] Gefen, p. 106.

[134] Jean-Louis Croze, "Augusta Holmès," *La Revue hebdomadaire*, 3 (1903): 304–17; Bernac, pp. 136–9; Horace Hennion, *Messager d'Indre-et-Loire*, 15–17 June 1899, quoted in Gefen, pp. 110–11.

[135] Bernac, p. 138.

[136] Gefen, p. 115.

[137] Ibid., p. 123.

[138] Regarding Augusta's travels and the estate's value see Feilhauer, p. 139, and Pichard du Page, p. 30.

[139] Feilhauer, p. 139; Gefen, pp. 116–17.

[140] Gefen, p. 25.

French writers.[141] He accordingly attended the Munich premiere of *Das Rheingold* and traveled with his wife, Major Holmes, and Augusta to Tribschen, where Wagner and Cosima were embarrassed by openly acknowledged marital difficulties closely resembling their own.[142] Augusta thus found an enthusiastic supporter for her forays into a Wagnerian compositional style in Mendès, who continued to revere Wagner even after 1870, when *Eine Kapitulation*, Wagner's vicious satire of France's surrender to the Prussians, alienated admirers.

After *La Revue fantaisiste* folded, its contributors published poetry in equally ephemeral periodicals and soon convened with like-minded older poets at the home of Charles-Marie-René Leconte de Lisle to discuss philosophy, aesthetics, and literature.[143] From their sessions emerged the idea of restoring French lyric poetry to the stature it enjoyed before romantic excess supposedly precipitated its decline. An opportunity to publish their original poetry arose when Mendès persuaded Louis-Xavier de Ricard to convert his financially ruinous journal, *L'Art*, into a purely literary publication. Thus was conceived *Le Parnasse contemporain*, three poetic anthologies named for the mountain towering above Apollo's temple at Delphi, where the priestess of the Greek god of poetry, music, and light dispensed truth. The title aptly reflected the contributors' enthusiasm for antiquity and dedication to restraint, precision, and objectivity, traits nineteenth-century authors associated with classical verse.[144] Holmès co-edited the second of three tomes that respectively appeared in 1866, 1871, and 1876, and hence was intimately familiar with the work of the Parnassians, as the group soon became known.[145]

The 99 contributors to *Le Parnasse contemporain* produced work encompassing diverse genres, styles, and literary subjects. Many Parnassians nonetheless shared common interests, including a defiance of the Second Empire's pervasive censorship, a rejection of the materialism that attended the rise of the bourgeoisie after 1830, and a concern with formal perfection that earned them a somewhat undeserved reputation as exponents of Gautier's precept of "art for art's sake." Classical antiquity likewise held a privileged position within the rich mosaic of Parnassian style and substance. Leconte de Lisle's devoted Hellenism motivated his followers to draw inspiration from ancient Greek religion, history, mythology, and literary symbols and forms.[146] Some merely derived picturesque subjects from classical antiquity, producing a kind of exoticism scarcely different from more typical French nineteenth-century evocations of African or Asian cultures.[147] Others, however, closely engaged with Greek poetry's philosophical ideals, searching for models of valor, majesty, and vigor that would rejuvenate French literature. Certainly among the latter must be numbered Augusta Holmès, whose

[141]   Turbow, pp. 151–2.

[142]   Léon Guichard, *Lettres à Judith Gautier par Richard et Cosima Wagner* (Paris, 1964), pp. 116–20.

[143]   Aaron Schaffer, *Parnassus in France: Currents and Cross-Currents in Nineteenth-Century French Lyric Poetry* (Austin, 1939), p. 48.

[144]   Ibid., pp. 49–50.

[145]   Gefen, p. 135.

[146]   Fernand Desonay, *Le Rêve hellénique chez les poètes parnassiens* (Paris, 1928), pp. 59–64.

[147]   Aaron Schaffer, *The Genres of Parnassian Poetry: A Study of the Parnassian Minors* (Baltimore, 1944), p. 137.

profound influence by the Parnassians manifested itself in her self-acknowledged attraction to Greek antiquity's heroes and gods and her cultivation of Parnassian images such as dreams, visions, and the personification of inanimate objects in texts for her vocal compositions.[148] But before she employed these images in new works of Wagnerian "virility," she and Mendès shared their third common experience, service in the Franco-Prussian War.

During the 1860s tensions between France and the German states had escalated owing to the rise of German nationalism, the Prussian military's growth, and the North German Confederation's establishment after Austria's defeat at Jena in 1866. But the catalyst for armed conflict was the announcement of the Hohenzollern Candidature in July 1870, when Leopold, Prince of Hohenzollern-Sigmaringen and husband of the Princess of Portugal, was offered the Spanish crown. Leopold would have taken orders from Berlin, allowing German armies to threaten two French borders. First minister Ollivier swiftly called for war credits on 15 July and gave the vastly overrated French army its first orders a week later, even as the Prussians mobilized over 1,000,000 soldiers, half of whom were immediately transported to France's eastern border.[149]

As both sides expected, the French attacked first and easily prevailed in a skirmish at Saarbrücken on 2 August 1870, even though they were poorly organized, ill equipped, inadequately trained, and hampered by chaotic railway schedules. When the Germans retaliated at Wissembourg on 4 August, however, the city fell within hours. Shocking and demoralizing defeats at other border cities culminated in the French army's surrender on 2 September at Sedan. Half an hour after the signing of the capitulation, the German alliance's Bavarian troops advanced on Paris, surrounding the city by the month's end.[150]

During the turbulent summer of 1870 Holmès and Mendès briefly led separate lives. Augusta emerged from seclusion, as a rare letter from the period suggests. On 3 June, just before the Candidature's announcement, Liszt inquired about her latest compositions in a note indicating she had previously communicated with him from her father's address in Versailles.[151] Catulle, on the other hand, spent the second half of July visiting Wagner and Cosima at Tribschen.[152] Faced with the imminent threat of war, he and his party returned to Paris by 25 August after negotiating a rail system paralyzed by military traffic.[153] Unable to leave the city without being considered a deserter, Catulle wrote to Cosima on 12 September, lamenting that his thoughts had turned to dying beneath the walls of Paris.[154] He instead joined the infantry and soon became inspector of the ambulance service. Augusta served as an attendant, remarkable work for any woman of her era, let alone the mother of an infant.[155]

---

[148]   Theeman, pp. 89, 94.

[149]   Michael Howard, *The Franco-Prussian War: The German Invasion of France, 1870–1871* (London, 2000), pp. 48, 56.

[150]   Ibid., pp. 222–3.

[151]   The entire letter appears in Gefen, p. 119.

[152]   Cosima Wagner, *Cosima Wagner's Diaries*, ed. Martin Gregor-Dellin and Dietrich Mack, trans. Geoffrey Skelton (2 vols, New York, 1978), vol. 2, pp. 246–50.

[153]   Howard, p. 255.

[154]   Wagner, vol. 2, p. 269.

[155]   Theeman, p. 71.

Nothing is known of their military activities, but they doubtless ministered to casualties of battles that ended with the occupation of Versailles on 5 October, the German army's entrenchment at Fontainebleau on 10 November, and the capture of Orléans (the climax of the civilian resistance known as the People's War) on 5 December.[156] So, too, must they have encountered victims of Paris's systematic bombardment, which began early in 1871 and concluded with an armistice on 28 January, though even such desperate circumstances failed to deter Augusta's music-making at her new address on the rue Galilée ten days earlier.[157] Few could celebrate, however, when the occupational government was established at Versailles late in February and German troops made three successive daily marches down the *Champs-Elysées* beginning on 1 March. Several days before this demoralizing spectacle, on 27 February 1871, Augusta set aside her unfinished cantata, *Prométhée*, a score articulating the advent of her "virile" musical style, her involvement with Parnassian poetry, and her reactions to warfare.

Two manuscripts held at the Salle de musique at the Bibliothèque nationale in Paris preserve the unpublished cantata (F-Pn Ms. 11917, F-Pn Ms. 5398). Both are essentially vocal scores containing parts for soloists, chorus, and piano, though Holmès conceived the work orchestrally, as cues for instruments such as trumpets and trombones, tremolo notation suitable only for strings, and the occasional third staff in the piano part verify. The first manuscript's title page bears the autograph date 27 February 1871.[158] Some of its concluding material appears without revision at the beginning of the second manuscript, possibly suggesting Holmès was preparing a fair copy of the score for unknown purposes. Ms. 5398 nonetheless ends abruptly with a descending chromatic scale in the bass line, several chords, and a few separate pitches. Otherwise both sources disclose few interruptions and only two large deleted passages, both replaced with alternatives on separate inserts. Sometimes, however, the accompaniment is either partially sketched or totally absent, while the cantata as a whole is simply incomplete. The unfinished manuscripts could scarcely have served to generate orchestral parts, notwithstanding Gérard Gefen's conjecture that if such parts ever existed, they no longer survive.[159] Their notation nonetheless reconciles well with Holmès's description of her compositional process as continuous and free of erasures or amendments.[160]

Had the cantata been completed it would have been very long and ambitious. Extant materials comprise three well-developed scenes, the third subdividing into three sections separated by instrumental interludes and featuring different characters. Preceded by an instrumental prelude, the cantata's five major divisions are: (1) a monologue for Prometheus; (2) a scene for Prometheus, the Oceanids, and their Queen; (3) a scene for Prometheus, men's and mixed choruses, a man, a woman, and anonymous vocal soloists; (4) a dialogue for Prometheus and the Queen of the Oceanids; and (5) an exchange between Prometheus and Mercury. The Oceanids were slated to return in an ensuing fragmentary section.

---

156   Howard, pp. 347, 299, 315.
157   Gefen, p. 126.
158   Without mentioning the manuscript's date, Gefen (p. 253) suggests 1870. Theeman (List of Works) catalogs the manuscript as undated.
159   Gefen, p. 253.
160   Bernac, p. 139.

Holmès's libretto reveals several decidedly Parnassian traits. Restraint and objectivity, perhaps less suited to a dramatic cantata than the poems of *Le Parnasse contemporain*, nonetheless color her depiction of Prometheus. He scarcely indulges in the self-pity and anger prominent in the myth's earlier romantic representations, especially compared to the laments and outbursts found in the three Goethe settings and Liszt's incidental music. Instead he narrates previous actions with detachment, acknowledging his crime, accepting divine punishment, and impassively enduring torment to promote humanity's welfare. He even remains stoic while other characters act more passionately, as when the Oceanids weep for him, their Queen expresses fear of the gods, and Mercury fails in persuading him to recant. A quintessentially Parnassian reliance on dreams plays no role in the cantata, although Prometheus vividly prophesies the future to the Oceanids: "On more propitious days, under brilliant skies, your eyes will see the end of my torments. And this dreadful god [Jupiter] … will implore for himself the one conquered today." His vision becomes almost palpable in a resplendent march with brass fanfares.

More concrete are manifestations of two common Parnassian literary devices, the personification of inanimate objects and textual parallelisms. In his opening monologue Prometheus addresses rivers, limpid springs, the earth, and the sun as "inanimate great ones," exhorting them to hear him acknowledge his crime and witness Jupiter's revenge against mankind. His attesters also include the wind and clouds, personified as sons of divine aether. Holmès's language imbues other inert forces with a living presence: in scene 3 a man and a woman invite divine flame to enter their souls; nature, formerly mankind's ruler, becomes humanity's subject after fire tames it; time is an educator capable of teaching the gods to cry; thunderbolts, rocks, the earth, and its silt remain faithful to Jupiter; and profound depths sing of the Titan's achievements. Parallelisms abound throughout scene 3, which begins as a men's chorus compares the smoke rising from newly forged metal to the celestial flame blazing in the night. In scene 5 Mercury asks if it is sweet for a god to suffer like the son of mortal races; Prometheus denigrates the Olympian messenger by inquiring if it is sweet for a god to serve. And the Titan's last utterance comprises a list of indirect commands: "Let slavish thunderbolts, let punishing rocks remain faithful to Jupiter; let the earth and its silt, the winter of death strike my rebellious flanks," but they will never elicit reactions from him. In addition, the libretto echoes lines in José-Maria de Hérédia's *Prométhée*, a poem published in the first volume of *Le Parnasse contemporain*, especially the reference to the Titan's flanks, the phrase "douleurs fraternelles," and a depiction of the Oceanids shedding tears.[161] Holmès thus frequently and prominently adopted characteristics of the literary movement that engrossed her attention while she composed the cantata.

The score also embodies modern musical techniques Holmès first employed during the late 1860s after encountering Wagner's music and making her pilgrimage to Tribschen. Such procedures include rapid contrasts of character, conspicuous and chromatic brass parts, advanced harmonies, and Wagner's typical blurring of distinctions among recitative, arioso, and aria. An abundance of developmental passages, especially canons and fugues, discredit Holmès's ill-deserved reputation as a composer incapable

---

[161]   José-Maria de Hérédia, *Prométhée*, in *Le Parnasse contemporain, Recueil de vers nouveaux* (3 vols, Paris, 1866), vol. 1, p. 16.

of elaborating themes through standard motivic techniques.[162] All these "virile" traits appear throughout the cantata, as a survey of its "scenes" demonstrates.

A long instrumental prelude of arresting complexity introduces the cantata. Above agitated tremolos a wide-ranging melody incorporates jagged leaps, bold reversals of direction, and hemiola patterns (Example 5.6, upper staff). The theme generates seven developmental episodes, starting with its harmonization with close-position chords. It then serves as the subject of two canons, one retaining the chordal harmonization and culminating in trumpet calls, the other reverting to plain melodic lines. Homophony returns when the theme's chordal version appears above widely arching arpeggios, but the lush layering soon reverts to the prelude's initial texture. After restatements of several introductory phrases, however, counterpoint resumes when the theme freely intertwines with a new melody. More tremolos support another canonic episode that leads to the theme's final presentation in largely parallel chords. The ambitious scale, dogged developmental strategies, daring melodic gestures, and textural contrasts not only reconcile well with the bold style Holmès adopted during the early 1870s, but also suggest the completed cantata would have achieved operatic proportions, as the elaborate nature of ensuing scenes confirms.

Example 5.6   Holmès *Prométhée*, Prélude, mm. 21–41

---

[162]   Theeman (p. 41), for example, cites Holmès's developmental weaknesses as the reason for her works' absence from the active repertoire.

The Titan's monologue (scene 1) entails three sections, a short recitative, a full-fledged aria, and an arioso that returns to recitative. Marked *Allegro con fuoco*, the opening recitative invokes the four classical elements (the personified rivers, earth, sun, and the wind and clouds), suggesting Holmès knew the Aeschylean drama, probably owing to literary proclivities she, her father, and Mendès shared. The recitative's dark key (B-flat minor), string tremolos, continued hemiola, and flourishes of virtuosic vocal writing (Example 5.7) are all notable because they contrast greatly with what follows. In the aria Prometheus relates he formerly ranked among the greatest of the gods, but he now suffers at their hands and has been hurled into an abyss with the other Titans. His narration abandons the recitative's fiery affect, adopting the parallel major key, revealing an unexpected *dolce* character, and supporting wide melodic arcs with a thick, homophonic accompaniment. Holmès thus cultivated contrasts her early critics considered "virile," and hence Wagnerian, attributes of her style. The closing arioso reverts to the parallel minor key and tremolos, but adds a recurrent sigh figure to depict the Titan's decision to endure punishment and take pity on mankind. Punctuating chords inaugurate the final recitative, in which Prometheus maintains fire is the source of life, love, liberty, and power—humanist associations developed later in the cantata.

Example 5.7   Holmès *Prométhée*, Title Character's First Recitative, mm. 1–4

Scene 2 is more intricate, involving another orchestral prelude, recitatives, choruses, and a march-like aria. Rippling arpeggios attend the Oceanids' arrival, evoking their aquatic habitat or, as the libretto soon reveals, their airborne journey on the wings of the wind. The arpeggios, supporting a dotted motive that gains force as the scene unfolds, firmly establish E-flat major (not coincidentally the key of Wagner's aqueous prelude to *Das Rheingold*), though more adventurous harmonies soon prevail. In an ensuing recitative Prometheus reacts to the rustling figuration, asking if visitors have come to see him nailed to his rock or if he hears the wings of his persecuting vulture. The accompaniment's triads and seventh chords articulate interlocking thirds (E-flat–G-flat, F–A-flat), another instance of daring harmonies. But simpler diatonic progressions and the rippling arpeggios appropriately recur in a chorus for the Oceanids, who dispel the Titan's fears and console his pain. Only when they recall hearing his anguished cries or their eyes fill with tears upon seeing him incarcerated does the prevailing diatonicism yield to bolder harmonies, including a modulation to A major, a tritone removed from the tonic.

Throughout the chorus Prometheus echoes the Oceanids' sentiments in interjections that utilize dotted rhythms from the scene's prelude. His final utterance—the gods no longer have weapons against mortals—alarms the Queen of the Oceanids, who demands to know the nature of his crime in a prosaic recitative. He answers in an expressly martial aria, replete with dotted rhythms in the bass line, an agitated, irregular pattern of afterbeats above, and a slower military cadence that maintains rhythmic equilibrium in a third staff. The accompaniment suits the lyrics immanently well: Prometheus admits he sealed his fate by climbing Mount Olympus to sit defiantly on Jupiter's throne. But when he discloses he gave mortals divine fire and lasting hope, the mode's enharmonic change from C-sharp minor to D-flat major, a slower harmonic rhythm, and cues for trombones (instruments long associated with sacred subjects) create a solemn, hymn-like setting. The aria's minor key and initial ferocity return when Prometheus accuses Jupiter of exacting revenge on innocent beings, a passage set in a Lisztian manner with chords whose roots outline an augmented triad. The aria ends as the Oceanids warn Prometheus of his complaint's futility and urge him to bow to Jupiter. In the scene's concluding march Prometheus impudently predicts his torments will soon end and Jupiter will bow before him. Critics would have undeniably considered the entire sequence "virile" had the cantata been performed.

Scene 3, the cantata's core, illuminates Holmès's reactions to the Franco-Prussian War. As the libretto subsequently clarifies, another prelude imitates hammers striking anvils by incessantly repeating an open fifth (D–A) in the rhythm of two sixteenth notes followed by an eighth rest, perhaps evoking a blacksmith's work less vividly than Wagner's portrayal of Mime's labor in *Das Rheingold*, but a clear point of comparison nevertheless. Rapid scalewise ascents likewise function mimetically, depicting smoke rising as iron is forged. Unaccompanied, Prometheus then claims profound immensity extols his deeds, whereupon anvil sounds resume as a men's chorus sings the following strophe in G minor:

> Supple, firm, well tempered,
> From fire issue swords
> That proud warriors value;
> Their laurels –
> Liberty, their native land,
> Enslaved by tyrants –
> Fire will deliver them,
> The weapon is there.

The Promethean flame's unique interpretation as the source of weapons obviously resonates with the circumstances of Paris, surrounded by German soldiers, an interim government threatening its freedom, and in dire need of "proud warriors" to deliver its citizens from tyranny.

But beyond furnishing a parallel to a historical situation, scene 3 reveals personal attitudes toward the war that Holmès doubtless harbored as an expectant or new mother. Abandoning its battle song, the men's chorus relates that parents and children gather around hearths in illuminated houses, guarded by fire as they sit watch. When D major returns, a berceuse's repetitive rocking provides a gentle homophonic background for a duet between a man and a woman. The man, responding to a knock at his door, invites a stranger to share meat from his flocks, purified as a sacrifice by fire. The woman replies as the berceuse modulates to A major: their children sleep in cradles while her husband speaks sweetly, awakening desires deep in her heart. As the swaying accompaniment shifts to E minor, the man exhorts the hearth's divine flame to enter their souls, vowing he and the woman will love each other eternally. Together they repeat his pledge five times. The intimate domestic image, plausibly idealizing autobiographical events, is fleeting. Augmented by women's voices, the chorus embarks on an astonishing fugue, asserting that divine arts are born of fire, and humanity, once nature's slave, is now its master. A double fugue, normally a scene's conclusion in cantatas and oratorios, instead leads to a passage for four soloists who solemnly proclaim a funeral pyre consumes the dead, giving wings to their souls. An instrumental interlude then implies the beginning of another scene, though no designation appears in the score.

Holmès encountered obstacles in the rest of the cantata, as several fragmentary passages indicate. A conventional recitative begins scene 4 as Prometheus inquires if the Queen of the Oceanids hears the nations praising his deeds. No voice has said his name, she answers, eliciting a retort whose text and music are incomplete. Likewise betraying compositional difficulties are two versions of the Queen's ensuing aria, one deleted, the other unfinished.[163] Both feature the same text, an indictment of humanity's offenses against Prometheus, namely forgetting his name, offering fiery sacrifices to evil Olympians, and ignoring his torment and altruism. The original setting, an Andante in F major with a chorale-like accompaniment in four parts, seems incongruous with the impassioned lyrics, a defect perhaps explaining its rejection. Better suited to the Queen's accusations are the second rendition's slightly more animated accompanimental patterns of downbeats and afterbeats and its darker tonality, C-sharp minor, the key of the Titan's martial aria in scene 2 and portions of scene 5. Holmès, perhaps exploiting one key too frequently, was apparently dissatisfied with her second attempt, since its accompaniment dwindles to a bass line as the aria ends, when the Queen urges Prometheus to rejoin the gods.

The Titan's blunt reply held greater appeal for Holmès. Laughing at Olympian fury, Prometheus vows never to roam with the gods, a pledge eliciting more vivid musical treatment than the Queen's charges against mankind. In a *recitativo accompagnato* recalling the cantata's opening key of B-flat minor and the Titan's characteristic dotted motive, agitated neighbor tones interrupt jagged vocal lines and relentlessly acquire the doubling of thirds, sixths, and complete triads. Terrified by the Titan's outburst, the Queen exclaims his vow has provoked divine retribution and heralds Mercury's arrival against a background of restless tremolos. Thus, within scene 4, relative states of completion and different intensities of Holmès's response to her libretto confirm her special aptitude for conceiving forceful music.

---

[163]   The first occupies fols 20–21 of Ms. 11917, the second a smaller inserted bifolium.

Scene 5, a multi-sectioned dialogue between Prometheus and Mercury, is largely complete, except for isolated passages merely comprising vocal and bass lines. After an instrumental segue, Mercury's unaccompanied demand for the thief of fire to obey him initiates a duet in a highly chromatic C-sharp minor. A passage marked *andante mosso* commences with driving dotted rhythms in an ascending bass line that supports syncopated chords, a vigorous accompaniment suiting Mercury's announcement that he comes in the name of gods betrayed by Prometheus, who must end his blasphemy. Modulating to the remote key of E-flat major for a new plot development, Mercury asks if Prometheus knows the future or the means of breaking divine rule. In a thinly sketched passage Prometheus advises Mercury to cease his mockery, predicts the Olympians will follow other fallen gods, and disavows knowledge of their demise and the hand that will cause it. Shifting from common time to compound meter, the duet concludes with a long exchange between the characters, accompanied by six-part chords that are repeated in continuous eighth notes. Mercury offers many reasons to recant, but Prometheus refutes them all. Enraged by such mad defiance, Mercury threatens humanity with a terrifying hurricane, predictably evoked by stormy tremolos and diminished seventh chords. The Oceanids briefly recapitulate their consolations from scene 1, declaring they will never desert Prometheus, whereupon the notation dwindles to several chords and two lone pitches, leaving the cantata without a denouement.

Why Holmès abandoned *Prométhée* remains speculative, though manuscript sources suggest three likely reasons. She obviously encountered problems in characterizing the Queen of the Oceanids, as two nondescript versions of an aria confirm. Tonal homogeneity—created by a preponderance of C-sharp minor, the enharmonically spelled major mode, and its relative minor—likewise probably caused her to forsake the score. And a static plot had not advanced significantly in five well-developed scenes: Prometheus remains shackled, exhorting the elements and Oceanids to witness his predicament, pointing to his beneficent deeds, and obstinately refusing to recant, despite entreaties from the Queen of the Oceanids and Mercury.

Initially, however, Holmès must have been strongly attracted to the myth. A youthful admirer of classical antiquity in Versailles, she developed her Hellenistic proclivities through contact with the Parnassians during the late 1860s and her relationship with their leader, Catulle Mendès, as traits of her libretto verify. Moreover, she cast Prometheus as romanticism's quintessentially defiant rebel and liberator, precisely the type of heroic subject she cultivated in a new, virile style to transform herself from a sovereign of the salon into a respected figure in Parisian concert venues. The myth prompted her to employ developmental procedures (as in the opening prelude and a choral fugue), extravagant melodic gestures (evinced by daring changes of direction in wide-ranging themes), bold harmonies and tonal plans (the latter notably based on interlocking thirds, tritones, and augmented triads), and extreme contrasts of character (epitomized by juxtaposing "cries of war" and "calls for liberty" in a men's chorus with a "song of love" in the ensuing domestic scene). Contemporary critics associated such techniques with Wagner, who encouraged Holmès to adopt a personal style rather than adhere to any school's precepts. *Prométhée*, like other choral works she wrote immediately after visiting Wagner at Tribschen, embodies this new style. And finally, *Prométhée* afforded Holmès opportunities to react to national and personal challenges, namely the fate of France in the Franco-Prussian War's aftermath and her new role as an infant's mother.

A fourth French representation of the myth articulates similar issues. Its libretto reflects the Parnassian movement's dissolution into Symbolism. Its music raises a persistent concern of French critics, Wagnerism. And it utilizes "virile" developmental processes, melodic gestures, harmonies, and contrasts, features scarcely surprising in any score based on the Prometheus legend. But discovering them in a work by Gabriel Fauré (1845–1924) confronts his traditional image as a composer of intimate piano pieces, refined chamber music, delicate sacred works, and exquisitely crafted songs.

Fauré

When Fauré retired at age 75 to focus exclusively on his final works, he was known throughout France as director of the Paris Conservatoire, member of the Académie, president of the Société nationale de musique, and critic for *Le Figaro*. He acquired fame, however, only after years of toiling in relative obscurity and composing for a few select admirers.[164] His *Prométhée*, a full-length *tragédie lyrique*, contributed to his burgeoning reputation, even while reflecting a style honed during the earliest stages of his training.

Born in provincial Pamiers, Fauré evinced musical aptitude as a child by playing the harmonium in the chapel affiliated with the Ecole normale at Montgauzy, where his father was appointed director in 1849. He soon enrolled in Paris at the Ecole de musique classique et religieuse, later renamed for its founding director Louis Niedermeyer, who sought to elevate contemporary church music's standards through study of plainchant and Renaissance polyphony and by purging sacred repertories of operatic influence.[165] Fauré consequently developed expertise in the church modes, which often colored his later scores. After Niedermeyer's death in 1861, Fauré became a protégé of Saint-Saëns, who supplemented the school's curriculum with contemporary music. Now acquainted with works by Schumann, Liszt, and Wagner, Fauré produced his first compositions, including the *Cantique de Jean Racine*, a prize-winning cantata for mixed chorus, string quartet, and harmonium that marked the end of his apprenticeship.

Fauré worked as a church organist, initially in the provinces, then in Paris, and served in the military during the Franco-Prussian War. After the Commune's turbulence subsided, he was appointed assistant organist at the prestigious Eglise de Saint Sulpice and frequented the salons of Saint-Saëns and Pauline Viardot, both of whom promoted his music in Parisian society's highest echelons. He nonetheless remained little known as a public figure well into the 1880s, rising to prominence only when he became an inspector of provincial conservatories (1892), succeeded Jules Massenet as professor of composition, counterpoint, and fugue at the Conservatoire

---

[164]   Jean-Michel Nectoux, *Gabriel Fauré: A Musical Life*, trans. Roger Nichols (Cambridge, 1991), p. 79.

[165]   Maurice Galerne, *L'Ecole Niedermeyer: Sa création, son but, son développement* (Paris, 1928), pp. 31–2.

(1896), and developed an international profile, especially in Italy and England.[166] The growth of Fauré's fame, however, arguably culminated with his enormously successful *Prométhée*, commissioned for an extraordinary festival in Béziers in southern France and premiered there in August 1900.

Early critics of *Prométhée* typically noticed its radical departures from Fauré's previous endeavors, which mostly comprised songs and chamber music, as Paul-Louis Garnier observed six weeks after the debut.[167] Fauré's large-scale mastery also surprised many other journalists who had previously believed he was "suited solely to sketching small, ingenious and exquisite pages of delicate intimacy," as Léopold Dauphin remarked a month later.[168] Indeed, Fauré was nicknamed the "Schumann français," an apt comparison based on both composers' predilections for piano music and songs early in their compositional evolutions.[169] Moreover, as composer Paul Dukas noted, Fauré had written practically nothing for the all-important French theater, except incidental music to the *Caligula* of Dumas *père* (1888) and *Shylock*, a Shakespearean adaptation (1889).[170] *Prométhée* accordingly represents a milestone in Fauré's career, when he unexpectedly developed serious theatrical ambitions that were consummated 13 years later in his opera *Pénélope*. His Promethean setting, however, is far more than a preliminary effort in an unexplored genre: it is an exceptional work with a unique theatrical history.

Prométhée debuted at an annual festival that attracted thousands of spectators to remote Béziers, an event produced by a confluence of several phenomena shaping nineteenth-century provincial culture, most conspicuously the economy, regional identity, entrepreneurial patronage of the arts, and the rise of popular theater. Located 100 kilometers from the Spanish border, near but not on the Mediterranean coast, Béziers had benefited from virtually uninterrupted prosperity in the local wine growing industry since the late eighteenth century. Indeed, even an outbreak of vine mildew in 1852 curtailed overproduction that had depressed grape prices for several consecutive years.[171] Another economic boon occurred in 1859, when several competing railways established Béziers as a hub connecting Toulouse, Montpellier, Nîmes, and Perpignan.[172] Concurrent setbacks in local textile factories and the

---

[166]   Robert Orledge, *Gabriel Fauré* (London, 1979), p. 15.

[167]   Paul-Louis Garnier, "Théâtre: *Prométhée* à Béziers," *La Revue blanche*, 15 September 1900, p. 142. See also Pierre Lalo, "A l'Hippodrome: Première représentation à Paris de *Prométhée*," *Le Temps*, 10 December 1907, p. 2; J. Saint-Jean, "Hippodrome et Académie nationale de musique: *Prométhée*," *La Nouvelle revue*, 1 January 1908, p. 140.

[168]   Léopold Dauphin, "Gabriel Fauré et le *Prométhée*," *La Vogue*, 15 October 1900, p. 59. See also Charles Koechlin, "Représentations de Béziers: *Prométhée*, de M. Gabriel Fauré," *Mercure de France*, 40 (1901): 550; Lalo, "A l'Hippodrome," p. 2; and Lalo, "A l'Académie nationale de musique: *Prométhée*, drame lyrique," *Le Temps*, 11 June 1917, p. 3.

[169]   See, among others, René Maizeroy, "Fêtes de Béziers: *Prométhée*," *Le Théâtre*, 43 (1900): 12.

[170]   Paul Dukas, *Les Ecrits de Paul Dukas sur la musique*, ed. Flavien Bonnet-Roy et al. (Paris, 1948), p. 507.

[171]   Marcel Nussy Saint-Saëns, "La Fondation du théâtre des arènes de Béziers: La Première du *Déjanire* le 18 Août 1898," *Etudes sur Pézenas et l'Hérault*, 9/2 (1980): 4.

[172]   Jean Sagnes (ed.), *Histoire de Béziers* (Toulouse, 1986), pp. 229–32.

passage of restrictive ordinances governing metallurgical production encouraged additional investments in viticulture.[173] Crowning the small city's good fortune was that the phylloxera infestation of the 1870s reached Béziers later than surrounding areas, and while the voracious insects bankrupted some small wineries, large firms suffered fewer losses.[174] Surviving establishments received government relief and adopted previously unavailable extermination methods. The local wine industry then flourished until labor disputes prompted its socialization in 1907.

The favorable economic climate predictably benefited the arts. In 1859 the local archaeological society inaugurated a museum of painting with a series of bullfights, a form of fundraising reflecting close cultural ties between Languedoc and Spain.[175] So successful were the bullfights in the open fields of the Champ de Mars that the city council voted to build a wooden arena to accommodate huge audiences. Three such structures were respectively left unfinished, demolished, and destroyed because of economic uncertainty induced by the phylloxera infestation, rapid urbanization, and fire. But in 1896 the council met the demands of citizens and a clamorous local press by hiring two contractors, Germain Antoine Gleyzes and Jean Joseph Sautel, to build an amphitheater with a concrete foundation and a capacity of 12,500 seats. The facility was essentially complete by the summer of 1898, though architectural details required work until 1901.

Commercialism may partially explain the construction of four arenas in Béziers, though municipal profits were usually small and went to charity. More convincingly accounting for the venue's immense popularity is that it came to symbolize regional identity. The Parisian press, opposed to the bullfights since their inception in 1859, eventually influenced the national legislature to issue an interdiction against them in 1895.[176] Southern royalists nonetheless staunchly defended the bullfights as manifestations of their Languedocian heritage: to prohibit them was to restrict the liberty of the ancient provinces. The general population likewise resented "the authoritarian whims of the central government," which, they maintained, sought to integrate the Meridion's inhabitants by suppressing indigenous practices. Soon the entire region from Nîmes to Toulouse was inflamed, prompting local authorities to hold town meetings that revealed late nineteenth-century Languedocians still shared fewer affinities with their northern compatriots than with their Catalonian contemporaries and distant Roman ancestors.[177] To flaunt the prohibition, defy northern politics, reinforce ancestral ties, and strengthen regional identity, the amphitheater cultivated classical subjects. Enjoying special favor were stories involving Hercules, who, some ancient Roman authorities claimed, sojourned in Béziers on his travels to the Strait of Gibraltar.

---

[173]   Marcel Hardtmeyer, "Evolution des valeurs et des structures viticoles dans le biterrois depuis 1789," in *Béziers et le biterrois* (Montpellier, 1971), p. 407.

[174]   Sagnes, p. 230.

[175]   Nussy Saint-Saëns (pp. 4–5) fully narrates the amphitheater's history.

[176]   Ibid., p. 4.

[177]   René Merle, "L'Identité occitane, brouillage de l'opposition de classe," in *L'Identité occitane: Réflexions théoriques et expériences* (Montpellier, 1990), pp. 167–78.

The animating force behind the bullfighting arena's conversion into a neo-Hellenic amphitheater was Fernand Castelbon de Beauxhostes (1859–1936), who owned a large wine estate near Béziers and preserved strong regional traditions of civic patronage. In 1897, for example, he founded the Société tauromachique de Béziers, a coalition of townspeople and politicians who worked to resolve a labor dispute delaying the arena's completion.[178] Castelbon doubtless considered the bullfights manifestations of regional identity, since he belonged to two liberal political organizations and befriended the radical leftist Louis Lafferre, an outspoken critic of state authority over local governments.[179] He also organized the local chapter of the Saint Cecilians, a nineteenth-century association dedicated to reforming the Catholic Church's music, and more famously founded and conducted La Lyre biterroise, a wind band deriving its name from the ancient Roman word for Béziers (Baeterrae). Comprised of talented amateurs from throughout the region, the group played in Barcelona in 1895, joining Spanish military regiments to form a band of 600 players. The acoustics of the Catalonian capital's amphitheater were disappointing,[180] but a year later, when 18,000 spectators enjoyed his group's performance in the marvelous acoustics of Valencia's ancient Roman arena, Castelbon became convinced of the viability of such venues:

> This was for me a revelation, or rather an explanation of the success obtained among the Greeks and Romans in open-air spectacles. Could these spectacles not be revived in France, in our Midi which has nothing to envy in the sun of Athens or Rome, since above all our Mediterranean population owes to their illustrious origins its natural taste for beauty in every form, the faculty of being emotionally moved, and the precious gift of understanding among all?[181]

Toward the goal of educating Languedocians in their classical heritage Castelbon devoted considerable financial resources and personal effort, often working with civic and religious leaders in Béziers.[182] He consequently earned the Spanish government's title of vice consul, and the Parisian press named him "the biterrois patron" and "the extravagant patron of Béziers."[183]

For the first open-air spectacle Castelbon turned to Saint-Saëns, who overcame his aversion to bullfights and tested the amphitheater's acoustics after performing an organ recital in Béziers on 7 May 1897. Favorably impressed, he agreed to inaugurate the venue with *Déjanire*, a tragedy based on an episode in the life of Hercules drawn from the *Trachiniae* of Sophocles.[184] Castelbon, having procured a celebrated composer's services, engaged regional performing groups for the debut

---

[178]   Nussy Saint-Saëns, p. 6.
[179]   Paul Pistre, *Francs-Maçons du Midi* (Perpignan, 1995), p. 143.
[180]   Nussy Saint-Saëns, p. 6.
[181]   Ibid.
[182]   Pistre, p. 152.
[183]   Gustave Larroumet, "Chronique théâtrale: Aux arènes de Béziers," *Le Temps*, 3 September 1900, p. 1; Robert Brussel, "La Représentation de *Prométhée*," *Le Figaro*, 6 December 1907, p. 5.
[184]   René Thorle, "Saint-Saëns intime," *Musica*, 6/57 (1907): 92–3.

on 28 August. He assembled 400 instrumentalists from La Lyre biterroise, its sister organization La Rallye biterroise, regiments stationed at Béziers and Montpellier, the municipal guard of Barcelona, and players from seven other cities; he recruited choristers, vocal soloists, and stage actors from local chapters of the Orphéon Society, the Chorale biterroise, the Théâtre du Liceo, this nearby city's conservatory, and Paris's Théâtre de l'Odéon.[185]

Enthusiasm spread from the musical community to the entire town, which installed new street lamps, repaired sidewalks, paved streets, and sponsored free public festivities such as a wine fountain in the central plaza.[186] Germain Bourjade, superintendent of bridges and streets, oversaw the construction and installation of the sets (designed by Marcel Jambon of the Paris Opéra), the dressing rooms, and the stage floor. Castelbon persuaded railway companies to run special excursion trains at reduced fares. Emile Baumann, an admirer of Saint-Saëns, subsequently praised Béziers for unity that revealed the city's best tendencies.[187] A community of just over 50,000 inhabitants indeed deserved accolades for supporting the project. But public involvement in local theatrical productions was a widespread cultural development throughout France during the nineteenth century.

During the Napoleonic era and for decades afterward, the state strictly regulated theaters by granting licenses and segregating genres by location. These conditions prevailed until 1864, when legislative reforms sanctioned free enterprise in the theatrical industry, although the theater's role in mass education and greater public access to cultural events genuinely concerned the liberal monarchy during the 1830s.[188] *Le Théâtre et le peuple*, published by Jules Bonnassies in 1872, marked progress toward a populist theater, reviving the Enlightenment ideal of state subsidies for municipal theaters, not just elitist urban institutions.[189] Parisian architect Eugène Emmanuel's proposal to build popular theaters with 3,000 affordable seats, advanced in 1879, likewise attests to growing interest in education and access.[190] Serious engagement with the issue, however, dates from the 1890s, as is confirmed by Maurice Pottecher's founding of the Théâtre du peuple at Bussang in 1899, the appearance of his influential essay of the same name and Romain Rolland's critical study of the subject in 1903, and the proliferation of amateur dramatic societies such as the Universités populaires.[191]

Populism especially suited the provinces, where small towns generally had only one theater that was built as a gesture of civic pride, as in Béziers. A mixed repertory necessarily evolved, comprising operas, melodramas, pantomimes, and conventional plays that appealed to prosperous bourgeois audiences.[192] In such venues local

---

[185] Nussy Saint-Saëns, p. 14.

[186] Ibid.

[187] Emile Baumann, *Les Grandes formes de la musique: L'Œuvre de Camille Saint-Saëns* (Paris, 1923), p. 161.

[188] John McCormick, *Popular Theatres of Nineteenth-Century France* (London, 1993), pp. 1–2, 13.

[189] Ibid., p. 4.

[190] Ibid., p. 5.

[191] Ibid., p. 3.

[192] Ibid., pp. 53–4.

citizens often performed with professionals, especially if orchestral players were required. Thus the Languedocian amphitheater's productions represented lavish contributions to populist theater's emergence in *fin-de-siècle* France. That the ancient Roman amphitheater in Orange received the central government's financial support and consequently acquired an "official character" only reinforced public perception of the arena in Béziers as a populist venue.[193]

The amphitheater decisively affected generic features of works commissioned for the festivals. Outdoor performance demanded loud instruments or large numbers of softer ones, hence the use of wind bands and 100 strings. The open space also encouraged antiphonal effects among separate orchestral groups that were located in a newly built pit, on both sides of the stage, and backstage. Fauré's extraordinary orchestration accordingly deployed three large instrumental masses mixing entire families of variously sized clarinets, saxophones, trumpets, and now obsolete saxhorns with strings that were divided into the traditional quartet (first and second violins, viola, and cello) and a second array of cellos and contrabasses that continuously doubled the bass line, regardless of which mixed group was playing. Even more striking was the arena's obligatory "curtain of harps," 18 of which were perched above the pit on a platform in an exaggerated evocation of the strumming of the lyre that accompanied declamation in antique drama.

Unfamiliar with military instruments, Fauré collaborated with Montpellier's regimental bandmaster Charles Eustace, who had assisted Saint-Saëns with *Déjanire*. Fauré orchestrated some passages for the strings, harps, and conventional wind instruments, but sent sketches of other excerpts to Eustace, who scored them fully and returned them to Fauré for revision.[194] Never engraved, the original version survives only in the composer's manuscripts and two fair copies held at the Bibliothèque nationale.[195] Its scoring was preserved as closely as possible for the Parisian debut of *Prométhée* in 1907, but for later performances beginning in 1917 Fauré's assistant, Jean Roger-Ducasse, arranged the massive work for a more conventional orchestra.

The amphitheater also governed the distribution of speech and song among dramatic personnel. Castelbon and Saint-Saëns had agreed that recalling Greek tragedy's practices was integral to the festival's success, establishing a precedent for Fauré. Actors consequently spoke main roles, including Prometheus and Pandora, while several minor characters and the chorus sang. *Prométhée* thus occupies an ambiguous generic space, alternating between spoken dialogue and discrete musical numbers in the time-honored manner of French *opéra comique* despite its serious subject, a strategy provoking copious critical response.[196] Some commentators

---

[193]   A. Mangeot, "A Béziers," *Le Monde musical*, 15 September 1901, p. 262.

[194]   Nectoux (pp. 195–6) describes the process fully.

[195]   F-Pn Ms. 17768 (1–6).

[196]   Dukas, p. 506; Dauphin, pp. 60–61; Lalo, "A l'Académie nationale," p. 3; Mangeot, pp. 263–4; Julien Tiersot, "Semaine théâtrale: Ancien Hippodrome—Première représentation de *Prométhée*," *Le Ménestrel*, 7 December 1907, n.p.; Henri de Curzon, "Paris: Le *Prométhée* de M. G. Fauré," *Le Guide musical*, 53/50 (1907): 779; Adolphe Jullien, "A l'Opéra: *Prométhée*, de M. Fauré," *Journal des débats*, 26 May 1917, p. 3; Jean Marnold, "Opéra national: *Prométhée*, tragédie lyrique de Jean Lorrain et A.-F. Hérold, musique de Gabriel Fauré," *Mercure de France*, 16 July 1917, p. 339.

believed the actors' declamation supported the arena's neoclassical pretensions, while others considered the alternation of music and speech a distraction. Attempting to discern a logical pattern in Fauré's allocation of song and speech, some reviewers asserted the gods sing and mortals declaim, a reductive view promulgated in the secondary literature.[197] Such claims are inaccurate, however, because Hermes speaks and two mortals, Andros and Aenoë, frequently sing. Dramatic exigency or operatic convention accordingly seem to have shaped roles, as when Hermes must converse with Pandora and Prometheus, or when Andros and Aenoë step forward to sing solos in larger choral numbers.

Fauré's mixture of dialogue and closed musical forms attracted notice because it was anachronistic in an era when Wagnerian continuity was the norm. Indeed, French Wagnerism's crisis was long past. For two decades after the Franco-Prussian War, French composers, critics, and audiences held conflicting attitudes toward Wagner, admiring his works for their advanced harmony, modern orchestration, and innate ability to convey extramusical associations, but reviling his nationalism and denigration of France, especially as he expressed them in *Eine Kapitulation*.[198] Older composers such as Saint-Saëns and Massenet had sought to absorb Wagnerian elements while preserving the French operatic legacy, but after the controversy climaxed in demonstrations against the Paris Opéra's productions of *Lohengrin* in 1887 and 1891, resistance collapsed. Wagner became the most frequently performed composer at the Opéra, and young French composers cultivated the *drame lyrique*, a term critics applied to operas that used leitmotifs, unfolded continuously, and were ideologically ambitious.[199]

Such criteria influenced opinions of *Prométhée*, as Wagnerian references in early reviews plainly indicate. One critic thought the singer who performed the role of Kratos could succeed in *Tristan und Isolde* or *Siegfried*.[200] Another dubbed Fauré the "master of Béziers," alluding to Wagner's nickname, "the master of Bayreuth."[201] Others identified Wagnerian features: the score was "full of leitmotifs," "modulated ceaselessly," and contained "modulations changing like veils of airy folds."[202] For one correspondent it embodied "the highest degree of absolute music, as Wagner said, which is applied harmoniously here to the contours of an antique bas-relief."[203] More telling than any critic's observation, however, was the confession Fauré made to his wife upon finishing *Prométhée*: "All that I have written seems awful to me, like an exaggerated imitation of Wagner."[204] A Wagnerian framework accordingly

---

[197] Dauphin, pp. 60–61; Tiersot, n.p. Later assessments include Martin Cooper, "Byways of French Opera: V.—The Operas of Gabriel Fauré," *The Monthly Musical Record*, 77/884 (1947): 34; Orledge, p. 130; Nectoux, (p. 197) mentions only Hermes as an exception.

[198] Steven Huebner, *French Opera at the Fin de Siècle: Wagnerism, Nationalism, and Style* (Oxford, 1999), p. 16.

[199] Ibid., p. 20.

[200] Garnier, p. 142.

[201] Koechlin, p. 550.

[202] Koechlin, p. 552. See also Lalo, "A l'Hippodrome," p. 2; Louis Laloy, "Notre troisième saison de guerre," *Le Pays*, 2 June 1917, p. 2.

[203] Marnold, p. 338.

[204] Gabriel Fauré, *Lettres intimes*, ed. Philippe Fauré-Fremiet (Paris, 1951), p. 39.

supplies an appropriate point of departure for a closer investigation of the libretto and music of *Prométhée*.

André-Ferdinand Hérold, a multifaceted neo-Hellenic author, and Jean Lorrain, a leading decadent poet, collaborated on the libretto. They again consulted Aeschylus, drawing not only on *Prometheus Bound*, but also on events that verifiably occurred in the two lost dramas of the Athenian's original trilogy.[205] Stage action is consequently more elaborate in *Prométhée* than in most nineteenth-century musical representations of the myth. Act I concerns the Titan's impending theft of fire, an action Andros, Aenoë, and mankind praise, but others condemn: Pandora loves him and fears his punishment; his mother Gaea considers his plan blasphemous; and Kratos (Power), Bia (Force), and Hephaestus decree his fate, causing Pandora to collapse as though dead. Act II emphasizes the Titan's punishment, though it digresses from Aeschylus when Aenoë and a chorus of lamenting women ceremoniously deposit Pandora's body in a cave. Then in a close Aeschylean paraphrase, Hephaestus regrets constraining Prometheus, but obeys Kratos and Bia, whereupon the Titan calls for witnesses to divine retribution and vows to endure eternal punishment. His tirade revives Pandora, who emerges from the cave in a daze, claiming her love for Prometheus will thwart the gods. Bia orders Pandora to abandon him, but she asks the Oceanids to transport her to the mountaintops, where she will condemn divine injustice. In Act III the principal characters maintain their attitudes, except Pandora, who attempts to persuade Prometheus to recant. Hermes, arriving amid thunder, announces the birth of Hercules, who will free Prometheus if Pandora gives mankind a box of gifts. Although Prometheus recognizes deceit, Pandora obeys Hermes and is heralded by humanity as the representative of the gods, thus ending the drama tragically.

The libretto's action is Aeschylean, but its language is not. Hérold and Lorrain were well-known *Symbolistes*, the poets, playwrights, and critics who succeeded the Parnassians and dominated *fin-de-siècle* literature.[206] Eschewing the meticulously descriptive Parnassian style to transcend objective experience, Symbolists sought a deeper reality by relying on suggestive language to create atmosphere or depict fleeting moods. Heavily influenced by Wagner, they found in his prose writings and music dramas—especially *Tristan* and *Parsifal*—a perfect fusion of sensuality and spirituality that resonated in their works.[207] Symbolists accordingly cultivated linguistic impenetrability and a sometimes "precious" vocabulary, traits inciting critical protest, most notably against Edouard Dujardin's decadent prose-poem *Amfortas*, his sumptuous translation of the first scene of *Das Rheingold*, and a hedonistic verbal paraphrase of the overture to *Tannhäuser* by Karl Huysmans.[208]

Symbolist characteristics suffuse the libretto of *Prométhée*, as two examples illustrate. In Act I proclivities for precious language emerge when Aenoë invites love to descend among men:

---

[205]   Jean Lorrain and A.-Ferdinand Hérold, *Prométhée, Tragédie lyrique en trois actes* (Paris, 1900), pp. 1–58.

[206]   Larroumet, p. 1.

[207]   Edouard Dujardin, "La Revue wagnérienne," *La Revue musicale*, 4 (1923): 149.

[208]   Turbow, p. 163.

Et toi, mystérieux parfum qui vas éclore,
Planante aile d'amour,
Jaillis comme un fleur d'aurore,
Descends comme un oiseau du jour![209]
[And you, mysterious perfume that begins to blossom, soaring wing of
love, burst forth like a flower of dawn, descend like a bird of day!]

The mixed sensual symbols (perfume, flowers, dawn, soaring) and pervasive
assonance are especially striking in their musico-dramatic context: comprising
an interlude in a men's chorus, the passage begins with martial exhortations for
Prometheus to fulfill his vow and ends by narrating his theft of fire with Greek
choric declamation. In Act III Pandora's plea to the Oceanids epitomizes linguistic
complexity:

O perles que le fleuve en le mouvant email
De ses flots roule et tord, pure Océanides
Aux doigt onglés de clair aiguail,
Prêtez le coquillage ourlé de vos oreilles
A ma voix![210]
[O pearls that the river in the shifting luster of its waves rolls and
twists, chaste Oceanids with fingers tipped in nails of clear dew,
lend the hemstitched shell-work of your ears to my voice!]

Because of its mixed images, esoteric vocabulary, and strained syntax, the passage
was "completely obscure and unintelligible when projected into the open air before
10,000 spectators," as one critic asserted.[211] Others nonetheless admired the libretto's
"superb structure," "fierce and sorrowful grandeur," and "energetic, magisterial
dialogue."[212] But later writers condemned "deplorable elegances," doubtless
influencing the libretto's now widespread assessment as "mediocre literature."[213]

The libretto also manifests Wagnerism by echoing the pseudo-Christian themes
of *Parsifal*. Pandora's death and resurrection present an obvious allegory of the
Christian soul, while Prometheus clearly embodies Christ. Aenoë refers to the Titan
as the "king of death," Bia calls him "the savior of men," and several characters pity
his "bloodied flesh," including Pandora, who weeps as he sheds "divine blood" after
Jupiter's eagle devours his liver.[214] Christian allusions likewise pervade contemporary
reviews, with the "bleeding flesh" of Edouard de Max, who portrayed the

---

[209]   Lorrain and Hérold, pp. 18–19.

[210]   Ibid., p. 43.

[211]   Mangeot, p. 264.

[212]   Arthur Dandelot, "*Prométhée* à Béziers," *Le Monde musical*, 15 September 1900,
p. 267; Garnier, p. 141; Edouard Gauthier, "Fêtes de Béziers: *Prométhée*," *La Rampe*, 16
September 1900, n.p.

[213]   Lalo, "A l'Hippodrome," p. 2 (littérature médiocre); Lalo, "A l'Académie nationale,"
p. 3 (déplorables elegances). For similar recent opinions, see Cooper, p. 33; Michel Desbruères,
"Le *Prométhée* de Jean Lorrain et André-Ferdinand Hérold," *Etudes fauréennes*, 20–21
(1983–4): 12, 16; Nectoux, p. 197.

[214]   Lorrain and Hérold, pp. 20, 30, 32, 43, 55.

Titan, attracting special notice.[215] One critic even identified Prometheus as "a god crucified five centuries before Christ's birth,"[216] an image reinforced by the Béziers production: Prometheus was imprisoned atop a huge rock pile comprising the set, just as Christ perished on Calvary; Max's costume, a toga exposing his limbs and chest, prompted journalists to describe him as naked or nude, the state in which Christ suffered and died; and Max struck poses unequivocally recalling the Crucifixion (Figure 5.1).

Figure 5.1   Cl. Boissonas et Taponnier, Edouard de Max as the Title Character
                    in Fauré's *Prométhée*
                    (Courtesy of the Music Library at the University of North Texas)

Christian overtones often colored *fin-de-siècle* operas, as Vincent d'Indy's *Fervaal* (1897) conspicuously illustrates. Parallels between Prometheus and Christ were likewise common in the era's literary treatments of the myth, including those of Camille du Locle, Ulrich Rudolph Schmid, Péladan, Stephen Philips, Stanislas

---

[215]   Maizeroy, p. 11.
[216]   Larroumet, p. 1. See also Maizeroy, p. 11.

Millet, and Guerra Junqueiro.[217] Indeed, a late nineteenth-century revival of the medieval exegetic tradition constituted one of several signs marking a decline in the Titan's romantic image as a rebel and outcast. This striking aspect of *Prométhée*, ignored in recent studies of Fauré's music, is even more notable because religious elements determined the keys of several numbers.

Two correlations between religious affect and tonality involve C minor, a dark key traditionally associated with the Mass for the Dead and contemplated by Fauré for his Requiem until he instead selected D minor.[218] C minor accordingly suits Gaea's divine condemnation of the Titan's blasphemy in her aria in Act I and the fear Andros expresses before the wrathful Olympians in Act III. F major links the eternal rest and peace of the Agnus Dei in Fauré's Requiem with identical sentiments in the chorus of Oceanids in Act III, a number aptly described as "a pagan Requiem."[219] D minor, identified with gravity and stately grandeur in the Requiem's Introit, Kyrie, and Libera me, fittingly inaugurates a trio in Act I, when three deities, Kratos, Bia, and Hephaestus, disclose the Titan's fate; the key is admittedly less congenial for the trio's angry ending. And Fauré ostensibly connected the distinctive key of F-sharp major with antique impulses in two short choral works with Renaissance dance titles, the *Pavane* and the *Passapied*, and the opening chorus of *Prométhée*, where primitive mankind emerges from caves singing primordial calls of "Eia." The passage occurs in the context of C major, thus creating bold tritone relationships at the drama's outset. Associative tonalities are admittedly less systematic in *Prométhée* than in some of Wagner's operas, but they nonetheless illustrate another of Fauré's Wagnerian affinities.

Recurrent leitmotifs in *Prométhée* have been considered more direct evidence of Fauré's Wagnerism since the Languedocian premiere.[220] Indeed, the score largely derives from just six motives (Example 5.8). The first, initiating the prelude and representing Prometheus, separates two ascending figures with a precipitous downward leap. Comprising diatonic fanfares, the second motive invariably accompanies references to the Olympians. The chromatic, sinuously contoured third motive denotes mankind's hopes. Fire is embodied in the fourth motive's repetitive leaps and nimble accompaniment, while the fifth motive's descending fifths attend Pandora's presence or actions. Introduced at the appropriate point in Gaea's aria, the sixth motive alludes to the Titan's punishment. The mere presence of six leitmotifs, however, scarcely makes a perfect Wagnerite of Fauré, who, like many French composers, valued Wagnerian referents, but adapted them to his own use.[221]

---

[217]   Trousson, pp. 421–5.
[218]   Nectoux, p. 116.
[219]   Ibid., p. 207.
[220]   Dauphin, p. 59; Koechlin, p. 552; Nectoux, pp. 199–202; Orledge, pp. 129–34.
[221]   Fauré acknowledged the Wagnerian system's supremacy while working on *Pénélope*. (Fauré, p. 144). Regarding various French composers' use of leitmotifs, see Huebner, pp. 64–5, 95–6, 242–4, 278–80, 342–3, 385–6, 422, 441, 472–3.

a. Prometheus

b. The Olympian Gods

c. Mankind's Hopes

d. Fire

e. Pandora

f. Punishment

Example 5.8   Six Principal Motives in Fauré's *Prométhée*

Fauré's leitmotifs typically undergo rhythmic variation, often within discrete numbers, as the first motive illustrates (Example 5.9a–e). After inaugurating the prelude, it assumes different guises in the ensuing chorus, exhibiting hemiola when men exalt the Titan's power (5.9a), changing mode and gaining rhythmic momentum as women liken him to joy (5.9b), growing longer as Aenoë equates him with hope (5.9c), and pervading the accompaniment when Aenoë expresses gratitude for his love of humanity (5.9d). Such manipulations produce continuity among passages based on variants of one motive, creating the "fluidity," "moving limpidity," and "undulating forms" that critics noticed, despite the score's division into separate numbers.[222]

a. Prometheus as Power

b. Prometheus as Joy

c. Prometheus as Hope

d. Love for Humanity

e. Motives in Counterpoint: Prometheus and Mankind's Hope

Example 5.9   Variations of the Prometheus Motive in Fauré's *Prométhée*

---

[222]   Dauphin, p. 65; Koechlin, p. 550; Lalo, "A l'Hippodrome," p. 2; Servières, p. 5; Saint-Jean, p. 140; Laloy, p. 2.

Example 5.10a   Fauré *Prométhée*, Act III, scene 4, mm. 10–14

Wagner occasionally observes similar practices, but more characteristically presents a succession of different motives, as in Wotan's monologue in Act II of *Die Walküre*, or repeats one motive that modulates incessantly but preserves its defining melodic and rhythmic traits, as in the same opera's penultimate instrumental passage, when Wotan protects the sleeping Brünnhilde with her armor. Fauré sometimes employed Wagner's standard technique of combining leitmotifs contrapuntally, as when the motives representing Prometheus and mankind's hope intertwine to begin the second chorus in Act I (5.9e), though he generally develops one motive in a series of consecutive rhythmic variations. His procedures consequently resemble those of his mentor, Saint-Saëns, and his fellow officer of the Société nationale, d'Indy, both of whom generated extended operatic passages through protracted manipulations of individual leitmotifs. Fauré's variations, however, usually correlate with textual events, whereas Saint-Saëns and d'Indy cultivated more abstract thematic development.[223]

Prométhée thus engages with three important facets of Wagnerism: its Symbolist language corroborates Wagner's impact on French literature and criticism, while its associative tonalities and leitmotifs illustrate widespread adoption and modification of quintessentially Wagnerian techniques. A Wagnerian perspective nonetheless cannot account for several radical tonal elements in *Prométhée* (Example 5.10a–d). Foremost among them is the modal writing that pervades many numbers, as a passage for the Oceanids demonstrates (5.10a). The principal melodic line's B-naturals create the Lydian mode, though the accompaniment's B-flats occasionally allude to the conventional key of F major. Elsewhere largely modal melodies produce pentatonicism, as in the cortège that accompanies the deposition of Pandora's body (5.10b). Modality is admittedly ubiquitous in Fauré's compositions, a stylistic trait he acquired during studies at the Ecole Niedermeyer and church appointments. But early critics deemed the score's use of the "ancient ecclesiastical tones" noteworthy, and Dukas even thought an "antique accent" was "especially appropriate to the primitive character" of several scenes, particularly the opening chorus.[224]

Example 5.10b   Fauré *Prométhée*, Act II, scene 1, mm. 76–8

[223]   Huebner, pp. 222, 342–3.

[224]   Marnold, p. 338; Dukas, p. 508; Lalo, "Béziers: *Prométhée*, tragédie lyrique de MM. Jean Lorrain et Ferdinand Hérold. Musique de M. Gabriel Fauré," *Le Temps*, 5 October 1900, p. 3; Tiersot, n.p.

Likewise incompatible with Wagnerian harmonic practices are isolated passages of essentially atonal counterpoint and impressionist allusions to the whole-tone scale, found respectively in Hephaestus' aria in Act II and his ensuing dialogue with Kratos and Bia (5.10c–d).[225] Although Fauré discounted such sonorities as "platitudinous," they bewildered his hosts when he inspected conservatories in southern France shortly before the opera's premiere and attracted early critical attention.[226] *Prométhée* emanated a "savage grandeur," evinced "an imperious and lively force, a sovereign power," and was "full of strength."[227] Its orchestration was "ferocious in character," a "primitive tonality" perfectly evoked the "first chorus's savagery," and Kratos and Bia expressed "hateful fury." Fauré, the composer of genteel songs and chamber music, had rarely cultivated such traits. Indeed, among many reviewers surprised by Fauré's mastery of new expressive techniques in a genre he had never explored, one claimed *Prométhée* revealed "a symphonist of incomparable power."[228]

Example 5.10c   Fauré *Prométhée*, Act II, scene 2, mm. 94–7

---

[225]   Wagner's atonal passages, such as the interlude following Wotan's exit in Act I of *Siegfried*, are more homophonic than contrapuntal. Regarding whole-tone allusions in the opening chorus of *Prométhée*, see Nectoux, p. 200.

[226]   Fauré, p. 34.

[227]   Koechlin, p. 550; Saint-Jean, p. 148.

[228]   Garnier, p. 142.

Example 5.10d   Fauré *Prométhée*, Act II, scene 2, mm. 227–33

Other numbers scarcely evince Wagnerism, but still draw Wagnerian comparisons.[229] The Oceanids, for example, supposedly resemble Wagner's Rhinemaidens because both are aquatic nymphs who prophesy impending doom. But they share little in common beyond a basic dramatic situation and a reliance on compound meter, the latter habitually used to depict flowing water. Fauré's sprites, singing their "bewitching" tune in the Lydian mode,[230] are embodiments of the native French operatic tradition of exoticism, antique counterparts to the choruses of gypsies, Brahmin priestesses, and Egyptian slaves who routinely tinted *fin-de-siècle* operas with *couleur locale*. Similarly, Fauré's Gaea and Wagner's Erda are both goddesses who emerge from the earth's depths to issue prohibitions, but aside from occasional craggy leaps in their vocal lines, their musical profiles diverge: Gaea is a mezzo-soprano whose tessitura gravitates toward the treble clef's upper region, while Erda is a low contralto; Gaea's declamation faithfully reflects textual nuances with a flexibility and incisiveness that identify her as a descendant of stately heroines in operas by Lully and Gluck. Moreover, Fauré's final apotheosis recalls the Revolutionary period's massive festival odes and the Napoleonic era's royalist oratorios, not Brünnhilde's immolation scene in Wagner's *Götterdämmerung*. Through Wagnerian comparisons, however, critics came to recognize power, force, and even savagery as components of Fauré's compositional arsenal.

Just as *Prométhée* inaugurated a new stage in Fauré's career, so it marked a decisive turn in the Languedocian amphitheater's fortunes. Festivals still attracted audiences after 1900, but their unadventurous repertoire comprised revivals of earlier productions, older operas, one newly commissioned conventional opera, plays with interpolated choruses or ballets, and several works by lesser known composers that preserved the ideal of declamation interspersed with substantive music. When a military regiment occupied the arena in 1907, classical tragedies were performed with minimal incidental music.[231] By 1911 costly maintenance and competition from new theaters instigated a civic resolution authorizing the amphitheater's demolition, an event postponed for 15 years. Castelbon, lamenting its demise, outlined the festival's achievements in an article that included a postscript by Saint-Saëns, who noted Béziers had provided a venue for young composers to enter the highly

---

[229] Orledge, p. 134; Nectoux, pp. 197–8, 202.

[230] Nectoux, p. 207.

[231] Nussy Saint-Saëns, pp. 17–18.

centralized world of French opera.[232] Mentioning no names, Saint-Saëns doubtless numbered his protégé Gabriel Fauré among the beneficiaries.

Prométhée's popularity was likewise brief. Its first two immensely successful performances in 1900 attracted over 14,000 spectators, but well under 10,000 attended the revival in 1901. In Paris it drew large audiences in 1907, when Castelbon's production benefited flood victims in provincial Hérault, and, after a ten-year hiatus, the reorchestrated *Prométhée* received 40 performances between the wars before disappearing from the active repertoire.[233] Although its extraordinary instrumentation and unusual mixture of speech and song have precluded all but a few performances in more recent times, *Prométhée* nonetheless articulates important cultural issues in *fin-de-siècle* France. Its remarkable performances occurred because of the provincial economy's continuous expansion throughout the nineteenth century, the civic patronage of wealthy merchants, and the construction of a bullfighting arena that reflected Languedoc's cultural ties to Catalonia. Temporarily suppressed by the central government, this manifestation of regional identity metamorphosed into a penchant for neoclassical drama, which again subverted northern hegemony by reminding Languedocians of their Mediterranean heritage. Neo-Hellenist theater's leading proponent in Béziers, Fernand Castelbon de Beauxhostes, prevailed by engaging the entire community in a collective effort that mirrored populist theater's widespread florescence following reforms of a domain previously governed by royal courts and bureaucratic legislation.

The confluence of such powerful cultural phenomena necessarily affected productions in Béziers. Amateur instrumentalists and singers constituted the orchestra and chorus, and principal characters interacted within conventions intended to emulate antiquity's theatrical practices. The resulting fusion of speech and song dictated an adoption of closed musical forms that elicited mixed critical reception because they violated prevailing norms of the Wagnerian *drame lyrique*. Reviews and Fauré's letters nonetheless indicate a Wagnerian framework is appropriate for evaluating the opera's Symbolist language, an attendant correlation between the libretto's religious elements and the tonalities of individual numbers, and distinctive leitmotivic procedures. Other radical traits, however, reconcile poorly with Wagnerian techniques, including pervasive modal writing, atonal counterpoint, and use of the whole-tone scale—attributes suggesting *Prométhée* adhered not to a Wagnerian model, but was instead, as Dukas astutely observed, "an antiquity perfumed with modernism."[234] Castelbon, the zealous neo-Hellenist and enterprising capitalist, would have undoubtedly embraced this description, since it alludes to Languedoc's Roman legacy and the score's progressive elements, which briefly placed Béziers in the vanguard of French musical venues. Critics perceived such modernism as boldness, power, and force, traits previously considered foreign to Fauré's refined style. These characteristics make *Prométhée* a pivotal work in the composer's evolution.

---

[232]   Fernand Castelbon de Beauxhostes and Camille Saint-Saëns, "Les Arènes de Béziers," *Musica*, 121 (1912): 194–5.

[233]   Nectoux, p. 549.

[234]   Dukas, p. 508.

Against the backdrop of historical events shaping nineteenth-century France, the Prometheus myth preserved its humanist legacy while periodically marking cultural, social, and political milestones. The Halévy brothers promoted myth's traditional role in educating a progressive society: Léon translated Aeschylus with "impassioned exactitude," and Fromental sought to revive the ethos of Greek antiquity's enharmonic genus. But as the July Monarchy's vibrancy faded, their *Prométhée enchaîné* embodied a rejection of romantic theatrical excess and a vogue for archaeology. Saint-Saëns's prize-winning *Les Noces de Prométhée* likewise perpetuated the legend's time-honored themes, with the Titan representing the archetypal inventor, and a fraternal mankind prevailing over adversity. Yet these broad themes also elucidate an allegory of France in the Industrial Age, when technological advances and sustained economic prosperity ended decades of political instability. Holmès's *Prométhée* retained Aeschylean vestiges, depicting Prometheus as the quintessentially romantic hero who willingly accepts punishment for his transgressions. Otherwise, however, her unfinished cantata adopts unique perspectives on the myth: the Titan's uncharacteristic stoicism and the literary techniques of personification and parallelism reflect Parnassian restraint; an intimate domestic scene expresses reactions to the Franco-Prussian War; and fire, symbolizing the power of weapons, animates the hearts of a young family confronting war's perils. Fauré's *Prométhée* again recalls Aeschylus, combining elements from every drama in the Athenian playwright's trilogy and seeking to recapture the atmosphere of classical antiquity's festivals. The *tragédie lyrique* nonetheless raises several contemporary issues, namely Languedoc's assertion of regional identity, collaborative patronage's success in the provinces, theatrical populism, and the advent of Symbolism. Mythographers generally consider myth an ambiguous language open to diverse interpretations, but rarely in modern times is the point so vividly illustrated as in the Titan's nineteenth-century French representations.

Three scores invoke the specter of Wagnerism. Only Halévy's cantata escaped its direct impact, since Wagner's music was virtually unknown in France during the 1840s. Saint-Saëns, however, experienced its effects when competition judges speculated Wagner had submitted his cantata. An ensuing scandal "threw Saint-Saëns into the limelight," but the erroneous ascription was based merely on wishful thinking and an "advanced use of brass instruments." Holmès, in contrast, embraced a Wagnerian idiom in several early choral works, including *Prométhée*, after visiting her idol at Tribschen. By cultivating heroic subjects and bold musical gestures, she transformed herself from a seductive, prodigious composer of salon music into a creator of large-scale works whose "virile" features drew Wagnerian comparisons from her peers and critics. Fauré's engagement with Wagnerism is strikingly similar: previously recognized for his songs and chamber music, he embarked on a new path in *Prométhée*, which critics lauded for its "power" and "force." The libretto's "impenetrable language" and fusion of sensuality and religion likewise illustrate Wagner's influence on the Symbolists.

French Wagnerism was scarcely unique. From the 1870s onward, Wagner's theories and operas precipitated volatile intellectual, literary, and musical developments throughout Europe and the Americas, usually duplicating the French pattern of resistance and selective assimilation. In England debates culminated during the 1890s, when decadent writers such as Oscar Wilde embraced Symbolism and critics such as Bernard Shaw promoted Wagner's music dramas and social agenda. In 1880, however, C. Hubert H. Parry faced charges of Wagnerism following the debut of his *Scenes from Shelley's* Prometheus Unbound. Parry's *Scenes* aroused contention partly because they signified Wagnerism's incursion upon an established British cultural institution, the Three Choirs Festival. But equally controversial was that the *Scenes*, like Fauré's *Prométhée*, include a religious element separating them from their French counterparts: atheism.

Chapter 6

Atheism, Wagnerism, and Eroticism in Parry's *Scenes from Shelley's* Prometheus Unbound

If we seek for a definite birthday for modern English music, September 7, 1880, when *Prometheus* saw the light at Gloucester and met with a distinctly mixed reception, has undoubtedly the best claim.[1]

For Ernest Walker, the premiere of C. Hubert H. Parry's *Scenes from Shelley's* Prometheus Unbound at the Three Choirs Festival in Gloucester in 1880 inaugurated an "English Renaissance" in music, a view widely embraced in British musical historiography after its publication in 1907.[2] Walker's observation, advanced merely as a rough division, nonetheless astutely identified the moment when English composers radically departed from a Victorian idiom derived from oratorios by Mendelssohn and Spohr—models so timeworn they were ridiculed in *The Mikado*.[3] Instead, young composers revitalized native traditions that had supposedly lain moribund since the seventeenth century, either by cultivating indigenous folk song, Renaissance polyphony, and the Baroque masque, or by adopting contemporary Continental techniques associated with Wagner, Liszt, and Brahms. Marking this development's onset, however, were premieres of two works by Parry, namely his Piano Concerto in F-sharp major, performed in London on 3 April 1880, and the *Scenes*, produced five months later.

Critics detected progressive traits in both scores. The concerto's key challenged the orchestra, while its formal innovations included the absence of a conventional ritornello at the beginning of the first movement, an unusual through-composed structure in the second, and the finale's cyclical design.[4] More audaciously, the *Scenes* confronted conservative Festival audiences with a libretto drawn from Shelley's lyric drama, which articulates the poet's metaphysical philosophy, social idealism, and—most importantly for Parry—atheism. Their equally bold music provoked

---

[1]   Ernest Walker, *A History of Music in England* (Oxford, 1907), p. 300.

[2]   Frank Howes, *The English Musical Renaissance* (New York, 1966), pp. 17–31; Meirion Hughes, *The English Musical Renaissance and the Press, 1850–1914: Watchmen of Music* (Aldershot, 2002), pp. 138–41.

[3]   The Mikado determines the music-hall singer's punishment: attending a series "Of masses and fugues and 'ops', By Bach interwoven with Spohr and Beethoven, At classical Monday Pops."

[4]   See Jeremy Dibble's truly magisterial biography, *C. Hubert H. Parry: His Life and Music* (Oxford, 1992), pp. 180–84.

accusations of Wagnerism, an issue as contentious and influential in late nineteenth-century England as it was in France. But in staid Victorian circles, Wagnerism's erotic connotations perhaps exacerbated anxiety over the incursion of Wagnerian precepts in insular musical traditions.

Atheism, Wagnerism, and eroticism seem incongruous with respect to Parry, who today is generally remembered for his unison setting of William Blake's *Jerusalem* and 14 major choral works completed between 1880 and 1908, including Anglican liturgical music. But in 1880, when circumstances finally allowed Parry to pursue a professional musical career at age 32, he expressed radical attitudes he later harbored as an accomplished composer, author, and collegiate administrator. Such lasting opinions formed in Parry's youth, reflecting his family background, education, and first professional activities.

The Parry wealth dated back three generations when Charles Hubert Hastings was born in 1848. His great-grandfather Thomas Parry, a distinguished naval officer, amassed a fortune after he was appointed director of the East India Company in 1783, a post his son Richard filled in 1813 following years in the Indian civil service. But it was Thomas Gambier Parry, Hubert's father, who in 1837 joined the landed gentry by purchasing a country seat, Highnam Court near Gloucester. In 1839 he married Isabella Fynes Clinton, the daughter of an aristocratic parliamentarian father and a mother of high ecclesiastical ancestry. During Continental travels the couple indulged mutual interests in religion, literature, and art, furnishing their estate with magnificent collectibles. Isabella died 12 days after the birth of Hubert, the youngest of three surviving children who had lost as many siblings during their parents' nine-year marriage. In 1851 Hubert's father married Ethelinda Lear, the austerely clerical daughter of the recently deceased Reverend Francis Lear, Dean of Salisbury. Religion then revealed a sterner guise in the Parry household.[5]

A gentrified social standing precluded a musical career for Hubert, though Highnam Court resounded with music. Parry's father, a competent keyboardist, composed and helped administer the Gloucester Festival; his brother Clinton was a skilled cellist and pianist; and his sister Lucy likewise played the piano. Before Parry finished preparatory studies at boarding schools in Malvern and Twyford in 1861, he had studied piano with local schoolmasters and composed chants, hymns, and secular songs.[6] Upon entering Eton, he notably strayed from the classical curriculum by indulging penchants for modern literature and music.[7] Involved with several musical societies devoted primarily to singing, he composed numerous songs, liturgical settings, piano and chamber miniatures, and larger keyboard works, all supervised by local organists. In January 1867 Parry passed examinations needed to enter Oxford with a Bachelor of Music, including obligatory exercises in species counterpoint.

Oxford provided no formal music training, but Parry participated in collegiate musical societies, informal student recitals, and chamber music soirees at professors' homes. In the summer of 1867 he studied orchestration with Henry Hugo Pierson,

[5]   Ibid., p. 7.
[6]   Emily Daymond, "On an Early Manuscript Book of Sir Hubert Parry's," *The R.C.M. Magazine*, 21/2 (1924): 75–9.
[7]   "An Eton Boy's Diary, 1864–1866," *Etoniana*, 103 (1946): 47.

a former Edinburgh professor then pursuing a career in Stuttgart,[8] whereupon Parry produced his first orchestral and large-scale chamber works. During his next term at Oxford he was the Exeter College Musical Society's *répétiteur* and composed Mendelssohnian part songs for its choristers.

But despite Parry's burgeoning musical achievements, including the Gloucester Festival's premiere of his *Intermezzo religioso* in 1868, his family assumed he would enter a business career upon graduation. He accordingly spent the summer of 1868 in Liège with one of his father's acquaintances, a Protestant minister, learning French, the indispensable language of Continental commerce. Vocational stability soon became urgent, partly because maintaining and improving Highnam Court had depleted family assets, but mostly because Parry and his childhood sweetheart, Maude Herbert, were engaged in the spring of 1870. Lady Herbert vehemently opposed her daughter's marriage outside the aristocracy, fearing Parry could not support Maude in the "luxury and comfort" she had enjoyed.[9] To prove otherwise, Parry embarked on an insurance career with the London firm of Lloyd's Register of Shipping months after writing final exams at Oxford in June 1870, an action his father arranged and heartily endorsed.

Employment at Lloyd's temporarily assuaged Lady Herbert and demanded Parry's full attention. But by July 1873, shortly after Hubert and Maude celebrated their first wedding anniversary, his responsibilities had grown routine and profits were down. Depressed business conditions allowed Parry to undertake regular piano instruction with Edward Dannreuther, an established virtuoso, recognized pedagogue, and zealous Wagnerite who, after some persuasion, advised Parry in composition. Dannreuther encouraged Parry to attend programs of recent Continental music, experiment with various compositional styles, and complete ambitious chamber and orchestral scores, including the *Großes Duo* for two pianos, which the Leipzig firm of Breitkopf & Härtel accepted for publication in 1877, a coup for any young British composer. In the same year, after a partner violated Lloyd's policy against borrowing money, Parry paid his portion of the debt, resigned, and pursued more promising musical opportunities.

Commissions for articles for the first edition of George Grove's *Dictionary of Music and Musicians* supplemented publication fees, beginning in 1875 with the entry for "arrangement." Indeed, Grove's requests for additional articles and editorial assistance doubtless bolstered Parry's decision to leave Lloyd's and concentrate exclusively on composing, writing, and teaching. Parry ultimately authored a series of distinguished articles and monographs, joined the Royal College of Music as professor of music history in 1883, succeeded Grove as its director in 1894, received honorary degrees from Cambridge and Oxford, and became a leading English composer of his generation. But his early professional efforts arguably culminated in his first major commission from the Gloucester Festival in 1880, when Shelley's *Prometheus Unbound* supplied a vehicle for defining religion's role in Parry's social philosophy.

Religion aroused strife in the Parry household, partly because its patriarch held inflexible attitudes. Thomas Gambier Parry's religious inclinations already attracted

---

8   Mssrs. Russell and Sons, "Hubert Parry," *Musical Times*, 39 (1898): 444.
9   For Lady Herbert's letter of 20 June 1870, see Dibble, pp. 74–6.

notice when he entered Cambridge in 1834,[10] but rather than pursuing the ministry, a profession suited to his social standing, he cultivated artistic leanings and settled at Highnam Court. Like many of the Victorian era's landed gentry, he subscribed to a fervent faith blending orthodoxy, morality, and social benevolence. He and Isabella accordingly considered erecting a chapel on their isolated estate to ensure its residents could attend services,[11] a plan sadly realized only after her death. Religious fervor apparently turned into moral intransigence after he married Ethelinda, reflecting her austerely clerical upbringing's influence. Assuming responsibility for his children's spiritual indoctrination, he supervised their study of the Bible and contemporary religious literature on Sunday afternoons,[12] but ironically failed to instill Clinton and Hubert with his faith.

Charles Clinton Parry, nearly eight years older than Hubert, expressed religious doubts as a teenager.[13] At Oxford, his outright rejection of Christianity headed a list of behaviors compromising his status as heir to the Parry estate: libertine conduct, lax studies, and the beginnings of acute alcoholism prompted three academic dismissals. His marriage in 1865 to a woman of lower social standing likewise encountered parental disapproval. But it was religion that precipitated an irreparable rift in 1877, when Clinton extolled Unitarianism and quoted modern biological theories in a letter that raised his father's "High Church ire to a terrible degree," as Hubert noted in his diary.[14] And it was religion's role in Clinton's imminent disinheritance that incited Hubert's similarly fateful declarations in 1873.

During his early years at Oxford, Hubert rejected Clinton's example, recording strict Anglican views in his diary in 1867.[15] Two years later, however, doubts surfaced during his sojourn in Liège, where he read Alfred de Musset's *L'Espoir en Dieu* (1838), a poetic contemplation of paganism and Christianity whose title he considered "a wonderful sort of motto for a man troubled with waverings of faith and yet still wanting to believe."[16] Parry, doubtless such a man, then finished his Oxford studies in 1870, attending lectures of the controversial naturalist and art historian John Ruskin, who taught at the radical Christian Socialist Working Men's College in London, emphasized art's social implications, and openly questioned Christian doctrine.[17] Ruskin blamed orthodox Christianity for the greed that corrupted British society and oppressed the lower classes, attitudes common in British "infidel" discourse from the 1840s onward.[18] His ideas indelibly impressed Parry, who necessarily developed new perspectives in relative secrecy.

---

[10] Dibble, p. 3.

[11] Ibid., p. 7.

[12] Ibid., pp. 13–14.

[13] Ibid., p. 17.

[14] Parry's diaries and most subsequently cited letters are preserved at the Shulbrede Priory, Lynchmere, Sussex [henceforward: ShP]. The cited diary entry is for 22 October 1877.

[15] Dibble, p. 47.

[16] ShP, Diary, 24 August 1869.

[17] J.F.C. Harrison, *A History of the Working Men's College, 1854–1954* (London, 1954), pp. 77–8.

[18] Susan Budd, *Varieties of Unbelief: Atheists and Agnostics in English Society, 1850–1960* (London, 1977), pp. 44–52.

Parry's lone confidant was Eddie Hamilton, an Eton and Oxford classmate who delivered messages to Maude during the couple's clandestine courtship.[19] They discovered additional solidarity in September 1870:

> ... Eddie and I had a walk together, wherein our conversation ... culminated in an ... expression of sympathy ... with regard to the 'High Churchism' in which we have been brought up and with which we are surrounded. That Eddie was of like manner with myself was ... of such satisfaction to us both that we allowed ... pent-up bitterness to flow from our mouths without reserve.[20]

Hamilton claimed "the 'charity' and 'religiousness' which everybody makes so much 'to do' about was too concerned with mere worldly pleasure and excitement." Parry concurred, believing practitioners of such charity and religion held as their "first object" the "approbation of their betters, that ... the righteousness which acts silently and inwardly has in them no part." Parry then scornfully condemned these hypocrites:

> Their inward conscience they are forced to silence for fear that it should teach them anything which would not seem to be in conformity with the tenets of the master they follow. They are forced to bury themselves in dogmatic theology; ... the search for truth is denied them. Their religion is no longer honest, pure and moral, but a determination to force upon themselves the opinions of their class, and to make the acme of their glory their own prominence in the party to which they belong. ... Everyone who endeavors to use ... reason is condemned as among the godless, ... as misbelievers, not worthy of the congregation of the faithful.

Parry now clearly embraced Ruskin's rationalist censure of class-based religion and was close to repudiating orthodoxy.

A month later, Parry and Hamilton heard Stopford Brooke—then Queen Victoria's Chaplain in Ordinary but by 1880 a secessionist Unitarian—preach "a scientific and very liberal sermon on the reconciliation of intellect and religion."[21] For Parry, "it was of all sermons the most to my mind that I ever have heard." He heartily approved one of Brooke's "most striking points," a definition of "true faith":

> When we are troubled with intellectual difficulties we are not to cast them away, ... but receive them in full belief that things which are obviously rational must be reconcilable to Christianity (otherwise religion would be mere hypocrisy).

In struggling to reconcile rationalism and faith, Parry had not yet categorically repudiated Christianity, despite earlier objections to "dogmatic theology." But his views quickly sharpened.

Five months after Parry began working at Lloyd's in November 1870, he stopped keeping detailed diaries for over two years,[22] making his religious evolution difficult to trace. Reading lists and summaries nonetheless disclose increasing interest in

---

[19]   Dibble, pp. 29, 67.

[20]   ShP, Diary, 30 September 1870. This and ensuing quotations appear on pp. 94–8 in the 1870 volume of Parry's diaries.

[21]   This and ensuing quotations appear in Parry's diary entry for 20 November 1870.

[22]   The gap occurs from 30 April 1871 to May 1873.

rationalist or radical literature. In 1871, for example, he read "sundry essays" by the philosopher David Hume (1711–76), who appealed to generations of British "blasphemers" by judging the evidence for miracles inferior to that for the "laws of nature," contending the belief in a supreme intelligence derives from imaginative instead of rational faculties, and tracing polytheism's evolution into degenerate monotheism.[23]

Throughout the 1870s Parry investigated similar or more explicit challenges to Christianity. In 1873 he read Samuel Butler's newly issued *The Fair Haven*, an assault on the Resurrection preserving the ironic tone of Butler's earlier utopian satire, *Erewhon* (1872), likewise on Parry's reading list. Also studied the year it was published was Matthew Arnold's *Literature and Dogma* (1873), a critique of biblical exegesis excoriating English sectarianism, materialism, and intellectual apathy. Parry recorded equally controversial titles the next year: *Supernatural Religion* (1874), a sensational examination of the Gospels, Acts of the Apostles, and evidence for miracles by the theological critic Walter Richard Cassels; *Phases of Faith* (1850), by Francis William Newman, a Calvinist turned deist whose dissenting opinions on ceremony and eternal punishment contrasted with those of his famous archbishop brother; and *A Naturalist's Voyage* (1839), Charles Darwin's chronicle of voyages on H.M.S. *Beagle*, which anticipated *On the Origin of Species* (1859) and its argument for man's natural, not divine, origin. In 1875 Parry read *First Principles* (1862) by Herbert Spencer, who derived evolutionary philosophy from Darwin and maintained individuals could act as they see fit, providing the liberty of others is not compromised, thus disputing the rule of divine law.

Such ideas undoubtedly exacerbated tensions within Parry's family. His mother-in-law was a new, outspoken convert to Catholicism, an object of special loathing.[24] Diatribes against Romanism permeate his diaries, resumed in 1873, as his opinion of Lady Herbert's regular priestly visitors illustrates:

> It has given me ... new insight into the amount of barefaced lying and shameless hypocrisy and deception human nature is capable of when religion is at issue, though I suppose no other religion ... professes and acts upon such a system as the Roman Catholic Church does.[25]

Parry also discovered "a good specimen of Roman Catholic lying" in the sensational testimony of a Salisbury clergyman's widow, who claimed her husband had converted to Catholicism with her, though another cleric supposedly destroyed corroborating letters to conceal the truth.[26] Undoubtedly intensifying his abhorrence of Romanism were the announcement of the doctrines of Papal Infallibility in 1870 and Lady Herbert's initial opposition to and lasting interference in his marriage, especially proselytizing. More grievous than her religious beliefs, however, were those of his father.

---

[23]   Regarding the first two points, see David Hume, *An Enquiry concerning Human Understanding: A Critical Edition*, ed. Tom L. Beauchamp (Oxford, 2000), pp. 83–111. The third is the central thesis of *The Natural History of Religion*, ed. H.E. Root (Stanford, 1957).

[24]   Dibble, p. 28.

[25]   ShP, Diary, 20 May 1873.

[26]   ShP, Diary, 19 June 1873.

The inevitable crisis arrived on 15 December 1873, when Parry revealed his views to his father, a drastic step justified in his diary:

> A few days before I left London I sent Possie a statement ... of my opinions, and history of them. ... My reason for doing so was that he had often hinted to me his intention of leaving Highnam to me because Clin had "thrown overboard his religion etc." So I told him that I had done the same ... in order that he might not do Clin an injustice through a false impression of me.[27]

Anticipating his father's reaction, Parry's epistle enumerated objectionable doctrines, namely original sin, hell, divine creation, and the story of Noah (his repudiation of the last two reflecting Darwin's influence):

> You know very well, and I think there is none that will deny it that as a boy I was of a very religious turn of mind. ... However, ... a part of religious training, which is so generally impressed upon young minds in religious families, was left out. I mean the indoctrination of the idea that ... when reason proved one thing and revelation said another, the former was seen to be leading astray, and it would be wicked to doubt the so called revelation. I consequently brought my reason to bear upon questions of faith very early. ... It was in this manner ... that I ceased to believe in the theory that we are all punished for the sin of our first progenitors, as altogether contradictory to the theory that God was good and beautiful. ... Along with this naturally went the idea of Hell—which I early thought an unfit conception for any rational being. Of course ... my unconscious heterodoxy should soon have to replace the story of the Creation as told in Genesis and Noah's Ark and the Flood and the early history of mankind ... as among the poetical conceptions of a barbaric people in a very early stage of development.[28]

But Hubert scarcely denied God's existence, in the modern sense of the term atheist:

> I believe in religion, but one so pure and simple that its chiefest maxim is "strive after virtue for itself". I believe that the theological part of Christianity and all dogmas connected with it are a mistake. ... I believe in God, and I believe that he is good, and I think that is the one form of "faith" that will always stick with me.[29]

Parry had plainly abandoned orthodoxy, but still espoused ethics compatible with the Christian example and, as later discussion demonstrates, tenets of Shelley's *Prometheus Unbound*.

On 19 December Thomas Gambier Parry acknowledged Hubert's integrity, but lamented an egregious loss:

> I value the honesty of your letter—and your honorable intention in repudiating all claims, on any ground of religious principle, superior to those of your eldest brother, in respect to the future possession of property. ... My eldest son has ... led a life too grievous to bear exposure. ... I had therefore set my heart—and based my hopes on you. — and now even you fail me. ... I am sure ... you could not wish *me* (by the circulation of that

---

[27]   ShP, Diary, December 1873. Dibble (p. 110) includes portions of the cited entry.
[28]   ShP, Letter to Thomas Gambier Parry, 15 December 1873. Dibble (pp. 110–13) includes larger extracts from this letter, but not the quotation's conclusion.
[29]   Dibble (p. 112) includes longer extracts from this quotation.

painful letter) ... to publish to our relations and friends that my loved son Hubert is an Infidel. — ! — You can little conceive the bitterness and horror of such an idea to me.[30]

Moreover, the anguished father attributed Hubert's betrayal to a character flaw, not a reasoned consideration of doctrine:

> I have ... noticed in you with painful anxiety a growing pride of intellect and great impatience of any opinion contrary to your own. ... I ... hope and pray ... Maude may escape this deadliest Poison of the Pride of Modern Life.[31]

Thus Hubert reached an unhappy plight, supposedly led astray by vanity, called an infidel, and admonished to remain silent. He accordingly confided in his diary and read additional radical literature, including David Friedrich Strauss's *Das Leben Jesu* (1836), which posited myth as the basis of the Gospels, George Eliot's evolutionist novels, and Algernon Swinburne's scandalously outspoken repudiations of Christianity. Hence Parry doubtless welcomed the opportunity to voice attitudes publicly by composing music for the *Prometheus Unbound* of Percy Bysshe Shelley (1792–1822), a central figure of British atheism.

In 1811, when Oxford expelled Shelley for printing a pamphlet entitled *The Necessity of Atheism*, such publications enjoyed a remarkably short history in Britain. Indeed, William Hammon and Matthew Turner had produced the first English avowal of "speculative" atheism, *An Answer to Dr. Priestley's Letters to a Philosophical Unbeliever*, only in 1782.[32] But a tradition of English atheism had already developed during the Reformation, when new religious alternatives, secularized education, and the Scientific Revolution's rationalism induced fear of unbelief and an attendant revival of the Classical Greek word atheism itself, which encompassed denials of God's existence, rejections of scriptural or ecclesiastical authority, and disputations of specific doctrines, and involved numerous labels such as infidel, freethinker, and, eventually, deist.[33] Atheists necessarily expressed views covertly, however, since publicly avowed unbelief remained a capital offense throughout Europe, as the lurid executions of Geoffroy Vallée (Paris, 1574) and Thomas Aikenhead (Edinburgh, 1697) attest.[34] Evidence of atheism consequently derives from accusations against authors, transcripts of trials for other offenses, claims of theologians who purportedly disputed doctrine with

---

[30]   ShP, Letter from Thomas Gambier Parry, 19 December 1873. Dibble (p. 112) includes portions of this quotation.

[31]   Ibid. Dibble (p. 113) includes this quotation's final phrase.

[32]   "Speculative" atheists employ reason, unlike "practical" atheists, who behave immorally, and "unthinking" atheists, who are ignorant, mentally incompetent, or unintelligent. See David Berman, *A History of Atheism in Britain: From Hobbes to Russell* (London, 1988), pp. 1–3.

[33]   Michael Hunter and David Wootton (eds), introduction to *Atheism from the Reformation to the Enlightenment* (Oxford, 1992), pp. 1–5; Wootton, "New Histories of Atheism," in Hunter and Wootton (eds), pp. 15, 25; Hunter, "The Problem of 'Atheism' in Early Modern England," *Transactions of the Royal Historical Society*, 5th Series, 35 (1985): 152–6.

[34]   Wootton, "New Histories," pp. 13–15, 26; Hunter, "'Aikenhead the Atheist': The Context and Consequences of Articulate Irreligion in the Late Seventeenth Century," in Hunter and Wootton (eds), pp. 221–53.

actual atheists, other second-hand statements, and literary stereotypes of atheists, to say nothing of the posthumous inquiry into Christopher Marlowe's blasphemy (1593) and official proceedings mounted against Sir Walter Raleigh (1594).[35] To defend themselves and disseminate their ideas, atheists naturally denied charges, met secretly, cultivated an oral tradition to thwart state censorship of books and letters, and ingeniously subverted their accusers' literary practices.[36] Orthodox believers often sought to refute controversial tenets in print, whereupon atheists extracted and published offending quotations under the believers' names, or wrote similar but carefully encoded tracts that allowed sympathetic readers to discern their true meaning.[37]

Circumstances changed significantly during and after the Civil War (1642–9), when widespread questioning of religious doctrine accompanied monarchical authority's collapse.[38] The Presbyterian-dominated Long Parliament of 1648 admittedly reacted with an infamously severe ordinance against blasphemy and atheism, but in 1650 the Rump effectively annulled it with two statutes that defended blasphemy and repealed all earlier Acts of Uniformity, though weekly attendance at some form of Sunday worship remained mandatory.[39] Likewise contributing to atheism's more unequivocal expression was that pre-censorship of the press ended in 1695, briefly lifting restraints on religious radicalism.[40] The seventeenth century's closing decades accordingly represent a point of departure for publicly professed irreligion.

A major figure in the new, more overtly articulated atheist discourse was Thomas Hobbes (1588–1679), whose writings respectively served irreligion's opponents and advocates as foil and authority.[41] Central to the debate was *The Leviathan* (1651), a political treatise that subordinated the church to the state by allocating the power to interpret Scripture to the civil sovereign, not an ecclesiastical authority, as was the case before Christianity's advent.[42] Equally drastic unorthodoxies, namely *The Leviathan's* repeated denials of the human mind's ability to conceive an idea, image, or the nature of God or comprehend God's word, negated the possibility of a "true religion."[43] Although Hobbes steadfastly refuted atheist charges, his treatise provoked death threats, vituperative rebuttals, and even an act of Parliament, none of which inhibited the propagation of his ideas.

Facing similar harassment, other late seventeenth-century authors still practiced literary subterfuge. The freethinker Charles Blount (1654–93), for example, published broadsheets of "offending" quotations from Hobbes and exposed heathen religious

---

[35]   Wootton, "New Histories," pp. 17, 27, 33; Hunter, "The Problem of 'Atheism'," p. 150.

[36]   Wootton, "New Histories," pp. 19–21, 26–7, 37–43; Berman, "Disclaimers as Offence Mechanisms in Charles Blount and John Toland," in Hunter and Wootton (eds), p. 260.

[37]   Charles Blount's *Last Saying, or Dying Legacy of Hobbs* (1680) offers a prime example.

[38]   Hunter and Wootton, Introduction, p. 6; Wootton, "New Histories," p. 47.

[39]   Richard Tuck, "The 'Christian Atheism' of Thomas Hobbes," in Hunter and Wootton (eds), p. 127.

[40]   Wootton, "New Histories," p. 47.

[41]   George T. Buckley, *Atheism in the English Renaissance* (Chicago, 1932), pp. 1–19, 31–42.

[42]   Thomas Hobbes, *Leviathan*, ed. J.C.A. Gaskin (Oxford, 1996), pp. 37–8.

[43]   Ibid., pp. 70, 73, 259, 262.

fallacies to reproach Christianity, though he also explicitly proposed alternatives to biblical history, blamed priests for Christianity's corruption, and defended ridicule and wit as legitimate tools in religious critiques.[44] Blount's disciple Charles Gildon (1665–1724) intermingled his own essays among his mentor's posthumous works (*Oracles of Reason*, 1695), but also autonomously rejected the doctrine of divine providence, considered the Creation a parable, doubted the chronology of Genesis, and questioned the Pentateuch's attribution to Moses.[45] Matching Hobbes in potency of influence was John Locke (1632–1704), who initially supported the Hobbist proposition regarding the state's authority over religion, but later contended the individual's judgment superseded that of the civil sovereign—a subordination of religion to reason that shaped eighteenth-century deism and Unitarianism.[46] Moreover, Locke proclaimed atheists existed and doubted the idea of God was innate to every human culture.[47] Locke's protégé John Toland (1670–1722) argued the state had invented religion for worldly purposes, thereby corrupting a primitive Christianity whose ethics he admired, despite his denial of Christ's divinity.[48] And Matthew Tindal (1657–1733) likewise echoed Locke's anticlericalism and advocacy of the individual's authority in judging religion.

In 1697 Parliament reinstated legislation against blasphemy and profaneness, again curbing published irreligious expression. Notable early eighteenth-century exceptions included the *Answer to Mr. Clarke's Third Defence* (1711) by Anthony Collins, who averred to prove God's existence but actually argued against it, and openly disputed the Messianic prophecies (*Grounds and Reasons of the Christian Thought*, 1724). Thomas Woolston (1669–1731), once a priest of the Church of England, likewise purported to defend Christianity, but through wit and ridicule denied proof of miracles, declared Christ a false prophet, and reduced Scripture to allegory. Such assaults on orthodoxy prompted Richard Blackmore (*The Creation*, 1712) to expand the definition of atheists from "those who have deny'd the Being of God," to anyone who "believes in a Deity, but affirms this Deity is not Eternal ... or ... showed no Wisdom, Design, or Prudence in the Formation, and no care or Providence in the government of the world."[49] Blackmore's inclusive label, aimed at growing ranks of deists, endured until at least 1869, when T.H. Huxley's newly coined term "agnostic" distinguished between deniers of God's existence and contesters of divine attributes.

During the Enlightenment—as deism flourished, anticlericalism spread, and democratic-revolutionary ideals eroded state censorship—another wave of overtly expressed atheism spread across Europe and the Atlantic, cresting in the first printed avowals of speculative atheism. In 1770 Paul Henri d'Holbach published his *Système de la nature* in Amsterdam, and in 1782 Hammon and Turner published its English

---

[44]   Berman, "Disclaimers as Offence Mechanisms," pp. 255–71; Roger D. Lund, *The Margins of Orthodoxy: Heterodox Writing and Cultural Response, 1660–1750* (Cambridge, 1995), pp. 22, 172, 227–9.

[45]   Gildon also expressed ideas compatible with Christianity and ultimately recanted his irreligious views. See Lund, p. 229.

[46]   Lund, pp. 73–5, 103.

[47]   Berman, *A History of Atheism*, p. 38.

[48]   Wootton, "New Histories," pp. 39–41; Berman, "Disclaimers as Offence Mechanisms," pp. 255–8.

[49]   Berman, *A History of Atheism*, p. 121.

counterpart, disputing God's existence and omnipresence and denying that morality requires belief in God or religion. Other late eighteenth-century authors such as Hume and Samuel Francis (*Watson Refuted*, 1796) continued to divest God of divine attributes and repudiate Scriptural validity. Other writers attacked institutionalized religion, led by William Godwin (Shelley's future father-in-law), who declared a "system of religion is a system of blind submission,"[50] and Thomas Paine, who condemned "all national institutions of churches" because they "terrify and enslave mankind and monopolize power and profit."[51] Eschewing politics, early English romantic poets experimented with atheism, largely responding to Benedict Spinoza's pantheism.[52] During the 1790s William Blake interpreted the Bible not as revelation, but as a source of allegory and metaphor, thus preferring imaginative over literal readings of Scripture. Samuel Taylor Coleridge reputedly denied God's existence, but expressed basically orthodox views in analyzing various modes of atheism (*Lectures on Revealed Religion*, 1795). And the arch-pantheist William Wordsworth refused to believe in a conciliatory afterlife until his brother's death precipitated a spiritual crisis. But the most "notoriously atheistic" romantic poet, and perhaps "the most famous British atheist," was Percy Bysshe Shelley.[53]

Shelley's atheism, though indebted to earlier writers, appears even more striking against its historical background. After 150 years of denials, subterfuge, and the subject's tempered poetic treatment, his brazen declarations and penetrating philosophical analyses transcended their precedents, notwithstanding bold statements by Enlightenment authors. At Eton (1804–10) his nickname, "Shelley the atheist," reflected his outspoken antagonism toward scholastic rather than ecclesiastical authority.[54] The epithet nonetheless followed him to Oxford in 1810, when he read radical texts by Godwin, Paine, and classical writers.[55] In Pliny's *De Deo* he encountered a rejection of any god's conception in any specific form or image; and in the *De rerum natura* of Lucretius, a staple of heterodox discourse, he found an indictment of pagan religions as superstitious belief systems that priests exploited to maintain power and accrue wealth. After scarcely five months at Oxford, Shelley anonymously published his pamphlet, *The Necessity of Atheism*. Several days later, on 25 March 1811, he and his ostensible collaborator, Thomas Jefferson Hogg, were dismissed for refusing to provide information about it, including its authorship.[56]

The pamphlet begins with an audaciously capitalized declaration: "THERE IS NO GOD."[57] And while Shelley immediately notes "this negation must be understood solely to affect a creative Deity—the hypothesis of a pervading spirit coeternal with the universe remains unshaken," these qualifications in no way compromise his argument.

---

[50]   Martin Priestman, *Romantic Atheism: Poetry and Freethought, 1780–1830* (Cambridge, 1999), p. 28.

[51]   Thomas Paine, *The Age of Reason*, in *The Complete Writings of Thomas Paine*, ed. Philip S. Foner (2 vols, New York, 1954), vol. 1, p. 464.

[52]   Priestman, pp. 82–6, 139, 157–71.

[53]   Priestman, p. 5; Berman, *A History of Atheism*, p. 145.

[54]   Newman Ivey White, *Shelley* (2 vols, New York, 1940), vol. 1, p. 37.

[55]   Ibid., vol. 1, p. 52.

[56]   Thomas Jefferson Hogg, *Shelley at Oxford* (London, 1904), pp. 219–29.

[57]   Percy Bysshe Shelley, *The Necessity of Atheism and Other Essays* (Buffalo, 1993), p. 31.

The deity's "creative" faculty is merely one attribute of a being whose existence Shelley systematically dismantles in the essay; and the "pervading Spirit" is simply "the exterminable spirit of life," as he later explained in his ideological poem *Queen Mab* (1813).[58] Shelley, like Locke, adopts an epistemological perspective, investigating the means and limitations of acquiring knowledge to expose religious fallacies. Emulating Enlightenment rationalists, he posits three sources of human knowledge: direct experience ("the senses"); reason ("the decision of the mind, founded on experience"); and indirect testimony ("the experience of others"). He summarily rejects the first, since "the God of theologians is incapable of local visibility" and thus presents no evidence to the senses.[59] The second is likewise dispatched because a mind confronted with two opposing propositions must believe "that which is least incomprehensible." Faced with alternative hypotheses regarding the creation and divine providence, Shelley reaches a devastating conclusion: "every reflecting mind must acknowledge that there is no proof of the existence of a Deity." Lacking proof, he chooses not to believe. Shelley's scrutiny also renders indirect testimony inadequate:

> It is only by hearsay (word of mouth passed down from generation to generation) that whole peoples adore the God of their fathers and of their priests: authority, confidence, submission and custom with them take the place of conviction or of proofs. All religious notions are founded solely on authority; all the religions of the world forbid examination and do not want one to reason.[60]

Testimony accordingly draws Shelley's twofold condemnation: it is based not on reason, but on imposed authority. Hence, religion's morality is objectionable.[61]

Scarcely a youthful indiscretion, *The Necessity of Atheism* foreshadows convictions Shelley articulated in verse and prose throughout his short life. *Queen Mab*, steeped in allusions to earlier atheistic tracts, repeats his acclamation, "There is no God," three times. The poem's sixth and seventh cantos and several appended essays again posit an "exterminable spirit of life" as the universe's sole animating force, but steadfastly maintain anything beyond this formulation is a human conceit designed to justify crimes of the powerful.[62] Shelley's most crushing and closely reasoned assault on belief in a deity, however, appears in *A Refutation of Deism* (1814). Like d'Holbach's *Système* and Hume's *Natural Religion*, the *Refutation* is cast as a dialogue, wherein a deist and a fideistic Christian assail each other's positions so successfully that neither can offer persuasive rebuttals. Whereas religious belief based on faith alone is shown to be merely false, the deistic contradiction between accepting God's existence and rejecting divine attributes is a "heresy" against reason, as Shelley verified in personal correspondence.[63]

---

[58]   Shelley, *Queen Mab*, in *The Complete Poetical Works of Percy Bysshe Shelley*, ed. Neville Rogers (4 vols, Oxford, 1972), vol. 1, p. 275.

[59]   Shelley, *The Necessity of Atheism*, pp. 32–7.

[60]   Ibid., pp. 38, 39.

[61]   See Shelley's letter of 16 May 1811 to Janetta Philipps in Frederick L. Jones (ed.), *The Letters of Percy Bysshe Shelley* (2 vols, Oxford, 1964), vol. 1, p. 88.

[62]   Shelley, *Queen Mab*, pp. 268–81.

[63]   See Shelley's letter to Hogg of 8 May 1811 in Jones (ed.), vol. 1, p. 77.

Atheism obviously emerges as the only viable alternative. And the epic poem *The Revolt of Islam* (1818) revives attacks against religious authority, condemning corrupt priests.

Shelley adhered to atheistic tenets in *Prometheus Unbound* (1818), conceived and completed in Italy, where he and his household hoped to escape creditors, find a favorable climate for his chronic health problems, and avoid the social intolerance his controversial writings and lifestyle incited.[64] Universally ranked among the nineteenth century's great literary achievements, the four-act lyric drama fuses Shelley's social philosophy, Neoplatonic tendencies, and idiosyncratic approaches to conflicts between materialism and idealism, physics and metaphysics, and science and religion. Its extraordinarily varied verse forms match its vast array of symbols, metaphors, allegories, and double-edged personifications. Among many examples, references to every form of water, from dew to clouds, define strata in an existential continuum stretching from the terrestrial to the celestial. Prometheus suffers from external punishment and internal psychological turmoil, alleviated only by the prospect of redemption through self-regeneration. Jupiter embodies both a tyrant and a flawed deity. Mercury, a messenger and tempter, entices Prometheus to accept Jupiter's forgiveness and rejoin the Olympians. And the Oceanid Asia, the Titan's lover, blatantly personifies nature. These principals interact with allegorical choruses of Furies, Echoes, Fawns, and Spirits.

Within this figurative milieu Shelley's irreligion is strikingly clear, thanks to a preface he published with the drama in 1820. Especially significant is his revelation of the Titan's identity:

> The only imaginary being resembling ... Prometheus, is Satan; and Prometheus is ... a more poetical character than Satan, because, in addition to courage, majesty, and firm and patient opposition to omnipotent force, he is ... exempt from the taints of ambition, envy, revenge, and a desire for personal aggrandizement, which, in the Hero of *Paradise Lost*, interfere with the interest. ... Prometheus is ... the highest perfection of moral and intellectual nature, impelled by the purest and truest of motives to the best and noblest deeds.[65]

The passage comprises an atheist manifesto: Satan is an "imaginary being," not a material biblical entity; Prometheus—the archetypal romantic hero imbued with virtuous traits and motivated by purity, truth, and noble goals—opposes omnipotent force—a transparent allusion to the Christian deity and the established church; and Shelley's satanic Prometheus scarcely resembles Milton's Lucifer, whose faults are ascribed to Jupiter, and hence to the Christian deity, as the drama unfolds. The preface nonetheless indicates Shelley admired Milton:

> We owe the great writers of the golden age of our literature to that fervid awakening of the public mind which shook to dust the oldest and most oppressive form of the Christian religion. We owe Milton to the progress and developement of the same spirit. Milton was ... a republican and bold inquirer into morals and religion.[66]

---

[64]   White, vol. 1, pp. 536–47.

[65]   Shelley, preface to *Prometheus Unbound*, in *Shelley's* Prometheus Unbound: *A Variorum Edition*, ed. Lawrence John Zillman (Seattle, 1959), pp. 120–21.

[66]   Ibid., pp. 123–4.

Shelley thereby conceived Prometheus as a rebel, as in Goethe's ode and the introduction to Beethoven's overture.

Shelley's drama develops the preface's theme of religious oppression. The Titan's opening monologue decries the "ill tyranny" of a "Mighty God" (I, 17–19).[67] Later a phantom recalls how Prometheus denounced Jupiter as a "malignant spirit," a "God and Lord" who maintains misery to force "all things of Earth and Heaven" to bow before him "in fear and worship" (I, 272–86). Religious subjugation is repeatedly condemned: Jupiter is "the tyrant of the world," whom "the nations, panic-stricken, served with blood, ... flattering the thing they feared," which rules them "like slaves" (III, iv, 183–206); and "Heaven's despotism" will end when Love casts power from its "awful throne" (IV, 554–7).

Forceful domination, however, is just one charge Shelley levels against religion. Anticlericalism emerges when Prometheus declares his "beloved race is trampled down" by Jupiter's "thought executing ministers," meaning priests who banned reason's application to doctrine (I, 385–6). "Hypocrisy and custom" also victimize humanity, making "minds the fanes of many a worship, now outworn," an allusion to religious ceremony (I, 621–2). Most harshly censured is the conception of God as the source of suffering, a deity who created "terror, madness, crime, remorse, ... pain, ... and Hell, or the sharp fear of Hell" and inflicted mankind with "famine, and then toil, and then disease, strife, wounds, and ghastly death unseen before"—an indictment of original sin (II, iv, 19–51).

Prometheus Unbound castigates Christianity, clerics, and specific orthodoxies, but it also imparts sentiments compatible with Christian ethics, like several of Shelley's late works.[68] Even while steadfastly rejecting established and revealed religion, Shelley admired Christ's example of conquering evil through forgiveness, of passively resisting violence. The drama most conspicuously endorses Christ's principles in the Chorus of Furies, which nonetheless repudiates the religion established after Christ's death:

> One came forth of gentle worth
> Smiling on the sanguine earth;
> His words outlived him, like swift poison
> Withering up truth, peace, and pity. ...
> Mark that outcry of despair!
> 'Tis his mild and gentle ghost
> Wailing for the faith he kindled. (I, 546–55)

Christ's message had been corrupted, but Shelley's Titan advocates its original form as his opening monologue concludes, announcing he is changed: he no longer harbors any evil wish, hate is dead within him, and he cannot remember his curse against Jupiter (I, 69–73). Thus the satanic Prometheus more nobly embodies Christian ethics than Jupiter, the tyrannical deity.

Shelley's attitudes uncannily resemble Parry's stance during the 1870s. Indeed, shortly after beginning work on the *Scenes*, Parry admitted he had been anxious "to cut [Shelley's text] down into shape," fearing he might not "find anything else that

---

[67]   Act, scene, and line numbers derive from Zillman's edition.
[68]   Carl Grabo, Prometheus Unbound: *An Interpretation* (Chapel Hill, 1935), pp. 15–16.

approaches [his] ideas."[69] Both men "threw over" their religion while at Oxford and abhorred hypocritical, class-based orthodoxy, clerical suppression of reason, and ceremonial trappings—the latter manifested in Parry's loathing of Romanism. They likewise rejected the concepts of original sin and hell, but embraced Christ's ethics, Shelley by advocating forgiveness as a means of overcoming evil, Parry by "striving after virtue." But before addressing how these shared convictions resonate in Parry's *Scenes*, a final stage of British atheism, culminating in two events that occurred shortly before the Gloucester Festival, provides context for the premiere.

Between 1820 and 1880 atheistic tenets proliferated as planks of the agendas of numerous movements concerned with personal liberty or social humanitarianism, particularly lower-class education.[70] Robert Taylor, for example, founded the Christian Evidence Society and attracted large audiences to his lectures on scriptural fallibility until he was convicted of blasphemy in 1827.[71] After his incarceration Taylor joined Richard Carlile, imprisoned in 1819 for reprinting Paine's *Age of Reason*, in establishing the Rotunda, a short-lived center of radical thought in London. Their activism and revival of earlier "infidel" writings marked the beginning of a cohesive, continuous atheist movement in England.[72]

Not until 1841, however, did the first important, avowedly atheistic periodical, the *Oracle of Reason*, begin publication under Charles Southwell's editorship.[73] Seeking to deny all supernatural agency, not merely refute scriptural truth, Southwell and George Jacob Holyoake, the journal's second editor, proselytized publicly and served time for blasphemy. But Holyoake's trial in 1842 united and galvanized the secular movement's factions under his leadership, a status he enhanced by founding *The Reasoner*, a periodical maintaining a small but long-lived circulation from 1846 to 1861. By then Holyoake had discovered another dynamic colleague in Charles Bradlaugh, founder of the propagandist *National Reformer* (1860) and the National Secular Society (1866).

Dedicated to protecting the legal rights of unbelievers and opposing the citizenry's blind submission to authority, Bradlaugh led the NSS to its largest membership and strongest influence in public affairs. But when the NSS zealously campaigned to repeal the blasphemy act in 1879, only 4,800 sympathizers signed the necessary petition, despite Bradlaugh's oratorical and authorial prowess.[74] His election to the House of Commons in 1880, however, marked the highpoint of nineteenth-century British atheism. A law prohibiting atheists from taking oaths denied Bradlaugh his seat in Parliament, precipitating public outrage until he won several ensuing by-elections and was allowed to take a non-religious

---

[69]   ShP, Diary, 1 March 1880.

[70]   F.B. Smith, "The Atheist Mission, 1840–1900," in Robert Robson (ed.), *Ideas and Institutions of Victorian Britain* (New York, 1967), p. 20.

[71]   Budd, p. 20.

[72]   Smith, pp. 201–2. The elitist South Place Society's tradition already dated back to the late eighteenth century. (Budd, p. 15.)

[73]   The poorly circulated *Theological Inquirer*, edited by Erasmus Perkins, ran for only a year in 1815. (Smith, pp. 201–5.)

[74]   Budd, p. 225.

affirmation. Thus two seminal events in British atheism's history occurred in 1879 and 1880, precisely when Parry composed his *Scenes*.

Parry began his first task, deriving a practical libretto from Shelley's massive drama, on 29 February, in consultation with Dannreuther.[75] Already by 2 March he recorded progress: "I paid D a visit ... to get his opinion on a form into which I have got the words of Prometheus, and he thinks it may do." Parry had worked assiduously, choosing only 314 of Shelley's 2,608 lines, a critical act based partly on achieving a measure of narrative coherence (Table 6.1). In Part I Prometheus berates Jupiter and is answered by a Voice from the Mountains; Mercury, attempting to learn the time of Jupiter's downfall, bribes the Titan with forgiveness; Furies and the Earth advise Prometheus to accept Mercury's offer, but Spirits predict a brighter future based on the principle of Love; and Prometheus, now beyond heaven's oppression, receives the Earth's consolation. In Part II Jupiter asserts his eternal power, but the apocalyptic Demogorgon hurls him into an abyss; a Spirit of the Hour notes sudden, profound changes in mankind, now freed from tyranny; and her companions usher in an eternity of paradise.

Table 6.1   The Libretto for Parry's *Scenes*, after Shelley's *Prometheus Unbound*

Part and Scene Number		Dramatis Personae Basic Musical Profile	Lines in Shelley's Text	
I	1	Orchestral Introduction		
		Prometheus (bass)	I:	1–11, 23–7, 30,
		Recitative – arioso		40–48, 50–52
		Voice from the Mountains	I:	74–7, 91–2
		Chorus (SATB)		
		Mercury (tenor) & Prometheus:	I:	350–55, 410–15,
		Recitative – arioso		424–32, 435–6
		Chorus of Furies	I:	443
		Chorus (SATB)		
		Interlude		
		Chorus (SATB)	I:	495–517,
				539–41, 560–63
	2	The Earth (contralto)	I:	656–63
		Arioso – aria-like		
		Chorus of Spirits	I:	672–91
		Women's chorus		
		Prometheus	I:	807–20
		Arioso – aria-like – recitative		
		Voices of Spirits	II, v:	48–71
		Chorus (SATB, soli, semi-chorus)		

---

[75]   ShP, Diary, 1880.

II	3	Jupiter (tenor)	III, i	1–6, 8–14, 16–20,
		Recitative – arioso – aria – recitative		24–8, 30–33
		Demogorgon	III, i:	52–6
		Men's chorus		
		Jupiter	III, i:	63–70, 74–83
		Recitative – arioso		
	4	Spirit of the Hour (soprano)	III, iv:	97–103, 106, 125,
		Aria – arioso		137–8, 142–3,
				160–61, 163
	5	Voice of Unseen Spirits: sopranos	IV:	1–8
		Dark Forms and Shadows: basses	IV:	9–29
		Voice of Unseen Spirits: tenors	IV:	48–55
		Semi-Chorus of the Hours: SAB	IV:	57–60, 65–8
		Spirits: SATB	IV:	69–80
		Hours: ATB	IV:	89–92
		Spirits: SATB	IV:	93–8, 117–28
		Spirits and Hours: SATB	IV:	129–34

Although loosely constructed, the plot preserves the irreligious views Shelley and Parry shared. Four passages focus on divine oppression, belief's imposition through fear, and humanity's repression by Jupiter's "truth entangling lines." The first, appearing in the Titan's opening monologue, alternates between accompanied recitative and more lyrical arioso phrases. It begins rather prosaically as Prometheus addresses Jupiter—pointedly named the monarch of Gods, Demons, and every Spirit except Prometheus—in declamatory, largely diatonic vocal lines supported by low tremolos and sustained chords. But marked changes occur when Prometheus orders Jupiter to contemplate the Earth, "made multitudinous with his slaves," who "toil with fear and self-contempt," burdened with "knee-worship, prayer and praise" (Example 6.1). The vocal line ascends in two long, melodic arches, ending a twelfth higher than where it began; its accelerating rhythms grow irregular; and the increasingly animated accompaniment's bass line abandons its pedal point to climb chromatically as woodwinds and upper strings play antiphonal triplet figures. Parry's urgent, almost eruptive setting plainly underscores Shelley's indictment of a despotic deity who subjugates worshippers through fear. Similarly, in the ensuing passage simple recitative prevails as Prometheus seeks compassion from the Earth, Sun, and Sea, but animation returns when he describes his torture by Jupiter. Thus divine authority's immorality receives twofold emphasis.

Example 6.1   Parry *Scenes from Shelley's* Prometheus Unbound, No. 1, mm. 57–67

Comprising the second irreligious passage, the penultimate section of the Chorus of Furies involves a doctrine rejected by composer and poet alike: hell. Previously the Furies saluted Prometheus with fanfares, remained silent during an orchestral interlude, exhorted the Titan to escape captivity in a rousing march, and discussed his flame in a canonic dialogue, excerpts either maintaining one volume (usually fortissimo) or making incremental crescendos as the choir's sections enter successively. But again changes transpire when the Furies instruct Prometheus to "leave hell's secrets half unchanted" to Jupiter, who is "more cruel ... with fear" than the Titan is filled "with hate" for his oppressor (Example 6.2). A sudden mezzo piano, doubtless responding to the word "secrets," twice swells to forte, first underscoring "cruel," then stressing "hate" and "fear"—dynamic vilifications of Jupiter, who created hell's torments. A unique choral texture exploiting the three uppermost parts (soprano, alto, tenor) likewise distinguishes the excerpt from its two immediate predecessors, which respectively feature four canonic voices and unison basses. The accompaniment's sequential structure, chromatic bass line, and pizzicato figuration also enhance the passage's distinctive profile. Indeed, following another orchestral interlude, the Furies sing an a cappella chorale, reprise their fanfares, and conclude with a varied march. Parry's vivid setting of the "secrets of hell" accordingly reflects his heterodox convictions.

The third passage documents Parry's sympathy with Shelley's indictment of religious authority. In the monologue inaugurating scene 3, Jupiter gloats that all have been "subdued" to him, except man's soul, which, "like an unextinguished fire," burns with "fierce reproach and doubt." Spiritual insurrection renders Jupiter's "antique empire insecure, though built on eldest faith, and hell's coeval, fear." Elsewhere *Prometheus Unbound* cultivates dense allegory, but these lines are unequivocal: England (the "antique empire") and the Anglican Church (the "eldest faith") maintain power through fear, hell's coeval. Parry again isolates and highlights the text's crucial lines. Jupiter's initial boast receives cursory treatment as secco recitative: strings punctuate the vocal line with pizzicato chords, and woodwinds add fragmentary ascending scales doubled in thirds. When he mentions subjugation through fear of punishment, however, arioso prevails (Example 6.3). Wide vocal arcs adopt regular rhythms; the accompaniment follows suit as violins replace woodwinds in exchanging scale fragments, violas reinforce each measure's first and last beats, and clarinets and bassoons sustain chords; and the tonality (F minor) remains stable. Then, as Jupiter bemoans humanity's perseverance despite his curses, the music becomes static, perhaps appropriately imitating perseverance. But rapidly repeated octaves in the strings, several chords interjected by bassoons and horns, and the vocal line's tendency to hover around one pitch, C, evince a less imaginative approach to persistence than the one taken toward divine punishment. Text of special importance to Parry again elicited a more intense setting.

Example 6.2   Parry *Scenes from Shelley's* Prometheus Unbound, No. 1, mm. 301–10

Example 6.3   Parry *Scenes from Shelley's* Prometheus Unbound, No. 3, mm. 37–56

Example 6.3 concluded.

The fourth passage not only contrasts with adjacent materials, but also exhibits internal characteristics affirming Parry's atheistic predilections. As scene 3 closes, a Spirit of the Hour sings the score's only genuine aria, comprising an instrumental introduction and four discrete sections. In the first, the Spirit claims a transformation "folded itself round the sphered world" the moment Jupiter fell. She then describes her travels "among the haunts and dwellings of mankind," where "thrones were kingless." In the third, most crucial passage, she observes men neither "fawned" nor "wrought [their] lips in truth entangling lines"—overtly castigating worship and scriptural fallacy. She concludes by proclaiming Love's triumph over pride, jealousy, envy, and shame.

Each passage's musical profile is naturally distinct. The first features long-breathed arching vocal lines, a repetitive syncopated figure in the first violins, and tremolos in the remaining upper strings. While the second preserves the cantabile vocal style, its accompaniment shifts to syncopated chords, chromatically embellished arpeggios, and echoes of vocal phrases in the low strings and woodwinds. Thus far slowly moving harmonies change every one to six measures, modestly supplementing tonic and dominant chords in F major with prolonged, recurrent tonicizations of the relative minor, D. Ensuing events establish the third section's unique status within the aria (Example 6.4). As the Spirit announces earthly thrones were kingless, another tonicization of D proceeds unexpectedly to E minor, a peculiar modal inflection heralding an ecclesiastical idiom's onset. The third section then adopts a translucent C major for a homophonic chorale, its fast-paced harmonies embellished with numerous suspensions and appoggiaturas, but almost no chromaticism. Thus the chorale, disclosing men no longer fawned, trampled, or gazed on another's eye of cold command, is a parody: it subverts a recognized religious idiom to repudiate a deity worshipped by mankind's fawning.

Example 6.4   Parry *Scenes from Shelley's* Prometheus Unbound, No. 4, mm. 39–54

Example 6.5   Parry *Scenes from Shelley's* Prometheus Unbound, No. 4, mm. 55–62

A deceptive cadence ends the chorale and inaugurates the aria's final section, which reorders, condenses, and varies all previous material. Most remarkable is this peroration's treatment of lines concerning scriptural fallacy (Example 6.5). Chromaticism merely embellished arpeggios in the aria's second section, but here governs the bass line, suggesting a fanciful parallel between serpentine harmonies and scriptural deceit. Then, after moving exclusively in semitones, the bass line supports a D-flat major triad in first inversion, locally the Neapolitan of C major, but within the aria as a whole, the key furthest from the tonic. The arrival on D-flat coincides with the Spirit's highest pitch in the entire aria (A-flat), making "lie" her most important word and reflecting Parry's repugnance to scriptural tenets he considered patently untrue.

The *Scenes* repeatedly indict Jupiter, the tormentor of "self-despising slaves of heaven," "Heaven's slaves," and "heaven-oppressed mortality." More telling than Parry's inclusion of these isolated phrases, however, is his omission of Shelley's endorsements of Christ's ethics. Admittedly, the Furies urge Prometheus to renounce hatred, and the Spirit proclaims Love has replaced Jupiter's tyrannical thunder. But Parry otherwise avoided the drama's conspicuous Christian allusions, thus reinforcing his strongly felt unbelief.

Two factors suggest the atheistic tenets of the *Scenes* would have aroused controversy in Gloucester. First, atheism was a topical issue, the campaign to rescind blasphemy laws and Bradlaugh's election having recently attracted widespread attention. Second, the Three Choirs Festival, like its counterparts throughout England, assembled choristers from churches and cathedrals, and it entailed religious ceremonies and sermons based on Scripture. Indeed, Francis Hueffer's review for *The Times* dwells on the inaugural homily's importance as a Festival institution, its subject (Psalm 57:8, "Awake up, my glory"), and its relevance to the charitable work that prompted the Festival's founding in 1724.[76] But in discussing Parry's libretto, Hueffer overlooked Shelley's atheism, instead declaring the choice of *Prometheus Unbound* "could not be sufficiently commended," since English composers typically set the native literature's "weakest stanzas" while ignoring its "untold treasures of lyrical impulse." Hueffer recorded no textual objections besides wishing Parry had restricted himself to Shelley's most lyrical episodes.

Other critics took similar approaches. The *Athenaeum*'s unsigned correspondent, Ebenezer Prout, simply described *Prometheus Unbound* as a "beautiful but mystic poem."[77] Robin Benson, a Parry supporter writing for the *Saturday Review*, emphasized the drama's Christian ethics, avowing no great work except the Passion dealt "so ideally with patience under pain, with courage against omnipotent force, with human love and the sympathy of nature."[78] Benson and Hueffer mentioned "the liberality of [the Festival's] musical entertainment," possibly alluding to Shelley's radicalism, but more likely referring to an imminent performance of a Catholic mass, Beethoven's *Missa solemnis*, in a Protestant cathedral, another controversy critics studiously avoided. But debate had arisen over whether the audience would stand at appropriate points in the mass, or whether Gloucester Cathedral should continue to host the Festival.[79] Parry's *Scenes*, on the other hand, were premiered in Shire Hall on the Festival's secular series and thus probably had little connection with journalistic references to liberality.

Scarcely coincidental, however, is that in June 1880 *Macmillan's Magazine* published a long article on Shelley by Stopford Brooke, whose sermon Parry had enjoyed in 1870.[80] Brooke discussed Shelley's religious unorthodoxies, noting his *Ode to Liberty* attacks "priestcraft" and *The Revolt of Islam* rails against the "sovereign right of God to destroy ... His subjects." But Brooke denied Shelley's

---

[76]   [Francis Hueffer], "The Glocester [*sic*] Musical Festival," *The Times*, 8 September 1880, p. 8.

[77]   [Ebenezer Prout], "The Week: Gloucester Musical Festival," *Athenaeum*, 11 September 1880, p. 346.

[78]   [Robin Benson], "Mr. Hubert Parry's *Prometheus Unbound*," *The Saturday Review of Politics, Literature, Science, and Art*, 11 September 1880, p. 334.

[79]   [Joseph Bennett], "Festival of the Three Choirs," *Daily Telegraph*, 9 September 1880, p. 4. See also Hueffer, p. 8. Already in 1875 the Dean and Chapter of Worcester considered the Festival irreconcilable with concepts of worship. See Barry Still (ed.), "The Nineteenth Century," in *Two Hundred and Fifty Years of the Three Choirs Festival* (Gloucester, 1977), p. 18.

[80]   Stopford A. Brooke, "Some Thoughts on Shelley," *Macmillan's Magazine*, 52 (1880): 124–35.

atheism, instead emphasizing his more benign attraction to pantheism, a strategy commentators often adopted in evading or obscuring Shelley's unpalatable ideas, especially during the height of Victorian moralism. Indeed, the almost eerie critical silence on the irreligious content of the *Scenes* suggests a studied avoidance of the libretto's controversies. Another issue, however, invariably attracted notice and usually derision: Parry's music manifested Wagnerism.

Wagnerism faced stiff opposition in England, particularly compared to its florescence in France before 1870. British critics and audiences preferred oratorios and concert music over opera, habitually deemed a degenerate art form.[81] And Wagner's intricate librettos undoubtedly challenged the English practice of performing German operas in Italian rather than the local language, as was customary in France. Wagner nonetheless mounted English campaigns in 1839, 1855, and 1877.

In August 1839 Wagner stopped in London en route from Riga to Paris, where he naïvely hoped to conquer the operatic establishment with his incomplete *Rienzi*. He could locate neither Sir Edward Bulwer-Lytton, author of the novel on which *Rienzi* is based, nor Sir George Smart, who was considering whether the Philharmonic Society would perform Wagner's overture *Rule Britannia*.[82] The London press had already publicized his Continental activities and would do so throughout the 1840s, but no Wagnerian composition was performed in England until 1854, when several concert organizations programmed selections from *Tannhäuser*.[83] G.A. Osborne's Amateur Choral Society presented the "Entrance of the Guests into the Wartburg," while the "New" Philharmonic and Louis Antoine Juillien's orchestra repeatedly played the overture. Entrenched critics, advocates of a Mendelssohnian model, naturally received the overture poorly.[84] Henry Chorley (*Athenaeum*), James W. Davison (*The Times*), Charles Gruneisen (*Morning Post, Athenaeum*), Campbell Clarke (*Daily Telegraph*), and Alfred J. Novello (*Musical Times*) achieved a consensus, variously decrying the overture as "queer stuff," "loud and empty," "much fuss about nothing," "a weak parody of the worst compositions" of Berlioz's imitators, and "an empty commonplace."[85] The overture's repeated performances nonetheless indicate modest popular acceptance, though the die was cast among journalists.

Wagner's second visit resulted from the Old Philharmonic Society's invitation to conduct eight concerts between March and June 1855. He remained virtually unknown to the public, notwithstanding previous Continental successes with *Rienzi*, *Der fliegende Holländer*, *Tannhäuser*, and *Lohengrin*, and despite his scandalous Swiss exile following his participation in the Dresden Uprising in 1849. Critics and an elite constituency, on the other hand, were following his career and reading his theoretical essays. Nevertheless, his primary duty was to conduct works by earlier Austro-German

[81]   William Morris, for example, considered opera "the most rococo and degraded of all forms of art." See Anne Dzamba Sessa, *Richard Wagner and the English* (Rutherford, 1979), p. 90.

[82]   Richard Wagner, *My Life*, trans. Andrew Gray, ed. Mary Whitthall (Cambridge, 1983), pp. 166–7.

[83]   Sessa, *Richard Wagner and the English*, p. 16.

[84]   Hughes, p. 7.

[85]   William Ashton Ellis, *Life of Richard Wagner* (6 vols, London, 1906), vol. 5, p. 51. Subsequent references are to volume 5.

composers, making his effectiveness on the podium the focus of many reviews. Wagner's own works, comprising excerpts from *Lohengrin* and the *Tannhäuser* overture, were originally scheduled only twice, on 26 March and 14 May. With many of the same critics or their equally conservative successors in place, reactions were predictable.

W.H. Glover, preserving Gruneisen's legacy at the *Morning Post*, considered Austro-German composers from Handel to Mendelssohn proper influences on British music, not Wagner's "corruption."[86] Chorley detected scarcely any "pretext of melody" in the *Lohengrin* selections, just as Davison found "not a vestige" of "rhythmical melody" in the *Tannhäuser* overture.[87] They instead heard "incessant noise," "pure cacophony," "an inflated display of extravagance," and "a curious piece of patchwork."[88] Only George Hogarth deemed Elsa's processional from *Lohengrin* "a nuptial celebration of the most gorgeous kind" and claimed the extracts, though lacking their theatrical context, still "had a great effect, and a most favourable reception," remarks undoubtedly colored by his loyalties as the Society's secretary.[89] The overture's performance on 11 June, added at Queen Victoria's command, strengthened objections: Henry Smart judged it "utterly antipathetic to Mozart's and Beethoven's symphonies," while Chorley alleged its repetition pleased subscribers even less than its first performance.[90]

An illuminating aspect of Wagner's reception in 1855 is that critics often held anachronistic expectations, believing his operas of the 1840s would embody theories he developed during the early 1850s. Glover, for example, discerned "no marked individuality in [*Lohengrin*], no epoch-making innovations, such as the very original literary works of the composer had taught us to look for, but instead a succession of very brilliantly-instrumented pieces, which contained nothing new."[91] Smart concurred, describing one Wagnerian tableau as "a vast and dreamy mind picture struggling to acquire material vitality," but whose musical realization was merely "a faint shadowing of his imaginings."[92] Thus, Wagner's music elicited two complaints: in rejecting earlier Austro-German models, especially Beethoven and Mendelssohn, it became unmelodic, unrhythmic, and noisy; yet it simultaneously failed to illustrate Wagner's revolutionary theories. Both issues would resurface during Wagner's final London sojourn and would ultimately shape attitudes toward Parry's *Scenes*.

Wagner's concerts, though garnering considerable attention, produced few tangible results. During the 1860s performances of his music in England merely consisted of isolated concert presentations of selections from *Tannhäuser*, *Die Meistersinger*, and *Rienzi*.[93] Beginning in 1867, however, it figured prominently in the repertoire of the Working Men's Society, a private organization led by three Liszt disciples—Karl Klindworth, Walter Bache, and Fritz Hartvigson—and Parry's

---

[86]   Ibid., p. 310.
[87]   Ibid., pp. 216, 281.
[88]   Ibid., pp. 307, 9, 282.
[89]   Ibid., p. 203.
[90]   Ibid., pp. 312, 314.
[91]   Ibid., p. 208.
[92]   Ibid., p. 213.
[93]   Percy A. Scholes, *The Mirror of Music, 1844–1944: A Century of Musical Life in Britain as Reflected in the Pages of the* Musical Times (2 vols, London, 1947), vol.1, p. 252.

future teacher, Dannreuther.[94] Their work, bolstered in 1869 when Hueffer began to support Wagner in *The Times*, prepared audiences for English Wagnerism's first genuine florescence during the 1870s.

The decade began auspiciously with the British premiere of a complete Wagner opera, *Der fliegende Holländer*, performed in Italian at Drury Lane in 1870. Three years later the newly founded Wagner Society, led by its first president and secretary, Dannreuther and Hueffer, sponsored six largely Wagnerian concerts at Hanover Square, which inspired Alfred Forman's seminal translations of Wagner's librettos. Popular interest supported Italian productions of *Lohengrin* at Drury Lane and Her Majesty's Theatre in 1875 and Drury Lane's *Tannhäuser* in 1876. That year English journalists covered the inaugural Bayreuth Festival, but several old-guard reporters remained intractable. Davison characterized the *Ring*'s orchestral music as "a chaos of sound, ... now more or less agreeable, now more or less the opposite."[95] Concurring were younger anti-Wagnerian critics who gradually replaced their predecessors during the 1870s, including Joseph Bennett (*Daily Telegraph*), Henry Lunn (*Musical Times*), and William A. Barrett (*Morning Post, Musical Times*).[96] Bennett, for example, called *Das Rheingold*'s mythological setting a "strange world" and castigated *Die Walküre*'s incestuous plot. In short, when Wagner visited London in 1877, audiences had experienced multiple opportunities to hear his operas in whole or part, and popular interest was increasing. Critics, however, remained doggedly resistant.

In May 1877 Wagner returned to London for six concerts devoted exclusively to his music, given during a span of just 14 days and filling the giant Royal Albert Hall to capacity. He was occupied with social engagements, including a royal luncheon, so the eminent conductor Hans Richter, entrusted the previous summer with the *Ring*'s premiere, fulfilled many podium duties. Unfavorable contract provisions doomed the venture financially, but reports of cheering and frequent encores confirm its popular success. The *Athenaeum*'s critic, presumably Gruneisen, nonetheless observed instrumental pieces always received such accolades, never vocal selections.[97] Similarly, the *Examiner*'s columnist admired the music, but deemed Wagner's theatrical elements superfluous and tedious, and his theories—a matter of public indifference—utter nonsense.[98] Hence, English audiences of the late 1870s apparently recognized Wagner's orchestral prowess, while critics remained intransigent—factors influencing perceptions of Parry's thoroughly choric *Scenes*.

Parry could scarcely have anticipated facing charges of Wagnerism prior to undertaking lessons with Dannreuther in November 1873. While at Oxford he had heard just two performances of the *Tannhäuser* overture, one with the Philharmonic Society in 1866, the other conducted by August Manns in 1867. "Some of it was very fine," Parry noted, "somewhat giving the sensation of chaos with creation and form beginning to be

[94] Sessa, *Richard Wagner and the English*, p. 26.
[95] Ibid., p. 31.
[96] Hughes, p. 7.
[97] Sessa, *Richard Wagner and the English*, p. 34.
[98] Max Moser, *Richard Wagner in der englischen Literatur des XIX. Jahrhunderts* (Bern, 1938), p. 12.

perceptible," but he "couldn't understand the reason of a great deal of it."[99] He remained equivocal after settling in London and completing his first hectic years at Lloyd's. Curious, he attended the Wagner Society's inaugural concerts early in 1873, even while hoping to study in Vienna with Brahms, who declined to take him as a pupil. Only then, after his half-sisters Beatrice and Linda Gambier Parry had secretly presented one of Parry's compositions to Dannreuther, did he approach the prospective teacher.[100]

Soon Parry became absorbed in Dannreuther's fervent Wagnerism. A frequent conductor of the Wagner Society's programs throughout the 1870s, Dannreuther belonged to Wagner's inner circle, having attended the groundbreaking ceremonies for the Bayreuth Festspielhaus in 1872.[101] He accordingly received first-hand news of the *Ring*'s progress and was among the first to obtain freshly printed scores of its latest installments. He also included analysis of Wagner's music in the freely constructed curriculum of his receptive students, including Parry. In 1875 Drury Lane's *Lohengrin* elicited Parry's forthright admiration:

> I think Wagner is right in his idea of what an opera should be. … A great deal of the music is perfectly wonderful … the story and situations are very dramatic and interesting, and leave a profound impression.[102]

He heard the same company's *Tannhäuser* in 1876, but by then he was immersed in the *Ring* and planned to attend the inaugural Bayreuth Festival with his teacher. Prepared by Dannreuther's exacting tutelage, Parry reacted effusively to the performances:

> I never was so perfectly satisfied in all my life. *Rheingold* was … perfect to my mind. The *Walküre* came up to my expectations which were of the very highest. Then *Siegfried* I found certainly hard to understand; and I did not enjoy it so much as the others. … *Götterdämmerung* … utterly surpassed my anticipations. I was in a whirl of excitement; and quite drunk with delight.[103]

Thus in just over three years the neophyte became an ardent Wagnerian, intoxicated with Wagnerism.

Parry remained zealous when Dannreuther hosted Wagner's third London sojourn in 1877. Although he recorded no impressions upon meeting Wagner, he described subsequent encounters with the composer and his music. Wagner, a brilliant conversationalist, entranced new acquaintances and old friends; his conducting was "quite marvelous"; *Lohengrin* was thoroughly enjoyable for Parry and Maude; and "Siegfrieds Tod" was not only "the greatest thing in the world," but had also made Parry "quite cold with ecstasy."[104] Steeped in burgeoning English Wagnerism, Parry turned to *Prometheus Unbound*.

Composed less than three years after Wagner left England in June 1877, the *Scenes* reveal his influence over basic organizational principles, text setting, and specific

---

[99]   ShP, Diary, 1 July 1867.
[100] Dibble, pp. 99–100.
[101] Sessa, *Richard Wagner and the English*, p. 29.
[102] ShP, Diary, 28 May 1875.
[103] ShP, Diary, monthly summary for August 1876.
[104] ShP, Diary, 16 May 1877.

instrumental techniques. Continuity ranks among the score's most obvious Wagnerian attributes. (Again see Table 6.1.) In Part I a single pause separates two "numbers," each so designated in the score and encompassing highly differentiated events. The first entails a majestic orchestral introduction, an agitated scena for Prometheus, his heated, declamatory dialogue with Mercury, an instrumental interlude, and the Chorus of Furies. In the second, equally diverse sections comprise a soliloquy for the Earth cast entirely as arioso and recitative, another interlude, a lively Chorus of the Spirits, a flexibly structured monologue for Prometheus, a lilting waltz for four Spirits, a contralto's subdued aria, and a diaphanous chorus for a half-choir. Part II, however, incorporates less variety in three numbers. Jupiter's long expostulation (No. 3), shifting among recitative, arioso, and genuine lyricism, is interrupted only when the Demogorgon announces the Olympian's downfall in unison, choral recitative. The Spirit of the Hour's previously described aria constitutes a set number (No. 4). And while changes in tempo, meter, and key articulate the finale (No. 5), conventions governing English choral music since Handel's day prevail: imitation culminates in tutti homophony, a repeated cliché justifying Parry's self-assessment of the finale as "abominably choppy."[105] Continuity was not unknown in earlier choral works popular in Britain during the nineteenth century, including the revered oratorios of Mendelssohn and Spohr, but in the *Scenes* it is the norm, not the exception.

These unbroken tableaux exhibit two broadly Wagnerian traits: orchestral interludes and pervasive vocal declamation. No interlude approaches Wagner's "Forest Murmurs" or "Siegfried's Rhine Journey" in stature, but two are especially effective. The first, separating the Titan's dialogue with Mercury from the Chorus of Furies, features chromatically embellished viola arpeggios that ascend despite occasional downward leaps. After passing to the violins, the arpeggios gradually acquire support from pizzicato low strings, chords and scales in the woodwinds, and brass fanfares, culminating in the Furies' entrance. Thus the interlude not only links two dissimilar passages, but also establishes a new character and marks a climax as the first set piece in the *Scenes* begins.

Another striking interlude likewise connects solo and choral excerpts, respectively the Earth's lyrical arioso and short recitative and the Chorus of Spirits, but functions differently. It initially counters the recitative's dissipation of lyricism by recalling two motives from the arioso, one emphasizing upward melodic leaps with dotted rhythms before making stepwise descents, the other involving syncopated scales. After a clarinet reverses the syncopated line's direction and joins other woodwinds in sustaining chords, both motives experience transformation in the chorus's prelude. The upward leaps lose their dotted rhythms, briefly yield to melodic skips, and resume their stepwise descents, while the syncopated scales undergo rhythmic diminution. Notably, the motivic links reinforce textual associations between the solo and choral passages: the Earth hopes the Spirits will comfort Prometheus; they fulfill her wish, prophesying the Titan's victory.

Declamation's preponderance in the *Scenes* suggests another Wagnerian affinity. In the first number, Prometheus intersperses just two aria-like passages in a monologue otherwise consisting of recitative and arioso, while he and

---

[105]   See Parry's letter to Dannreuther of 13 July [1880], now held at the Bodleian Library, Oxford University. Bod. MS Eng. Letters e. 117.

Mercury converse entirely in accompanied recitative. The next two numbers are comparably proportioned: the Earth sings only 19 lyrical measures before shifting to declamation; Prometheus inserts one short lyrical passage between lengthy sections of arioso and recitative; and Jupiter's aria is prefaced by recitative and followed by the Demogorgon's choric declamation, further recitative, more arioso, and an aria-like conclusion. Although the two closing numbers are more conventional, flexible text setting in the Spirit of the Hour's aria deserves Jeremy Dibble's praise as an especially successful application of Wagnerian methods.[106]

Another fine example, the second number's soliloquy for Prometheus, is nonetheless more Wagnerian because it appears in a long, continuous scene, not as an independent set piece. This monologue comprises an arioso, an aria-like excerpt, and a recitative. In the arioso the Titan's thoughts turn from the Spirits who comforted him in the preceding chorus to Asia, his Oceanid lover (Example 6.6). Enhancing continuity between the chorus and arioso is additional development of two earlier motives: the syncopated scales, altered by diminution in the chorus, revert to their original longer note values; several measures later, the motive involving upward leaps and stepwise descents alternates between the accompaniment's tenor and bass voices. Parry's malleable text setting proceeds from equal note values as Prometheus observes the fairly shaped Spirits, to irregular rhythms matching his conflicted ruminations on vain hope and love, and finally to an animated outpouring of feelings for Asia. Phrase lengths vary with each idea, ranging from less than two measures to as many as six. Escalating chromaticism likewise increases momentum.

The aria-like excerpt unfolds over a drone embellished only by its lower chromatic neighbor, mirroring the Titan's contemplation of a quiet morning after a sleepless night with harmonic stasis. Although such stability precludes the contrasting cadential patterns essential to classical phrase structure, the passage's design is otherwise periodic. Arching woodwind melodies and wider vocal arcs divide respectively into regular four- and two-measure segments. Recitative nonetheless soon returns as Prometheus, transcending earthly consolations and heaven's torments, ponders his destiny as the savior of a suffering mankind. The third section accordingly reinstates vocal declamation, replete with many repeated pitches, turbulent dotted rhythms, and increasingly angular melodic lines. Intrusive tutti orchestral chords, sustained chords in the strings, and tremolos matching the Titan's agitation successively accompany choppy vocal phrases.

Thus the monologue's fluid global sequence shifts seamlessly among arioso, aria, and recitative, matching Shelley's nuanced textual structures with variously asymmetrical and regular phrases. Enhancing the setting's plasticity are numerous tempo changes, many indicated in printed editions, others only in manuscript sources.[107] But as Dibble astutely demonstrates, the *Scenes* contain little pliant,

---

[106]   Dibble, p. 191.

[107]   The passage's printed marking, "Ma poco più sostenuto," is modified twice by the word ritardando and once each by tranquillo, largamente, and adagio. A vocal score now held at the Shulbrede Priory also includes handwritten advice not to proceed "too fast" (twice) and to move "much faster" in the tranquillo section.

Example 6.6   Parry *Scenes from Shelley's* Prometheus Unbound, No. 2, mm. 96–111

pseudo-Wagnerian declamation.[108] Phrasing is more often periodic, predictably in choral passages, but even in solo sections such as the central excerpt from the Titan's monologue. Moreover, short, frequently repetitive phrases are foreign to the quintessentially Wagnerian notion of "endless melody." The differing approaches naturally originate in the respective texts. From the 1850s onward, Wagner's own librettos replaced end rhyme with alliteration and root rhyme (*Stabreim*), producing irregular meters and line lengths. Shelley's verse forms, in contrast, exhibit incredible variety, but essentially regular internal construction. Parry would scarcely have distorted Shelley's poetry to emulate Wagnerian declamation, but his frequent adherence to textual rhythms imbues the *Scenes*, at a fundamental level, with a decidedly un-Wagnerian quality.

Two instrumental techniques likewise evince pale imitations of Wagner. Only one of Parry's melodic ideas truly merits the designation leitmotif, Wagnerian music drama's definitive thematic substance.[109] Muted cellos present it in the introductory prelude, following several solemn woodwind chords (Example 6.7). Temporarily lacking textual associations, it is treated canonically, a rare procedure in Wagner's music, except in *Die Meistersinger*, where counterpoint ridicules pedantry. The motive acquires explicit meaning after the opening monologue, when the choric Voice of the Mountains grafts the trope, "thrice three hundred thousand years," onto it. During that vast time, the Voice discloses, mountains never bowed their snowy crests until the Titan's unrest compelled them to do so. Thus the leitmotif links passing eons with submission to the will of Prometheus, an association preserved in his dialogue with Mercury, where Jupiter's downfall is predicted, and in the Olympian's monologue, where it occurs. Leitmotivic segments, namely its upward leaps and stepwise descents, permeate the second number, as previously mentioned. Such fragments, however, are basically nondescript, admittedly unifying disparate sections and enhancing continuity, but scarcely constituting a Wagnerian complex of musico-textual referents.

Example 6.7   Parry *Scenes from Shelley's* Prometheus Unbound, No. 1, mm. 5–10

Parry's orchestration invites further Wagnerian comparisons, as Dibble again discerns.[110] Low bassoons and horns in Jupiter's monologue recall parts of *Siegfried*, notably the Act I prelude and Fafner's scenes. Divisi first violins, tremolos in the remaining upper strings, and harp arpeggios accompany the Spirit of the Hour, suggesting affinities

---

[108]   Dibble, pp. 187–8.
[109]   Ibid., pp. 192–3.
[110]   Ibid., p. 188.

with passages in *Lohengrin*, especially Elsa's narrative. Additionally, the flickering tremolos, snarling low trombones, and piccolo shrieks attending the Furies evoke Wagner's "Magic Fire Music." Innovative orchestration, however, is again rare in the *Scenes*. Typically strings observe score order, with winds providing judicious color. Prosaic *colla parte* writing suffuses choral passages, where upper strings and high woodwinds double women's voices, and low strings, bassoons, and brasses reinforce men's parts. Nevertheless, invariably competent and often imaginative instrumentation confirms Parry's success in fulfilling his first major commission.

From a modern perspective, the *Scenes* rather mildly manifest Wagnerism. Noteworthy continuity in Part I is less pronounced in Part II. Pervasive declamation approaches Wagner's free melodic style, but vocal lines more typically accommodate Shelley's regular meters and line lengths. A single leitmotif confirms Parry's understanding of Wagner's technique, as his contemporaneous work on the relevant entry in *Grove's Dictionary* confirms, but hardly qualifies as a full-fledged engagement with it.[111] And although Parry's scoring glimmers with Wagnerian effects, it is often generic. Early critics occasionally acknowledged Parry's assimilation of Wagner's precepts was limited, but they more frequently believed the *Scenes* embodied virulent, full-blown Wagnerism.

All five reviewers attending the premiere mentioned Parry's Wagnerism, but only two adopted a relatively neutral tone.[112] Hueffer, the ardent Wagnerite, merely stated Parry was "unmistakably of Wagner's school," though he divulged his predilections by dubiously claiming the brief orchestral introduction to the *Scenes* resembled the "marvelous prelude to *Tristan und Isolde*" in terms of structure and "oneness of sentiment." Prout likewise simply asserted "the composer shows a strong leaning to the modern German school ... as exemplified in one direction by ... Brahms and in another by ... Wagner." Parry's recent instrumental works illustrated the influence of the former, whereas the *Scenes* were "written under the inspiration of *Tristan und Isolde*." Two journalists expressed anti-Wagnerian prejudices openly. Bennett demeaned the "young disciple of the modern German School," as "something more than an amateur and something less at present than a master, even in the eccentric school of his adoption." And Barrett admonished Parry for embracing Wagner's "mannerism" instead of "the Mendelssohnian model." Only Robin Benson equivocated: "it would be difficult to determine [Parry's] genealogy. We have found passages ... which suggest Beethoven and Wagner have gone before; but he does not appeal to us in their language." Critical consensus nonetheless placed Parry in Wagner's camp.

Both intolerant critics thought Wagnerism had impeded Parry's compositional development. According to Bennett, "had the composer been less fettered by the school to which he has wedded himself his real poetical feeling would have been more constantly evidenced." Even more withering was Bennett's insinuation that

---

[111]   C. Hubert H. Parry, "leit-motif," in *A Dictionary of Music and Musicians*, ed. George Grove and J.A. Fuller-Maitland (4 vols, London, 1879), vol. 2, pp. 115–18.

[112]   To previously cited reviews by Hueffer, Benson, and Bennett may be added [Bennett], "Festival of the Three Cities," *Musical World*, 11 September 1880, pp. 575–8 (largely a verbatim reprint of part of Bennett's article in the *Daily Telegraph*); [Bennett] "The Gloucester Musical Festival: From our Special Correspondent," *Musical Times*, 1 October 1880, pp. 498–9; William A. Barrett, *Morning Post*, 9 September 1880, quoted in Hughes, p. 141.

Parry, having accepted the "doctrines of an original thinker," was not a "real creator." Barrett echoed these sentiments by alluding to *Macbeth*: "it may therefore be hoped that in his next attempt he may be induced to abandon a borrowed garb which sits badly upon him and only too clearly betrays the shape of the former wearer." Both reviewers thus believed Wagnerian techniques poorly suited Parry's natural gifts, which would fully evolve if released from Wagner's inhibiting influence.

Three journalists commended Parry's careful treatment of Shelley's text, but protested the declamatory style of the *Scenes*. Hueffer conceded Parry had set the words "with laudable attention to their poetic [and] metrical significance" and acknowledged "the close connexion of Mr. Parry's music with the words it tends to illustrate." But fulfilling these conditions in "detached bits of monologue and dialogue" was inadequate:

> The declamatory type of music, paradoxically though the statement may sound, requires an infinitely greater fund of melody than the ordinary humdrum style of Italian opera. This melody … is always potentially present, being heard now in the orchestra, now in the voice parts. Without it the declamation is dry and void of interest. It is in this "endless melody" … that Mr. Parry seems somewhat deficient.

Thus Hueffer, the self-professed Wagnerian, accurately discerned Parry's declamation lacked a supporting web of leitmotifs.

Benson likewise offered praise and censure, observing Parry had "contrived to endow Shelley's verse with under-currents of added melody without impairing an accent." But he emphasized this point "because the very learning and detail, the accurate adjustment of music to each single word, and the number of minor climaxes … may convey an impression of instability, and restlessness, and want of coherence in the parts." Moreover, "a calm, rhythmical melody of eight bars" in the Titan's declamatory opening monologue briefly "made the audience feel how safe they were, under the composer's guidance." Prout adopted an identical stance: "every word, every change of sentiment" had received "its appropriate expression," yet textual fidelity had again spawned problems:

> A chief fault of the work is the absence of contrast and repose. … Mr. Parry keeps his music too continually at high pressure … until one feels that an eight-bar phrase with nothing but tonic and dominant harmony would be an absolute relief.

Two critics accordingly condemned Parry's declamation because it eschewed periodic phrasing, whereas a third blamed undeveloped leitmotivic technique. Bennett alone insisted "the words [were] set with such a total disregard of the effect of the music upon the hearers as almost to make us believe that the composer had ignored the necessity of such considerations altogether."

No other feature of the *Scenes* experienced such intense scrutiny, although Parry's orchestration drew several complaints. Prout noticed it was "at times a little overloaded," and Benson remarked it "was so full that we lost for a moment the solo voice" in the opening monologue. Neither journalist equated thick scoring with Wagnerism, whereas Bennett considered Parry's "oppressively heavy orchestration" a capital Wagnerian offense.

Critics denounced Parry's declamation and orchestration, but nonetheless accorded the *Scenes* a general, if qualified, approval. Hueffer praised the finale's "excellent contrapuntal writing," "cantabile passages of great sweetness," and "climax of almost dithyrambic enthusiasm." Benson, deeming the score's "power and originality beyond question," professed "no great vocal work by a modern English composer exists of equal pretension." Prout credited Parry with "much real poetic feeling and with no ordinary dramatic power," but doubted he had uniformly succeeded "in rising to the height of his subject." Even the intractable Bennett admitted the *Scenes* "had moments of real beauty," though he observed a "dullness which gradually spread over the large audience was made even more apparent by these transient gleams of light." Hueffer, however, maintained "the reception of Mr. Parry's work ... was most favorable." Critics of both polemic persuasions judged the score difficult, complicated, and ambitious—obstacles the performers overcame with great aplomb, as the reviewers likewise universally agreed.

Criticism of the *Scenes* often perpetuated long-standing traditions of English Wagner reception. Just as early reviewers found the *Tannhäuser* overture loud, empty, and cacophonous, so one later journalist condemned Parry's membership in an "eccentric school." Similarly, descriptions of Wagner's overture as an unmelodic patchwork resonated in denunciations of Parry's timid leitmotivic technique and "detached bits of monologue and dialogue." And a Mendelssohnian model dominated reviews for over three decades. Despite the Wagner Society's founding in 1867, the production and popularity of complete Wagner operas during the 1870s, and Wagner's celebrated visit to London in 1877, critics scarcely changed their views at the Gloucester Festival.

Parry, too, was initially skeptical. Ambivalent about the *Tannhäuser* overture and rejected by Brahms, he embraced Wagnerism only after his half-sisters arranged lessons with Dannreuther, under whose guidance he came to admire Wagner's music, attend the first Bayreuth Festival, meet Wagner, and adopt Wagnerian techniques in several works of the late 1870s. In the *Scenes*, Wagnerism's manifestations include continuity among diverse sections, orchestral interludes, declamation, a prominent though solitary leitmotif, and ambitious orchestration. But critics, beyond recognizing problems with Parry's declamation, pointedly noted he cultivated a Wagnerian rather than a Mendelssohnian idiom. Indeed, they soon dubbed Parry a "disciple of Wagner," an affiliation some feared would stunt his natural talent.

Contemporary objections to Parry's Wagnerism rested primarily on aspects of musical style, namely melodic technique, declamation, and internal coherence. Another time-honored tradition in British Wagnerism, however, plausibly influenced the reception of the *Scenes*, if not among critics, then at least among Parry's acquaintances, as his correspondence will ultimately confirm. Thus warranting brief consideration is Wagnerian eroticism—a mainstay of British Wagnerism long before and after the Gloucester Festival.

Wagner first influenced English literature during the 1860s, as in France. The earliest British Wagnerites, however, were neither poets nor journalists, but two diplomats assigned to the Viennese embassy, Edward Bulwer-Lytton and Julian

Fane.[113] Admiring Wagner's music, they collaborated on *Tannhäuser, or, the Battle of the Bards*, published pseudonymously in 1861. Their synopsis of Wagner's libretto in English verse is scarcely distinguished poetry and rarely departs from Wagner's plot, factors inducing hostile criticism. But their emphasis of the opera's eroticism, as the following extracts illustrate, foreshadows a trend that dominated English literary circles well into the 1890s:

> Woe to the man who wanders in the vast
> Of those unhallow'd solitudes, if Sin,
> Quickening the lust of carnal appetite,
> Lurk secret in his heart; for all their caves
> Echo weird strains of magic, direful-sweet,
> That lap the wanton sense in blissful ease;
> While through the ear a reptile music creeps,
> And, blandly-busy, round about the soul
> Weaves its full web of sounds. …
> Away adown the ever-darkening caves, …
> Away into the mountain's mystic womb,
> To where, reclining on her stupious couch
> All the fair length of her lascivious limbs,
> Languid in the light from roseate tapers flung,
> Incensed with perfumes, tended on by fays,
> The lustful Queen, waiting damnation, holds
> Her bestial revels. …
> Slaves of their bodies, in the sloughs of Sin
> They roll contented, wallowing in the arms
> Of their libidinous goddess.[114]

Thus a magical, direful-sweet, reptilian sound web ensnares wanton senses and the soul itself, just as Venus synaesthetically entangles her lovers in fleshy limbs, candlelight, and perfume.

Such sensuality anticipated works by William Morris, Algernon Swinburne, and John Payne, affiliates of the Pre-Raphaelite Brotherhood during the 1850s. The Brotherhood's artists, poets, and critics espoused ideals resembling those of Wagner.[115] They shared his aversion to materialism, which degraded the arts; they rejected the Renaissance painter Raphael as a model and embraced earlier art of the Middle Ages (hence the Brotherhood's name), just as Wagner's librettos favored medieval subjects; and they fused moral seriousness, often embodied in religious themes, with sensuous mysticism, just as Wagner amalgamated religious redemption and carnality in *Tannhäuser*, *Lohengrin*, and, ultimately, *Parsifal*. These affinities reached a notorious

---

[113]　Moser, p. 23.

[114]　Edward Bulwer-Lytton and Julian Fane, *Tannhäuser, or, The Battle of the Bards* (London, 1861), pp. 6, 7, 11.

[115]　Sessa, *Richard Wagner and the English*, p. 89.

zenith during the 1890s among the so-called decadents, particularly Aubrey Beardsley and Oscar Wilde,[116] but the earlier trio had already solidified the tradition.

Swinburne, Morris, and Payne, like Bulwer-Lytton and Fane, rendered the Tannhäuser saga in verse. Swinburne's *Laus Veneris* (1864), published perhaps before its author knew Wagner's music, nonetheless blends religion and sensuality in an uncannily Wagnerian manner. Leaving the Venusberg, Tannhäuser concedes the Lord is great and fair, though less beautiful than Venus' "wonderfully woven hair," and her mouth was lovelier than the divine kiss that healed him.[117] Morris also describes the goddess's sensual body in *Hill of Venus*, part of a cycle of romances published in 1870:

> Naked, alone, unsmiling, there she stood
> No cloud to raise her from the earth, her feet
> Touching the grass that his touched, and her blood
> Throbbing as his throbbed through her bosom sweet.[118]

Payne's *The Building of a Dream* (1870) depicts the Venusberg as a magnificent golden city where maidens dazzle Tannhäuser with their beauty. Venus lives joyfully with him until he returns to the mortal world to die, overcome with ennui.

All three poets remained Wagnerites: Swinburne, whose works Parry read during the 1870s, employed another Wagnerian subject and leitmotivic references in *Tristram of Lyonnesse* (1882); Morris adhered more faithfully than Wagner to Icelandic myths in *Sigurd the Volsung* (1876); and Payne emulated *Lohengrin* in *Sir Floris* (1870) and praised Wagner in *Songs of Life and Death* (1872). But prior to the Gloucester Festival of 1880 English literature's most pervasive Wagnerian images involved *Tannhäuser*'s eroticism. Thus two critical traditions potentially influenced the reception of the *Scenes*: journalists scorned Wagnerian cacophony and its threat to Mendelssohnian hegemony, and poets mingled moral seriousness with sensuality.

Music critics also discussed Wagnerian eroticism. During the inaugural Bayreuth Festival, for example, Bennett reasserted his preference for moral plots based on "human interest," not incestuous demigods.[119] Davison, normally Bennett's ally, reacted positively to the 1876 *Ring*, lauding "Wagner's marvelous facility in giving expression, after his individual manner, to the emotions of passionate love."[120] Otherwise Wagner threatened Victorian virtues, especially when *Tristan und Isolde*, *Die Meistersinger*, and the complete *Ring* debuted in London in 1882. Anticipating Drury Lane's production of *Tristan*, H.F. Frost condemned the libretto as "a hideously

---

[116] Emma Sutton, *Aubrey Beardsley and British Wagnerism in the 1890s* (Oxford, 2002), pp. 1–23.

[117] Algernon Swinburne, *Laus Veneris: Poems and Ballads by Algernon Charles Swinburne* (Portland, Me., 1899), p. 18.

[118] William Morris, *The Earthly Paradise, A Poem*, 9th edn (4 vols, London, 1891), vol. 4, p. 388.

[119] Sessa, *Richard Wagner and the English*, p. 32.

[120] Ibid.

immoral book,"[121] dwelling on Isolde's ambiguous infidelity and discouraging the adoption of a Wagnerian model in explicitly masochistic language: the music drama induced "mental exhaustion" by arousing "intense emotional pleasure" that was actually "more akin to pain."[122] H.W.L. Hime's *Wagnerism: A Protest*, likewise published in 1882, chastised Wagner for depicting the incestuous Siegmund and Sieglinde without expressing "some censure of their conduct"—a "real deformity of the poem" compromising "morality and decency."[123] And as English audiences grew increasingly aware of Wagner's personal life, including his suspicious relationship with Mathilde Wesendonck and his extra-marital affair with Cosima, an aura of moral ignobility surrounded him. His revolutionary activities and publicly avowed anti-Semitism only supported perceptions of his work as sinful and sexually immoral, views common among British and American critics well into the twentieth century and still contentious in recent Wagner reception.[124]

Shelley aroused similar controversies, as Brooke's previously mentioned article acknowledged. Indeed, Shelley's rejection of "the ordinary religious views of English society" was accompanied by his shocking advocacy of free love over institutionalized matrimony, his elopement with Harriet Westbrook (an innkeeper's 16-year-old daughter), their marriage's collapse, another elopement with Mary Godwin, their triangular relationship with her half-sister, and his rakish affairs in Italy. *Prometheus Unbound*, though unburdened by his libertinism, is laden with sexual symbols, the most overtly erotic appearing in a conversation between Asia and her sister Panthea.[125] While sleeping at the Titan's feet, Panthea dreamt his faint voice intoxicated her with joy; his immortal shape's overpowering light was eclipsed by love, which emanated as steam from his soft flowing limbs, passion-parted lips, and keen eyes; and an all-dissolving power enveloped her until she did not see, hear, or move, but felt only his presence flow and mingle through her blood until it passed (II, i, 57–82).

Panthea's orgasmic narration epitomizes the flagrant sensuality typical of Shelley's lyric poems, but Parry omitted it from his *Scenes*. He likewise avoided other conspicuously erotic passages in *Prometheus Unbound*, such as Panthea's awakening of her sister Ione's quiescent sexuality with a homoerotic kiss and Jupiter's contrasting recollection of his passionless rape of Thetis. Indeed, the *Scenes* contain only two brief erotic utterances. The first again employs orgasmic imagery, though from a masculine perspective. In his second monologue Prometheus relates that when his "being overflowed," Asia was "like a golden chalice to bright wine, which else had sunk into thirsty dust" (I, 807–11), lines evoking Wagnerian eroticism with a previously described outpouring of animated arioso writing and increased chromaticism (Example 6.5). The second occurs in the aria for the Spirit of the Hour,

[121] H.F. Frost, "Some Remarks on Richard Wagner's Music-Drama *Tristan und Isolde*," *Proceedings of the Royal Music Association*, 8 (1882): 148.

[122] Ibid., pp. 160–61.

[123] H.W.L. Hime, *Wagnerism: A Protest* (London, 1882), pp. 23–4.

[124] Sessa, "At Wagner's Shrine: British and American Wagnerians," in Large and Weber (eds), *Wagnerism in European Culture and Politics*, p. 246.

[125] Nathaniel Brown, *Sexuality and Feminism in Shelley* (Cambridge, Mass., 1979), p. 61.

who becomes "dizzy with delight" when a transforming love dissolves into the sky, air, and sunlight, enfolding the world. Parry's diaphanous setting of a second female envelopment recalls *Lohengrin*, bearing only mildly erotic connotations.

Early critics—doubtless aware of Shelley's attitudes regarding sexuality, his poetry's sensuality, and Wagnerian eroticism's impact on English literature—detected no related offenses in the *Scenes*, duplicating their evasion of Shelley's atheism. That Parry's Wagnerism also connoted eroticism is accordingly substantiated not by journalists, but by a friend. Hugh Montgomery, a fellow musical enthusiast at Oxford who hosted an "Essay and Discussion Club" Parry attended starting in 1875, perceived Wagnerism's dangers after Parry's overture, *Gillem de Cabestanh*, was performed at the Crystal Palace on 15 March 1879. After reading reviews, Montgomery wrote Parry, employing blatantly sexual language:

> All I hear promises well … for your power and originality, but the remarks point to that quality in your work which makes Wagner so unsatisfactory to me and immoral in the effect he produces on my emotional condition. A tendency to promiscuous intercourse with all sorts of loose keys instead of that faithful cleaving to one only … to which one is accustomed in the respectable masters.[126]

Wagner's immorality was neither political nor erotic, Montgomery posits, but musical. Wagnerian tonality's "promiscuous intercourse"—its intermingling of licentious keys—betrayed respectable harmonic fidelity. Montgomery was probably disheartened 16 months later, when critics of the *Scenes* recognized "a disciple of Wagner's school." His testimony nonetheless indicates Wagnerism and eroticism were linked, at least in Parry's social circles.

Atheism and Wagnerism, the chief issues raised by Parry's *Scenes*, occupy extremely different positions in his life. As a child and student, his religious views were consistent with his era, social standing, and orthodox family background. But doubts surfaced by age 21, when he began a lifelong engagement with controversial authors ranging from Hume to Darwin. Contributing to his rejection of institutionalized religion were his father's inflexibility, his brother's avowed unbelief, and his loathing of Romanism. Parry revealed his convictions to his father in 1873, but they remained a family secret for years, since unbelief still bore a heavy stigma. After all, England's first published avowals of atheism dated back only a century, following over 200 years of persecution and literary subterfuge. Even in Parry's day heterodox social movements sought to educate the lower classes, hardly a country squire's pursuit.

Parry nonetheless discovered the perfect vehicle for articulating his principles in Shelley's lyric drama, confiding to his diary that nothing else approached his own ideas. Shelley's daring proclamations in essays and poems, including *Prometheus Unbound*, closely resembled Parry's opinions on the examination of faith through reason, religious tyranny, anticlericalism, original sin, and hell. The *Scenes* reflect Parry's views on divine authority's inherent evil, hell, institutionalized religion, and the "lie" of revealed doctrine by highlighting crucial lyrics with unique textures, agitated figuration, dynamics, accents, changes of tessitura, and a parodied chorale.

---

[126]   Dibble (p. 172) includes the extract from Montgomery's letter of 20 April 1879, now held at the Shulbrede Priory.

Equally significant, however, is Parry's pronounced tendency to distance himself from Shelley's admiration for Christ's ethics. Critics were undoubtedly familiar with Shelley's unorthodoxies, and audiences would have remembered the highly publicized attempt to rescind the blasphemy laws in 1879 and Charles Bradlaugh's election to Parliament in 1880. Nevertheless, Parry's bold declarations went largely unnoticed.

Parry's irreligious views lasted his entire life.[127] He begrudgingly allowed but refused to attend his daughters' baptisms. Beginning in 1896, he presided over Highnam Court, was accordingly obliged to serve on the local parish council, and attended church services only to set an ethical example for servants and estate workers, whose rural isolation precluded access to other institutions capable of ministering to their humanitarian needs. But he abstained from reciting the Athanasian Creed during the liturgy and steadfastly embraced Darwinism, even in his scholarly endeavors, as the title and premise of the second edition of his best-known monograph, *The Evolution of the Art of Music*, verifies. Thus Parry arrived at a permanent affirmation of atheistic precepts from a strict but conventional background.

His Wagnerism differed significantly. As a student Parry was unfamiliar with Wagner's music, especially compared to his thorough religious indoctrination, but he probably knew critics had deemed it cacophonous, unmelodic, and disjointed, notwithstanding its pale illustration of Wagnerian theory. Ambivalent until he encountered Dannreuther, Parry then studied Wagner's scores intensely, attended performances in London and Bayreuth, and met Wagner. Ensuing experiments in the *Scenes* yielded continuity between disparate sections, orchestral interludes, declamation, and elaborate orchestration. But by modern standards, the *Scenes* only mildly embody Wagnerism: set numbers predominate in Part II; phrasing is often periodic; and one leitmotif recurs just several times. Critics, however, considered these tendencies virulent Wagnerian manifestations capable of inhibiting Parry's development. Especially problematic was Parry's careful, detailed text setting, which nonetheless lacked the vitality of Wagner's "endless melody." In other words, Parry's declamation failed to illustrate Wagner's theories, a charge earlier journalists had leveled against *Tannhäuser* and *Lohengrin*. Likewise objectionable were heavy orchestration and a dearth of cohesion among "detached bits of monologue and dialogue," but most reviewers still broadly praised the score's ambition.

In contrast to unbelief's permanence in Parry's life, Wagnerism only temporarily influenced his music. He admittedly planned to adopt Wagnerian techniques in his incomplete opera *Guenever* (1886) and developed leitmotifs systematically in his oratorio *Job* (1892), to name just two mature works authenticating Wagner's lingering influence. But even while composing and long after completing the *Scenes*, Parry cultivated a Brahmsian idiom in numerous orchestral and chamber works. As his Wagnerism subsided, critics who opposed it began to praise his compositions as products of a genuinely English school, while Wagnerites reacted coolly to his Brahmsian scores.[128] The *Scenes* accordingly represent an experimental stage in Parry's compositional development, with few noteworthy successors.

---

[127]   Dibble, pp. 159, 351, 392.
[128]   Hughes, p. 49.

If the *Scenes* are somewhat anomalous in Parry's *œuvre*, their reputation as a harbinger of an English musical renaissance may seem undeserved. They were performed only twice during Parry's lifetime, first in Gloucester, then in Cambridge in 1881, when their Wagnerian traits unsettled Stanford.[129] And notable exceptions to their infrequent performance since Parry's death comprise the BBC's observance of their centennial and a recording preserved at Indiana University.[130] Meirion Hughes plausibly argues that early in the 1900s, when the Renaissance construct appeared in Walker's monograph and Fuller-Maitland's article on Parry in the second edition of *Grove's Dictionary*, Parry was no longer considered progressive, especially compared to Elgar, whom critics touted as Richard Strauss's British counterpart.[131] Parry's partisans then marked the renaissance's onset with the indisputably progressive *Scenes*.

Such polemics doubtless colored the historiography of the *Scenes*. But critics and Parry's friend Montgomery immediately recognized the score's power, originality, ambition, and complexity—rare qualities in earlier nineteenth-century British choral repertoire. Moreover, as Hughes concedes, the Renaissance construct originated in 1882, when the anti-Wagnerian Bennett admitted Parry's Symphony in G furnished "capital proof that English music [had] arrived at a Renaissance period."[132] Thus contemporary assessments, particularly Benson's claim that "no greater work by a modern English composer exists of equal pretension," acknowledged Parry departed from Mendelssohnian paradigms during the early 1880s. He thereby set precedents for his oratorios and works by emerging English composers, including Stanford, Holst, Elgar, and Vaughan Williams. Parry's representation of the Prometheus myth should therefore be deemed not a stylistic aberration, but a vehicle for expressing personal ideals, testing contemporary compositional techniques, and advancing new models for English music.

---

[129] Dibble, pp. 195–6.

[130] Hughes, p. 158. The tape recording's bibliographical record (TP .P2638 D1.1 in the Orchard Collection) includes no information other than it was a donation.

[131] Hughes, pp. 150–51. Fuller-Maitland claimed Parry's otherwise unsuccessful cantata "undoubtedly marks an epoch in the history of English music, and the type of composition of which it was the first specimen has had great consequences in the development of our national art." See J.A. Fuller-Maitland, "Parry, Sir Charles Hubert Hastings," in J.A. Fuller-Maitland (ed.), *Grove's Dictionary of Music and Musicians*, 2nd edn (5 vols, London, 1904–10), vol. 3, p. 625.

[132] [Bennett], "Birmingham Musical Festival," *Daily Telegraph*, 4 September 1882, p. 3.

Chapter 7

Conservatism Assimilates the Prometheus Myth: Concert Overtures by Bargiel and Goldmark

As popular as the Prometheus myth was during the romantic era, it rarely inspired autonomous instrumental compositions intended exclusively for concert performance. Beethoven's ballet and Liszt's incidental music originated in the theater, although the overtures from both scores admittedly enjoyed limited independence on orchestral programs. Nearly every remaining work involved a text: Reichardt, Schubert, and Wolf set Goethe's ode; French composers gravitated toward cantatas or stage works with topical librettos; and Parry likewise met a specific occasion's demands by turning to Shelley's lyric drama. Additional cantatas by French, Belgian, German, and Italian composers, another incidental score, a burlesque, and even a set of trivial waltzes for solo piano confirm nineteenth-century predilections for theatrical or dramatic representations of the legend.[1]

This dearth seems surprising, since the vivid narrative offers an ideal vehicle for addressing one of the period's quintessential and most passionately disputed issues: program music, or the purely instrumental depiction of nonmusical subjects typically drawn from literature, history, the visual arts, or natural landscapes. During the 1850s the topic engendered highly partisan debates between two factions. Program music's leading advocates included Wagner, who considered extramusical associations the means whereby a composition's otherwise ineffable essence was externalized for listeners, a process culminating in the music drama; Liszt, who sought to rejuvenate and universalize the tradition of German instrumental music by infusing his symphonic poems and program symphonies with European literature's substance; and Franz Brendel, the editor of the *Neue Zeitschrift für Musik*, who championed the music drama and symphonic poem as pinnacles of historical evolution.[2]

---

[1]   Ferdinando Paër, Peter Benoit, André Messager, Gerhard Schjelderup, and Heinrich Hofmann wrote the cantatas; John Barnett compiled the burlesque's music; Edgar Kelley provided incidental music for Aeschylus; and Joseph Lanner composed the waltzes. To these may be added the finale of Charles Alkan's *Grande Sonate*.

[2]   Carl Dahlhaus, *The Idea of Absolute Music*, trans. Roger Lustig (Chicago, 1989), pp. 18–27; Berthold Hoeckner, *Programming the Absolute: Nineteenth-Century German Music and the Hermeneutics of the Moment* (Princeton, 2002), p. 155.

Their foremost opponent, the critic Eduard Hanslick, began writing for Viennese periodicals in 1848, soon became music editor of Vienna's leading newspaper, the *Neue freie Presse*, and ultimately earned a professorship at Vienna University. In his influential treatise, *Vom Musikalisch-Schönen* [On the Musically Beautiful, 1854], Hanslick appropriated Wagner's term "absolute music," which signified instrumental music's objectless imprecision, as opposed to the objective precision vocal music achieved through its text.[3] For Hanslick, musical structure was no mere vessel for conveying ideas, feelings, or subjects; instead, "tonally moving forms" (tönend bewegte Formen) comprised music's only genuine substance.[4] Explanatory programs or mottos were consequently either superfluous or detrimental because they failed to illuminate form or compromised instrumental music's autonomy. Hanslick gained powerful allies in 1860, when Brahms, Joachim, and the composer-conductors Julius Grimm and Bernhard Scholz published a manifesto in the *Berliner Musik-Zeitung Echo* denouncing the "products, leaders, and pupils of the so-called 'New German' School [Brendel's constellation of Wagner, Liszt, Berlioz, and their disciples] as entirely contrary to the innermost essence of music."[5] Thus the lines between "programmaticists" and "absolutists" were clearly drawn.

The controversy was scarcely new. Instrumental depictions aroused little strife during the seventeenth and early eighteenth centuries, when composers borrowed techniques from vocal genres to portray central emotions or affects, as in biblical sonatas by Kuhnau and Biber, or imitated physical motions and natural sounds, as in pieces by French clavecinists. Nor were illustrative orchestral passages in operas and oratorios contentious. By the mid-eighteenth century, however, representing material objects in vocal and instrumental music was judged inferior to imitating human emotions or "characters."[6] Views sharpened as the century progressed until even the revered Haydn suffered derision for depicting natural sounds in his late oratorios. The problem more acutely affected the symphony, whose burgeoning status as the premiere instrumental genre was threatened by titles or mottos that inevitably kindled expectations of material imitation.[7] Hence Beethoven famously prefaced his "Pastoral" Symphony with the subtitle, *Mehr Ausdruck der Empfindung als Mahlerei* [More the expression of emotion than tone-painting], rationalizing conventions already deemed factious as the nineteenth century dawned. Ignoring such qualms, the period's largely receptive audiences enjoyed over 200 "characteristic symphonies" that reenacted battles, hunts, storms, and ceremonies of mourning and celebration.[8] Nevertheless, romantic composers remained suspicious, especially in Germany.

---

[3]   Dahlhaus, *The Idea of Absolute Music*, p. 18.

[4]   Regarding this distinction's relationship to Hegel's conception of instrumental music as "contentless," see Hoeckner, pp. 163–4.

[5]   See the reprinted manifesto in Hans Kalbeck, *Johannes Brahms*, 8 vols in 4 (Berlin, 1912–14), vol. 1/2, pp. 404–5.

[6]   Richard Will, *The Characteristic Symphony in the Age of Haydn and Beethoven* (Cambridge, 2002), pp. 130–33.

[7]   Ibid., p. 129.

[8]   Ibid., pp. 242–93. Will indexes 225 works.

Felix Mendelssohn-Bartholdy and Robert Schumann, heirs to the Austro-German musical legacy after the deaths of Weber (1826), Beethoven (1827), and Schubert (1828), were circumspect regarding programs. Mendelssohn attached descriptive or literary titles to overtures and symphonies, but repeatedly avoided furnishing details about individual compositions, including the Overture to *A Midsummer Night's Dream*.[9] Judging musical meaning "too specific" to be conveyed in ordinary words, Mendelssohn was ultimately an absolutist who, as he acknowledged, occasionally indulged in *Mahlerei*, but no more so than Beethoven.[10] Schumann, in measured contrast, viewed Beethoven's "characteristic" forays as precedents for exploring "states of the soul," aided by literary allusions.[11] He nonetheless asserted he sometimes conceived titles for his piano works of the 1830s after completing them, thus discounting their literary affinities. Well-known annotations in his copy of Jean Paul's *Flegeljahre* nonetheless belie Schumann's claim, correlating specific episodes in the novel with the constituent pieces of his *Papillons*. Schumann also suppressed subtitles found in the "Rhenish" Symphony's manuscript sources when he published the score in 1851. Two years later he contributed his valedictory essay to the *Neue Zeitschrift für Musik*, the periodical he founded in 1834, edited for ten years, and sold to Brendel as his health began to fade. In "Neue Bahnen" [New Paths] he anointed Brahms as the "chosen one" who would "give expression to his time in ideal fashion,"[12] thereby ironically endorsing a nascent absolutist in a journal already serving as an organ of the as yet unnamed New German School.

Mendelssohn and Schumann died prematurely, before the controversy engendered rancorous debate. Their uneasy rapprochement between absolutism and programmaticism nonetheless influenced their successors, who range in posthumous fame from celebrated luminaries such as Antonín Dvořák to lesser-known composers such as Niels Gade. Two of the latter entered the equivocal middle ground between absolute and program music with Promethean overtures. Woldemar Bargiel (1828–97), an indirect relative of Schumann and a colleague of Brahms and Joachim, joined the absolutists. His *Ouverture zu Prometheus für grosses Orchester*, Op. 18 (1852) perpetuates the patrician ideals of the Leipzig Conservatory, a bastion of conservatism where he studied at Schumann's recommendation. Yet it also advances certain formal conventions of overtures by Mendelssohn, his mentor at the Conservatory, and aspires to the monumentality of Beethoven's middle-period overtures, as a musical quotation demonstrates. Just as importantly, Bargiel's overture replaced Liszt's *Prometheus* during a festival of the Allgemeiner deutscher Musikverein, a venue held by the programmatic faction, and may accordingly be read as a conservative critique of the New German School's "products." Carl Goldmark (1830–1915), remembered today for his opera *Die Königin von Saba* [The Queen of Sheba, 1875], espoused Wagnerism during the 1860s, incorporating Wagnerian traits

---

[9]   R. Larry Todd, *Mendelssohn:* The Hebrides *and other Overtures*, Cambridge Music Handbooks, ed. Julian Rushton (Cambridge, 1993), pp. 70–71.

[10]   Ibid., p. 43. Beethoven's *Fidelio* and *Leonore* overtures were Mendelssohn's precedents..

[11]   Leon Plantinga, *Schumann as Critic* (New Haven, 1967), pp. 94–6.

[12]   Robert Schumann, *On Music and Musicians*, ed. Konrad Wolff, trans. Paul Rosenfeld (Berkeley, 1983), p. 253.

in his scores, supporting Wagner as a critic, and advocating the founding of Vienna's Wagner Society. Later, however, Goldmark recanted his opinions, declined to join the Society, and befriended Brahms. His *Ouverture zum* Gefesselten Prometheus *des Aeschylos*, Op. 38 (1889) accordingly reflects a shift from overt to attenuated programmaticism. Both overtures thus appropriate a progressive subject—Prometheus, mankind's champion—to promote a conservative agenda.

Bargiel

Nearly forgotten today, Bargiel was famous during his lifetime as a widely performed composer, distinguished teacher, and conductor of prestigious ensembles in Cologne, Rotterdam, and his native Berlin. In childhood he began piano, harmony, and perhaps organ and violin lessons with his father, August Adolph Bargiel, who ran a music boarding school in Berlin.[13] After August died in 1838, the ten-year-old Woldemar continued his training at Berlin Cathedral, where he studied organ, violin, and counterpoint, the latter with the eminent theorist Siegfried Wilhelm Dehn, and sang in a choir directed by Mendelssohn and August Grell.[14] His mother, Mariane (née Tromlitz) Wieck, had performed as pianist and singer in Leipzig's Gewandhaus, impressive credentials allowing her to support her family as a music teacher following August's death.[15] She had divorced the piano pedagogue Friedrich Wieck in 1824, five years after the birth of their second child, Clara, who would become one of the century's greatest pianists and Schumann's wife. Thus Woldemar was Clara's half-brother and Schumann's brother-in-law.

The Schumanns decisively influenced Bargiel's career. After their marriage in 1840, they monitored his talent's progress when he and his siblings regularly visited Leipzig, affording Mariane respite from single parenthood.[16] In 1846 Bargiel heeded Robert's vocational advice and entered the Leipzig Conservatory with a scholarship arranged by Mendelssohn, now the school's inaugural director, who had assembled a largely conservative faculty.[17] Bargiel received orthodox training in counterpoint with Moritz Hauptmann, composition with Gade and Julius Rietz, piano with Ignaz Moscheles and Louis Plaidy, and violin with Ferdinand David and Joachim,[18] most of whom subsequently condemned Liszt's program music when it was performed

---

[13]   Karl Debruis van Bruyck, "Woldemar Bargiel," *Niederrheinische Musik-Zeitung für Kunstfreunde und Künstler*, 7 (1859): 405–6.

[14]   Bernhard Hoeft, *Berühmte Männer und Frauen Berlins und ihre Grabstätten* (Berlin, 1919), p. 175.

[15]   Joachim Draheim, "Schumanns Schwager Woldemar Bargiel als Komponist," in Bernhard R. Appell (ed.), *Schumann Forschungen*, vol. 2, *"Neue Bahnen": Robert Schumann und seine musikalische Zeitgenossen* (Mainz, 1997), p. 144.

[16]   Robert Schumann, *Tagebücher*, ed. Gerd Nauhaus (3 vols, Leipzig, 1988), vol. 2, pp. 94, 232–4, 404; vol. 3, pp. 220–21, 464–5, 501–2, 514, 522, 531, 598–601.

[17]   van Bruyck, "Biographisches: Woldemar Bargiel," *Musikalisches Wochenblatt*, 2 (1871): 424.

[18]   Edward Dannreuther and Elisabeth Schmiedel, "Bargiel, Woldemar," in *The New Grove Dictionary of Music and Musicians*, vol. 2, p. 727.

in Leipzig throughout the 1850s. After Bargiel graduated, the Schumanns remained mentors. Robert recommended his compositions to publishers and numbered him among "the most aspiring artists of recent times" when he revised "New Paths" for inclusion in his collected writings in 1856.[19] Clara played his works during private soirees and fostered his relationship with Brahms. With such powerful support, Bargiel was poised to flourish professionally.

In 1850 Bargiel returned to Berlin to teach privately. His grueling composition curriculum entailed harmony, chorales, canons, and fugues, while his ambitious piano repertoire comprised technical exercises, Czerny's etudes, Clementi's *Gradus ad Parnassum*, the *Well-Tempered Clavier*, nearly every Beethoven sonata, and scores by Schumann, Chopin, and others.[20] Bargiel's rigor secured piano and theory appointments at the Cologne Conservatory in 1859. Six years later he assumed the directorship of the Maatschappij tot Bevordering der Toonkunst, Rotterdam's premiere musical institute, spurring the Bach revival in the Low Countries by programming excerpts from the *St. Matthew Passion* in 1870.[21] That year he married into a prominent Dutch musical family and would probably have remained in Rotterdam, but in 1874 Joachim requested he teach composition at Berlin's Hochschule für Musik. Bargiel accepted, becoming professor at the Akademie der Künste, directing the Berliner Bachverein, collaborating with Brahms in editing the complete works of Chopin and Schumann, and producing distinguished students, including the pianist Leopold Godowsky, the Liszt scholar Peter Raabe, and the musicologist Johannes Wolf, all before succumbing to a heart attack in 1897.[22]

Bargiel was a close colleague of Schumann, Brahms, and Joachim, but not their mere epigone. Scores completed as a student in Leipzig and young teacher in Berlin predictably disclose influences of his brother-in-law and the Conservatory's faculty. His individual style nonetheless developed quickly, as critics often noted. In 1851 a reviewer for the *Signale für die musikalische Welt* praised the clearly expressed content of Bargiel's first published opus, a set of character pieces, especially the "anguished yearning" of the first.[23] Writing for the *Niederrheinische Musik-Zeitung* in 1859, Karl Debruis van Bruyck likewise cited "sober pathos" as "the overriding

---

[19]   See, for example, Schumann's letter to Raimund Härtel in *Robert Schumann's Briefe, Neue Folge*, ed. F. Gustav Jansen (Leipzig, 1886), p. 385; Schumann named no composers when he published "Neue Bahnen" in the *Neue Zeitschrift* in 1853, but added them in his collected writings. His oft-quoted phrase, "hochaufstrebenden Künstlern der jüngsten Zeit," appears in *Gesammelte Schriften über Musik und Musiker von Robert Schumann*, ed. Martin Kreisig (2 vols, Leipzig, 1914), vol. 2, p. 301.

[20]   Ernest Rudorff, *Aus den Tagen der Romantik: Bildnis einer deutschen Familie*, ed. Elisabeth Rudorff (Leipzig, 1938), pp. 213–14.

[21]   Emile Wennekes, "Nachwelt im Nachbarland: Aspekte der Bach-Pflege in den Niederlanden, ca. 1850–2000," *Rijdschrift van de Koninklijke Vereniging voor Nederlandse Muziekgeschidenis*, 50/1–2 (2000): 111, 114.

[22]   Dannreuther and Schmiedel, p. 727; Sabine Stahr, "Bargiel, (George Louis August) Woldemar," in Ludwig Fischer (ed.), *Die Musik in Geschichte und Gegenwart: Personenteil*, 2nd edn (14 vols, Kassel, 1994-), vol. 2, pp. 246–7.

[23]   Ker., "Zwei neue Componisten und ihre ersten Werke," *Signale für die musikalische Welt*, 9/21 (1851): 194.

fundamental tone" of Bargiel's music.[24] A year later van Bruyck lauded Bargiel's "individually distinct forms," which, more so than Schumann's works, emphasized "elaboration of detail" and exhibited "surprising harmonic combinations."[25] Hermann Deiters, contributing to the *Allgemeine musikalische Zeitung*, acknowledged the debt Bargiel's first few opus numbers owed Schumann, but also maintained his originality had emerged as early as 1854 in his Suite in C major, Op. 7 and his *Fantasiestücke*, Op. 9.[26] His "truly creative talent," Deiters avowed, derived from his "sense of melodic charm, rhythmic proportion, innate harmonic beauty," and, once again, "a pathetic element, dark, somber, but with the glow of passion," all emanating from "the magic circle of his individual thoughts and musings."[27] Perhaps both writers underscored Bargiel's individuality as part of an ongoing critical campaign to validate a moderate Schumann school steeped in the expression of inner content, distinct from more conservative Mendelssohnians and more progressive New Germans, but Bargiel's mentors also noticed his swift development.[28]

After performing his Piano Trio in F major, Op. 6 for invited auditors on 28 May 1852, Clara Schumann told him it was "haunted ... by a bit of Mendelssohn, but at the same time everything is so characteristically your own that one takes great pleasure in it."[29] Robert reacted enthusiastically to another private reading on 31 January 1853, deeming the trio the "most characteristically personal of his earlier works, marking absolutely enormous progress."[30] Joachim likewise discerned Bargiel's growth between 1849, when his String Octet's first movement impressed the Leipzig Conservatory's faculty, and September 1852, when additional movements "significantly complemented [and] strengthened it."[31] In 1853 Joachim commended Bargiel's *Characterstücke*, Op. 8, particularly the reharmonization of successive statements of the second movement's opening theme, which Joachim considered "just as new as it is beautiful."[32] And Brahms, after scrutinizing Bargiel's *Characterstücke*, Op. 1 and *Bagatellen*, Op. 4 in August 1854, exclaimed, "What fine first works, and what rapid progress," a compliment he repeated five months later regarding Bargiel's Opp. 8 and 9.[33]

---

[24]   van Bruyck, "Woldemar Bargiel," (1859): 406.

[25]   van Bruyck, "Woldemar Bargiel," *Deutsche Musik-Zeitung*, 1 (1860): 4.

[26]   Hermann Deiters, "Woldemar Bargiel," *Allgemeine musikalische Zeitung*, 2/27 (1864): 466–8.

[27]   Ibid., 2/26, p. 443.

[28]   See the editor's commentary to Adolf Schubring, "Schumanniana No. 4: The Present Musical Epoch and Robert Schumann's Position in Music History [1861]," in R. Larry Todd (ed.), *Schumann and his World* (Princeton, 1994), p. 362.

[29]   See her otherwise unpublished letter of 5 June 1852 to Woldemar in Draheim, p. 149.

[30]   See his otherwise unpublished letter of 1 February 1853 to Mariane Bargiel in Draheim, p. 149.

[31]   Johannes Joachim and Andreas Moser (eds), *Briefe von und an Joseph Joachim* (3 vols, Berlin, 1911), vol. 1, p. 34.

[32]   Ibid., vol. 1, p. 71.

[33]   *Johannes Brahms: Life and Letters*, ed. Styra Avins, trans. Josef Eisinger and Styra Avins (Oxford, 1997), pp. 60, 84.

Schumann and Joachim acted as consultants for Bargiel's first orchestral compositions. As early as 16 November 1849, Schumann reluctantly judged an overture Bargiel had sent him impractical for performance, despite much that was characteristically his own.[34] Schumann urged Bargiel to exploit powerful middle registers of instruments, particularly the oboe, and avoid extreme ranges. A month later Bargiel acknowledged Schumann's advice, conceded the overture was his first effort in orchestration, and vowed to improve.[35] In March 1853, after gaining experience by transcribing the overture to Schumann's opera, *Genoveva*, for piano four-hands, Bargiel presented his mentor with his *Ouverture zu Prometheus*.[36] It apparently elicited approval, since Bargiel subsequently sent it to Joachim, who studied the score in January 1854, admired "the magnificent work most deeply," but deferred writing more about it because of pressing engagements.[37] Three months later Joachim apologized for not returning the overture, praised its "noble power of spirit," and again postponed discussing details until their reunion the following summer.[38] Joachim's tantalizing analysis thus went unrecorded, although he and Schumann probably offered further counsel regarding the overture, not only because Bargiel revised it three times before publishing it in 1865, but also because Joachim's plan to write a Prometheus symphony reflects keen interest in the subject.[39]

Concert overtures were relatively new when Bargiel turned to the genre. Early in the nineteenth century, overtures by Beethoven, Cherubini, Weber, and others often appeared in concert venues, briefly introducing programs that featured long virtuoso concertos and even longer symphonies with increasing regularity.[40] These works, however, typically originated in the theater, as in Beethoven's *Leonore* and *Coriolanus* Overtures, Cherubini's *Les Deux journées*, and Weber's *Der Beherrscher der Geister*, or in festive occasions, as in Beethoven's *Namensfeier* and *Die Weihe des Hauses* and Weber's *Jubel-Ouvertüre*.[41] The first major composer to write truly autonomous concert overtures and indisputably provide models for later contributors to the genre was Mendelssohn. As a teenager he completed several theatrical and occasional overtures, but in 1826, probably inspired by A.W. Schlegel's reissued Shakespearean translations, he composed his Overture to *A Midsummer Night's Dream* with no prospect of the play's performance.[42]

---

[34] *Robert Schumann's Briefe, Neue Folge*, pp. 316–17. Three manuscripts at the Staatsbiblothek zu Berlin Preußischer Kulturbesitz (D-Bsb Mus. Ms. Autogr. W. Bargiel 4, 5, and 6 N) indicate the overture (apparently a revision of the one first presented to Schumann) existed in three versions, the first and second dated December 1852 and lacking any reference to Prometheus, the third October 1854; Bargiel revised the score for its premiere in Aachen in 1859. See Bärbel Pelker, *Die deutsche Konzertouvertüre (1825–1865): Werkkatalog und Rezeptionsdokumente* (2 vols, Frankfurt, 1993), vol. 1, pp. 92–4.

[35] See his otherwise unpublished letter of 17 December 1879 in Draheim, p. 147.

[36] Draheim, p. 148.

[37] Johannes Joachim and Moser, vol. 1, p. 166.

[38] Ibid., vol. 1, pp. 188–9.

[39] Ibid., vol. 1, p. 208.

[40] Thomas Grey, "The Orchestral Music," in Douglass Seaton (ed.), *The Mendelssohn Companion* (Westport, Conn., 2001), p. 461.

[41] Todd, p. 2.

[42] Ibid., pp. 11–12.

Indeed, the opportunity to embellish Shakespeare's comedy with incidental music did not arise until 1843, when Ludwig Tieck produced it in Berlin. Thus the overture was neither theatrical nor occasional in nature, but instead evoked or embodied salient aspects of its subject, most obviously the fleet-footed scampering of fairies, Shakespeare's paired lovers, and Bottom's braying.[43] The score accordingly functioned not as an overture "to" the play, as Thomas Grey observes, but rather as a "surrogate" for it, and consequently assumed responsibility for conveying the drama's essence.[44]

Mendelssohn's later concert overtures and Berlioz's contemporary counterparts functioned similarly. *Meeresstille und glückliche Fahrt* (1828) was no prologue to Goethe's coupled poems, nor did Berlioz's *Waverley* (1828) and *Rob Roy* (1831) preface readings of Scott's novels. They instead invoked essential literary ideas with musical depictions of various degrees of materiality. Mendelssohn then radically eliminated a literary subject in *The Hebrides* (1830), an overture verifiably inspired by western Scotland's bleak landscape, specifically a grotto on the island of Staffa nicknamed Fingal's Cave, not John Macpherson's Ossianic epic, *Fingal* (1763), despite resonances between compositional features and the poem's incidents or setting.[45] The score is consequently more often discreet than explicit in representing primitive scenery with stark parallel fifths, swelling ocean waves with repetitive yet varied figuration, and the grotto's open space with harmonic stasis and textural transparency. *Die schöne Melusine* (1833) likewise eschews or obscures a connection with one literary model. Franz Grillparzer's version of the oft-told story of a water nymph's ill-fated encounter with a mortal prince is frequently posited as the score's stimulus, but Mendelssohn disclaimed any single literary source while admonishing his sister Fanny in tones only half facetious for asking which of the tale's renderings was pertinent.[46] Musical events broadly correlate with narrative episodes, but Mendelssohn abjured precise poetic associations, confirming his non-imitational aesthetic. He ultimately reverted to dramatic overtures "to" stage works at the Berlin court, including Victor Hugo's play, *Ruy Blas* (1839).

As encapsulations of literary works or landscapes, concert overtures infused an orchestral medium normally cast in sonata form with romanticism's "poetic" content. In accommodating this new content, however, the standard sonata design typically underwent various structural "deformations," as James Hepokoski designates them, while themes often experienced transformation, a practice rooted in Beethoven's symphonies and already apparent in Mendelssohn's scores.[47] The basic Mendelssohnian concept of the concert overture as a poetic subject's embodiment,

---

[43]   Todd (pp. 72–3) refers to A.B. Marx's account of the overture, which specifies associations for six motives.

[44]   Grey, p. 461.

[45]   While visiting Scotland in 1829, Mendelssohn sketched the overture's opening in a letter to his family. See Grey, p. 470. Todd (pp. 79–91) discounts correspondences between the overture and Macpherson's poem.

[46]   Felix Mendelssohn Bartholdy, *Briefe aus den Jahren 1833 bis 1847*, ed. Paul Mendelssohn Bartholdy and Carl Mendelssohn Bartholdy (2 vols, Leipzig, 1863), vol. 2, pp. 36–7.

[47]   Hepokoski derives five structural "deformations" from the traditional discipline of *Formenlehre* in *Sibelius: Symphony No. 5*, Cambridge Music Handbooks, ed. Julian Rushton (Cambridge, 1993), pp. 5–8.

plus sonata form's attendant modifications, clearly inform many scores that were inspired by *A Midsummer Night's Dream*, *Meeresstille und glückliche Fahrt*, and *The Hebrides*, especially after Mendelssohn published them as independent compositions, bound in one volume, in 1835.[48] Bargiel's overture, like those of his mentors, furnishes a prime example.

Bargiel's title, *Ouverture zu Prometheus für grosses Orchester* [Overture to Prometheus for large Orchestra], alludes to no specific literary model. Whether the Titan is bound or unbound is not even indicated, as the Cologne critic Ludwig Bischoff noted after hearing the overture in 1865.[49] Likewise omitted is any authorial reference comparable to Goldmark's Aeschylean invocation. Nor does the title unequivocally suggest a German or English romantic version of the myth that German readers of the 1850s may have known, including those of Goethe, Schlegel, Shelley, and Byron. A distinct referent's absence instead implies the overture conveys the legend's essential content, requiring listeners to associate presumably familiar narrative episodes with unfolding musical events. The process involves recognizing categories of characteristic music such as the martial, mournful, pastoral, and hymn-like. Bargiel accordingly avoided a precise stipulation, like Mendelssohn, while seeking to embody a poetic subject, like Schumann. And like many contemporaries, he employed a common deformation of sonata form and thematic transformation.

Table 7.1   Formal Divisions in Bargiel's *Ouverture zum Prometheus für grosses Orchester*, Op. 16

INTRODUCTION: Maestoso					
Theme:	a	b	a′		
Topics	martial	lyrical-pastoral	martial		
	heroic	tattoo	heroic		
	primitivism	retransition to martial			
EXPOSITION: Allegro Moderato ma passionato					stringendo
Th:	Principal (1)	Principal (2)	Transition	Subordinate	Closing
T:	pathos	agitation	dissolution	hymn	pastoral
	lament	fanfares		anthem	anthem
DEVELOPMENT: Tempo I di Allegro					
Th:	Introduction's fanfare, transformed				
T:	Martial transformed by pathos, internalized perspective				
RECAPITULATION					
Th:	Principal (1)	Principal (2)	Transition	Subordinate	Closing

---

48   Todd, p. 1.

49   [Ludwig Bischoff], "Siebentes Gesellschaft-Concert in Köln im Gürzenich," *Niederrheinische Musik-Zeitung für Kunstfreunde und Künstler*, 12 (1865): 38. "The title itself, however, leaves us in doubt whether the composer has in mind the *Prometheus Bound* of Aeschylus or some other poem (Goethe's *Prometheus*?)."

T:	Lament shortened	agitation fanfares	dissolution	hymn anthem	anthem amplified
CODA:	1/1 meter		Maestoso		Più moto
Th:	fanfares/rapid bass		martial introduction		fanfares
T:	*Sturmmarsch*		martial-heroic		
			primitive/pastoral omitted		

The overture preserves and enhances conventional sonata form's symmetry (Table 7.1). Its slow introduction supplies thematic material that recurs twice, first as the primary motive of a brief passage serving as a development section, then in the longer coda. Formal events in the main body of the work observe customary order. A standard exposition's clearly differentiated principal theme, transition, subordinate theme, and closing area appear in the recapitulation with one change, an abbreviation of the principal and subordinate themes typical of Mendelssohn's symphonic scores.[50] Otherwise the recapitulation merely transposes the exposition and varies several details of orchestration and part writing. Thus Bargiel's overture exemplifies Hepokoski's second deformation:

> *The introduction-coda frame.* This procedure gives the effect of subordinating 'sonata activity' to the overriding contents of an encasing introduction and coda (whose identity may also intrude into certain inner sections of the 'sonata'). A common result is the furnishing of two levels of aesthetic presence, for example ... that of a fuller, more emphatic framing-reality – or even that of a metaphorically 'present' narrator – which unfolds a subordinate sonata-process, that is eventually absorbed back into the original, fuller presence at its end.[51]

Bargiel's design—shaped by an "emphatic framing reality" that usurps a development's role and thereby subordinates "sonata activity" to its own, fuller self-realization in a coda—had notable precedents that Bargiel undoubtedly knew: the first movement of Mendelssohn's "Scottish" Symphony; his Overture to *A Midsummer Night's Dream*, with its celebrated opening woodwind chords; the first movement of Schubert's Ninth Symphony, rediscovered by Schumann in Vienna in 1838, conducted by Mendelssohn at the Gewandhaus in 1839, and extolled in the *Neue Zeitschrift für Musik* in 1840; and the archetypal opening movement of Beethoven's "Pathétique" Sonata.[52] The character, order, and transformation of the overture's component parts—plus an unusual tonal plan—illuminate Bargiel's reading of the myth.

Comprising 49 of the overture's 550 measures, the introduction's open ternary form (ABA′) observes classical practice by leading from the tonic to the dominant. As a critic for the *Allgemeine musikalische Zeitung* noted, its first section establishes a martial character with diatonic harmonies in C major, common-time meter,

---

[50]   Grey, p. 475.

[51]   Hepokoski, p. 6.

[52]   Regarding the respective references to Mendelssohn, Schumann, and Beethoven, see Todd, pp. 73, 96–7; Robert Schumann, *Schumann on Music: A Selection from the Writings*, ed. Henry Pleasants (New York, 1988), pp. 163–8; Hepokoski, p. 94.

Example 7.1   Bargiel *Ouverture zu Prometheus für grosses Orchester*, mm. 1-10.

Example 7.1 concluded.

accented dotted rhythms, triadic triplet fanfares, periodic phrasing suited to a slow march, and prominent brasses and timpani (Example 7.1).[53] But as the bass line descends from C to B-flat to A, the seemingly deliberate primitivism of parallel fifths colors the overtly military topic, plausibly evoking the subject's antiquity, just as Mendelssohn's comparably raw voice leading depicts Scotland's primal landscape. Four measures later the bass line's longer descent (C–B-flat–A–A-flat–G) foreshadows the exposition's opening key (C minor) through modal borrowing and underpins a quotation from Beethoven's Promethean overture, as later discussion demonstrates. The character of the introduction's contrasting central section is equally clear (Example 7.2). Forte dynamics suddenly decrease to piano, while the full orchestra yields to paired horns playing in parallel thirds above a dominant pedal. The instrumentation, melodic parallelism, and drone suggest a pastoral idiom, as the entry of bucolic oboes and clarinets, likewise coupled in thirds, confirms. Another credible antique association would link sylvan musical features with Arcadian images frequently encountered in eighteenth- and nineteenth-century mythological paintings. Pianissimo timpani strokes nonetheless taint the idyllic interlude with dotted tattoo figures traditionally played on muffled side drums during funeral processions.

The introduction's primary gestures reveal essential traits of Bargiel's Prometheus. He is heroic, as military music inevitably implies; but his heroism is tempered by a pastoral agent, often the means whereby protagonists overcome obstacles to self-realization, and a mournful element that ostensibly embodies some darker aspect of the myth, perhaps the Titan's laments during his punishment.[54] More broadly, the martial procession is communal, as its tutti orchestration affirms, whereas the pastoral mode typically suits individual expression, as reduced scoring indicates, and affords "a metaphorically 'present' narrator" entry into the discourse. Both engagements—heroism's mediation by pastoral and funereal agents, and the dialogue between community and individual—gain importance in the impending sonata form, but only after a transition, featuring layered scales that display the tattoo's rhythms, leads to the martial-heroic opening's condensed reprise.

Although the introduction ends with a minor ninth (A-flat) repeatedly embellishing the dominant triad, the exposition's parallel minor mode still seems somewhat unexpected following long martial and pastoral episodes in C major. Redolent of the pathos of Beethoven's aptly subtitled sonata and the "Eroica's" *Marcia funebre*, the somber key of C minor allowed Bargiel to cultivate his music's "overriding fundamental tone." Fittingly, the principal theme resembles a lament (Example 7.3). Its melodic profile, involving two stepwise descents (E-flat–D, D–C) interrupted by a leap, recalls madrigalesque depictions of sobbing, an effect enhanced by tenebrous orchestration exploiting low strings and the darkest woodwinds, clarinets and bassoons. An equally pathos-laden response from the first violins prominently features

---

53   [unsigned], "Recensionen: Musik für Orchester (Woldemar Bargiel: *Ouvertüre zu Prometheus für grosses Orchester*)," *Allgemeine musikalische Zeitung*, 3/5 (1865): 9. "A broadly disposed introduction ... in the rhythms of a slow march begins the work."

54   Ibid. "A solo of two horns in C, accompanied by solemn short drum rolls and answered by oboes and clarinets, then seems to want to produce a milder element."

Example 7.2   Bargiel *Ouverture zu Prometheus für grosses Orchester*, mm. 19–26

a tritone (C–F-sharp), the harsh, quintessential interval of mournful outcries. As the remaining strings restate the theme, the first violins incessantly repeat their answer, while the woodwinds play sustained sigh figures—literal exhalations emphasized by hairpin dynamics. The precipitous tempo, however, imbues the theme with a breathlessness more fully realized in the ensuing tutti passage's agitation. Tracing wide, largely triadic arcs, the strings play continuous tremolos that externalize another psychological state, equating rapid, repetitive physical movements with inner turmoil. Brasses respond by reiterating one pitch in dotted rhythms, abstractions of the introduction's martial triadic fanfares. Occasionally interrupted by ascending scales in the strings, the agitated calls and militant replies alternate expansively, developing motives through imitation and reducing the interval between antiphonal statements—a passage the reviewer for the *Allgemeine musikalische Zeitung* linked with the Titan's misfortunes and defiance.[55] Less materially, but still within a heroic context, the principal theme's commonly encountered bifurcation suggests the individual's plight (the lament) has acquired communal proportions (tutti), a reading compatible with extreme contrasts in literary epics.

Example 7.3   Bargiel *Ouverture zu Prometheus für grosses Orchester*, mm. 60–67

---

55   Ibid. "… the overture is occupied partly with demonic, gloomy, sorrowful minor sounds that seem to want to indicate the Titan's revolt against the humanity-hating Zeus, penetrated with chromatically mournful melodies that perhaps should also suggest suffering."

The tutti's ending converts the major tonic triad into a secondary dominant of F minor, a peculiar harmonic inflection portending unusual events in the exposition's tonal trajectory and initiating a dissipative process that constitutes the transition's main activity. After a horn fanfare punctuates the lament's slow-moving motives, woodwinds fulfill the transition's all-important function, establishing the new key. The woodwinds repeat chords in progressively slower note values, modulating with considerable surface chromaticism from F minor to D-flat major, where the subordinate theme unfolds idiosyncratically in the overture's Neapolitan key.

Advancing the heroic narrative's progress, the subordinate theme serves the broad purpose of reintegration, made especially necessary by the dissolutive transition. A new synthesis emerges as the orchestra emulates hymnody, the quintessential style of choral utterances in religious ceremonies (Example 7.4). The theme's chorale-like texture consists of four real parts, with a fifth doubling one voice or moving among lines. Confirming the religious topic are an organ-like pedal point, four-measure phrasing, and a wordless strophic structure. Strings and bassoons play the opening stanza; woodwinds join the first violins in another verse as the second violins and violas add animated triplets; and brasses reinforce the third statement. Thus the hymn strengthens during three increasingly elaborate presentations that duplicate the instrumental sequence of Beethoven's *Ode to Joy* and the principal theme Brahms later adopted in his First Symphony's finale. It accordingly retraces a familiar path from an individual's intimate prayer to the congregation's unanimous anthem, an integrative process nonetheless remaining incomplete. Pervasive chromaticism and occasionally ambiguous tonality, both foreign to celebratory chorales such as the well-known examples of Beethoven and Brahms, require simplification and clarification. And the key, D-flat major, is far removed from the anticipated dominant, G, or relative major, E-flat. The ensuing passage addresses both issues.

The concluding area, marked *poco a poco stringendo e crescendo*, contains little new thematic material. Instead, short chorale motives rise sequentially, alternating with nondescript figuration that gradually coalesces in brass fanfares. As momentum increases, the hymn's first complete phrase rematerializes in a diatonic, pastoral guise, replete with open fifths played by bucolic horns and clarinets (Example 7.5). Musical pastoralisms, increasingly pervasive fanfares, and repeated *stringendo* markings imbue the hymn with secular qualities better suited to public ceremonies than church services. The hymn accordingly mediates between the lament and its dissolution on the one hand, and martial heroism's restoration on the other. Moreover, the advent of the hymn's pastoral incarnation coincides with similarly integrative tonal events. When the bass line shifts from D-flat to C, horns and clarinets tonicize F, the key that ended the first theme's tutti passage, though the implicit resolution is now to the major, not the minor mode. After F major briefly reappears, the bass line descends chromatically to D, where a long pedal tone prepares G, the overture's dominant. Fortissimo woodwind chords, brass fanfares, and string arpeggios then herald the arrival of sonata form's conventional secondary key. A private, devotional hymn's transformation into a public, secular celebration, plus a purging of chromaticism in achieving a tonal goal, indicate progress toward reintegration, though impending events suggest a reconciliation of such epic contrasts requires another perspective.

As dynamics plunge to pianissimo, clarinets and bassoons play a two-octave scalewise descent in parallel thirds, adopting increasingly slower rhythms until only

Example 7.4   Bargiel *Ouverture zu Prometheus für grosses Orchester*, mm. 166–86

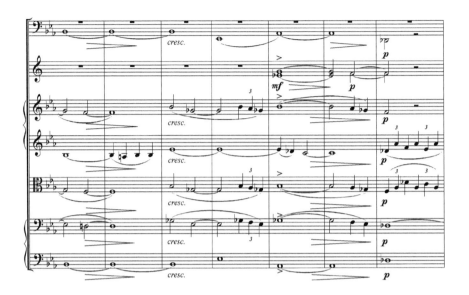

Example 7.4 concluded.

Hörner in C.

Example 7.5   Bargiel *Ouverture zu Prometheus für grosses Orchester*,
             mm. 220–23

a dominant pedal tone reverberates. Then, precisely when convention mandates development of the sonata form's themes, the introduction's fanfares return, again played by trumpets and manipulated rhythmically to reproduce the overture's inaugural tempo, but otherwise transformed (Example 7.6). Their tonic minor key recalls the principal theme's pathos, an allusion strengthened by falling semitones in responsorial trombones, instruments associated with solemn religious rites, especially the requiem. Only the fanfares and the trombones' initial chords barely exceed the accompaniment's subdued dynamics, maintained by *sempre pianissimo* markings as the ersatz development proceeds. Moreover, thinly scored tremolos and pedal points support the fanfares, not the full orchestra, internalizing the introduction's communal procession. Thus the "metaphorically 'present' narrator" reemerges at a crucial juncture in the sonata process, invoking an archetypal parallel in heroic narratives, whereby the protagonist's introspection yields a new perspective on a situation or action. In the Prometheus myth, the Titan's laments and pleas for personal deliverance shift to eternal defiance against the Olympians and altruism toward humanity, a reading congruent with the recapitulation's formal variants.

A facile tonic reprise seems imminent when the initial trumpet fanfare outlines a six-four chord in C minor, but the trombones deflect the tonality toward D minor, where woodwinds restate the fanfare sequentially. After the D-minor triad acquires a lowered fifth (A-flat) and a new root (B-natural), the resulting diminished seventh chord tonicizes another six-four and dominant that resolve to F minor. Still marked pianissimo, the recapitulation begins surreptitiously in the subdominant, a common strategy of classical composers, notably Mozart and Schubert. Slightly more unusual yet consistent with Mendelssohnian practice is that the principal theme begins in its fifteenth measure, thereby omitting many stepwise descents and plaintive tritones that originally defined the lament. Instead, only ten of the theme's lyrical measures are restated before the tutti comprising its second part erupts in C minor. Tonal displacement and thematic compression accordingly reduce the lament's status in the heroic action.

Much of the remaining recapitulation, as noted, merely transposes previous material, although tonal irregularities support the heroic narrative. The agitated, martial tutti ends forcefully in C minor, perhaps simply furnishing tonal closure the exposition lacks, but also feasibly suggesting inner turmoil and militant defiance are more stable attributes of Bargiel's Prometheus than the lament's pathos. A mode change could readily facilitate the subordinate theme's presentation in the parallel major, a tactic Beethoven's Symphony in C minor famously deploys. Instead the transition modulates to the relative major, E-flat, where the hymn's first two verses recur without significant variation. Its third, emphatic brass setting, however, is missing. These tonal and formal

Example 7.6   Bargiel *Ouverture zu Prometheus für grosses Orchester*, mm. 282–9

anomalies function analogously. E-flat major is closely related to the tonic, especially compared to the exposition's foray into D-flat, but not the tonic itself, demanding further tonal resolution to integrate the subordinate theme into the sonata structure. Similarly, the hymn must don its celebratory guise to regain its standing as a secular, communal anthem. The concluding area achieves both goals.

All the concluding area's motives and fanfares recur in the major mode above a pedal tone on G, thus prolonging anticipation of the major tonic. Soon, however, the hymn's first phrase emerges with its pastoral traits restored, played by horns and trumpets, not clarinets and horns as in the exposition. The recapitulation's tasks accordingly seem complete: the subordinate theme has appeared in the tonic with brassy scoring. But because these events transpire above a dominant pedal, final resolution awaits the bass line's arrival on C, which initiates a two-part coda.

Rather than collapsing in the diminuendo and scalewise descent that ended the exposition, the concluding area gains momentum with an accelerando, fortissimo brass fanfares, and ascending scales in the strings. The coda then restores the maestoso introduction's major key signature, but not its tempo (Example 7.7). Instead the new meter signature and metronome marking establish a pace approximately twice that of the exposition's allegro. As brass fanfares regain triadic outlines, strings repeat a short stepwise descent (C–B–A–G) 16 times. Thus the coda embodies the double-time attack or *Sturmmarsch* encountered in characteristic battle symphonies, whose conclusions often depict synchronized movements of massed soldiers charging to victory.[56] A comparable assault closes Beethoven's Fifth Symphony (Presto), likewise marking a heroic trajectory's final phase.[57] Bargiel's march, however, leads not to Beethoven's notoriously repetitive tonic chords, but rather to the maestoso introduction's reprise, varied only by the bass line's arpeggiation in dotted rhythms. The metaphorical narrative presence thus returns in its original martial guise, suggesting the hero's quest has come full circle after negotiating stages of grief, agitation, dissolution, reintegration, reevaluation, and reconstitution. Accordingly omitted are the funereal and pastoral elements that instigated discourse between the individual and the communal as the overture began. Instead the coda ends with antiphonal fanfares, played by one choir of brasses and timpani and another of strings and woodwinds, and unison tonic chords.

Bargiel's overture adeptly defines and manipulates standard topics, especially considering it is his earliest orchestral work. Its sequence of diverse characters—martial, pastoral, funereal, pathos-laden, agitated, plus the hymn and the *Sturmmarsch*—easily reconciles with an abstraction of the Prometheus myth. Immediately established as a hero, the Titan endures trials, regroups, reconsiders past events, casts aside personal tribulations, and attains self-realization through benevolence toward humanity, reproducing stages in the archetypal heroic narrative. In a common deformation of sonata form, the main body of the overture is enclosed within a framing introduction and coda whose martial fanfare experiences

---

[56]   Will, p. 193.

[57]   Beethoven's *Egmont* Overture likewise concludes with a *Sturmmarsch*. An anonymous reviewer ("Recensionen: Musik für Orchester," p. 9) drew another apt comparison with the central section of Chopin's Polonaise in A-flat major.

Example 7.7   Bargiel *Ouverture zu Prometheus für grosses Orchester*, mm. 493–6

transformation in a truncated development section, signifying the protagonist's internalization of a formerly communal gesture. Another transformation converts the congregational hymn into a universal anthem, again illustrating a shift between private and collective domains. The overture's generalized extramusical content, its subordination of sonata activity to a structural deformation, and the recapitulation's thematic compression have notable precedents in Mendelssohn's symphonic works, confirming Bargiel's successful assimilation of his mentor's practices. Another palpable influence nonetheless accounts for the overture's monumental tone: Beethoven.

Two previously mentioned features of Bargiel's score recall passages in two Beethoven finales, namely the thrice-stated hymn, as in the Ninth Symphony, and the coda's *Sturmmarsch*, as in the Fifth. More broadly, the fully orchestrated military procession, the principal theme's pathos, and extreme contrasts among formal sections have many counterparts in Beethoven's middle-period works, which provided imposing models for nineteenth-century composers. Bargiel and his colleagues were aware of Beethoven's orchestral legacy and its bearing on the concert overture, as Joachim affirmed in a letter he attached to his *Hamlet-Ouverture* and sent to Bargiel on 7 April 1853:

Hamlet is usually called an unmusical subject; people observe Hamlet reflects a great deal. But this reflecting is ... the necessary escape from the restlessness that constantly disturbs his inner self. What drives him—the eternally powerful urge toward action, the deep sorrow connected with it, that this grand longing toward realization of innermost life in outward relationships must powerlessly bleed to death in futility—has doubtless penetrated every human heart, is a universally human feeling, and therefore musical.

Beethoven is the eternal model; he was more than any other a profound judge of the human soul. He is the musical Shakespeare. ... His themes remain his only friends his entire spiritual life; they accompany him everywhere as confidantes, and thus the entire warmth of his rich feeling automatically imprints itself on them. Hence the variety, the liveliness of the structures, which captivates us so magically ..., which his works exhale upon us with such foreboding.[58]

Thus Beethoven's expression of inner psychological states through audible musical representation furnished a broad aesthetic paradigm for overtures by two members of Schumann's circle. But a final, extremely specific manifestation of Beethoven's influence appears in Bargiel's score. The introduction's disruptive descending bass line supports harmonies that duplicate the opening of Beethoven's Promethean overture, passing from the tonic to the dominant, tonicizing and resolving to the subdominant, and reestablishing the dominant with an augmented sixth chord, an infamous progression listeners attuned to the mythic subject should have recognized (Example 7.8). Nineteenth-century critics, however, failed to notice it on several occasions.

Before the overture's publication in 1865, it received only three performances, in Aachen (1861), Cologne (1864), and Leipzig (1865).[59] The conservative Cologne critic Ludwig Bischoff rebuked Bargiel for cultivating "all too serious, indeed, melancholy subjects," which hindered an appreciation of "clear beautiful form, as with Haydn and others," and instead caused "the general public" to accustom itself to "sonorous impressions and garish effects" and regard "instrumental noise as beautiful."[60] Following the performance by Leipzig's Euterpe Musikverein, an initialed critique in the *Neue Zeitschrift für Musik* predictably disclosed contrasting, progressive views. Its author insisted the aesthetic-technical sense of the overture remained unclear because Bargiel had forced poetic substance into an old form without summarizing the subject.[61] Detecting defiant resistance, wild rebellion, hopeless brooding, and a premonition of rescue and final victory, the journalist claimed the twofold representation of triumph in the dominant and tonic (at the end of the exposition and in the coda) betrayed a lack of inner psychological necessity. Despite generally favorable reactions, the Euterpe Society's dominant conservative faction greeted the overture with whistles, finding its subordinate theme reminiscent of *Tannhäuser*.

Circumstances were reversed in 1885 when Bargiel's score encroached on a progressive venue. As the devoted Liszt pupil August Göllerich recorded, it replaced *Prometheus*, Liszt's symphonic poem, as a prelude to the attendant Herder choruses

---

58   Joachim and Moser, vol. 1, pp. 46–7.
59   Pelker, p. 94. Other performances of the overture occurred in Munich (1869), Prague (1871), Gürzenich (1875), and Leipzig (1880).
60   [Bischoff], p. 38.
61   St., "Correspondenz," *Neue Zeitschrift für Musik*, 61/4 (1865): 31.

Example 7.8   Bargiel *Ouverture zu Prometheus für grosses Orchester*, mm. 14–17

during an annual festival of the Allgemeiner deutscher Musikverein held in Karlsruhe.[62]
Liszt, who in 1861 had co-founded the society as a progressive haven, initially opposed
the scheduling of his music in Karlsruhe, reminding the festival's chairman, Felix
Mottl, that he had never misused the society for frequent performances of his works,
though conceding the *Prometheus* choruses had become staples on its programs.[63] Liszt
relented in time to sanction and attend the concert,[64] but Richard Pohl, author of the
text that connected the choruses during concert performances, maintained an icy silence
regarding Bargiel's overture in an extensive review for the *Neue Zeitschrift für Musik*.[65]

A conservative, absolutist work had infiltrated a bastion of the music of the future.
Its broad poetic content, clear sonata form, competent but conventional orchestration,
and limited reliance on thematic transformation doubtless seemed incongruous amid the
festival's repertoire of compositions by Berlioz, Wagner, Saint-Saëns, Bruckner, and Liszt.
The Beethoven quotation, a vestige of the classical symphonic legacy representing the
limits of programmatic associations and harmonic audacity, must have been an affront, or
perhaps a lesson, to progressive Karlsruhe audiences. Thus the *Ouverture zu Prometheus*,
at least on this occasion, may have provided a cautionary example for unreceptive listeners.
Bargiel's incursion into hostile territory corroborates his lifelong adherence to one set
of aesthetics, developed through early contact with Schumann, studies at the Leipzig
Conservatory, and professional associations with Joachim. His overture, though an early
work, verifies his loyalties. Such is not true of Carl Goldmark, who promoted Wagnerism
in his early writings but later realigned himself with Brahms. His overture accordingly
evinces conflicting impulses regarding explicit poetic content, material imitation, and
sonata form's deformation. It also reveals a very different portrayal of Prometheus.

Goldmark

The claim that Goldmark personified Vienna's transformation from the mere seat of
a pre-revolutionary empire into a modern metropolis, first advanced in Ferdinand
Scherber's preface to Goldmark's autobiography, has informed secondary studies
of the composer.[66] Indeed, beginning in the 1860s his evolution from a promising
virtuoso violinist into one of the Danube monarchy's "most prominent representatives"
mirrored a flowering of cosmopolitan liberalism and economic development that
created New Vienna.[67] Magnificently varied cultural products reflected the era's
predilections for artistic opulence, refined taste, and sensual pleasure. Most tangibly,

---

[62]   August Göllerich, *Franz Liszt: Sonderausgabe der von Richard Strauss
herausgegebenen Sammlung* Die Musik (Berlin, 1908), p. 105.

[63]   *Franz Liszts Briefe*, vol. 8, pp. 416–17.

[64]   Ibid., vol. 7, p. 423.

[65]   Richard Pohl, "Die zweiundzwanstigste Tonkünstler-Versammlung des Allgemeinen
Deutschen Musikvereins in Karlsruhe," *Neue Zeitschrift für Musik*, 81/24 (1885): 262–4.

[66]   Ferdinand Scherber, preface to *Notes from the Life of a Viennese Composer* by Carl
Goldmark, trans. Alice Goldmark Brandeis (New York, 1927), p. vii.

[67]   Gerald Schlag, *Geleitwort* [preface] to *Carl Goldmark (1830–1915): Opernkomponist
der Donaumonarchie, Ausstellung des Burgenländischen Landesmuseums, 10. Juli–15.
September 1996* (Eisenstadt, 1996), n.p.; Gerhard J. Winkler, "Carl Goldmark und die

the new Ringstraße encircled a refurbished inner city with "a riot of gold and color," celebrated when the lavish Hofoper opened in 1869.[68] Soon Hans Makart decorated the Ringstraße's buildings with vibrant, monumental murals whose antique subjects have drawn comparisons with the sumptuous exoticism of Goldmark's best-known work, *Die Königin von Saba*, premiered at the Hofoper in 1875.[69]

But indulgent sensuality, which sank into decadence by the century's end, comprised just one part of the city's rich cultural milieu. Historicism's advent not only helped preserve the legacy of Viennese musical classicism, but also influenced local acceptance of Brahms, recognized as a North-German traditionalist practically the moment he settled in Vienna in 1863.[70] And although Francis Joseph ascended to the emperor's throne amid decisive victories against the Hungarians during the Revolution of 1848 and suppressed nationalist ambitions until he reluctantly accepted a dual monarchy in 1867, his decades-long reign was a period when German, Slavic, and Hungarian artists mingled in the imperial capital.[71] Goldmark's life and music echo these mixed trends: he imitated Mendelssohn and revered Brahms, but assimilated Wagnerian techniques; and his scores disclose traces of the synagogue's liturgy, Hungarian popular and folk idioms, and, in his later years, Impressionism.[72] Thus Goldmark's reputation as the Austro-Hungarian monarchy's leading musical representative rests on works that simultaneously embody the epoch's opulence and amalgamate the Empire's heterogeneous musical dialects. His achievement is even more remarkable in view of his humble origins and his career's deliberate pace.

Born on 18 May 1830 in Deszthely in western Hungary, Goldmark and his family moved to Németkerestúr (now Deutschkreutz in easternmost Austria) near Ödenburg (Sopron) in 1834.[73] He was consequently raised in the present-day Austrian Burgenland, the region that produced Haydn, Liszt, and Joachim. In adulthood he adopted an Austrian national identity, as he confirmed in a vehement appeal for Hanslick to intercede when the Hofoper initially rejected *Die Königin von Saba*.[74] His father was a cantor and notary, positions inadequate to support a wife and 12 of

---

Moderne," in Helen Geyer et al. (eds), *"Denn in jenen Tönen lebt es": Wolfgang Marggraf zum 65* (Weimar, 1999), p. 231.

   [68]   Scherber, p. ix; Max Graf, *Legende einer Musikstadt* (Vienna, 1949), p. 219.

   [69]   Scherber, p. ix; Winkler, "Carl Goldmark: Ein biographischer Abriß," in *Carl Goldmark (1830–1915): Opernkomponist der Donaumonarchie*, p. 9; Winkler, "Carl Goldmark und die Moderne," pp. 230–31.

   [70]   Winkler, "Carl Goldmark und die Moderne," p. 231.

   [71]   Max Graf, p. 215.

   [72]   Regarding Goldmark's limited use of Hungarian idioms, see Maria Párkai-Eckhardt, "Einflusse der ungarischen Musik bei Goldmark," in Susanne Antonicek and Otto Biba (eds), *Brahms-Kongress Wien 1983* (Tutzing, 1988), pp. 427–8. No comparable study of traditional Jewish idioms in Goldmark's music exists, although standard secondary sources invariably refer to the subject. See, for example, Wilhelm Pfannkuch and Gerhard J. Winkler, "Goldmark, Karl," in the *New Grove Dictionary of Music and Musicians*, vol. 10, p. 99.

   [73]   István Kecskeméti clarifies the geographical intricacies in "Liszt und Goldmark im *Ausstellungsalbum ungarischer Tondichter, 1885*," in Renate Grasberger et al. (eds), *Bruckner Symposion: Bruckner und die Musik der Romantik* (Linz, 1989), p. 87.

   [74]   The entire letter is translated in Goldmark, pp. 221–3. See also Scherber, pp. vii–viii.

20 children who survived infancy. Poverty and the town's small size perhaps limited Goldmark's educational opportunities, but his assertion that he had no schooling whatsoever until age 12 is suspect.[75] A cantor's son would have unquestionably learned Hebrew at an early age, especially in an Orthodox community boasting a brand new synagogue and a regionally acclaimed Talmud school.[76] Hence Goldmark's declaration probably pertains to his first formal German-language studies and as such corroborates his thorough assimilation in Austrian culture.[77]

Goldmark's musical education also began inauspiciously at age 11 with violin lessons from a synagogue chorister who coincidentally played the instrument.[78] Impressive progress led to serious studies with the more qualified Anton Eipeldauer at a school connected with the Musikverein in Ödenburg, a two-hour walk from Németkerestúr the 12-year-old Goldmark made twice weekly.[79] A year later his debut on one of the society's concerts was so successful that his parents, determining he should pursue a musical vocation, arranged further training with the noted Viennese pedagogue Leopold Jansa.[80] But despite prudent financial measures, Goldmark's father could pay Jansa's fees for less than two years, obliging his son to consider another profession.[81] In the autumn of 1847 Goldmark entered Vienna's Polytechnic University, but also gained admission to the Conservatory. Disinclined toward general studies, he concentrated on violin lessons with Josef Böhm, whose illustrious pupils included Joachim and Leopold Auer, and theory and harmony instruction with Gottfried Preyer.[82] The latter comprised his first and last systematic training in composition.

On 13 March 1848 revolution broke out in Vienna, closing all institutions of higher learning that traditionally harbored student radicals.[83] Goldmark returned to Németkerestúr on 26 May, never to resume his formal education.[84] Instead he performed for several years in theater orchestras in Ödenburg (1848–9) and Budapest (1850–51), supplementing meager wages with summer employment in Raab, a spa town, in 1849, when his participation in patriotic Hungarian plays and appearance as a soloist on a concert benefiting wounded Hungarian soldiers placed him under suspicion after the Austro-Russian alliance routed the Hungarian army.[85] Indeed, Russian officers detained and nearly executed him, allegedly for insulting Emperor Francis.[86] A calmer seasonal stint in Ofen in 1850 reflected a gradual process of political stabilization that allowed Goldmark to return to Vienna in 1851.

---

[75]   Goldmark, pp. 21–4.
[76]   Winkler, "Carl Goldmark: Ein biographischer Abriß," p. 11.
[77]   Winkler, "Carl Goldmark und die Moderne," p. 232. Likewise signifying Goldmark's assimilation was his denial of a connection between the exoticism of *Die Königin von Saba* and music of the synagogue. See Otto Keller, *Carl Goldmark* (Leipzig, [1901]), p. 17.
[78]   Goldmark, p. 24.
[79]   Ibid.
[80]   Ibid., pp. 30–32.
[81]   Ibid., p. 37.
[82]   Ibid., pp. 44–5.
[83]   Ibid., p. 49.
[84]   Ibid., p. 42.
[85]   Ibid., pp. 61–3, 76–8.
[86]   Ibid., pp. 69–75.

Performing in Viennese theater orchestras until 1857, Goldmark sought collegial advice regarding the idiomatic use of instruments in early works that contributed to his emerging reputation as a composer.[87] He simultaneously earned respect as a teacher, not only of the violin, but also of the piano, a surprising accomplishment since Goldmark claimed he first played the instrument during his brief sojourn in Budapest.[88] Encouraged by mounting success, he hired members of the Hofoper to perform his new compositions, namely an overture, a piano quartet, two lieder, and a psalm setting. The audience hailed the concert on 12 March 1858 with a "friendly reception," though critical response was decidedly mixed.[89] A reviewer for the *Wiener Zeitung* qualified his assessment of Goldmark as the most promising of three new composers who had entered the public arena that season:

> [The piano quartet] may lack the higher artistic character which is granted only occasionally to the chosen few, yet it is ambitious and tastefully fashioned. … Less good may be said of the overture, which suffers from various formal defects; the psalm, like the quartet, discloses Mendelssohn's predominant influence, and of the two lieder … the first, *Der Trompeter an der Katzbach*, if somewhat dry, nonetheless offers … a certain sensible character. Everyone is permitted an attempt if it only proceeds in a not entirely unjustified direction, but Herr Goldmark will probably not deny that in the area of musical production, especially in purely instrumental forms, very few more laurels are to be won presently.[90]

Goldmark later admitted these early works lacked originality and the psalm was "pure Mendelssohn and nothing else," but adverse criticism produced meaningful effects.[91]

After his debut Goldmark lived in Budapest with a sister and her husband, supplementing household income with fees from a few music lessons. He was accordingly free to undertake rigorous daily studies of orthodox compositional treatises by A.B. Marx and Simon Sechter, Eduard Richter's recent counterpoint textbook, Bach's *Well-Tempered Clavier*, and Beethoven's late works.[92] Armed with a new, self-taught technique and bolstered by favorable reactions to a concert of his music in Pest, he permanently returned to Vienna in 1860.[93] His growing renown as a teacher and composer of instrumental works culminated in 1875 with the premiere of *Die Königin von Saba*, initially a modest success that soon acquired a cult following and remained a staple of the operatic repertory in Vienna and Budapest until the 1930s.[94] Although four later operas never achieved similar popularity, they were produced at major European opera houses, and Goldmark's orchestral works, especially the Overtures to *Sakuntala* (1865) and *Penthesilea* (1879) and the "Rustic

---

[87]   Ibid., p. 96.

[88]   Caroline von Gomperz-Bettelheim, "Aus meinem Jugendjahren," in Helene Bettelheim-Gabillon (ed.), *Caroline von Gomperz-Bettelheim: Biographische Blätter* (Vienna, 1915), pp. 2–4.

[89]   Goldmark, p. 101.

[90]   Keller (pp. 7–9) reprints most of the review.

[91]   Goldmark, p. 102.

[92]   Ibid., p. 106.

[93]   Keller, p. 9.

[94]   Robert Werbe, "Königin für 277 Abende: Goldmarks Oper und ihr wienerisches Schicksal," *Österreichische Musikzeitschrift*, 34 (1979): 192–201.

Wedding" Symphony (*Ländliche Hochzeit*, 1876), were widely performed. An esteemed figure in Vienna's cultural life, he received the Ritterkreuz of the Order of St. Leopold in 1896 and numerous international honors after 1900.[95]

Goldmark's rise from provincial poverty to cosmopolitan prestige shaped his basic approach to Prometheus. It not only affected his compositional style, aesthetics, and attitude toward programmaticism, all of which changed as he absorbed new influences, but also contrasted with Bargiel's background, thus producing a different critical orientation. Both composers were theatrical musicians, Goldmark an orchestral player, Bargiel a conductor, but otherwise their careers diverged. Goldmark experienced frequent interruptions in his violin training and was largely self-taught, whereas Bargiel's talent was nurtured by renowned mentors and systematically developed at a conservatory. Goldmark consequently exploited several musical traditions, achieving versatility and success in chamber and symphonic music, numerous songs, many works written for Vienna's choral societies, and especially opera. Bargiel conversely avoided opera, like most *Schumannianer*, and cultivated Schumannesque character pieces, chamber music, and symphonic genres. Bargiel's attendant lifelong adherence to a relatively conservative aesthetic of expressing inner psychological content without explicit specification or overt imitation likewise markedly differs from Goldmark's more flexible engagement with absolute and program music. Goldmark's stance began its evolution in the late 1850s, during his migrations between Vienna and Budapest.

After his compositional debut in 1858, Goldmark admitted he lacked originality, had imitated Mendelssohn, and accordingly withdrew to Budapest, where he steeped himself in conservative theory and composition treatises, Bach's preludes and fugues, and Beethoven's late works. Endeavoring to improve his technique, strengthen his "intellectual capacity," and develop his "melodic sense," Goldmark also articulated an emerging perspective in an unpublished essay, "Eine Ansicht über Fortschritt" [An Opinion on Progress].[96] The 15-page manuscript, dated 11 July 1858, addresses a central idea in the debate over absolute and program music, which had already been argued notoriously in Hanslick's *Vom Musikalisch-Schönen* and Liszt's essay on Berlioz's *Harold en Italie*, and would be distilled a year later in Brendel's divisive phrase, "New German School."[97]

Goldmark begins by rejecting the notion "that in the area of purely instrumental composition nothing significant or new is to be created," perhaps merely reacting to previously quoted comments in the *Wiener Zeitung*.[98] That absolute music's potential was exhausted, however, is precisely the doctrine Liszt, Wagner, and younger New Germans propounded in seeking to revive a supposedly moribund medium through infusions of literary or linguistic substance. Hence the "Opinion" initially reconciles with a primary tenet of absolutism, but it soon advances a "gently harbored"

[95]   Winkler, "Carl Goldmark: Ein biographischer Abriß," pp. 15–19.

[96]   Goldmark, p. 106. The autograph, preserved at the Hungarian State Opera House (Magyar Állami Operaház, H-Bo, Sign. 78.12), is listed as no. 9 in *Carl Goldmark (1830–1915): Opernkomponist der Donaumonarchie*, p. 26.

[97]   Liszt's young colleagues were known as "New Germans" long before Brendel published "Zur Anbahnung einer Verständigung: Vortrag zur Eröffnung der Tonkünstler Versammlung," *Neue Zeitschrift für Musik*, 50 (1859): 265–75.

[98]   Portions of Goldmark's essay appear in Winkler, "Carl Goldmark und die Moderne," pp. 239–40.

outlook that attempts to mediate between factional discourses. Again conceivably responding to critical recognition of his Mendelssohnian affinities, Goldmark asserts, "no actual progress in relation to the creative medium may be attributed" to the German composer, who had nonetheless produced "an original type of melody" based on distinctive treatments of the minor scale. These modes, which Goldmark likewise detected in the Hungarian operas of Erkel and Doppler, had already begun to animate nationalist musical cultures—an avenue Goldmark rarely explored. Thus the "Opinion" seeks a middle ground between the absolutist denial of instrumental music's decline and the circumscribed potential of Mendelssohnian aesthetics.

After returning to Vienna Goldmark preserved moderate views, but between the wider extremes of Wagner and Brahms. Although Vienna offered few opportunities to hear Wagner's music during the early 1860s, Goldmark developed Wagnerian sympathies. In 1861 three New Germans—Peter Cornelius and Carl Tausig, both Liszt protégés, and Ferdinand Peter Laurencin d'Armond, a critic for the *Neue Zeitschrift für Musik* who had replied to Hanslick's *Vom Musikalisch-Schönen* in 1859—attended a second Viennese concert of Goldmark's works.[99] Cornelius recognized "a disciple of the new era," a title Goldmark gladly accepted, and with the new acolyte frequently discussed modern music, especially Wagner's operas.[100] A year later, when Cornelius corrected proofs of *Tristan und Isolde* for its impending production in Vienna, he and Tausig performed the score for Goldmark, who admired its "rich, absolutely new and daring harmonies." Goldmark likewise reacted enthusiastically to a fully staged *Lohengrin* and orchestral excerpts from Wagnerian operas, all presented while their composer resided in Vienna in 1861 and 1862. During this period, when he met Wagner for the first and only time, Goldmark praised *Tannhäuser*, *Lohengrin*, and selections from the *Ring* and *Die Meistersinger*.[101] Advocating a minority opinion toward these progressive works, Goldmark and his colleagues were shunned at concerts[102] and, as composers, risked incurring the wrath of Hanslick, whom Wagner had recently ridiculed in *Die Meistersinger*.[103] Goldmark thus jeopardized his career in 1861 and 1862 by advocating the founding of Vienna's Wagner Society, advising the Hofoper on the proper staging of Wagner's operas, and extolling Wagner's music in reviews for the *Österreichische constitutionelle Zeitung*, signed—perhaps recognizably—with his surname's last two letters, "rk."[104]

Goldmark's Wagnerism was nonetheless short-lived. He ceased writing reviews after 1862 and declined to join Vienna's Akademischer Wagnerverein in 1873, perhaps because its roster included his name without his consent.[105] Thus he alienated Wagnerites and later suffered their adverse criticism. Ultimately Goldmark rejected Wagnerism in his writings and professional associations. In "Gedanken über Form und

---

[99]   Ferdinand Peter Laurencin d'Armond, *Dr. Eduard Hanslick's Lehre* Vom Musikalisch-Schönen, *eine Abwehr* (Leipzig, 1859).

[100] Goldmark, pp. 132–4.

[101] Ibid., pp. 145–6.

[102] Ibid., pp. 138–9.

[103] Barry Millington, *Wagner* (Princeton, 1984), p. 247.

[104] Winkler, "Carl Goldmark: Ein biographischer Abriß," p. 18.

[105] Goldmark, p. 139.

Stil (eine Abwehr)" [Thoughts on Form and Style (a Defense)], a second unpublished essay written in 1896, Goldmark urged younger composers not to become epigones, but remain "los von Wagner" [free from Wagner].[106] And after Gustav Mahler assumed the Hofoper's directorship in 1897, Goldmark declined his invitation to *Tristan und Isolde*, having already experienced Wagner's dangerous influence.[107]

Nevertheless, Goldmark was unquestionably indebted to Wagner and arguably distanced himself from Mendelssohn through familiarity with Wagner's music.[108] *Die Königin von Saba*, for example, prompts comparisons with *Tannhäuser* and *Lohengrin* because it combines rich chromaticism, vocal declamation, several recurrent leitmotifs, and largely continuous dramaturgy with occasional set pieces, characteristics traceable to a common source, Meyerbeer's grand operas.[109] Some of Goldmark's later operas disclose Wagnerian traits, notably the mysticism of *Merlin* and the monumentality of *Die Kriegsgefangene*, whereas others recall the earlier German romantic tradition of Marschner and Lortzing with closed forms.[110] Recently critics have advanced Wagnerian or Lisztian models for the orchestration of Goldmark's non-operatic works,[111] although Goldmark maintained Berlioz, Brendel's third New German, taught him "many new possibilities of the orchestra."[112] And while Goldmark heard Liszt perform several times, met him once, and even received his compliments after a concert featuring selections from *Die Königin von Saba*, they never developed close relations.[113] Goldmark instead avoided affiliations with the New Germans, resisted their influence, and sought independence between polarized factions.

Indicative of Goldmark's precariously balanced position are his relationships with the nineteenth century's principal absolutists, Brahms and Hanslick. Goldmark remembered meeting Brahms in 1860 or 1861, before the German composer performed his Piano Quartet in A major and the *Variations and Fugue on a Theme by Handel* in Vienna on 29 November 1862.[114] In reviewing the concert, Goldmark claimed the latter work alone "would have sufficed to recognize [his] significant talent."[115] In 25 variations, Goldmark explained, Brahms had created "practically every range of mood of arousable human feeling, from the tender, naïve, and even humorous, to the somber [and] mournfully pathetic." Although less impressed by the quartet, Goldmark conceded it was "a significant work, full of significant ideas." Thus Goldmark the journalist recognized Brahms's genius precisely when he was lauding Wagner's accomplishments.

The Viennese émigrés became and remained friends until Brahms died in 1897, when Goldmark was among his last visitors. Together they socialized, vacationed in the Austrian Alps, and journeyed to Italy when *Die Königin von Saba* was produced

106   Goldmark's essay is quoted in Winkler, "Carl Goldmark und die Moderne," p. 248.
107   Harald Graf, "Carl Goldmark: Beziehung zu den Zeitgenossen," *Studia musicologica*, 30/3–4 (1997): 399.
108   J.A. Fuller Maitland, *Masters of German Music* (New York, 1894), p. 142.
109   Winkler, "Carl Goldmark: Ein biographischer Abriß," pp. 18–19.
110   Keller, p. 20.
111   Harald Graf, p. 380.
112   Goldmark, p. 114.
113   Ibid., pp. 45, 111, 203, 226.
114   Ibid., p. 152.
115   Harald Graf (pp. 382–3) reproduces generous extracts from Goldmark's review.

in Rome in 1878.[116] But while Brahms enjoyed Goldmark's company, valued his collegiality, and called him "the dearest of all men," he was unenthused about Goldmark's compositions, which perhaps too often indulged exotic or programmatic tendencies;[117] nor did he reciprocate when Goldmark dedicated the Overture to *Penthesilea* to him in 1879.[118] Conversely, Brahmsian strains echoed throughout Goldmark's mature choral and chamber works, corroborating his absolutist inclinations. Goldmark realized their contrasting temperaments precluded mutual admiration: the "character of their intercourse varied constantly, ... cordial, warm, and friendly one day, cold, reserved, and unresponsive the next."[119] Their bond nonetheless survived a period of estrangement after Brahms questioned whether Goldmark's use of a "Protestant" text (Psalm 113) was appropriate for a Jewish composer.[120]

Fraught with similar complexities are Goldmark's interactions with Hanslick and the critic's opinions of his music. In 1858 Goldmark sent Hanslick the overture that was to be performed on his debut concert in Vienna, hoping an endorsement would encourage a patron's sponsorship. Hanslick's verdict—the score evinced talent but was immature—impressed Goldmark's benefactor, who purchased a large block of tickets.[121] Goldmark again petitioned Hanslick in 1875 when the Hofoper management rejected *Die Königin von Saba*, fearing it would duplicate previous failures by Austrian composers.[122] Hanslick could have interceded as a member of the Unterrichtsministerium [Ministry of Education], an agency that promoted native artists and awarded stipends to young talent, but apparently did not. Goldmark instead attributed the opera's subsequent acceptance to spirited reception of its entrance march and chorus, which Hanslick deemed the score's only numbers fit for performance, when the Gesellschaft der Musikfreunde programmed them.[123] Goldmark wisely bore no grudge: after the opera's triumph catapulted him to fame, he also served the ministry, siding with Hanslick and Brahms in choosing the stipend winners in 1883.[124]

Hanslick praised Goldmark's originality while censuring his Wagnerian proclivities, a balanced view amid pervasive factionalism. "*Die Königin von Saba* scarcely belongs to the Wagner school," Hanslick observed, "despite many indirect influences of Wagner and isolated reminiscences of him. It is independently conceived."[125] Meyerbeer and Wagner influenced Goldmark's second opera, *Merlin*, whose composer had copied neither, but instead learned much from each. Moreover, *Merlin* "was not heavily impregnated with a Wagnerian essence," nor was its moderate use of declamation and leitmotifs comparable to Wagner's practice in

---

[116] Goldmark, pp. 251–3.

[117] See Goldmark, p. 160; Harald Graf, p. 385; Richard Heuberger, *Erinnerungen an Johannes Brahms*, ed. Kurt Hofmann (Tutzing, 1971), p. 72; Johannes Brahms, *Briefwechsel*, ed. Andreas Moser (16 vols, Tutzing, 1974), vol. 1, p. 32.

[118] Harald Graf, p. 386.

[119] Goldmark, p. 157.

[120] Ibid., pp. 155–7.

[121] Ibid., p. 100.

[122] Several sources reprint the letter, including Goldmark, pp. 221–3.

[123] Ibid., pp. 224–6.

[124] Harald Graf, p. 375.

[125] Eduard Hanslick, *Musikalische Stationen* (Berlin, 1880), p. 302.

Tristan.[126] But Goldmark's third opera, *Das Heimchen am Herd*, earned Hanslick's heartiest endorsement because its return to "old forms of strophic songs, arias, duets, and choruses" demonstrated "music could not exist without the laws of form and symmetry unless it was allowed to degenerate into mere sensuality and pathological irritation of the nerves"—an indictment of Wagner.[127] Thus Goldmark's operas escaped Hanslick's scorn by eschewing Wagner's most egregious techniques.

The same was essentially true of Goldmark's instrumental compositions. In 1865 Hanslick judged *Sakuntala*, Goldmark's earliest extant overture, "the best work the gifted ... composer has hitherto produced. Fresh and characteristic in invention, of clear arrangement and fine detail, the overture exhibits decisive clarity compared to Goldmark's earlier confused and wallowing talent. Only a few passages recall the previous love of dissonance and pathetic lack of clarity."[128] Plainly Hanslick focused on the score's formal properties, but he also mentioned its expressive content in another review in 1878. *Sakuntala* was "an ingenious composition, which, through the insatiable repetition of its principal motive, becomes an ingenious form of torture. The mournful character of these five closely interwoven notes follows us even in dreams."[129] On both occasions, however, Hanslick pointedly ignored the overture's literary subject, Kālidāsa's popular Sanskrit drama.

Hanslick more thoroughly addressed Goldmark's programmaticism in 1880, when he critiqued the composer's second overture, *Penthesilea*, a title derived from Heinrich Kleist's recounting of the exploits of an Amazon warrior slain by Achilles. Initially encountering the overture in an arrangement for piano four-hands, Hanslick and his partner "thought they would fall off the piano bench" after playing the first two chords, whose dissonance evoked "the cry of victims struck with the sharp lash of a whip; Wagner's Valkyries gallop in more discreetly than Goldmark's Amazons."[130] Once over his initial shock, however, Hanslick acknowledged "this fearful anacrusis sounds less painful in the orchestra and introduces a tone painting that produces a harsh but meaningful effect—which is indeed what a composer who undertakes a musical rendering of Kleist's famous tragedy should (and wants to) produce." Whether anyone should actually pursue such goals naturally remained questionable: "Must it be?" Hanslick asked, quoting the motto attached to the finale of Beethoven's String Quartet, Op. 135. The answer was yes in the case of Goldmark, who followed "no mere whim, but rather an overpowering inner urge." Hanslick's magnanimity, however, scarcely precluded complaints about Goldmark's next two overtures: the Wagnerian harmonies of *Im Frühling* were unexpected representations of a spring thunderstorm, and *Sappho* was "a primeval forest of dissonance."[131]

---

[126]   Hanslick, *Musikalisches Skizzenbuch: Neue Kritiken und Schilderungen* (Berlin, 1895), pp. 76–7.

[127]   Keller (p. 20) quotes Hanslick's comments.

[128]   Keller (p. 10) quotes Hanslick's review of the fourth Philharmonic concert of the 1865–6 season.

[129]   Hanslick, *Concerte, Componisten und Virtuosen der letzten fünfzehn Jahre, 1870–1885* (Berlin, 1886), p. 212.

[130]   Ibid., pp. 282–3.

[131]   Hanslick, *Aus dem Tagebuche eines Musikers* (Berlin, 1892), p. 271.

Hanslick extended his tolerance to the *Ouverture zum* Gefesselten Prometheus *des Aeschylos*, deeming it "one of the best, most mature of Goldmark's compositions."[132] Its appeal was not merely "its burning energy of expression; there is actually something important in terms of musical meaning." Initially, however, the literary subject aroused Hanslick's suspicion:

> ... Goldmark loves chiefly tragic material, sorrowful, implacable struggle, and he is not timid in expressing this love. I was consequently unable to avoid some apprehension when Goldmark expressly chose *Prometheus Bound*. Would the loathsome vulture that pecks at Prometheus' liver not also simultaneously bite at our ears? Instead of the hero, would not his brother Epimetheus appear, causing everything to emanate from Pandora's infamous box? Nothing of this happened. Despite this composition's incisive tragedy, glowing red-hot in the fire of the most vigorous orchestra, I noticed nothing downright repulsive or ugly. ... Goldmark's merit is that he loses himself not in pedantic depictive details, but instead keeps his eye on the larger whole and has created a musical artwork from his dangerous substance.[133]

Goldmark thus achieved parity between form and content without compromising "the musically beautiful" with ugliness, a virtue Hanslick extolled even while conceding the composer remained a "poet of tragic conflict and struggle."[134] Hanslick's remarks explain his broadly favorable judgment, contributing to an analysis also informed by comparisons with Bargiel's score and Goldmark's engagement with Wagnerian and Brahmsian compositional principles.

While their overtures share important commonalities, Bargiel and Goldmark differ regarding their basic programmatic orientation. Bargiel merely identifies a general subject, whereas Goldmark specifies a source, the *Prometheus Bound* of Aeschylus—neither a radical nor progressive strategy, but one affecting his overture's expressive content. Prometheus is vanquished, imprisoned, and condemned to exile and torture as Aeschylus' play concludes, affirming Goldmark's preference for "tragic conflict and struggle," as Hanslick noted. Goldmark's overture, however, scarcely mirrors the Aeschylean plot with a series of overtly imitative episodes, as in some of the New German School's explicitly narrational products. It instead embodies salient character traits of the protagonist that have ostensibly perceivable counterparts in the drama, just as Bargiel's score reflects well-known facets of the Titan's persona with familiar musical topics. And like Bargiel, Goldmark closely observes sonata form's conventions, though several exceptional procedures reveal noteworthy similarities and differences between the two overtures. Indeed, Goldmark emphasized the preservation of musical structure's integrity whenever a program was involved in a third unpublished essay, "Über musikalischen Fortschritt: Eine Mahnung" [On Musical Progress: A Warning, 1905], declaring a score would "lose its clarity and the musical form its impact" if a literary source demanded repetition.[135] Goldmark's aesthetic thus

---

[132] Ibid., p. 298.
[133] Ibid., pp. 299–300.
[134] Keller (pp. 22–3) quotes Hanslick's comment.
[135] Winkler ("Carl Goldmark und die Moderne," p. 236) quotes the essay.

reconciles with absolutism, partially explaining Hanslick's balanced opinions of his works. Nevertheless, one outburst of graphic imitation unmistakably refers to the Aeschylean narrative, illuminating Goldmark's representation of the myth.

Table 7.2   Formal Divisions in Goldmark's *Ouverture zum* Gefesselten Prometheus *des Aeschylos für Orchester*, Op. 38

INTRODUCTION: Adagio. Feierlich still und ruhig			
Theme: a_1	a_2	b_1	b_2
Comments: imitative reverie	tutti, brasses, tutti: cortege	lyrical, imitative	triadic returns in coda

EXPOSITION: Allegro con brio		Poco meno	Tempo
Th: Principal	Transition	Subordinate 1	Subordinate 2
C: *Sturm und Drang* agitation	nondescript scales, triplet figure, princ. theme, 7-note syncopation, disintegration	lyrical dialogue folk-like song	Wagnerian lied

DEVELOPMENT				
Episode 1	2	3	4	5
C: princ. theme sub. theme 2	sub. theme 2 triplet figure	princ. theme canon	princ. theme, 3 fragments, abstractions	pedal tones, princ. theme

RECAPITULATION			
Th: Principal	Transition	Subordinate 1	Subordinate 2
C: *Sturm und Drang* agitation shortened	as in exposition	lyrical dialogue folk-like song	lied, song, lied

CODA	Più presto, alla breve	Poco animato	
Section	1	2	3	4
C:	fragments, princ. theme, arpeggios, block chords	bass line and afterbeats, triads with lied's dotted rhythms	block chords *Sturmmarsch*	timpani rolls, fanfares, return of introduction, sustained tonic triad

Beyond disclosing essentially moderate programmaticism, the overtures reveal strikingly similar forms distinguished by notable variants (Table 7.2). Both begin with slow, polythematic introductions, but while Bargiel's open (modulatory) structure is ternary, Goldmark's closed design is bipartite. In each score the introduction resurfaces in the coda, creating a framework that suggests a metaphorical narrative presence. Goldmark's introduction, however, makes no recurrence in the development. In both expositions principal themes and transitions predictably lead to secondary areas, but Goldmark, rather than adopting a contrasting subordinate theme and a concluding area based on the principal subject, presents two new melodies in rapid succession, linking them harmonically in antecedent-consequent fashion. Moreover, this subordinate theme group begins traditionally in the dominant, not Bargiel's Neapolitan, before it, too, modulates to a remote key. Goldmark's development section is likewise more conventional, subjecting the exposition's themes to Beethovenesque motivic foreshortening rather than transforming the introduction. Both recapitulations truncate principal subjects and expand secondary themes, the former process more obvious in Bargiel's overture, the latter more notable in Goldmark's score. And Goldmark's longer coda includes the principal theme's reprise, several new, relatively nondescript passages, the Aeschylean outburst, and a final peroration. These structural features and additional tonal variants provide insights into Goldmark's programmaticism.

The introduction commences not with Bargiel's martial fanfares, but with a passage marked *Adagio, feierlich still und ruhig* [Slowly, solemnly quiet and peaceful, Example 7.9]. Enhancing the serene atmosphere is a single dynamic indication, *pp sempre*, in every orchestral part, each of which enters with an imitative figure comprising an upward leap and a scalewise descent. After the figure rises through the strings and woodwinds, suspensions embellish scalewise descents above a tonic pedal on C, perhaps evoking sounds of church polyphony or attendant notions of antiquity. This measured prefatory gesture scarcely corresponds to the Aeschylean play's impassioned opening dialogue, in which Force compels Hephaestus to chain Prometheus to the cliff where he will spend eternity. Instead it produces an almost contemplative tranquility that Hanslick likened to "a solemn, calm sea."[136] The best and perhaps only possible parallel in Aeschylus is the Titan's first monologue, spoken after he has been bound and abandoned.

---

[136] This and Hanslick's remaining comments appear in *Aus dem Tagebuche eines Musikers*, pp. 298–300.

Example 7.9   Goldmark *Ouverture zum* Gefesselten Prometheus *des Aeschylos*,
                 mm. 1–9

Prometheus begins by summoning the four elements to witness the harm the gods have done him in calm, stately language compatible with the overture's reflective opening.[137] A deeper correlation between the four elements and Goldmark's identically numbered imitative lines may seem fanciful, but ensuing musical events suggest further counterparts in the monologue. During the imitative passage's restatement in the dominant, the full orchestra intrudes in C minor with fortissimo block chords that are repeated in double-dotted rhythms and punctuated by triadic fanfares. A funeral cortege's easily recognized tread remains unmistakable as military brasses offer a pianissimo response exhibiting a lament's hallmark traits, namely repetitive neighbor-tone motion in the inner voices and a descending chromatic bass line (Example 7.10). The cortege proceeds with another fortissimo tutti statement, less the flutes and low brasses, until syncopation dissolves its regular rhythms. Quiet solemnity has plainly been broken by mournful allusions, duplicating a sequence in Aeschylus: after Prometheus invokes the elements, he cries out, bemoaning his pain, disgrace, and sorrowful destiny, composing himself only when the sound of rustling wings distracts him. Thus far the introduction reconciles well with Goldmark's literary source, a claim less easily made as it continues.

Example 7.10   Goldmark *Ouverture zum* Gefesselten Prometheus *des Aeschylos*, mm. 19–21

Above syncopated chords in D-flat major, woodwinds exchange imitative melodic strands that hover on high notes, descend and reascend diatonically through the interval of a sixth, and conclude with embellished upward leaps. Marked *dolce espressivo*, the patently lyrical passage momentarily eludes programmatic associations. Its polyphonic texture suggests neither the individual narrative presence that pastoralism evokes at the same point in Bargiel's overture, nor the Aeschylean narrative's impending episode, the Titan's dialogue with the

---

[137]   Aeschylus, *Prometheus Bound*, trans. Paul Roche, p. 29.

Oceanids, who speak in unison, not individually. Goldmark's lyrical effusion may instead allude to the next lines in the Titan's monologue, which disclose he can foresee the future in its entirety. Indeed, the lyrical passage foreshadows much later musical events: its final measures return in the coda and hence comprise the overture's "emphatic framing reality," its "metaphorically present narrator." The introduction's ending helps clarify the allusion. As woodwinds and strings repeat the lyrical tune's fragments, harmonies drift from D-flat, through A-flat minor, and into G major, where sonata form's conventions dictate the introduction should conclude. Intense chromaticism, however, thwarts expectations (Example 7.11). Descending through an octave of a largely chromatic scale, the violins reach G-natural, where a sforzando emphasizes an augmented triad—a striking effect that is not only repeated immediately, but also amplified in the coda. A final imitative dialogue between the clarinet and flute then reinstates the previous section's lyricism and the opening reverie's C-major tonality. The restoration of peace has only one equivalent in Aeschylus: Hercules will free Prometheus after eons of incarceration and suffering, an explication ultimately supported by the coda's outburst of graphic representation. Meanwhile, however, the introduction has ended improperly in the major tonic, a dilemma remedied when a fortissimo augmented sixth chord abruptly prepares the dominant.

Marked *Allegro con brio*, the exposition begins with a familiar topic— the psychological agitation embodied in the principal theme of Liszt's symphonic poem and the transition in Bargiel's overture. After unison strings and woodwinds encircle the dominant with syncopated scale fragments, the violins, horns, and bassoons announce a principal theme epitomizing inner turmoil (Example 7.12): its key is C minor; the expressive indication, *heftig*, means violent or fierce; the violin's G string produces coarse tones; long notes change position within the measure, destabilizing the meter; and the spare texture comprises a unison theme and frenzied tremolos. This *Sturm und Drang* conflict could represent the Titan's internal anguish or his audible tirades against Zeus, the latter implied by Hanslick's characterization of the "sharply delineated theme" as "defiant." A fully orchestrated response is somewhat stabilized by primary harmonies, regularly placed long notes, and repetitive triplet figures emphasizing the dominant with neighbor tones. But the modulation to a secondary key begins as tutti chords tonicize E-flat major and a canon in A-flat minor restores the theme's erratic traits.

Although distinguished by the expressive marking *breit* [broadly], the transition begins nondescriptly with sequential ascending scales, chromatic versions of prosaic figuration routinely effecting modulations in classical symphonies. More distinctively, the repetitive triplet figure reemerges, the principal theme's restatement is harmonized with a new tonicization of G, and canonic treatment of seven pitches of the chromatic scale annihilates metric regularity with asymmetrical accents before G major coalesces. Goldmark's transition thus intensifies the principal theme's agitation until it dissolves, a process governing the equivalent passage in Bargiel's overture. Reintegration may accordingly constitute the subordinate theme group's goal.

Example 7.11   Goldmark *Ouverture zum* Gefesselten Prometheus *des Aeschylos*,
mm. 42–52

Example 7.11 concluded.

Example 7.12   Goldmark *Ouverture zum* Gefesselten Prometheus *des Aeschylos*,
mm. 57–62

The first of two integrated yet contrasting themes restores tonal and rhythmic order
(Example 7.13). Above gently syncopated chords vaguely recalling earlier unrest, a
mellifluous oboe solo diatonically embellishes the dominant triad, unfolding in regular
four-measure phrases at a slightly slower tempo (*Poco meno*). The oboe's second phrase
reaches a half cadence in B-flat major, foreshadowing the key of the subordinate group's
second theme, though a solo clarinet's abbreviated repetition of the theme promptly
reinstates the dominant. Unlike Bargiel's hymn, but better than any previous passage
in Goldmark's score, the theme suits individual expression. Indeed, its solos, regular
phrasing, diatonicism, and sublimated accompaniment support its characterization as
a song, perhaps one rather folk-like in nature, as Hanslick confirmed in describing it as
"remarkably tender, almost idyllic." The wordless lied's subject nonetheless remains
obscure, since Aeschylus emphasizes the Titan's tribulations, his condemnation and
defiance of Zeus, and mankind's misfortunes. Granted, the Greek tragedian also
portrays Prometheus as a gentle philosopher who nurtures humanity, teaches essential
skills, and pities Io. But Goldmark's lyrical woodwind solos evoke no specific images,
instead offering momentary repose before intensity renews, as Hanslick observed.
Entrusting other exegetes with determining whether the subordinate theme represented

the "memory of earlier happiness or the hope of deliverance," the critic ratified one of his fundamental aesthetic precepts by claiming the idyllic interlude "temporarily interrupts and allays the torment of the shackled Prometheus, allowing both him and us to draw a breath. This contrast was musically necessary; in an orchestral work we first desire music and only then tragedy, insofar as it is reconcilable with the former." For Hanslick, formal considerations outweighed the theme's elusive programmatic role.

Resuming the original tempo, the subordinate group's second theme begins in B-flat major, fulfilling the harmonic promise of the oboe solo's second phrase. The new theme's presentation in two increasingly elaborate orchestral guises resembles the strophic design of Bargiel's hymn, but its remaining features better accord with another secular song, producing a generic bond between the theme group's constituent parts. Other than its repetition scheme, however, the second lied differs from the first (Example 7.14a). Its opening two-measure phrase, played by violins above chromatic counterpoint, arpeggiated triplets, and sustained primary chords, signals a periodic answer will follow, an implication briefly realized when the first measure recurs in the third. Nevertheless, the new phrase expands into ten sequentially structured measures of Wagnerian endless melody, which, notwithstanding veiled allusions to G major and C minor, suspend functional tonality through escalated chromaticism, directionless six-four chords, unresolved secondary dominants and seventh chords, and a half cadence obscured by harmonic elision (a dominant seventh chord implies A minor as the supertonic of G, but proceeds directly to the dominant). Likewise sequentially structured, the theme's more elaborately orchestrated second stanza descends a third, from D-flat to B-Flat, but eschews incipient periodicity by starting with the long-breathed phrase. Goldmark's latent Wagnerism accordingly emerges in a veritable love song whose main motive recalls the leitmotif heard as Isolde reveals Tantris, the knight whose wounds she once healed, was actually Tristan, who now forces her to marry the king of her enemies (Example 7.14b). That both motives suggest renewed vigor seems coincidental, though Goldmark's chromaticism, sequences, swelling dynamics, and reinstated tempo doubtless herald another stage in the narrative. But if the subordinate group's second theme bears any explicit association, perhaps it marks the Titan's shift from self-absorption to altruism toward mankind, a well-known attribute expounded in his Aeschylean monologues.

Although terse, the development is conventional. Its five episodes manipulate the exposition's themes with contrapuntal combination, motivic foreshortening, rhythmic displacement, transposition, re-harmonization, and new orchestration—standard techniques that contrast with Bargiel's transformation of the slow introduction's materials. The first episode, juxtaposing the principal theme's imitative statements with the Wagnerian lied's chromatic countermelody, modulates from G-flat major, through a modally ambivalent B-flat, to an ephemeral G minor. Next, a fragment of the Wagnerian lied and the transition's triplet figures move sequentially to D-flat, F, and back to G. Again briefly stabilizing G minor, the third episode subjects the principal theme to a canon between the first and second violins. In the fourth and most complex episode three fragments of the principal theme acquire the arpeggiated accompaniment of the Wagnerian lied's second strophe and experience rhythmic displacement, foreshortening, and canonic or freely contrapuntal treatment. Rapid modulations match the feverish motivic interplay, leaping from G minor to D-flat and A major before passing through B minor to C. Having explored much of the exposition's motivic potential, the development ends as pedal points on A, C, and G support sequential abstractions of the principal theme's double-dotted rhythms. Tension increases as strings and woodwinds ascend through a two-octave chromatic scale, horns and timpani sustain a dominant pedal, piano dynamics swell to fortissimo, and an accelerando all anticipate the recapitulation.

Example 7.13   Goldmark *Ouverture zum* Gefesselten Prometheus *des Aeschylos*, mm. 116–23

Example 7.14a   Goldmark *Ouverture zum* Gefesselten Prometheus *des Aeschylos*,
              mm. 130–41

Example 7.14b   Wagner *Tristan und Isolde*, Act I, scene 3, mm. 143–52

Goldmark's developmental procedures fulfill formalist expectations, elevating the exposition's harmonic tension with the aid of motivic operations. More specifically, Goldmark's exposition intensifies the normal tonic-dominant friction with the subordinate theme group's modulations to B-flat and D-flat, keys the development more fully investigates and juxtaposes with the dominant in a dual modality (G major and minor). The tonal-motivic scenario also discharges the development's traditional programmatic duty to depict conflict or struggle. Indeed, musical narrations of military heroism routinely liken developmental turmoil to the protagonist's engagement in battle, as the first movement of Beethoven's "Eroica" Symphony illustrates.[138] Aeschylus supplies abundant grist for reading Goldmark's development as a representation of the Titan's defiance of Zeus, violent imprisonment, anguish over mankind's abuse, and self-doubts regarding his ability to endure punishment. Perhaps more importantly, the development's exhaustion of the exposition's tonal and motivic resources implies the recapitulation will alleviate previous tensions, an objective Goldmark and Bargiel achieve by altering the balance between the exposition's themes.

The recapitulation discards 14 of the principal theme's 32 measures, eliminating the brief preface that encircles the dominant with syncopated scale fragments and the final passage restoring the theme's metric irregularity. Thus one omission reduces agitation, while the other preserves the rhythmic stability acquired in the fully orchestrated response to the theme's initial presentation. Transposed to remain in the tonic, the transition ends in a half cadence, anticipating the subordinate theme's conventional reprise. Otherwise, minor changes in orchestration scarcely vary the literally recapitulated theme and transition.

Beginning normally enough in the major tonic, two statements of the subordinate theme group's folk-like song respectively replace the oboe with clarinet and cellos and substitute a flute for the clarinet. The newly harmonized second statement, however, reaches a half cadence in E-flat, not the expected C major, precipitating an expansion of the subordinate group's second theme. Three stanzas of the Wagnerian lied widen and then close the tonal rift, moving from G-flat major, through an especially chromatic strophe in B-flat, to a diatonic C major. While the appearance of every theme in the tonic fulfills the recapitulation's obligation to reduce large-scale harmonic tension, the brevity, simplicity, and subdued dynamics of the Wagnerian lied's C-major stanza unsatisfactorily resolve the global tonal drama, requiring elaboration. Unexpectedly, the folksong returns in C major, played by a clarinet as it was in the exposition, but accompanied by sustained rather than syncopated chords and delicate arpeggios in the flutes and pizzicato cellos, thus losing its vestigial rhythmic agitation and redressing the earlier discrepancy in scoring. The Wagnerian lied then recurs, passing from A-flat, through a circle of fifths, to F, where it assumes forte dynamics and its most opulent orchestration (Example 7.15). Thus the subordinate group climaxes in the subdominant, balancing dominant emphasis throughout the form. Programmatically, an enraptured song overwhelms agitation and pastoralism.

---

[138]   Will, pp. 188–215, especially 209–10.

Example 7.15   Goldmark *Ouverture zum* Gefesselten Prometheus *des Aeschylos*,
mm. 310–14

Example 7.15 concluded.

Short-lived equilibrium dissipates as the Wagnerian lied's bass line descends chromatically from C to F, where a Neapolitan triad and resurgent tremolos inaugurate the coda. Comprising 140 of the overture's 454 measures, the coda recalls previous themes amid intermittently nondescript passages. It begins with fragments of the principal theme recognizably drawn from the development's fourth episode, but then prosaically arpeggiates a dominant seventh that implies E major as a tonic, yet resolves to E-flat minor. Two recurrences of the principal theme's first two measures quickly reinstate C minor, where common time shifts to alla breve meter and additional commonplace figuration has no antecedent in the score. An ascending chromatic bass line merely supports afterbeats that are embellished by neighbor tones until insistent dotted rhythms vaguely recall the Wagnerian lied in B major. Triadic melodic outlines, however, more closely resemble fanfares than the lied's supple profile. Following a sequential passage Hanslick noticed because its novel scoring requires four trombones to traverse rapid chromatic ascents in parallel diminished seventh chords, a mundane series of block chords and a prolonged crescendo herald a decisive return of C minor. Marked fortissimo, the tutti orchestra finally announces the principal theme, transformed by augmented rhythmic values, an extra passing tone, and a reversal of its anacrusis from an upper to a lower neighbor. A stylized *Sturmmarsch* then preserves the minor tonic as its bass line's ostinato moves ever faster and its upper voices produce a frenzy of increasingly compressed scale fragments. Thus far the coda relies largely on clichéd figuration but nonetheless generates tremendous forward momentum, abetted by a liberal dose of bombast. Its frequently nondescript material, however, does little to advance the program: initial agitation, embodied in fragmentary references to the principal theme, fails to coalesce against an inchoate backdrop, despite a renewal of frenetic activity. In greatest possible contrast, the aforementioned outburst of graphic imitation provides a clearer perspective.

The *Sturmmarsch*, seemingly foredoomed to conclude the overture with a musical enactment of titanic fury, instead culminates in an apocalypse (Example 7.16). Tacet since the onset of cut time, timpani silence the orchestra with a fortissimo roll and rapid diminuendo, a barrage with exactly one counterpart in Aeschylus: the stage direction for "a universal bombardment of thunder and lightning" that causes Prometheus and the Oceanids to disappear.[139] Hermes, the Olympian messenger, had threatened Prometheus with punitive thunder when he inquired how Zeus' reign would end.[140] Prometheus knew his alliance with Hercules would precipitate the oppressor's downfall, but defiantly withheld the information. Hermes then predicted "threefold devastation" beyond escape: with thunder and lightning Zeus would shatter the cliff where Prometheus was shackled, entombing him in rock for eons of darkness; after reemerging into sunlight, Prometheus would be tortured by Zeus' eagle; and this persecution would end only when another god assumed the Titan's burden, an unwitting reference to Hercules.[141] Goldmark's timpani roll graphically represents the first dark prophecy's fulfillment, but it does not conclude the overture,

---

[139] Aeschylus, p. 79.
[140] Ibid., p. 72.
[141] Ibid., p. 76.

unlike the bombardment that closes the Aeschylean tragedy. A denouement instead alludes to further events in the Promethean narrative.

Accompanied by tremolos and repeated timpani thunderclaps, trumpets and trombones proclaim a fanfare new to the overture, doubtless evoking Zeus' majesty (Example 7.16, mm. 389–92). Two fanfares articulate plagal cadences, a conceivable though facile ending for the overture. At a third cadence, however, the bass line's F avoids returning to C, the tonic, to descend through an octave of the chromatic scale, harmonized extraordinarily with augmented triads above every other pitch (Example 7.17). The augmented triads initiate the narrative frame's closure, recalling their striking disruption of the slow introduction, where sforzandos likewise reinforced them. Amplified far beyond their incipient form, they suspend functional harmony in an atonal *Götterdämmerung*, a limbo failing to provoke even Hanslick, who wittily shrugged, "with pure triads one can just as little a Prometheus make as a revolution with rose water." The essentially atonal void perhaps embodies the second prophecy of Hermes, the Titan's imprisonment in a timeless abyss; but it definitely requires tonal resolution, which soon takes the form of an augmented sixth chord's regular progression to the overture's dominant, G, and an authentic cadence in C major. Then, above a sustained tonic chord embellished by indolent neighbor tones, the clarinet and flute engage in the imitative, triadic dialogue that closed the introduction, again restoring peace and fulfilling the third, unwitting prophecy of Hermes: Hercules will free Prometheus.

Viewed comprehensively, Goldmark's overture combines readily identifiable topics, explicit imitation of literary episodes, ambiguously programmatic passages, and nondescript excerpts, the latter apparent in transitions and the coda. Its distinctively mixed approach to musical representation thus reflects Goldmark's similarly eclectic aesthetics, attendant symbiosis of compositional styles, and simultaneous admiration for Wagner and Brahms. Among its Wagnerian features, the chromatic harmonies of the subordinate group's second theme and the coda's augmented triads are the most striking, although equally noteworthy are the Wagnerian lied's expansive phrase structure, the timpani's graphic evocation of the Aeschylean apocalypse, and adventurous brass writing. These traits probably would have disgruntled Brahms, who may have nonetheless respected the overture's formal clarity, skillful counterpoint, and finely sculpted melodies, especially the subordinate group's first theme, whose folk-like charms pervade his own music. Hanslick maintained the balanced perspective he adopted regarding Goldmark's other concert overtures, overlooking the most overt chromaticism and wincing only at occasional whip-like lashes of dissonance. He plainly realized these Wagnerian manifestations were offset by formal symmetry, traditional tonal-thematic sonata processes, conventional developmental strategies, and finely crafted instrumentation. Indeed, Hanslick may have plausibly considered the overture's contrasts a means whereby Goldmark successfully depicted "tragic struggle and conflict."

Example 7.16   Goldmark *Ouverture zum* Gefesselten Prometheus *des Aeschylos*,
              mm. 387–96

Example 7.16 concluded.

Example 7.17   Goldmark *Ouverture zum* Gefesselten Prometheus *des Aeschylos*, mm. 401–16

Example 7.17 concluded.

But Goldmark's score is no mere conflation of Wagner and Brahms, deliberately weighted to assuage Hanslick. It exemplifies principles the self-educated composer adopted while living in Budapest, where he studied theoretical treatises, Bach, and Beethoven to master counterpoint and develop his "melodic sense." Evincing his success are the overture's fluently deployed imitation and exquisite woodwind solos, which rank Goldmark with Schubert, Dvořák, and Tchaikovsky among the nineteenth century's leading melodists. Its programmaticism likewise confirms Goldmark's adherence to a moderate aesthetic codified in three unpublished essays on musical progress, the first again written in Budapest: the overture preserves formal clarity and integrity, even while transparently referring to its specified literary source. Goldmark's self-reliance also surfaced in questions he asked colleagues to enhance his talent in orchestration, which is too often credited solely to Wagner's influence. But his chromatic brass parts actually compare with those of Berlioz, whom Goldmark himself acknowledged, as the coda's previously mentioned trombone writing illustrates. The overture, a refined synthesis of diverse elements ranging from the monumental to the intimate, accordingly embodies Vienna's opulence during the Danube monarchy.

Bargiel and Goldmark structured their overtures comparably, encasing sonata forms between thematically linked introductions and codas. Both likewise chose a modally fluid key of C for their Promethean representations, perhaps observing a tonal convention that extends from Beethoven's balletic overture to Anton Bruckner's Eighth Symphony, which bears a Promethean subtitle in secondary commentaries. Despite outward similarities, however, the overtures portray the myth differently, as their composers' disparate backgrounds and distinct aesthetics predictably suggest. Bargiel specified no literary source, instead cultivating a heroic archetype that grants Prometheus a decidedly martial victory. Goldmark, in contrast, designated the *Prometheus Bound* of Aeschylus as his model and accordingly imbued his score with "tragic struggle and conflict," mitigated only by the promise of redemption.

Different approaches are immediately apparent. Bargiel's introduction discloses his score's complete trajectory: martial heroism, tinged with antique primitivism, will achieve transformation through a pastoral agent inflected with ominous tattoos. Conversely, Goldmark's introduction evokes serenity that a funeral cortege interrupts, just as the ensuing lyrical woodwind dialogue yields to augmented triads the coda will amplify. Bargiel's Titan is a military hero; Goldmark's is contemplative, awaiting redemption in a distant future. Both expositions begin similarly, but soon diverge. Bargiel's breathless lament grows into full-fledged agitation before expiring in dissolution, a sequence Goldmark simplifies by omitting the lament. Both subordinate themes attain partial reintegration, again via different means. Bargiel's intimate chorale becomes a celebratory anthem, a process of externalization facilitated by the pastoral agent's recurrence, whereas Goldmark's folksong and Wagnerian lied maintain interior perspectives. The developments accordingly deploy opposing tactics. Bargiel's reprise of the introduction's slow march, now thinly scored and colored by minor-mode pathos, internalizes conflict, requiring a new outlook on heroism. Goldmark's development externalizes conflict, revealing the exposition's potential to arrive at an analogous summons for new balance. Compressed recapitulations diminish Bargiel's lament and Goldmark's agitation, precipitating expansions of Bargiel's hymn, now infused with pastoralism and militarism, and Goldmark's songs, which overwhelm agitation with opulent scoring and large-scale tonal equilibrium produced by subdominant emphasis. Undoubtedly reflecting sonata form's exigencies, both scores reach similar narrative junctures, but their substantive codas again diverge. In Bargiel's straightforward ending a *Sturmmarsch* prepares the introduction's final, purely heroic appearance, untainted by pastoralism or tattoos. Goldmark's more elaborate coda reinstates an ill-formed agitation, grows into a frenzied *Sturmmarsch*, and culminates in an Aeschylean cataclysm—the material imitation of Zeus' thunderbolt. In an atonal denouement, the framing introductory gestures return, promising redemption after exile. Thus the overtures advance distinctive versions of the myth, notwithstanding formal similarities and points of narrative contact.

That the Prometheus myth successfully accommodates disparate interpretations partially explains its appeal to nineteenth-century composers, yet its versatility may also account for a dearth of related autonomous instrumental works. Messages other Promethean scores conveyed were perhaps so urgent they demanded explicit articulation: Beethoven envisioned a liberator during revolutionary times; Reichardt, Schubert, and Wolf mirrored Goethe's artistic and metaphysical rebellion; Liszt emphasized Herder's humanitarianism; French composers reflected their nation's classical heritage, economic prowess, military defeat, and regionalist aspirations; and Parry voiced religious controversy. Pertinent issues remained lasting concerns for the composers, their cultures, and their societies. The concert overture's programmatic ambiguities may have accordingly inhibited orchestral representations of the myth. Indeed, Mendelssohn conceived the concert overture as a vehicle for encapsulating dramatic, literary, or scenic content with broad musical allusions, not with material imitation's objective precision. Nevertheless, Bargiel and Goldmark effectively portrayed their subjects, albeit in different ways. Bargiel, subscribing to Mendelssohn's formal precepts and non-imitational aesthetic, produced a generic narrative suited to depicting heroic triumph over adversity. Goldmark, however, sometimes resorted to materiality, correlating musical and literary events without antagonizing Hanslick, the era's preeminent formalist. Thus both composers negotiated a precarious middle ground between absolutism and programmaticism, assimilating the Prometheus myth to a conservative cause without losing fundamental aspects of its progressive message in a leading controversy of nineteenth-century music.

Select Bibliography

Aeschylus, *Prometheus Bound: A New Translation, Introduction, Commentary*, trans. Paul Roche (Wauconda, Ill.: Bolchazy-Carducci Publishers, 1990).

Albrecht, Theodore (trans. and ed.), *Letters to Beethoven and Other Correspondence* (3 vols, Lincoln: University of Nebraska Press, 1996).

Allanbrook, Wye Jamison, "Dance as Expression in Mozart Opera" (Ph.D. diss., Stanford University, 1974).

Angiolini, Gaspare, *Dissertation sur les ballets pantomimes des anciens*, ed. Walter Toscanini (Milan: n.p., 1956).

——, Prefaces to *Don Juan* and *Sémiramis* by Christoph Willibald Gluck, in *Libretti: Die originalen Textbücher der bis 1990 in der Gluck-Gesamtausgabe erschienenen Bühnenwerke, Textbücher verschollener Werke*, ed. Klaus Hortschansky (Kassel: Bärenreiter, 1995).

Anonymous, "Recensionen: Musik für Orchester (Woldemar Bargiel: *Ouvertüre zu Prometheus für grosses Orchester*)," *Allgemeine musikalische Zeitung*, 3/5 (1865): 9–13.

——, "The Great French Exhibition," *The Times*, 6 May 1867, p. 10.

Barnard, F.M., *Herder's Social and Political Thought* (Oxford: Clarendon Press, 1965).

Barnard, Frederick A.P., *Paris Universal Exposition, 1867: Report on Machinery and Process of the Industrial Arts* (New York: D. Van Nostrand, 1869).

Beethoven, Ludwig van, *Ein Notierungsbuch von Beethoven aus dem Besitze der Preußischer Staatsbibliothek zu Berlin*, ed. Karl Lothar Mikulicz (Wiesbaden: Breitkopf & Härtel, 1927; reprint, Hildesheim: Georg Olms Verlag, 1972).

Berman, David, *A History of Atheism in Britain: From Hobbes to Russell* (London: Croom Helm Ltd., 1988).

Bernac, Jean, "Interview with Mademoiselle Augusta Holmès," *The Strand Musical Magazine*, 5 (1897): 136–9.

Bertagnolli, Paul A., "A Newly Discovered Source for Franz Liszt's *Chöre zu Herder's Entfesseltem Prometheus*," *Journal of Musicology*, 19/1 (Winter 2002): 125–70.

[Bischoff, Ludwig], "Siebentes Gesellschaft-Concert in Köln im Gürzenich," *Niederrheinische Musik-Zeitung für Kunstfreunde und Künstler*, 12 (1865): 38–9.

Blumenberg, Hans, *Work on Myth*, trans. Robert M. Wallace (Cambridge, Mass.: MIT Press, 1990).

Braemer, Edith Abel, *Goethes* Prometheus *und die Grundposition des Sturm und Drang* (Weimar: Arion Verlag, 1959).

Browning, Elizabeth Barrett, *The Complete Works of Elizabeth Barrett Browning*, ed. Charlotte Porter and Helen A. Clarke (6 vols, New York: Thomas Y. Crowell & Co., 1900).

Bruyck, Karl Debruis van, "Woldemar Bargiel," *Niederrheinische Musik-Zeitung für Kunstfreunde und Künstler*, 7 (1859): 405–6.

Budd, Susan, *Varieties of Unbelief: Atheists and Agnostics in English Society, 1850–1960* (London: Heinemann Educational Books Ltd., 1977).

Byron, Lord George Gordon, *The Poetical Works of Byron*, ed. Robert F. Gleckner (Boston: Houghton Mifflin Company, 1975).

Carner, Mosco, *Hugo Wolf Songs* (London: British Broadcasting Corporation, 1982).

Clapham, J.H., *The Economic Development of France and Germany (1815–1914)* (Cambridge: Cambridge University Press, 1966).

Comettant, Oscar, *La Musique, les musiciens et les instruments de musique chez les differents peuples du monde, Ouvrage enrichi de texts musicaux, orné de 150 dessins d'instruments rares et curieux, Archives complètes de tous les documents qui se rattachent à l'Exposition internationale de 1867* (Paris: Michel Lévy frères, 1869).

Cooper, Martin, "Byways of French Opera: V.—The Operas of Gabriel Fauré," *The Monthly Musical Record*, 77/884 (1947): 32–6.

Dahlhaus, Carl, "Liszts *Bergsymphonie* und die Idee der symphonischen Dichtung," *Jahrbuch des staatlichen Instituts für Musikforschung*, 1975 (1976): 96–130.

——, *The Idea of Absolute Music*, trans. Roger Lustig (Chicago: University of Chicago Press, 1989).

Dannreuther, Edward and Schmiedel, Elisabeth, "Bargiel, Woldemar," in *The New Grove Dictionary of Music and Musicians*, ed. Stanley Sadie and John Tyrrell, 2nd edn (New York: Grove, 2001), vol. 2, p. 727.

Dauphin, Léopold, "Gabriel Fauré et le *Prométhée*," *La Vogue*, 15 October 1900, pp. 59–65.

Dentu, E. and Petit, Pierre (eds), *L'Exposition universelle de 1867 illustrée* (2 vols, Paris: Commission impériale, 1867).

Deutsch, Otto Erich, *Schubert: A Documentary Biography*, trans. Eric Blom (London: J.M. Dent & Sons Ltd., 1946).

Dibble, Jeremy, *C. Hubert H. Parry: His Life and Music* (Oxford: Clarendon Press, 1992).

Draheim, Joachim, "Schumanns Schwager Woldemar Bargiel als Komponist," in Bernhard R. Appell (ed.), *Schumann Forschungen*, vol. 2, *"Neue Bahnen": Robert Schumann und seine musikalische Zeitgenossen* (Mainz: Schott, 1997), pp. 144–53.

Dukas, Paul, *Les Ecrits de Paul Dukas sur la musique*, ed. Flavien Bonnet-Roy et al. (Paris: Société d'Editions françaises et internationales, 1948).

Ergang, Robert Reinhold, *Herder and the Foundations of German Nationalism* (New York: Columbia University Press, 1931).

Fauré, Gabriel, *Lettres intimes*, ed. Philippe Fauré-Fremiet (Paris: Grasset, 1951).

Feilhauer, Ingeborg, "Augusta Holmès und die Französische Revolution," *Musica*, 43/2 (1989): 138–44.

Fischer-Dieskau, Dietrich, *Schubert's Songs: A Biographical Study*, trans. Kenneth S. Whitton (New York: Alfred A. Knopf, 1978).

——, *"Weil nicht alle Blütenträume reiften": Johann Friedrich Reichardt, Hofkapellmeister dreier Preußenkönige, Porträt und Selbstporträt* (Stuttgart: Deutsche Verlags-Anstalt, 1992).

Floros, Constantin, *Beethovens Eroica und Prometheus-Musik* (Wilhelmshaven: Heinrichshofen, 1978).

Foucault, Michel, "A Preface to Transgression," in Donald F. Bouchard (ed.), *Language, Counter-Memory, Practice: Selected Essays and Interviews*, trans. Donald F. Bouchard and Sherry Simon (Ithaca: Cornell University Press, 1977), pp. 29–52.

——, *Discipline and Punish: The Birth of the Prison*, trans. Alan Sheridan (New York: Vintage, 1975).

——, "The Ethic of Care for the Self as a Practice of Freedom," trans. J.D. Gauthier, in James Bernauer and David Rasmussen (eds), *The Final Foucault* (Cambridge, Mass.: MIT Press, 1988), pp. 1–20.

——, "The Order of Discourse," trans. Ian McLeod, in Robert Young (ed.), *Untying the Text: A Post-Structuralist Reader* (London: Routledge & Kegan Paul, 1981), pp. 48–78.

Garnier, Paul-Louis, "Théâtre: *Prométhée* à Béziers," *La Revue blanche*, 15 September 1900, pp. 142–3.

Gefen, Gérard, *Augusta Holmès, l'outrancière* (Paris: Pierre Belfond, 1987).

Gillespie, Gerald, "Prometheus in the Romantic Age," in Gerhart Hoffmeister (ed.), *European Romanticism: Literary Cross-Currents, Modes, and Models* (Detroit: Wayne State University Press, 1990), pp. 197–210.

Goldmark, Carl, *Notes from the Life of a Viennese Composer*, trans. Alice Goldmark Brandeis (New York: Albert and Charles Boni, 1927).

Grabócz, Márta, *Morphologie des œuvres pour piano de Liszt: Influence du programme sur l'évolution des formes* (Budapest: MTA Zenetudományi Intézet, 1986).

Graf, Max, *Legende einer Musikstadt* (Vienna: Österreichische Buchgemeinschaft, 1949).

Graf, Harald, "Carl Goldmark: Beziehung zu den Zeitgenossen," *Studia musicologica*, 30/3–4 (1997): 371–407.

Grey, Thomas, "The Orchestral Music," in Douglass Seaton (ed.), *The Mendelssohn Companion* (Westport, Conn.: Greenwood Press, 2001), pp. 395–550.

Haas, Robert, "Der Wiener Bühnentanz von 1740 bis 1767," *Jahrbuch der Musikbibliothek Peters*, 44 (1937): 77–93.

Halévy, Léon, *La Grèce tragique: Chefs-d'œuvre d'Eschyle, de Sophocle et d'Euripide traduits en vers* (3 vols, Paris: Hachette, 1849).

Hanslick, Eduard, *Aus dem Opernleben der Gegenwart* (Berlin: A. Hofmann, 1884).

——, *Aus dem Tagebuche eines Musikers* (Berlin: Allgemeiner Verein für deutsche Literatur, 1892).

Harris-Warrick, Rebecca, "Ballet," in Stanley Sadie and John Tyrrell (eds), *The New Grove Dictionary of Music and Musicians*, 2nd edn (New York: Grove, 2001), vol. 2, pp. 565–96.

Hecker, Max (ed.), "Die Briefe Johann Friedrich Reichardts an Goethe aus dem Goethe- und Schiller-Archiv," *Jahrbuch der Goethe-Gesellschaft*, 11 (1925): 203–29.

Hepokoski, James, *Sibelius: Symphony No. 5*, Cambridge Music Handbooks, ed. Julian Rushton (Cambridge: Cambridge University Press, 1993).

Herder, Johann Gottfried, *Herders Sämmtliche Werke*, ed. Bernhard Suphan (33 vols, Berlin: Weidmannsche Buchhandlung, 1877–1913).

Hesiod, *Theogony, Works and Days, Shield*, trans. Apostolos N. Athanassakis (Baltimore: The Johns Hopkins University Press, 1983).

Hirsch, Marjorie Wing, *Schubert's Dramatic Lieder* (Cambridge: Cambridge University Press, 1993).

Hoeckner, Berthold, *Programming the Absolute: Nineteenth-Century German Music and the Hermeneutics of the Moment* (Princeton: Princeton University Press, 2002).

Howard, Michael, *The Franco-Prussian War: The German Invasion of France, 1870–1871* (London: Routledge, 2000).

Huebner, Steven, *French Opera at the Fin de Siècle: Wagnerism, Nationalism, and Style* (Oxford: Oxford University Press, 1999).

[Hueffer, Francis], "The Glocester [*sic*] Musical Festival," *The Times*, 8 September 1880, p. 8.

Hughes, Meirion, *The English Musical Renaissance and the Press, 1850–1914: Watchmen of Music* (Aldershot: Ashgate Publishing Limited, 2002).

Hunter, Michael, "The Problem of 'Atheism' in Early Modern England," *Transactions of the Royal Historical Society*, 5th Series, 35 (1985): 135–57.

Hunter, Michael and Wootton, David (eds), *Atheism from the Reformation to the Enlightenment* (Oxford: Clarendon Press, 1992).

Joachim, Johannes and Moser, Andreas (eds), *Briefe von und an Joseph Joachim* (3 vols, Berlin: Julius Bard, 1911).

Johns, Keith T., *The Symphonic Poems of Franz Liszt*, ed. Michael Saffle, Franz Liszt Studies Series, no. 3 (Stuyvesant, NY: Pendragon Press, 1997).

Keller, Otto, *Carl Goldmark* (Leipzig: Hermann Seemann, [1901]).

Koechlin, Charles, "Représentations de Béziers: *Prométhée*, de M. Gabriel Fauré," *Mercure de France*, 40 (1901): 550–54.

Kramer, Lawrence, "Hugo Wolf: Subjectivity in the Fin-de-Siècle Lied," in Rufus Hallmark (ed.), *German Lieder in the Nineteenth Century* (New York: Schirmer Books, 1996), pp. 186–217.

Krüger, Manfred, *J.G. Noverre und das "Ballet d'action"* (Emsdetten: Lechte, 1963).

Lalo, Pierre, "A l'Académie nationale de musique: *Prométhée*, drame lyrique," *Le Temps*, 11 June 1917, p. 3.

——, "A l'Hippodrome: Première représentation à Paris de *Prométhée*," *Le Temps*, 10 December 1907, p. 2.

Laloy, Louis, "Notre troisième saison de guerre," *Le Pays*, 2 June 1917, p. 2.

Larroumet, Gustave, "Chronique théâtrale: Aux arènes de Béziers," *Le Temps*, 3 September 1900, pp. 1–2.

Levinson, André, "Le Ballet de *Prométhée*: Beethoven et Viganò," *La Revue musicale*, 8/6 (1927): 87–97.

——, *Meister des Balletts*, trans. Reinhold von Walter (Potsdam: Müller & Co., 1923).

Liszt, Franz, *Franz Liszts Briefe*, comp. and ed. La Mara [Marie Lipsius] (8 vols, Leipzig, 1893–1905).

——, Preface to *Prométhée, Poème symphonique* (Leipzig: Breitkopf & Härtel, 1856).

Lloyd, Moya and Thacker, Andrew, "Introduction: Strategies of Transgression," in *The Impact of Michel Foucault on the Social Sciences and Humanities* (New York: St. Martin's Press, Inc., 1997), pp. 1–9.

Lorrain, Jean and Hérold, A.-Ferdinand, *Prométhée, Tragédie lyrique en trois actes* (Paris: Société de Mercure de France, 1900).

Lund, Roger D., *The Margins of Orthodoxy: Heterodox Writing and Cultural Response, 1660–1750* (Cambridge: Cambridge University Press, 1995).

Lynham, David, *The Chevalier Noverre: Father of the Modern Ballet* (London: Dance Books, 1972).

Maizeroy, René, "Fêtes de Béziers: *Prométhée*," *Le Théâtre*, 43 (1900): 10–14.

Mangeot, A., "A Béziers," *Le Monde musical*, 15 September 1901, pp. 262–5.

Marnold, Jean, "Opéra national: *Prométhée*, tragédie lyrique de Jean Lorrain et A.-F. Hérold, musique de Gabriel Fauré," *Mercure de France*, 16 July 1917, pp. 336–40.

McKay, Elizabeth Norman, *Franz Schubert: A Biography* (Oxford: Clarendon Press, 1996).

Merrick, Paul, *Revolution and Religion in the Music of Liszt* (Cambridge: Cambridge University Press, 1987).

Monter, Emile Mathieu de, "Festival pour l'exécution de la cantate couronnée au Concours international de composition musical," *Revue et gazette musicale de Paris*, 34/36 (1867): 285–7.

Moore, Lillian, *Artists of the Dance* (New York: Dance Horizons Incorporated, 1975).

Moser, Max, *Richard Wagner in der englischen Literatur des XIX. Jahrhunderts* (Bern: Verlag A. Franke, Ag., 1938).

Nectoux, Jean-Michel, *Gabriel Fauré: A Musical Life*, trans. Roger Nichols (Cambridge: Cambridge University Press, 1991).

Nettl, Paul, *The Dance in Classical Music* (New York: Philosophical Library, 1963).

Nostrand, Howard Lee, *Le Théâtre antique et à l'antique en France de 1840 à 1900* (Paris: Librairie Droz, 1934).

Noverre, Jean-George, *Letters on Dancing and Ballets*, trans. Cyril W. Beaumont (New York: Dance Horizons, Inc., 1966).

Nussy Saint-Saëns, Marcel, "La Fondation du théâtre des arènes de Béziers: La Première du *Déjanire* le 18 Août 1898," *Etudes sur Pézenas et l'Hérault*, 9/2 (1980): 3–22.

O'Brien, Patrick and Keyder, Caglar, *Economic Growth in Britain and France (1780–1914): Two Paths to the Twentieth Century* (London: George Allen & Unwin, 1978).

Orledge, Robert, *Gabriel Fauré* (London: Eulenburg Books, 1979).

Pasler, Jann, "The Ironies of Gender, or Virility and Politics in the Music of Augusta Holmès," *Women & Music: A Journal of Gender and Culture*, 2 (1998): 1–25.

Pelker, Bärbel, *Die deutsche Konzertouvertüre (1825–1865): Werkkatalog und Rezeptionsdokumente* (2 vols, Frankfurt: Peter Lang, 1993).

Peyre, Henri, *Bibliographie critique de l'hellénisme en France de 1843 à 1870* (New Haven: Yale University Press, 1932).

Pichard du Page, René, *Une Musicienne versaillaise: Augusta Holmès* (Paris: Librairie Fischbacher, 1921).

Pistre, Paul, *Francs-Maçons du Midi* (Perpignan: Editions Mare nostrum, 1995).

Pratt, Hodgson (ed.), *Modern Industries: A Series of Reports on Industry and Manufactures as Represented in the Paris Exhibition in 1867* (London: Macmillan and Co., 1868).

Priestman, Martin, *Romantic Atheism: Poetry and Freethought, 1780–1830* (Cambridge: Cambridge University Press, 1999).

Prunières, Henry, "Salvatore Viganò," *Revue musicale*, Numéro spécial (1 December 1921): 71–94.

Ramann, Lina, *Franz Liszt als Künstler und Mensch* (3 vols, Leipzig: Breitkopf & Härtel, 1880–94).

Rees, Brian, *Camille Saint-Saëns: A Life* (London: Chatto & Windus, 1999).

Reichardt, Johann Friedrich, "Ueber Klopstocks komponierte Oden," *Musikalisches Kunstmagazin*, 1 (1782): 22–3, 62–8.

Reichart, Sarah Bennett, "The Influence of Eighteenth-Century Social Dance on the Viennese Classical Style" (Ph.D. diss., City University of New York, 1984).

Riemann, Hugo, "Beethovens Prometheus Musik: Ein Variationenwerk," *Die Musik*, 9/13–14 (1909–10): 19–34, 107–25.

Ritorni, Carlo, *Commentarii della vita e delle opere coredrammatiche di Salvatore Viganò* (Milan: Guglielmini e Rednelli, 1838).

Rolland, Romain, *Musicians of To-Day*, trans. Mary Blaiklock (Freeport: Books for Libraries Press, 1969).

Rust, Friedrich, "Ueber Salvatore Viganò's Originalscenarium zu L. v. Beethovens Ballet *Die Geschöpfe des Prometheus*," *Neue Berliner Musikzeitung*, 45 (1891): 124–5, 133–4, 143–4, 152–4.

Sagnes, Jean (ed.), *Histoire de Béziers* (Toulouse: Editions privat, 1986).

Saint-Jean, J., "Hippodrome et Académie nationale de musique: *Prométhée*," *La Nouvelle revue*, 1 January 1908, pp. 140–41.

Saint-Saëns, Camille, *Musical Memories*, trans. Edwin Gile Rich (Boston: Small, Maynard & Company Publishers, 1919).

Salmen, Walter, Foreword to *Goethes Lieder, Oden, Balladen und Romanzen* (Munich: G. Henle Verlag, 1970), pp. [i–ii].

——, *Johann Friedrich Reichardt: Komponist, Schriftsteller, Kapellmeister und Verwaltungsbeamter der Goethezeit* (Freiburg: Atlantis Verlag, 1963).

Sams, Eric, *The Songs of Hugo Wolf* (London: Eulenburg Books, 1983).

Saran, Franz, *Goethes Mahomet und Prometheus* (Halle: Max Niemeyer, 1914).

Schindler, Anton, *Beethoven as I Knew Him*, ed. Donald MacArdle, trans. Constance S. Jolly (Chapel Hill: University of North Carolina Press, 1966).

Schlegel, August Wilhelm, *Lectures on Dramatic Art and Literature*, trans. John Black (London: George Bell & Sons, 1909).

Schumann, Robert, *Robert Schumann's Briefe, Neue Folge*, ed. F. Gustav Jansen (Leipzig: Breitkopf & Härtel, 1886).

Searle, John R., *Speech Acts: An Essay in the Philosophy of Language* (Cambridge: Cambridge University Press, 1969).

Senner, Wayne M. (ed.), *The Critical Reception of Beethoven's Compositions by His German Contemporaries* (Lincoln: University of Nebraska Press, 1999).

Servières, Georges, *La Musique française moderne* (Paris: G. Havard fils, 1897).

Sessa, Anne Dzamba, *Richard Wagner and the English* (Rutherford: Fairleigh Dickenson University Press, 1979).

Sewall, William H., Jr., *Work and Revolution in France: The Language of Labor from the Old Regime to 1848* (Cambridge: Cambridge University Press, 1980).

Shelley, Mary, *Frankenstein: Complete, Authoritative Text with Biographical, Historical, and Cultural Contexts, Critical History, and Essays from Contemporary Critical Perspectives*, ed. Johanna M. Smith (Boston: Bedford/St. Martin's, 2000).

Shelley, Percy Bysshe, *Shelley's* Prometheus Unbound*: A Variorum Edition*, ed. Lawrence John Zillman (Seattle: University of Washington Press, 1959).

——, *The Necessity of Atheism and Other Essays* (Buffalo: Prometheus Books, 1993).

Simons, Jon, *Foucault and the Political* (London: Routledge, 1995).

Smart, Mary Ann, *Mimomania: Music and Gesture in Nineteenth-Century Opera* (Berkeley: University of California Press, 2004).

Smith, F.B., "The Atheist Mission, 1840–1900," in Robert Robson (ed.), *Ideas and Institutions of Victorian Britain* (New York: Barnes & Noble, 1967), pp. 205–35.

Solomon, Maynard, *Beethoven*, 2nd rev. edn (New York: Schirmer Books, 1998).

Solonière, Eugène de, *La Femme compositeur* (Paris: La Critique, 1895).

Studd, Stephen, *Saint-Saëns: A Critical Biography* (London: Cygnus Arts, 1999).

Thayer, Alexander Wheelock, *Thayer's Life of Beethoven*, ed. Elliot Forbes (Princeton: Princeton University Press, 1964).

Theeman, Nancy Sarah, "The Life and Songs of Augusta Holmès" (Ph.D. diss., University of Maryland, 1983).

Tiersot, Julien, "Semaine théâtrale: Ancien Hippodrome—Première représentation de *Prométhée*," *Le Ménestrel*, 7 December 1907, n.p.

Todd, R. Larry, *Mendelssohn:* The Hebrides *and other Overtures*, Cambridge Music Handbooks, ed. Julian Rushton (Cambridge: Cambridge University Press, 1993).

Torkowitz, Dieter, "Innovation und Tradition, zur Genesis eines Quartenakkords: Über Liszt's *Prometheus* Akkord," *Die Musikforschung*, 33/3 (1980): 291–302.

Trousson, Raymond, *Le Thème de Prométhée dans la littérature européenne* (2 vols, Geneva: Librairie Droz, 1964).

Turbow, Gerald D., "Art and Politics: Wagnerism in France," in David C. Large and William Weber (eds), *Wagnerism in European Culture and Politics* (Ithaca: Cornell University Press, 1984), pp. 134–66.

Vincent, Alexandre-Joseph-Hidulphe, *Notice sur divers manuscrits grecs relatifs à la musique, Comprenant une traduction française et des commentaires* (Paris: Imprimerie royale, 1847).

Wagner, Cosima, *Cosima Wagner's Diaries*, ed. Martin Gregor-Dellin and Dietrich Mack, trans. Geoffrey Skelton (2 vols, New York: Harcourt Brace Jovanovich, 1978).

Walker, Alan, *Franz Liszt* (3 vols, Ithaca: Cornell University Press, 1983–96).

Walker, Frank, *Hugo Wolf: A Biography* (New York: Alfred A. Knopf, 1952).

Watson, Derek, *Liszt* (New York: Schirmer Books, 1989).

Wellbery, David E., *The Specular Moment: Goethe's Early Lyric and the Beginnings of Romanticism* (Stanford: Stanford University Press, 1996).

White, Newman Ivey, *Shelley* (2 vols, New York: Alfred A. Knopf, 1940).

Whitton, Kenneth S., *Schubert and Goethe: The Unseen Bond* (Portland, Ore.: Amadeus Press, 1999).

Will, Richard, *The Characteristic Symphony in the Age of Haydn and Beethoven* (Cambridge: Cambridge University Press, 2002).

Winkler, Gerhard J., "Carl Goldmark: Ein biographischer Abriß," in Gerald Schlag (ed.), *Carl Goldmark (1830–1915): Opernkomponist der Donaumonarchie, Ausstellung des Burgenländischen Landesmuseums, 10. Juli–15. September 1996* (Eisenstadt: Burgenländische Landesmuseen, 1996), pp. 9–19.

——, "Carl Goldmark und die Moderne," in Helen Geyer et al. (eds), *"Denn in jenen Tönen lebt es": Wolfgang Marggraf zum 65* (Weimar: Hochschule für Musik Franz Liszt, 1999), pp. 229–43.

Winter, Marian Hannah, *The Pre-Romantic Ballet* (New York: Pitman Publishing Corporation, 1974).

Index

References to music examples and illustrations are in bold.

Lightning Source UK Ltd.
Milton Keynes UK
UKHW022021170320
360518UK00005B/50